Evolutionary Psychology,
Public Policy
and Personal Decisions

ॐ

Evolutionary Psychology, Public Policy and Personal Decisions

Edited by

Charles Crawford
Department of Psychology
Simon Fraser University

Catherine Salmon
Department of Psychology
University of Redlands

 LAWRENCE ERLBAUM ASSOCIATES, PUBLISHERS
2004   Mahwah, New Jersey   London

Lawrence Erlbaum Associates, Inc., Publishers
10 Industrial Avenue
Mahwah, New Jersey 07430

Cover design by Kathryn Houghtaling Lacey

Library of Congress Cataloging-in-Publication Data

Evolutionary psychology, public policy and personal decisions /
   edited by Charles Crawford, Catherine Salmon.
       p.   cm.
Sequel to: Handbook of evolutionary psychology.
Includes bibliographical references and index.
ISBN 0-8058-4377-9 (cloth : alk. paper)
ISBN 0-8058-4946-7 (pbk. : alk. paper)
1. Evolutionary psychology.   I. Crawford, Charles (Charles B.)
   II. Salmon, Catherine.
BF698.95.E96   2004
155.7—dc21   2003054726
                                                                    CIP

Books published by Lawrence Erlbaum Associates are printed on acid-
free paper, and their bindings are chosen for strength and durability.

Printed in the United States of America
10 9 8 7 6 5 4 3 2 1

Contents

∾

v

Part II: Cognitive and Affective Psychological Processes

Part III: Real-World Applications

         Perspectives and Public Policy
         Kingsley R. Browne

14   Is Psychopathy a Pathology or a Life Strategy?   293
         Implications for Social Policy
         Kirsten N. Barr & Vernon L. Quinsey

15   Cultivating Morality and Constructing Moral   319
         Systems: How to Make Silk Purses From
         Sows' Ears
         Dennis L. Krebs

16   Darwinism and Public Policy: The View   343
         From Political Science
         Robert S. Robins

         Author Index   353

         Subject Index   365

Preface

∞

During the last 15 years, empirical and theoretical scientists and scholars have produced considerable empirical and theoretical knowledge on how Darwin's theory of evolution by natural selection can be used in the study of human behavior. So far, this knowledge has had little impact on policymakers and legislators. Lawmakers, Supreme Court justices, and managers seldom consult evolutionary psychologists to help with their deliberations. When faced with personal decisions, few individuals ask themselves how a Darwinian perspective might help them. The aim of this volume is to start the process of using the theories and findings of evolutionary psychology to help make the world a better place to live in, as well as to help people adjust to and deal with the realities of their evolved human nature.

There are many conceptions of public policy. In this book, public policies mean laws enacted by legislative bodies, judicial interpretations of these laws and administrative procedures designed to implement them, as well as policies devised by corporations, public and private institutions, unions, and professional societies that enable them to conform to laws and their interpretations. Personal decisions are those that enable the ongoing behavior of individuals as they go about their daily lives, making friends, doing their jobs, finding mates, caring for their children, planning holidays, going to the movies, or scheming for advantage. Many factors (e.g., ability, financial resources, customs, and gender) constrain personal decisions. In state societies, public policies are one of the major constraints on personal decisions.

This book had its beginning in a series of eight lectures on public policy and personal decisions that occurred at Simon Fraser University during 2000 and 2001. Because of the interest the series generated, a variety of scholars and scientists who had not participated in the lecture series were asked to contribute to this volume. All the contributors to this volume believe that developing a society based on moral principles—yet one that is relatively livable—involves understanding evolved human nature. Darwin's closing paragraph of *The Descent of Man* suggested a role for using evolutionary theory to help people understand themselves. His "indelible stamp" of human phylogenetic heritage informs all evolutionary approaches to the study of human behavior. This volume is based on the premise that using evolutionary psychology to help people understand themselves can help them produce a world that is a better place to live and deal with the realities of that world.

The book is divided into three parts. The application of Darwin's thinking to human behavior has become an industry that includes cultural and physical anthropologists, economists, philosophers, sociologists, biologists, and psychologists. The focus of the four chapters in part I is on the logic of evolutionary theory and how the scientists and scholars who call themselves evolutionary psychologists use evolutionary theory in their work. Evolutionary psychologists concern themselves with evolved behavior producing mechanisms and how they interact with the current environment to produce individuals' everyday behavior. Part II explores some of the evolved cognitive and affective mechanisms that are relevant to public policy and private decisions. It includes chapters on mentalism and antimentalism in psychological science, and continues with chapters on self-deception and decision making, emotions as guides to current actions, the impact of ancestral reproductive motivations on current behavior, and concludes with a chapter on evolutionary psychology and the rules of primary obligations.

The material in parts I and II provides an intellectual basis for the chapters in part III of the book, which deals with the application of evolutionary psychology to a variety of substantive areas related to public policy and personal decisions. It begins with a chapter on family conflict and violence and the marital relationship, and continues with chapters on sex differences in human sexuality, why men do not pay child support, life history perspectives on rape, women in the workplace, and psychopathy as a pathology or a life history strategy. It concludes with a chapter on the implications of evolutionary explanations of morality for public policy. A political scientist completes the book with a commentary on evolutionary psychology and public policy.

Funds to support the lecture series that gave rise to the book were provided by the Simon Fraser SSHRC Small Grants Committee, the Simon Fraser Institute for the Humanities, the Deans of Arts and Continuing Studies, as well as the biology and psychology departments. The second editor was also supported by a Michael Smith Foundation for Health Research Postdoctoral fellowship. Graduate students, Erica Nance and Laura Dane, and undergraduates, Myriam Juda and Kaliya

Muntean, helped make the lecture series run smoothly, and Maria Janicki was her usual helpful self. Special thanks go to Gladys We, who designed the poster and Web site used to advertise the lecture series. We thank everyone else who helped with the lecture series and this book that grew from it.

PART I

Methodological and Philosophic Considerations

∾

The four chapters making up this section focus on the logic of evolutionary theory and how evolutionary psychologists use the theory of natural selection in their attempts to understand human motivations and behavior. The more human beings know about their evolved human nature, the better they will understand how to control their behavior and to create viable policies to achieve specific ends.

Crawford's chapter (chap. 1) provides an introduction to the possible ways in which evolutionary psychology can have a beneficial impact on the creation and implementation of public and private policy. The role of naturalistic and moralistic fallacies in hindering the development of sound public policies is discussed, as well as the implications of implementing beliefs about the nature of ancestrally evolved mental mechanisms.

Misconceptions about what evolutionary psychology is and about the nature of evolution by natural selection itself abound in popular and scientific writings. In chapter 2, Crawford and Salmon provide an introduction to the theory of evolution by natural selection and how evolutionary psychologists use it. Darwin's theory of sexual selection, the importance of kinship in the evolution of sociality and within family conflict, reciprocity, and the role of genetic variation and the modern environment in the production of current behavior are explained. The authors emphasize how natural selection produces adaptations that enable organisms to obtain and process information about their environment and use it to adjust their behavior to the varying environmental circumstances they encounter.

Although the Darwinian approach to studying behavior is commonly perceived as portraying most interactions as selfish, ruthless struggles to pass on genes, evolutionary models developed in the last 30 years have shown that altruistic and cooperative behavior can be selected for when it is preferentially directed toward relatives, or at least those who are likely to return the favor. In recent years, however, evolutionary theorists have begun to questions the limitations of these two "selfish" views of cooperative behavior, especially with regard to long-term relationships. In chapter 3, Janicki reviews recent theoretical and empirical developments that seem to uncover a more positive side to evolved human nature.

There are many philosophic issues that trouble those involved in the application of evolutionary theory to the study of human behavior. Holcomb (chap. 4) suggests that the framing of problems as naturalistic and/or moralistic fallacies should be rejected. He calls for a new "mutual engagement" model in which evolutionary psychologists and critics engage each other's ideas seriously, rather than turning their arguments into a muddle of moral and empirical statements.

Public Policy
and Personal Decisions:
The Evolutionary Context

Charles Crawford
Simon Fraser University

Most people would like to live in a society founded on moral principles that would help guide their interactions with their friends, neighbors, and acquaintances, and even with their enemies. But most individuals also resist constraints on their behavior that frustrate their attempts to achieve their personal goals and desires. This dilemma is often reflected in the importance of public policy and personal decisions in people's lives. In this book, public policies refers to laws enacted by legislative bodies, judicial interpretations of these laws and administrative procedures designed to implement them, as well as to policies devised by corporations, public and personal institutions, unions, and professional societies that enable them to conform to laws and their interpretations. For example, all state societies have laws dealing with crimes such as theft, murder, and rape, as well as the regulation of commerce, marriage, and other family relationships. Similarly, businesses and public institutions (e.g., hospitals, churches, and schools) must have policies on accounting, safety, and harassment that conform to government policies.

Personal decisions are those that enable the ongoing behavior of individuals as they go about their daily lives, making friends, doing their jobs, finding mates, caring for their children, planning holidays, going to the movies, and scheming for advantage. Many factors (e.g., ability, financial resources, customs, gender) constrain personal decisions. In state societies, public policies are one of the major constraints on personal decisions. However, the impact of public policy for personal decisions varies greatly with space and time. During the Middle Ages, church and state authorities proscribed the decisions of western Europeans on a wide range of topics ranging from appropriate clothing and places to live to church attendance and who individuals could and could not marry.

About 250 years ago, many thinkers in what are now called the Western democracies began resisting state and church interventions in the private lives of citizens. However, in many parts of the world, the state and/or the church still play important roles in the daily affairs of citizens. Moreover, in recent decades, many special interest groups in the Western democracies have begun demanding state intervention promoting the welfare of women, children, workers, minorities, animals, and the environment. This trend seems likely to continue. If it is to be productive, then it should be based on a sound understanding of the psychology of human beings.

There is an intimate relation between public policy and personal decisions. Many public policies arise because of personal decisions (e.g., the decision to view sexually explicit or aggressive material, become intimate with children or members of the same sex, adopt a baby, marry a cousin or mother-in-law, self-administer intoxicating and mind altering substances, employ young children, prevent women from voting, add a room on a house, start a new business, or to pay employees the least possible wage) that impinge on the rights and privileges others believe citizens ought to, or ought not to, possess. Moreover, even if personal decisions do not, themselves, directly violate a law or policy, their consequences sometimes activate public policy processes. This can happen when the consequences of individuals' decisions bring them into conflict with official policy. Normally, the choice of a child's stepparent is a personal decision. Although most stepparents are good parents, there is considerable evidence that when a parent abuses a child, a stepparent is likely involved (Daly & Wilson, 1998). Hence, the personal choice of a new mate may lead to actions that activate public policies concerned with the care and abuse of children. Many people believe in freedom of artistic expression. However, some research (Stossel, 1997) suggests that violence on TV leads to children becoming more violent. Such findings suggest to some that there should be restrictions on what can be shown on TV. Although many in the Western democracies believe that sex between consenting adults is a personal matter, many believe that prostitution is harmful to women, and hence, that men's use of prostitutes should be constrained (Jeffreys, 1997). Do such findings and claims suggest a role for more state intervention in regulating what individuals may or may not do? If they do, then what kinds of knowledge should be used in constructing the interventions?

Legalistic (Hammurabi, Napoleon, John Rawls), religious (Moses, Mohammed, Buddha), economic (Adam Smith, Karl Marx, Milton Friedman), philosophic (Plato, Karl Popper, Isaiah Berlin), and biological (Herbert Spencer, Cesare Lombroso, Stephen J. Gould) approaches to resolving issues in public policy and personal decisions have been advocated at different times and in different places. Biological approaches have always been controversial. However, they have been particularly controversial since the publication of *Sociobiology: The New Synthesis* (Wilson, 1975). Wilson surveyed the biological basis of social behaviors in species ranging from insects to humans. His argument that Darwin's Theory of

Evolution by Natural Selection must eventually play an important role in any comprehensive explanation of human behavior incensed social scientists and worried social reformers (Barlow & Silverberg, 1980; Caplan, 1978; H. Rose & S. Rose, 2000). The contents of this volume reflect the proposition that public policy and personal decisions can benefit from an understanding of the aspects of human nature that were shaped across evolutionary time by natural selection.

SCIENTIFIC AND MORAL REALMS

There are two realms that must be considered when developing public policy and making personal decisions. One is the empirical world of the senses. It includes the domain of scientific empirical observations and the scientific theories used to help discover and explain them, the factual historical record, as well as the results of everyday experience. The other is the domain of moral values that have been developed by theologians, moral philosophers, and politicians to help humans deal with the contingencies of human experience. However, it also includes the personal value systems of individuals.

Those who attempt to use Darwin's theory to contribute to solutions for social ills or in making personal decisions are often accused of leaping the chasm from the empirical and scientific to the moral realm (Barash, 1982). This leap is sometimes referred to as the *naturalistic fallacy*—using what is to justify what ought to be. Consider two possible evolutionary examples: (a) "Women, more than men, evolved as the primary caretakers of children; therefore, they have traits, such as nurturance and empathy, that make them superior caregivers, and hence women ought to be favored as teachers and nurses." (b) "Since the demands of hunting, warfare, and male–male competition caused men to evolve larger size, greater physical strength, and greater aggressiveness than women, men ought to be preferred as policemen and infantry men." Clearly, these statements are erroneous. From the perspective of logic we cannot reason from what is to what ought to be. Although, on average, men are larger, more aggressive, and more competitive than women in all known cultures, it cannot be concluded from this fact that men ought to exceed women on these attributes, and that these attributes ought to determine their roles in life. Empirical and moral realms are logically distinct.

However, recognizing that this reasoning is faulty can lead thinking astray if it prompts the conclusion that the empirical observations appearing to justify its claims are invalid, that the state of nature suggesting it ought to be changed, or that it can easily be changed. For example, identifying the claim "Men are larger than women, therefore, they ought to be larger" as fallacious does not imply that men are not larger than women, that the world would be a better place if men were not larger, or that women can easily be expanded or men shrunk. Similarly, identifying the claim that "Men are more aggressive than women, therefore, they ought to be more aggressive" as fallacious does not imply that men are not more aggressive than women, that they ought not to be more aggressive, that the world would be a better place if men were not more aggressive, or that it is easy to construct a world where men are not more aggressive than women. Although the scientific and moral realms are logically distinct, human suffering can result if it is then assumed that this implies that factual knowledge and scientific findings ought not to play an important role in informing social policy.

Although this fallacy in reasoning can be pernicious, another fallacy can be equally noxious. It is the fallacy of assuming that "What ought to be is" or "What ought to be can be" (Crawford, 1999). A prominent example is "Racial differences in intelligence ought not to exist; therefore, they do not exist; hence, anyone finding such differences must be using poor research methods or be politically motivated in their research." There are many other examples in contemporary thought. One that comes to mind is "Sex ought to be mutually enjoyable and personally enhancing. Aggressive sexuality is not compatible with this ought. Therefore, sexuality cannot be the motivation for rape, and hence rape must be motivated by men's desire to dominate women." This type of reasoning leads to ideological or moralistic fallacies—leaping the chasm from the moral to the empirical realms. Although moral values cannot determine objective, scientific reality, anyone putting forth arguments or findings challenging this form of thinking can expect a rough intellectual ride.

It is, however, legitimate for a society to use scientific research to help it attain moral, political, and social goals. Indeed, one of the goals of much scientific inquiry is the development of improved living conditions. A moralistic fallacy occurs when those goals are allowed to dominate the methods and findings of the knowledge producing processes. The classic example is the Catholic church's persecution of Galileo because of his scientific methods, findings, and conclusions about the nature of the universe and human beings' place in it. However, there are equally egregious modern examples. The best is the theory of the Russian agriculturist Trofim Denisovich Lysenko and its official acceptance by the communist party of the Soviet Union in 1948.

Lysenko was the son of a Ukrainian peasant whose theory of the inheritance of acquired characteristics came to dominate Soviet genetics, and research on plant and animal breeding, as well as many other aspects of Soviet biology (Medvedev, 1969; Sheehan, 1993). The underlying theme of his work was the plasticity of the life cycle. He claimed that plants went through various stages of development, and during each phase, their environmental requirements differed sharply. Knowledge of the different phases of development and their environmental requirements could enable human direction of this development through control of the environment. He rejected the existence of genes and argued that the basis of heredity did not lie in some special self-reproducing substance. Heredity, through the internalization of external conditions, was based on the interaction between the organism and its environment (Sheehan, 1993).

Lysenko's theory developed in a pragmatic and intuitive way as a rationalization of agricultural practice and as a reflection of the ideological climate and the very real development needs in the Soviet Union during the 1930s and 1940s, rather than through the rigorous application of the scientific method (Sheehan, 1993). As the struggle between Lysenko and his supporters with the geneticists and their supporters intensified, scientific and philosophical arguments increasingly gave way to political ones. The pursuit of genetics was spoken of as synonymous with adherence to the cause of reaction, and was identified with racism and fascism. The result was the destruction of Soviet scientific genetics and a tragedy for Russian agriculture, as well as for many Soviet geneticists. Many lost their jobs, some died in prison, and others were shot. When science and scholarship are politicized, those whose work is not seen as supporting the official goals are often seen as morally degenerate and deserving of severe punishment.

Some of the greatest tragedies of history have their origins in moralistic attempts to impose an ideology on a whole population. Up to 60 million people died because of Lenin's and Stalin's determination to impose communism in Russia (Davies, 1996; Yakovlov, 2002). The attempt to impose a strict Muslim code on Afghanistan is the most recent example of the costs of imposing an ideology on a whole nation. "What ought to be, can be" can have noxious consequences when applied with excessive zeal. There are moralistic fallacies that are much less pernicious than Lysenkoism. However, they take their toll. Some of these are discussed in the coming chapters.

EVOLUTIONARY PSYCHOLOGY

During the last 15 years, evolutionary psychology has developed considerably. It is a discipline concerned with the problems and stresses that hominid and primate ancestors encountered, the psychological mechanisms natural selection shaped to deal with these stresses, and the way those ancient mechanisms work now (Crawford & Anderson, 1989). Consider some examples. Life in the ancestral environment was not always easy. The modern social safety net—not to mention teachers, social workers, lawyers, and doctors—was not available to help solve people's problems. But, evolution by natural selection was there to design solutions for some of them. The process was slow, but it shaped a being with a vast array of problem-solving abilities.

One of the greatest challenges human ancestors faced was choosing a mate with characteristics that would contribute to the production of healthy and vigorous children. There is now considerable evidence that waist-to-hip ratio in women (Singh, 1993; Streeter & McBurney, 2003) and facial symmetry in men (Thornhill & Gangestad, 1993) are indicators of long-term prospects for good health. Therefore, natural selection may have produced a tendency in men to find women with small waists attractive and a propensity in women to be attracted to men with symmetric facial features. These tendencies are still part of our human nature, and their presence helps explain why small-waisted women and symmetric men help advertisers sell their products on TV.

Fair exchange of favors underpins many human activities ranging from marriage, interacting with neighbors and local businesses, through employer–employee relationships, civil servant–citizen interactions, and international trade. The essence of reciprocity is that a donor pays a cost to "help" a recipient who benefits from the help. At a later time, the roles are reversed and the recipient pays a cost to repay the favor. Consider two ancestral hunters, A and B, whose hunting success for game essential for their families' survival varies from week to week. If Hunter A shares his game with his friend, then he pays a cost because he may not have had to hunt quite so diligently if he had not shared. However, the cost may be small because of the fixed costs of hunting. Hunter B's hungry family may benefit greatly from the shared meat. The next week, Hunter A's hunting fails, but his family is fed by hunter B who has paid a small cost to feed Hunter A's family. Both families benefit greatly from the sharing and, across evolutionary time, psychological mechanisms for engaging in reciprocal helping may evolve (Trivers, 1985).

However, reciprocal systems have a weakness that can make them unstable. It can pay individuals and institutions to cheat on exchanges—to take the benefits of an exchange, but not to reciprocate when roles are reversed (Trivers, 1985). Consider some examples. An employer and her employees agree on a fair employment contract. An employee can cheat the employer by coming to work late. The employer can cheat the employees by paying them a day late and collecting interest on the delayed payments. A government agrees to provide police and fire protection services to its citizens in return for taxes. The government employees can cheat by asking for bribes to carry out their duties. The citizens can cheat on the amount of taxes they pay. A group of nations agree to eliminate tariffs to help promote international trade. Everyone benefits from the reduction. However, if one nation could find a way of secretly imposing tariffs that the other nations could not detect, then its citizens would benefit from selling its goods to the other nations, while being secretly protected from their competition.

All reciprocal systems, whether they are individual psyches, businesses, governments, or alliances of nations require mechanisms for protecting themselves against cheaters reaping the benefits of reciprocity, while avoiding its costs. Economists call it the free rider problem. Evolutionary psychologists have found good evidence for the evolution of specialized psychological mechanisms for engaging in reciprocal exchanges (Cosmides & Tooby, 1992). It includes evidence that people have evolved mechanisms for detecting cheaters on reciprocal exchanges. These psychological mechanisms enabled human ancestors to reap the benefits of gains in trade. In the modern world, they underpin people's sense of justice and make the international economy possible. Those with personal, economic, and political philosophies that do not have mechanisms for detecting and responding to cheaters that undermine them can expect trouble and exploitation. To many it seemed that a system with an ideology including principles such as "From each according to his abilities, to each according to his needs" would be vulnerable to various types of cheating on reciprocal relationships, and hence that it might not persist. Therefore, it was not surprising when communism ran into great trouble. Similarly, it is not surprising that even the complex and highly developed legal system in Western democracies has difficulty preventing various types of corporate cheating.

Technically speaking, when talking about the formation and functioning of psychological mechanisms in the context of evolution by natural selection, the discussion is about psychological adaptations. They are innate specialized information-processing mechanisms realized in the neural hardware of the nervous system. When activated by appropriate problem content from the external or internal environments, they focus attention, organize perception and memory, and call up specialized procedural knowledge that leads to domain-appropriate inferences, judgments, and choices (Cosmides & Tooby, 1989). They were shaped by the costs and benefits of the behaviors they produced in response to problems humans, and their primate ancestors, encountered. Their current operation reflects the ancestral costs and benefits that shaped them rather than those that may be appropriate to the current environment (Crawford, 1998). Evolutionary psychologists argue that the mental processes involved in human mate choice (Buss, 1994, 2000), detecting cheaters on social contracts (Cosmides, 1989), fear of spiders (Marks, 1987), landscape preferences (Orians & Heerwagen, 1992), facial expression involved in emotional communication (Ekman, 1973), and discriminating between kin and nonkin (Porter, 1987) are only a few of the many mental adaptations produced by natural selection to solve problems human ancestors faced.

ALTERNATIVE BELIEFS ABOUT THE SPECIALIZATION OF PSYCHOLOGICAL MECHANISMS

Those who fear using knowledge about how human beings' biological heritage influences their current behavior in the development of public policy worry that it may require people to learn to live with cheating on social contracts, unequal representation of women in the most prestigious jobs, rape, spousal abuse, the domination of the weak by the strong, and other noxious or morally undesirable behaviors (Allen et al., 1975; H. Rose & S. Rose, 2000). Their desire to produce a better world and their belief that human nature is very malleable leads them to claim that "What ought to be, can be" with only minimal human costs, or that if the human costs are non trivial, then the end justifies the means.

Consider the outcomes when possible hypotheses about states of human nature are considered in conjunction with possible beliefs about those states. The logic can be simplified by considering only two of the many possible states of nature and beliefs about it. The first is that the human psyche is comprised of evolved general purpose mental mechanisms. Hence, people's intellects, emotional, and motivational systems are very malleable. If this is the true state of nature, then although evolved aspects of human ancestral evolutionary heritage exist, they have minimal influence on individual's current thoughts, feelings, and behavior. Many contemporary social scientists and policymakers take this view of the human psyche.

The second possible state of nature is that many aspects of people's psyches are strongly affected by evolved specialized abilities and propensities. Symons (1987) characterized this view when he wrote, "Complex, specialized, species-typical brain/mind mechanisms are precisely what a Darwinian view of life should lead us to anticipate" (p. 143). His chapter helped to establish evolutionary psychology as a coherent approach to understanding human behavior. If this statement describes the state of evolved human nature, then human ancestral evolutionary heritage has a powerful influence on current beliefs, motives, and actions. Finally, individuals may choose to accept or reject either alternative. The two sets of alternatives generate four possibilities. Table 1.1 shows the four possibilities and indicates some results of each of them.

Suppose that people's psyches are actually very malleable, but for some reason—say poor research or conservative political motives—social policies are developed on the assumption that their psyches are strongly conditioned by ancestral biological heritage. What might be some consequences for public policy? Consider two possibilities. If a society were to act on the assumption that human psyches are strongly influenced by their evolutionary heritage and also that this

TABLE 1.1

**Outcomes of the Ancestrally Evolved General Purpose
Versus Specialized Mental Mechanisms Debate**

Possible Beliefs About Nature of Ancestrally Evolved Mental Mechanisms	Possible States of Nature: Evolved Emotional and Reasoning Mental Mechanisms	
	Evolved General Purpose Mechanisms	**Evolved Special Purpose Mechanisms**
Behaviors produced by general purpose emotional and reasoning mental mechanisms	*Correct decision:* *Public polices that work* • Great flexibility in setting societal goals and methods for achieving them • Utopias: Waldon II • Dystopias: 1984 Brave New World • Cultural imperialism	*Incorrect Decision:* *Public policies that fail* • Belief in untrue American dream leads to frustration and aggression • Prohibition laws that are difficult to enforce (e.g., infanticide & alcohol laws) • Fall of communism • Difficulties in devising rape law reforms that work • Special interest groups that undermine free trade
Behaviors produced by special purpose emotional and reasoning mental mechanisms	*Incorrect decision:* *Public policies that fail* • Coercive laws to control behavior • Absence of needed laws to help control behavior • Eugenics laws • Miscegenation laws • Apartheid laws	*Correct decision:* *Public policies that work* • Racism • Sexism • Schools that fit needs of students • Socialized medicine • Guaranteed annual income • Unemployment insurance

implies they must be biologically programmed to be aggressive, nasty, and brutish, then acting on this incorrect belief could cause unnecessary suffering. Laws restricting sex roles might be enacted. Social classes might be considered biological castes with biologically imposed limitations and abilities that must determine educational and employment policies. Inappropriate laws preventing interclass and interracial adoption and marriage might be enacted. War might be regarded as inevitable. However, an alternative possibility is that because of the assumption that biological heritage shapes much of people's behavior, the society might see little need to avail itself of institutions and laws for regulating the behavior of its citizens. Bees, wasps, and ants do not need to develop laws and institutions to help make their societies better places to live, the argument might go, so why do people need laws to control aggression, rape, murder, and fraud? Clearly, this error could have serious consequences. Those who worry about the consequences of hastily moving from research to practice are correct to fear what could happen if a society wrongly believes that ancestral history has a strong influence on people's current behavior.

Second, suppose that a society correctly believed that human psyches are very malleable. Then the abilities and propensities of individuals are socially constructed and all sorts of educational and social interventions seem easily attainable. The society apparently has great freedom in deciding the values and lifestyles its citizens pursue. Many who worry about the consequences of using information about individual's evolved natures see this as the ideal situation because public policy can then be used to accomplish great things. Skinner's (1948) controversial Utopian vision, *Waldon II*, described an ideal society where conditioning and learning schedules are used to shape behavior. This provides a recent literary example. However, some worry about how the particular great things to be achieved are chosen and about the methods for achieving them. The ideals of communism are noble. So far, most attempts to achieve them have ended in tragedy. Others worry that this alternative could be the prerequisite for dystopias, such as those described in *Brave New World* and *1984*. Still others wonder if the inhabitants of such worlds could develop the mental capacities to have any objections to such dystopian places (Crawford, 1979). The socially constructed world may not be benign or Utopian.

Third, suppose human psyches are biologically conditioned and that people's current behavior is strongly affected by their evolutionary heritage, but that a society decides to reject this state of nature and act on the assumption that human psyches are comprised of a few general purpose mechanisms and are therefore very malleable. Acceptance of this assumption might again be due to poor research or political motivations. What might be some consequences of this error for public policy and individual decisions? Public polices may be adopted that mandate or encourage individuals to do things some will be very uncomfortable doing. Some will be expected to undertake tasks they find difficult or impossible to accomplish. They will feel guilty when they cannot do what is expected of them. They may receive harsh punishments when they fail, because their failures may be seen as the result of lack of commitment and loyalty rather than lack of ability or different interests and life goals. The result may be frustration, aggression, depression, and even punishment for wrongdoing. Mental illnesses, deviant lifestyles, and unusual responses to difficult situations may be regarded as moral problems to be corrected by re-education and punishment.

Those who worry about the consequences of making moralistic fallacies fear the suffering this outcome can produce. The distress the imposition of communism produced on Russia has already been mentioned. Consider two other examples taken from history. Infanticide has been common throughout human history. Although there are many reasons for infanticide in both state and nonstate societies, some hunter-gatherer societies regard the practice as a mother's right (Scrimshaw, 1984). Western European societies regard it as sinful and illegal. Many women on the continent were hanged for the crime. However, even all-male British juries were unwilling to convict poor, young, single women for killing their newborn babies. British authorities were outraged: Not only were clearly guilty women going free, but the flouting of the law was also undermining the legal system. For four centuries, British lawmakers made numerous changes to the law in attempts to get more convictions for infanticide (Hoffer & Hull, 1981). However, none were successful, and in 1922 the law was medicalized. Nevertheless, infanticide by women is still a troublesome legal, medical, and social issue.

There has been a revolution in rape law in the United Sates and a number of other Western democracies during the last 30 years. The most common changes involved: redefining rape and replacing it with a graded series of offences related to aggravating conditions, eliminating the condition that the victim's testimony be corroborated, eliminating the condition that the victim must physically resist her assailant, and placing restrictions on the introduction of evidence about the victim's prior sexual conduct (Spohn, 1999). Although reformers had great hopes for rape law reform, for the most part, these hopes have not been realized, and most reformers no longer believe that rape law reform will have a major impact on rape. Reformers attribute the lack of success to laws that do not sufficiently constrain the discretion exercised by juries and other decision makers in the justice system and/ or provide them with adequate incentives to change their behavior (Sphon & Horney, 1992). This analysis is reminiscent of the views of the British law lords who kept revising the infanticide laws for 400 years in attempts to get more convictions for infanticide. Finally, Renner and Yurchesyn (1994) proposed that sexual robbery may be a better metaphor for rape than assault, and suggested a return to the older metaphor of a woman's sexuality as property, but with shift of ownership from her father or husband or another male to the women herself.

It would seem that the punitive British attempts to deal with infanticide were based on the belief that infanticide was entirely a moral problem that could be dealt with through punishment. Would the attempt to devise a communistic system that occurred in many parts of the world have been more successful if its architects had a more realistic understanding of human nature? Would those involved in rape law reform be more successful if they took evolved human nature into consideration?

Finally, suppose that human nature is characterized by biologically evolved specialized psychological mechanisms and that a society correctly acts on this belief. One consequence could be social Darwinism: a society where competition is rife and the strong dominate the weak. However, evolved propensities for cooperation, helping, and altruism exist in many nonhuman species (Wilson, 1975). There is much evidence that they also exist in humans. A society that developed under this state of nature could have a social safety net, public medical care, a guaranteed annual income, a justice system that insured fair treatment for citizens, and a school system designed to meet the needs of individual children (Crawford, 1979). The fears of those who worry that admitting a role for evolutionary history in understanding human nature in order help make a better world may not be justified.

EVOLUTIONARY PSYCHOLOGY AND PUBLIC POLICY

Evolutionary psychology is based on the assumption that psychological mechanisms that evolved to solve problems encountered by human ancestors in their long-gone environment are involved in producing current behaviors and institutions. These mental mechanisms evolved because they contributed to reproductive success across eons of time. However, all organisms live in infinitesimal segments of evolutionary time. Because environmental conditions in any infinitesimal segment of time may not be representative of those that shaped an adaptation, they may not contribute to reproductive success in any particular time segment. Hence, reproductive success cannot be used as a criterion for evaluating the observed functioning of an adaptation or judging how well it is helping individuals adjust to their current environment. When the focus is on the adequacy of an adaptation's functioning in the current environment, the focus must be on well-being, that is, on how well an ancestral psychological adaptation is contributing to physical and psychological health, and individuals' ability to function as healthy, well-adjusted, and productive members of their society.

Table 1.2 provides an expanded version of Crawford and Anderson's (1989; Crawford, 1998) classification of how behavioral adaptations function in ancestral and current environments. The *ancestral* dimension is defined in terms of adaptive and maladaptive, where adaptive refers to ancestral reproductive fitness of an adaptation relative to an alternative form of the adaptation measured across eons of evolutionary time. The *current* dimension is defined in terms of malfunctioning of adaptations designed by natural selection to contribute to ancestral fitness through the solution of an environmentally imposed problem (Wakefield, 1992a, 1992b). Hence, the ancestral dimension of the table is defined in terms of whether an adaptation could or could not have contributed to ancestral reproductive success, whereas the current dimension is defined in terms of whether the adaptation does or does not contribute to current well-being. The result is a 2×2 classification that produces true pathologies, pseudopathologies, quasi- normal behaviors, and adaptive-culturally variable behaviors. *True pathologies* (e.g., infantile autism, schizophrenia, brother–sister incest, brain damage caused memory loss, Korsakoff's syndrome, pellagra,

TABLE 1.2
A Classification of Behavior with Respect to Adaptation Functioning in Ancestral and Current Environments

Contribution to Expected Ancestral Fitness	Contribution to Current Health and Well-being	
	No	Yes
No	*True pathologies*	*Quasi-normal behaviors*
	Autism	Freedom of speech
	Brother–sister incest	Close birth spacing
	Phenylketonuria	Adoption of unrelated children
	Schizophrenia	Innocent until proven guilty
	Child abuse and neglect	Equality of sexes
	Korsakoff's syndrome	Exclusive homosexuality
	Down syndrome	Democratic government
	Pellagra	Female infantry
	Scurvy	House husbands
	Brain damage caused memory loss	Monogamy
	Huntington's chorea	Polyandry
		Communism
Yes	*Pseudopathologies*	*Adaptive-culturally variable behaviors*
	Taste for sugar & fat caused obesity	Athletic sports
	Wife abuse	Favoring kin
	Anorexic behavior	Gossip
	Nepotism	Sexual jealousy
	Prostitution	Pornography
	Teenage gangs	Self-deception
	Sexual harassment	Beauty in mate choice
	Infanticide	Courtship behaviors
	Rape	Facial expressions
	Father–stepdaughter marriages	Reciprocal exchanges
	Teenage gangs	Polygyny

Note: Modified from Crawford, C. B. (1998). Environments and adaptations: Then and now. In C. B. Crawford & D. Krebs (Eds.), *Handbook of evolutionary psychology: Ideas, issues, and applications* (p. 283). Hillsdale, NJ: Lawrence Erlbaum Associates. Modified with permission from Lawrence Erlbaum Associates.

and scurvy) did not contribute to ancestral reproductive success and they do not contribute to current well-being. Here, well-being is analogous to the adequacy of an engineering design for dealing with current environmental stress. True pathologies result from the disruption of major adaptations that were, and are, necessary for survival, reproduction, and well-being. They are always pathological. Most true pathologies are medical problems and can be best dealt with in that context. However, some may be due to unusual rearing patterns of children. For example, evidence from Israeli Kibbutz reared children (Shepher, 1983) and *sim pau* marriages (Wolf, 1995) in southern China suggests that intimate rearing of boys and girls, as in sharing the same bathroom and seeing each other nude, during the first few years of life inoculates them against sexual attraction as adults. Hence, by this reasoning, some instances of brother–sister incest may be due to the lack of intimate contact between them when they are young children. Similarly, a cause of child abuse and neglect may be inadequate rearing of the abusers.

Pseudopathologies are behaviors that have their origin in adaptations that evolved in response to problems human ancestors encountered, but for one reason or another are no longer healthy, morally acceptable, or culturally valued (Crawford & Anderson, 1989).

For example, the taste for sugar and fat likely evolved to motivate human ancestors to do the physical work and take the risks necessary to obtain these vital nutrients. However, people can now obtain them with little physical effort and few risks. As a consequence, some individuals consume too much of them, resulting in obesity (Nesse & Williams, 1994). Ancestral females and males may have exchanged sex for resources and protection (Symons, 1979). If this is the case, then modern prostitution may be a distorted and exaggerated form of this exchange due to some women needing resources and protection and some men lacking sexual access to women through normal courtship. Ancestral males who unknowingly reared other male's children would have had less reproductive success than men who had not been cuckolded. Therefore, natural selection may have produced male sexual propriety to help men avoid cuckoldry (Buss, 2000). In a modern environment where wives are in frequent contact with strange men, it can contribute to wife abuse (Tracy & Crawford, 1999).

Pseudopathologies have their basis in evolved adaptations, thus they may be difficult to eradicate from a society. For example, if obesity has its basis in ancestral adaptations that made sugar and fat taste good enough to motivate ancestors to do the work and take the risks of obtaining them, then eliminating obesity may be a difficult task. An evolutionary psychologist might predict that eliminating obesity should be more difficult than eliminating smoking, because the former likely has its basis in an evolved specialized adaptation whereas the latter likely does not. Similarly, if infanticide, prostitution, male pornography, sexual harassment, and wife abuse have their origins in evolved ancestral specialized emotional and motivational adaptations, then completely eliminating them may be difficult. Moreover, strenuous attempts to eliminate them may produce new pseudopathologies. For example, if prostitution has its origin in ancestral trading of sex for resources and protection, then strenuous legalistic attempts to eliminate it may increase the rate of shoplifting by women, the use of pornography by men, and may even attenuate some of the motivations that enable the family. Attempts to eliminate infanticide by women through coercive laws may lead to an increase in depression and suicide.

From the prospective of evolutionary psychology, zero tolerance may not be the most effective way of reducing the incidence of pseudopathologies or the suffering they cause. The route should be through understanding the functioning of the evolved, specialized psychological mechanisms producing them and how environmental interventions can influence the functioning of these mechanisms.

Quasi-normal behaviors are those that would have been rare or nonexistent in an ancestral environment because of their long-term fitness costs, but that have become socially acceptable to a significant proportion of the population of a particular society (Crawford & Anderson, 1989). The adoption of genetically unrelated children that would have detracted from ancestral fitness is not only socially acceptable, but is culturally valued in many parts of the world. Late childbearing and close birth spacing, which would have reduced ancestral lifetime reproductive success, is the norm in most modern industrialized cultures. Polyandry, a mating system that is unlikely to have existed in the Pleistocene, is acceptable and encouraged in a few societies (Daly & Wilson, 1983).

A variety of circumstances may produce quasi-normal behaviors. A new technology may alter the cost–benefit ratio of a behavior resulting in an infrequent behavior becoming more prevalent. Birth control may alter the cost and benefit of sexual behavior so that widespread recreational sex becomes possible and socially acceptable to many people in a society. Close birth spacing, which would have been detrimental to ancestral women's fitness, may become socially acceptable when a new technology makes it possible to replace mother's milk as the primary food for babies, and thereby reduce the fitness cost of closely spaced children. If the current psychological cost–benefit ratio for a behavior is positive for a particular society, then it may become acceptable and even encouraged in that society.

In general, quasi-normal behaviors are not as problematic as either true pathologies or pseudopathologies. Whether they become social problems depends on the values of the societies where they exist, the way those values are enforced, and the speed with which those values are changing. Nevertheless, there are at least three reasons why quasi-normal behaviors may cause problems for individuals exhibiting them and for those with whom they associate (Crawford, 1998; Crawford & Anderson, 1989).

First, the environmental conditions producing quasi-normal behaviors may produce conflicting or ambiguous inputs to psychological mechanisms, both in the individuals exhibiting them and their associates, resulting in emotional conflicts. A woman who engages in recreational sex may experience emotional conflict because other adaptations related to sexual behavior (e.g., those involved in the desire for children and long-term intimacy) may be telling her psyche the behavior is too costly. Moreover, the behavior may bring her into conflict with her parents and grandparents who want her to have children.

Second, because the current behavior is a fortuitous effect of an adaptation that evolved to do something else, the cues from the environment producing it may be inadequate for a fully functional behavior. Rearing a genetically unrelated, adopted child can be even more stressful than rearing a biological child (Silk, 1990). The reason may be that some of the ancestral cues involved in parental attachment to biological children are absent for an adopted child. From an evolutionary perspective, the stress in rearing an adopted child may be caused by the adopted child producing physical and behavioral inputs to systems of psychological mechanisms in the parents, friends, and relatives of the parents, as well as in the child, which are interpreted in ways that produce emotional conflict and stress.

Third, no matter how well a quasi-normal behavior is accepted in a particular culture, there will likely be some individuals who do not find it conducive to their well-being and happiness. Many of the women in polyandrous societies who do not find husbands, and some of the men who must share wives, may not be as accepting of polyandry as the elders of the society who arrange the marriages. Poor people may not view the costs and benefits of the stock market in quite the same way as Wall Street brokers and Japanese tycoons. Grandparents may not be as enthusiastic about their grandchildren being cared for in day-care centers as are their daughters.

Finally, societal standards may change across time, moving a particular behavior in and out of the range of acceptability. Fifty years ago, divorce, day-care centers, and homosexuality were not as acceptable as they are today in most Western democracies. Twenty years ago, the stock market was not as valued in Russia and China as it is now.

Quasi-normal behaviors are among the most important characteristics of all human societies. Yet, they can be a source of trouble and stress. If a society values its quasi-normal institutions such as monogamy, equality of the sexes, democratic government, communism, freedom of speech, the stock market, and innocent until proven guilty, then it must find ways of maintaining them. From the perspective of evolutionary psychology, this might involve designing them to use known psychological adaptations for producing human sociality, such as kinship, reciprocity, and mate choice.

In most cases, adaptations carry out the tasks they were designed to accomplish by natural selection. If they did not, then humans would be an extinct, or at least an endangered species. The adaptations producing these activities and behaviors are *adaptive-culturally variables* (Crawford, 1998). They are adaptive because they are currently doing the things natural selection designed them to do. They are variable because they do it in a relatively wide variety of environmental circumstances. Human hearts are still pumping blood and human eyes are still seeing. Mating and parenting systems are still enabling people to find adequate mates and rear their children. Human systems of reciprocal altruism are still enabling people to engage in complex social interactions. However, people's hearts are pumping blood at altitudes different from those where humans evolved. People's eyes are seeing sights their distant ancestors would not have imagined. Language adaptation is enabling people in Brazil to speak Portuguese, while those in Sweden learn Swedish. A mildly polygynous mating adaptation has given rise to various types of polygyny in many cultures, and monogamy in others (Buss, 1994; Daly & Wilson, 1998). Reciprocal systems vary considerably across different cultures, but they are the primary basis of sociality in all cultures. Although such adaptations are culturally variable in their expression, they are rugged. The list in Table 1.2 could be expanded almost infinitely.

Adaptive-culturally variable behaviors are robust. If some great environmental disaster eliminated one of them, such as spoken language, courtship, or reciprocal exchanges between individuals and groups, then new forms would be invented within a few generations. Nevertheless, they can produce problems because all adaptations have costs. Gossip, for example, is an important form of communication in all societies (Dunbar, 1996). Yet, it can be a source of conflict. Courtship behaviors are essential for finding mates (Buss, 2000), but they can result in conflict and violence. Marriage is not an easy street. In a fast moving world, a danger is that social and cultural change can move a behavior from being an adaptive-culturally variable to being pseudopathological. All the pseudopathological behaviors listed in Table 1.2 have their basis in adaptive mechanisms. A society must monitor many of them so that their costs do not escalate and make them even more noxious.

CHANGING BEHAVIORS: THE ROLE OF PUNISHMENT AND ADJUSTING ENVIRONMENTAL CIRCUMSTANCES

Humans have a strong tendency to punish behaviors they disapprove of as a way of changing or eliminating them. This proclivity may have some validity. Adaptations evolved in response to the costs and benefits of the ancestral behaviors they produced. Hence, increasing the costs of current behaviors may influence their occurrence. Most legal systems rely heavily on some form of punishment. Virtually all forms of punishment have a current fitness cost associated with them. Yet, there are problems associated with punishment as a public policy. Punishment can be expensive. There are more Black American men in prison than in colleges and universities. It costs more to send a man to prison than to an institution of higher education (Hutsler, 1995).

It can be difficult to implement severe punishments, especially in democratic societies. The difficulty of enforcing infanticide and rape laws has already been mentioned. However, there are many other examples. During the 1990s, Canadian courts were unable to enforce the abortion laws that were still on the books. A large number of offences were punishable by death in England during the 17th, 18th, and 19th centuries. Yet, few people were actually hanged because a variety of methods for reducing the severity of sentences came into existence. For example, a capital sentence might be reduced to transportation to Australia or some other distant part of the empire if the offender could recite the Lord's Prayer (Laurence, 1960).

Racial, religious, and class conflicts are endemic in human history. Members of dominant groups have often used severe punishments as weapons in their struggle with subordinate groups rather than attempting to understand their needs. This can happen even in advanced democratic nations. Occasionally, humans seem to lose control of their senses and go on punishment rampages for what later appear as minor offenses. The best example is the witch trials that occurred in Europe during the 16th and 17th centuries (Bostridge, 1997). Moreover, political purges of one kind or another are not an uncommon occurrence in human history. Stalin's show trials are not the only example.

Finally, it is not easy to design and implement human punishments. Zimbardo (Haney, Banks, & Zimbardo, 1973) created a mock prison in a laboratory basement. Twenty-one healthy male undergraduate volunteers were randomly divided into groups of guards and prisoners. Soon the "guards" and "prisoners" became totally absorbed in their respective roles. The guards grew more aggressive. The prisoners became passive and apathetic. The behavior of the participants became so noxious that the experiment had to be terminated after only 6 days. Devil's Island was not, and is not, the only infamous prison.

From the perspective of evolutionary psychology, all behaviors are either direct or indirect effects of evolved adaptations. Hence, programs for changing current behaviors should be based on an understanding of how ancestral environmental conditions involved in the development and functioning of the relevant adaptation relate to present environmental circumstances. One of the reasons for the lack of efficacy of many punishment regimes is that the relevant ancestral adaptations may not "recognize" the punishment as detrimental to fitness. If this is the case, then the punishment may be "seen" as a threat unrelated to the troublesome behavior the punisher is trying to change. The result may be aggression and frustration leading to even more troublesome behavior.

Economic thinking guides a great deal of public policy making, research, and action. It assumes that people always act rationally, that they are always motivated by self-interest, that choice is always good, and that there is never a free lunch (Weaver, 2002). The "likelihood of a free lunch" is the only one of these assumptions accepted by evolutionary psychologists. Evolutionary psychologists focus on the evolved emotional, motivational, and cognitive psychological processes that contributed to the survival and reproduction of human ancestors and how they function in this ever-changing world.

During the last 15 years, a great deal of knowledge about evolutionary psychology has been developed by empirical and theoretical researchers (Barkow, Cosmides, & Tooby, 1992; Crawford & Krebs, 1998). So far, this knowledge has had little impact on policymakers and legislators. Supreme Court justices and managers seldom consult evolutionary psychologists to help with their deliberations. When faced with personal decisions, few individuals ask themselves how a Darwinian perspective might help them. The aim of this volume is to start the process of using theories and findings of evolutionary psychology to help make the world a better place to live.

The contributors to this volume believe that developing a society based on moral principles, yet one that is relatively livable, involves understanding evolved human nature. Darwin's closing paragraph of *The Descent of Man* suggests a role for using evolutionary theory to help understand ourselves:

> Man with all his noble qualities, with sympathy that feels for the most debased, with benevolence which extends not only to other men but to the humblest of living creatures, with his god-like intellect which has penetrated into the movements and constitution of the solar system—with all these exalted powers—still bears in his bodily frame the indelible stamp of his lowly origin. (Darwin, 1871/1981, Vol. 2, p. 405)

His "indelible stamp" on human phylogenetic heritage informs all evolutionary approaches to the study of human behavior. This volume is based on the premise that using evolutionary psychology to help understand people can help them produce a world that is a better place to live.

The book is divided into three parts. The first part deals with basic issues in the application of the modern synthetic theory of evolution to the study of human behavior. It is designed to inform those who desire an overview of how Darwin's Theory of Evolution by Natural Selection is being used in the study of human behavior. The second part explores some of the evolved cognitive and affective mechanisms that are relevant to public policy and private decisions. The third part of the book deals with the application of evolutionary thinking to a number of substantive areas.

REFERENCES

Allen, E., Beckwith, B., Beckwith, J., Chorover, S., Culver, D., Duncan, M., Gould, S., Hubbard, R., Inouye, H., Leeds, A., Lewontin, R., Madansky, C., Miller, L., Pyeritz, R., Rosenthal, M., & Schreier, H. (1975). Against "sociobiology." *New York Review of Books*, November 13, pp. 182, 184–186.

Barash, D. (1982). *Sociobiology and behavior* (2nd ed.). New York: Elsevier.

Barkow, J., Cosmides, L., & Tooby, J. (1992). *The adapted mind: Evolutionary psychology and the generation of culture.* New York: Oxford University Press.

Barlow, G., & Silverberg, J. (Eds.). (1980). *Sociobiology: Beyond nature/nurture: Reports, definitions, and debate: AAAS Selected Symposium.* Boulder, CO: Westview Press.

Bostridge, I. (1997). *Witchcraft and its transformations c. 1650–c. 1750.* New York: Oxford University Press.

Buss, D. (1994). *The evolution of desire: Strategies of human mating.* New York: Basic Books.

Buss, D. (2000). *Dangerous passions: Why jealousy is as necessary as love and sex.* New York: The Free Press.

Caplan, A. (Ed.). (1978). *The sociobiology debate: Readings from the ethical and scientific issues concerning sociobiology.* New York: Harper & Row.

Cosmides, L. (1989). The logic of social exchange: Has natural selection shaped how humans reason? Studies with the Wason selection task. *Cognition, 31,* 187–276.

Cosmides, L., & Tooby, J. (1989). Evolutionary psychology and the generation of culture: Part II. Case study: A computational theory of social exchange. *Ethology and Sociobiology, 10,* 51–97.

Cosmides, L., & Tooby, J. (1992). Cognitive adaptations for social exchange. In J. Barkow, L. Cosmides, & J. Tooby (Eds.), *The adapted mind: Evolutionary psychology and the generation of culture* (pp. 163–228). New York: Oxford University Press.

Crawford, C. B. (1979). George Washington, Abraham Lincoln and Arthur Jensen: Are they compatible? *American Psychologist, 34*, 664–672.

Crawford, C. B. (1998a). The theory of evolution in the study of human behaviour: An introduction and overview. In C. B. Crawford & D. Krebs (Eds.), *Handbook of evolutionary psychology: Ideas, issues and applications* (pp. 3–41). Hillsdale, NJ: Lawrence Erlbaum Associates.

Crawford, C. B. (1998b). Environments and adaptations: Then and now. In C. B. Crawford & D. Krebs (Eds.), *Handbook of evolutionary psychology: Ideas, issues and applications*. Hillsdale, NJ: Lawrence Erlbaum Associates.

Crawford, C. B. (1999). [Review of the book *Uniting psychology and biology: Integrative perspectives on human development*]. *Evolution and Human Behavior, 20*, 137–139.

Crawford, C. B., & Anderson, J. L. (1989). Sociobiology: An environmentalist discipline? *American Psychologist, 44*, 1449–1459.

Crawford, C. B., & Krebs, D. (Eds.). (1998). *Handbook of evolutionary psychology: Ideas, issues, and applications*. Hillsdale, NJ: Lawrence Erlbaum Associates.

Daly, M., & Wilson, M. (1983). *Sex, evolution, and behavior* (2nd ed.). Boston: PWS Publishers.

Daly, M., & Wilson, M. (1998). The social psychology of family violence. In C. B. Crawford & D. Krebs (Eds.), *Handbook of evolutionary psychology: Ideas, issues, and applications* (pp. 431–456). Hillsdale, NJ: Lawrence Erlbaum Associates.

Darwin, C. (1871). *The descent of man, and selection in relation to sex*. London: Murray.

Darwin, C. (1981). *The descent of man, and selection in relation to sex*. Princeton: Princeton University Press. (Original work published 1871)

Davies, N. (1996). *Europe; A history*. New York: Oxford University Press.

Dunbar, R. (1996). *Grooming, gossip, and the evolution of language*. London: Faber & Faber.

Ekman, P. (1973). Cross cultural studies of facial expression. In P. Ekman (Ed.), *Darwin and facial expression: A century of research in review* (pp. 169–222). New York: Academic Press.

Haney, C., Banks, C., & Zimbardo, P. (1973). A study of prisoners and guards in a simulated prison. Naval Research Reviews, Dept. of the Navy. In E. Aronson (Ed.), *Readings about the social animal* (6th ed., pp. 52–67). New York: Freeman.

Hoffer, C., & Hull, N. (1981). *Murdering mothers: Infanticide in England and New England (1558–1803)*. New York: University Press.

Hutsler, J. (1995). Youth sport facts and demographics. Retrieved September 30, 2002, from *North American Youth Sport Institute*, http.//www.naysi.com

Jeffreys, S. (1997). *The idea of prostitution*. Melbourne: Australia: Spinifex.

Laurence, J. (1960). *A history of capital punishment*. New York: Citadel.

Marks, L. (1987). *Fears, phobias, and rituals: Panic anxiety and their disorders*. New York: Oxford University Press.

Medvedev, Z. (1969). *The rise and fall of T. D. Lysenko*. New York: Columbia University Press.

Nesse, R., & Williams, G. (1994). *Why we get sick: The new science of Darwinian medicine*. New York: Random House.

Orians, G., & Heerwagen, J. (1992). Evolved response to landscapes. In J. Barkow, L. Cosmides, & J. Tooby (Eds.), *The adapted mind: Evolutionary psychology and the generation of culture* (pp. 555–579). New York: Oxford University Press.

Porter, R. H. (1987). Kin recognition: Functions and mediating mechanisms. In C. B. Crawford, M. Smith, & D. Krebs (Eds.), *Sociobiology and psychology: Ideas, issues and applications* (pp. 175–204). Hillsdale, NJ: Lawrence Erlbaum Associates.

Renner, K., & Yurchesyn, K. (1994). Sexual robbery: The missing concept in the search for an appropriate legal metaphor for sexual aggression. *Canadian Journal of Behavioural Science, 26*, 41–51.

Rose, H., & Rose, S. (Eds.). (2000). *Alas, poor Darwin: Arguments against evolutionary psychology*. New York: Harmony Books.

Scrimshaw, S. (1984). Infanticide in human populations: Societal and individual concerns. In G. Hausfater & S. Hrdy (Eds.), *Infanticide: Comparative and evolutionary perspectives* (pp. 439–462). New York: Aldine.

Sheehan, H. (1993). *Marxism and the philosophy of science: A critical history.* Atlantic Highlands, NJ: Humanities Press International.

Shepher, J. (1983). *Incest: A biosocial approach.* New York: Academic Press.

Silk, J. B. (1990). Human adoption in evolutionary perspective. *Human Nature, 1,* 25–52.

Singh, D. (1993). Adaptive significance of female physical attractiveness: Role of waist-to-hip ratio. *Journal of Social and Personality Psychology, 65,* 293–307.

Skinner, B. F. (1948). *Waldon II.* New York: Macmillan.

Spohn, C. (1999). The rape reform movement: The traditional common law and rape law reforms. *Jurimetrics, 39,* 119–130.

Spohn, C., & Horney, J. (1992). *Rape law reform: a grassroots revolution and its impact.* New York: Plenum.

Stossel, S. (1997, May). The man who counts the killings. *Atlantic Monthly, 279,* 86–104.

Streeter, S., & McBurney, D. (2003). Waist-to Hip Ratio and attractiveness: New evidence and a critique of "a critical test." *Evolution and Human Behavior, 24,* 88–98.

Symons, D. (1987). If we're all Darwinians, what's the fuss about? In C. B. Crawford, M. Smith, & D. Krebs (Eds.), *Sociobiology and psychology: Ideas, issues, and applications* (pp. 121–146). Hillsdale, NJ: Lawrence Erlbaum Associates.

Symons, D. (1979). *The evolution of human sexuality.* New York: Oxford University Press.

Thornhill, R., & Gangestad, S. (1993). Human facial beauty: Averageness, symmetry, and parasite resistance. *Human Nature, 4,* 237–239.

Tracy, K., & Crawford, C. B. (1999). Wife beating in evolutionary perspective. In D. Counts, J. Brown, & J. Campbell (Eds.), *To have and to hit: Cultural perspectives on wife abuse* (pp. 27–42). Urbana, IL: University of Illinois Press.

Trivers, R. L. (1985). *Social evolution.* Menlo Park, CA: Benjamin/Cummings.

Wakefield, J. (1992a). The concept of mental disorder: On the boundary between biological facts and social values. *American Psychologist, 47,* 373–388.

Wakefield, J. (1992b). Disorder as harmful dysfunction: A conceptual critique of the DSM-III'R's definition of mental disorder. *Psychological Review, 99,* 232–247.

Weaver, B (2002). Psychology and public policy. *APS Observer, Convention Issue, 15,* 11–12.

Wilson, E. (1975). *Sociobiology: The new synthesis.* Cambridge, MA: Harvard University Press.

Wolf, A. (1995). *Sexual attraction and childhood association: A Chinese brief for Edward Westermark.* Stanford: Stanford University Press.

Yakovlov, A. N. (2002). *A century of violence in Soviet Russia.* New Haven, CT: Yale University Press.

The Essence
of Evolutionary Psychology:
An Introduction

Charles Crawford
Simon Fraser University

Catherine Salmon
University of Redlands

E arly in the 20th century, thinkers such as William James, John Dewy, and Sigmund Freud embraced Darwinism with enthusiasm. But for the past 75 years, a major activity of those involved in the study of human behavior has been "de-biologising" it. Neo-behaviorism, social learning theory, cognitive theory, modern psychoanalysis, and more recently, a variety of postmodernist explanations, as well as politically liberal approaches to the amelioration of social problems, currently dominate the thinking of many academics. Most individuals taking these approaches see little value in ancestral history, human nature, or innate mental mechanisms in developing explanations for human behavior.

During the later part of the 19th and the early part of the 20th century, there was a strong emphasis on improving society and the lot of those living in it. Because they accepted Jean-Baptiste Lamark's theory of the inheritance of acquired characteristics, many academic-minded reformers turned to evolutionary theory as a means to reform. They believed that acquired habits, such as prudence, diligence, and restraint, which contributed to successful reproduction in one generation, would be favored by natural selection, and within a few generations people could all be living in a better society. But two events occurred just after the turn of the century that crushed these hopes (Degler, 1991).

First, Weisman put forth convincing arguments, supported by some empirical data, that traits acquired during the lifetime of an individual cannot be inherited by their offspring. If Weisman was correct, evolution by natural selection did not offer the quick fixes for solving societal problems that early social Darwinists, such as Herbert Spencer, had expected. Second, the rediscovery of Mendal's laws seemed to provide a sound scientific basis for explaining the biological inheritance of a wide variety of physical and behavioral traits, and suggested that selective breeding of humans could lead to an improvement in society. Weisman's and Mendel's discoveries, combined with the desire to produce a better world, sent reformers in two directions (Degler, 1991). Some were attracted to genetic explanations of differences between individuals and groups, and eventually to eugenics, and others were attracted to the *tabula rasa* view of human nature. The controversy surrounding Herrnstein and Murray's (1994) *The Bell Curve: Intelligence and Class Structure in American Life*, Thornhill and Palmer's (2000) *A Natural History of Rape*, and Pinker's (2002) *The Blank Slate* suggests that the intellectual and scientific struggle between these approaches continues, and that the *tabula rasa* view dominates the thinking of the majority of scientists involved in the study of human behavior.

In addition to the political reasons for the widespread resistance to incorporating ideas from evolutionary theory into thinking about human behavior, until recently a major scientific reason for the wariness was that the theory did not provide a repertoire of useful constructs for formulating detailed explanations of human and animal behavior. Therefore, when the theory of evolution was employed, it was often used as a convenient framework for discussing adaptiveness or as a way of integrating diverse ideas, rather than as a paradigm for developing testable explanations of behavior. During the last three decades, however, the modern synthesis has been enriched by concepts such as inclusive fitness, kin selection, reciprocity theory, and the evolution of life histories, which have made it more applicable to behavior. New techniques for analyzing the formation and nature of adaptations have been developed, such as the theory of evolutionarily stable strategies and optimality theory. Moreover, during the past 15 years, a new discipline focused on the naturally selected design of the mental mechanisms that make up the "mind" has begun to emerge (Cosmides & Tooby, 1987). It is known as Darwinian, or evolutionary, psychology.

This chapter first reviews the logic of the Theory of Evolution by Natural Selection and discusses several issues concerned with its use. It then briefly describes kinship, reciprocity, sexual selection, and the significance of ancestral history. The role of genetics in developing evolutionary explanations is also discussed.

THE LOGIC OF NATURAL SELECTION

An adaptation is an anatomical structure, a physiological process, or a behavior pattern that contributed to ancestral individuals' ability to survive and reproduce in competition with other members of their species. Natural selection, the process that shapes adaptations, is the differential production or survival of offspring by genetically different members of the population (Williams, 1966; E. O. Wilson, 1975). Darwin's (1859) logic may be explained in terms of the following assumptions and inferences:

Assumption 1: Species are capable of overproducing offspring.

Assumption 2: The size of populations of individuals tends to remain relatively stable over time.

Assumption 3: Resources for supporting individuals are limited.

   Inference 1: A struggle for existence among individuals ensues.

Assumption 4: Individuals differ on traits (i.e., adaptations) that enable them to survive and reproduce.

Assumption 5: At least some of the variation in these traits is genetically heritable.

   Inference 2: There is differential production or survival of offspring by genetically different members of the population, which is by definition natural selection.

   Inference 3: Through many generations evolution of traits that are more adaptive than others will occur through natural selection.

In short, some feature of the environment, perhaps the arrival of a new predator or a change in climate, poses a problem for organisms. Genetically based variants, such as longer legs or thicker fur, contribute to reproduction and survival. The previous assumptions and inferences explain how natural selection provides the solution. Preexisting adaptations, sometimes called preadaptations, provide both stepping stones and limits to the solutions natural selection can produce (Gould, 1982). Hence, there are constraints on the "perfection" of the solution natural selection can provide.

This view might be called the phenotypic view of evolution, because the focus is on the anatomical structures, physiological processes, or the behavior patterns that helped solve the problems faced by the organism. Although at least some of the phenotypic variation must be heritable for natural selection to occur, genetic concepts are not referred to explicitly. It is also possible, however, to describe evolution by natural selection in terms of changes in allele frequencies caused by selection, mutation, migration, genetic drift, and other processes. Some scientists favor this more quantitative approach because it enables them to construct precise models of evolutionary processes that may be tested through experimental research, field studies, or computer model simulations. Others believe that the focus of evolutionary work must be on the formation of adaptations. They tend to favor the phenotypic view. However, the two descriptions are complementary and together make up the modern synthetic theory of evolution.

SOME COMMON MISCONCEPTIONS ABOUT NATURAL SELECTION

Circularity

There are some who still believe that the logic of evolution by natural selection is circular—the fittest survive because they are the fittest. However, this view is incorrect (Sober, 1984). Note that in the previous description of Darwin's logic, the definitions of both adaptation and natural selection are independent of the assumptions. If the definitions are accepted and it is possible to document the validity of the assumptions, then evolution by natural selection follows logically. Darwin extensively documented the validity of the assumptions and since his time massive additional evidence for their validity has accumulated (see Ridley, 1993).

Nature of Competition

The first three assumptions and their inference do not require that nature be "red in tooth and claw." Differential production or survival of offspring by genetically different members of a population is the basis of evolution by natural selection. Animals use a variety of subtle and not so subtle strategies for competing with members of their species. For example, juvenile Florida scrub jays apparently increase their fitness by deferring reproduction for up to 7 years in order to assist their parents in raising additional broods of siblings (Woolfenden & Fitzpatrick, 1984). Hamilton (1971) argued that individual animals in aggregations position themselves in such a way that their risk of predation, relative to others in the aggregation, is minimized.

Genetic Preprogramming of Evolved Traits

Although Assumptions 4 and 5 require that some trait variation be genetically conditioned for natural selection to occur, they do not imply that the development of evolved traits is genetically preprogrammed. If the ontogeny of a trait is influenced by environmental factors, then biologists refer to it as a *facultative trait* and label the genes involved in its development *facultative genes*. The white crowned sparrow, for example, must hear an adult male sparrow sing while it is a nestling and it must itself sing as a juvenile if it is to sing a complete song as an adult (Konishi, 1965; Marler, 1984). Moreover, the young sparrow does not, and indeed cannot, learn the song of another species. Apparently, this developmental process ensures that the species' song is learned, but that it can be adjusted to local dialects.

Acting for the Good of the Group

> Though occasionally, in the territorial or rival fights, by some mishap a horn may penetrate an eye or a tooth an artery, we have never found that the *aim* of aggression was the extermination of fellow members of the species concerned. (Lorenz, 1966, p. 47, italics added)

This quotation illustrates Lorenz' assumption, shared by many others, that individuals evolve to act for the good of the group. Similarly, Wynne-Edwards (1962) argued that selection acts on groups rather than on individuals. Models of group selection, although attractive to those attempting to understand the paradox of the existence of "helping" behavior in many species and the inability of "individual fitness"-based evolutionary theory to explain its evolution, have usually foundered on the problem of "cheating" (Williams, 1966).

Consider a number of groups, each made up of individuals who sacrifice some of their reproductive fitness for the good of other group members, competing with each other. Here a sacrifice is defined as any action, such as the provision of food, care, or protection to other group members, that reduces the reproductive success of the performer and increases the reproductive success of the recipient(s). Groups made up of such "altruistic" individuals may prosper. However, an individual group member possessing a mutation that programmed, or enabled the learning of, the acceptance of helping behavior without reciprocation would leave more offspring than altruistic members of the group. Groups or species made up of individuals acting for the common good would be undermined by mutation from within and by immigration from without. As a result, for group selection to be a viable evolutionary process, groups must appear and disappear at an unrealistically high rate (Maynard Smith, 1976). Although attempts to develop more sophisticated models of group selection are underway (Sober & D. S. Wilson, 1998), they do not yet provide a viable alternative to individual and kin selection.

Incompatibility of Evolutionary and Nonevolutionary Explanations

Must evolutionary and nonevolutionary explanations make different predictions? To answer this question, consider two sets of explanations. The first set contains explanations that were explicitly constructed with evolutionary theory in mind. The second set contains explanations that were developed without any explicit knowledge of evolutionary theory. However, some of these latter explanations, such as commonsense explanations like "Blood is thicker than water," and "It is a wise father that knows his own child," are compatible with evolutionary theory, although they were devised without knowledge of it. But, other members of this second set, such as those designed to explain *true altruism*, where fitness costs outweigh benefits, are incompatible with the logic of evolution by natural selection. Thus, the greater set of all explanations that are compatible with evolutionary theory includes all of Set 1, and some overlap from Set 2.

Explanations that are not compatible with evolutionary theory may be thought of as "warp drive" explanations, because warp drive is what the crew of the Starship Enterprise use when they wish to violate Einstein's theory of relativity to travel faster than the speed of light. Developing explanations of physical phenomena that violate Einstein's theory of relativity is risky, as is developing explanations about behavior that violate Darwin's theory of evolution by natural selection. Hence, it is likely that any good explanation of behavior will be compatible with an evolutionary explanation, even if it was not explicitly developed from an evolutionary perspective. Although a good explanation of behavior need not have been explicitly constructed from an evolutionary perspective, the contributors to this volume are committed to the proposition that an explicit consideration of evolutionary theory will improve the quality of explanations of human behavior.

Why do they believe this? Explicit evolutionary thinking can sometimes eliminate certain kinds of errors in thinking about behavior (Symons, 1987). For example, explanations that implicitly assume organisms have evolved to act for the good of their group or species should be treated with considerable skepticism. In addition, use of the theory can sometimes help to prevent people from making and accepting *moralistic fallacies*, where individuals assume that what *ought* to be actually *is*. Consider some examples. Stepparents ought to treat their natural and stepchildren equally. However, when Daly and Wilson (1980) applied evolutionary thinking to the problem of child abuse, they found that stepparents were a major source of abuse. There ought not to be conflict within families, but Trivers (1974) used evolutionary theory to help with understanding the within-family conflict that has proved perplexing for generations. Recently, Haig (1993, 2002) argued for the occurrence of mother–offspring conflict during gestation. Men and women ought to have the same intellectual abilities. But Silverman and Eals (1992) were able to use evolutionary thinking to predict and explain gender differences in some perceptual abilities. A rigorous application of evolutionary theory may help to identify and deal with other *oughts* that contradict reality.

But most important, the theory of evolution can be used to help scholars and scientists develop substantive testable predictions about human behavior. Cosmides (1989) used it to make predictions about content effects in logical reasoning. Silverman and Eals (1992) used it to make predictions about gender differences in spatial abilities. Singh (1993) used it to make predictions about preferences for body images. Buss (1994) used it to make predictions about gender differences in mate choice criteria and tactics for acquiring mates. Orians and Heerwagen (1992) used it to make predictions about evoked responses to landscapes. The majority of this book is devoted to the discussion of recent research in which various aspects of evolutionary theory were used to explore aspects of human psychology relevant to issues of public and personal policy.

Although Darwin's logic of natural selection provides the basis of all evolutionary explanations, a number of concepts that were not fully developed in his thinking have been more completely refined during the last few years. They include sexual selection, kinship theory, and reciprocity. They surface and are more fully explored in later chapters in this book.

SEXUAL SELECTION

Human males and females differ in anatomy, physiology, and behavior. There are at least two sources of selection pressure that interact and complement each other in producing this evolved sexual dimorphism. The production and rearing of offspring may have caused some specialization of roles for ancestral males and females that resulted in selection for sexual dimorphism in physical body size, behavior, and brain development (Kimura, 1987; Tooby & DeVore, 1987). The other evolutionary explanation for sexual dimorphism is Darwin's theory of sexual selection.

Sexual selection refers to differences in the ability of individuals with different genotypes to acquire matings. If, for example, tall and short males have similar survival, but tall males obtain more matings than short males, then sexual selection is said to be acting on the males. Darwin (1871) argued that sexual selection involves two processes that are usually referred to as *intrasexual selection* and *intersexual selection.*

In intrasexual selection, competition between the members of one sex (usually males) for access to the other sex (usually females) produces selection pressure for increased physical size, organs of threat, and aggressiveness in members of the competing sex, as well as differences between males and females on these traits. Male elephant seals, for example, compete vigorously among themselves for access to females. They are about 60% larger than females and about four times as heavy. Although most males never get near a female during their entire lives, a few male elephant seals may have as many as a hundred females in their harems (LeBoeuf, 1974). The males make no investment in individual offspring, whereas the females provide large quantities of rich milk that contribute to rapid growth of the young. Intersexual, or epigamic, selection, is the result of the members of one sex (usually females) generating competition between members of the other sex by "expressing" choice for a mating partner. The competition results in the elaboration of the traits members of the choosy sex "desire." The tail of the male peacock provides the classic example.

But why do males compete for females, and do females ever compete for males? Trivers and Willard (1973) attempted to develop a more general scheme for considering sexually selected traits than the one Darwin employed. He developed the notion of relative *parental investment*, where parental investment is defined as behavior of a parent toward an offspring that contributes to the offspring's reproduction at the cost of the parent's investment in other offspring. Because the females of most species put relatively greater minimal investment into individual offspring than do males, they are limited in the additional offspring that additional matings can provide to them. Males, because they put less minimal investment into individual offspring than do females, are less limited in the benefits of additional matings. Thus, females are a limiting resource for males, and males can benefit by competing among themselves for access to that resource. Males are usually, but not always, the sexually selected sex.

Exceptions that prove the rule are provided by organisms with sex role reversal such as seahorses, certain frogs, and several species of marsh and shorebirds (including jacanas and phalaropes). In these species, although males make a small investment in sperm, their relative minimal parental investment is large because they take sole responsibility for parental care (Alcock, 1993). As a result, the females have evolved to be larger and/or more colorful than the males and to compete among themselves for access to males.

But relative parental investment does not seem to explain why females are often so choosy. Several explanations have been offered. Darwin suggested that the females of some species had a sense of beauty. In his "sexy sons" explanation of female choice, Fisher (1930) argued that females can evolve to favor an arbitrary trait if their sons exhibit the trait and their daughters favor males who exhibit it. Zahavi (1975) argued that certain traits are attractive to females because they provide a handicap that indicates something about the quality of male genes. Thus the large, brightly colored tail of the peacock may be saying to the female "Look at my large and beautiful tail. It takes a lot of my resources to grow it. It is cumbersome to maneuver and it may attract predators. But the fact that I have it, despite these costs, shows that I am a vigorous and healthy male and you should choose to mate with me rather than with a male who has a dull, droopy tail." At first, the "sexy sons" and "handicap" arguments were greeted with skepticism. But, during the last few years, the role of ancestral parasites in the evolution of sexuality, the differences between males' and females' reproductive tactics, and how the members of each sex evaluate prospective mating partners has helped with understanding how apparent handicaps may provide clues about the fitness of their possessors. Miller (2000) reviewed the latest thinking on the origins of sexual dimorphism and its importance in explaining gender differences in behavior.

Are humans a sexually selected species? Men are about 7% larger than women. They are more physically aggressive than women. They die off faster than women at all ages and they do not live as long as women. They take risks that women consider foolhardy. Men vary more than women in the number of children they produce. Women often invest more in their children than do men. Throughout history, most men have mated monogamously. However, a sample of 849 societies found that 83% are either usually or occasionally polygynous, 16% are monogamous, and 0.5% are polyandrous (Daly & Wilson, 1983). Even in monogamous societies, such as the Hutterites, variance of male reproductive success exceeds that of females (Crawford, 1984). This evidence indicates that humans are a moderately sexually selected species. Several chapters in this book rely on the theory of sexual selection for their explanations. Browne (chap. 13) uses it in his work on gender differences in the workplace. Wilson and Daly (chap. 9) use it to help explain family violence, and Shackelford and Weekes-Shackelford (chap. 11) use it to illuminate the problems with getting men to pay child support. It also has implications for Salmon's (chap. 10) work on pornography.

THE NATURE OF KINSHIP

Altruistic behavior, which can be defined as "self destructive behavior performed for the benefit of others" (E. O. Wilson, 1975, p. 578), has long been a paradox for evolutionary theorists. According to the logic of natural selection, it should not evolve, but it is widespread in nature. Darwin believed that the existence of "neuter insects," the sterile castes in the bees, wasps, and ants, might be fatal to his theory. However, Hamilton (1964) elaborated Darwin's solution to the problem and expressed it in the language of modern population biology: "The social behavior of a species evolves in such a way that in each distinct behavior evoking situation the individual will *seem* [italics added] to value his neighbors' fitness against his own according to the coefficients of relationship appropriate to that situation" (p. 19). Hamilton saw that biological altruism can evolve, even though it reduces the reproductive fitness of the donor of the help, if it aids the donor's genetic kin, some of whom must inherit the helping allele from a common ancestor of the donor.

The previous statement can be expressed as an equation:

$$Br_1 > Cr_2$$

where $B =$ the benefit to the recipient
          $r_1 =$ the genetic correlation between
                the donor and the recipient's offspring
          $C =$ the cost to the donor
          $r_2 =$ the genetic correlation between the donor
                and its own offspring

In this equation, r_1 and r_2 represent the probabilities that the individuals in question have an allele that is a copy of one in a common ancestor. Such an allele is described as *identical by common descent*. These probabilities are called genetic correlations or coefficients of relatedness between individuals. Br_1 is the indirect benefit to the donor through the recipient's additional offspring. Cr_2 is the direct cost to the helper because of its forgone offspring.

Consider the case of an individual who possesses a helping allele A for giving up one offspring to help a half sibling produce three additional offspring. This allele was inherited from the parent of the two sibs. When a gamete is produced, a segregation occurs and only one of each pair of chromosomes is passed on to the fertilized egg. Therefore, the probability that any particular allele in a parent is passed on to an offspring is 0.5. There are two genetic segregations between donors and any of their three additional nieces or nephews that were produced *because* of the help. Therefore, there is a $0.5 \cdot 0.5 = 0.25$ chance that any one of them inherits the helping allele possessed by the donor, who is their uncle or aunt. But there is only one segregation between donors and their one, forgone, offspring, resulting in a genetic correlation of 0.5. Putting these numbers in to Hamilton's equation produces

$$3(0.25) > 1(0.50)$$
$$0.75 > 0.50.$$

Therefore, natural selection can favor the evolution of mechanisms for producing this *altruistic* behavior. Note that both sides of the equation refer to changes in the donor's fitness because of the *altruistic* act. The right side indicates the direct cost to the donor through offspring not produced, whereas the left side indicates the indirect benefits to the donor through offspring that a genetic relative was able to rear because of the help. Thus, Hamilton's altruism is really a special kind of *selfishness*. Those looking to evolutionary theory to provide an explanation for *true altruism*, a behavior that reduces the inclusive fitness of the performer while benefiting that of the recipient, will not find it in Hamilton's equation. As becomes evident later, in the current environment, the action of mechanisms for implementing Hamilton's *selfishness* can result in something like *true altruism*.

Within-Family Conflict

Trivers (1974) used Hamilton's argument that the behavior of an individual, whether it be a parent, a child, or a grandparent, is shaped by natural selection to maximize the probability that copies of alleles it carries are replicated through its behavior, to analyze within-family conflict. Figure 2.1 can be used to compute the probabilities that parents, grandparents, and children possess an allele (say *A*, or *a*) that is a copy of an allele possessed by a common ancestor. These probabilities are computed by raising 0.5 (the probability that *A* or *a* is passed on when a gamete is formed) to the power of the number of genetic segregations (represented in Fig. 2.1 as arrows) connecting two individuals.

Because the probability of the focal individual replicating its allele(s) through its own offspring is 0.5 and through its sibling's offspring (its niece or nephew) is only 0.25, natural selection will favor focal individuals that seek an unequal share of their parent's (labeled grandparent in the figure) resources. But because the parent (grandparent) is equally related to all its children and grandchildren, it will be selected to resist the focal individual's demands.

When the offspring is young, the parent can maximize its fitness by investing in the current offspring at the expense of additional offspring, who would be future siblings of the current offspring. When the offspring is old, it can maximize its fitness if it defers parental investment in itself in favor of parental investment in additional younger siblings. Conflict is most intense at intermediate ages of the focal offspring. During this period, the parent's fitness is increased more by investing in additional offspring, while the focal offspring's fitness is increased more by continued parental investment. Thus, the intensity of within-family conflict varies both as a function of genetic relationships and the relative ages of individuals in the family.

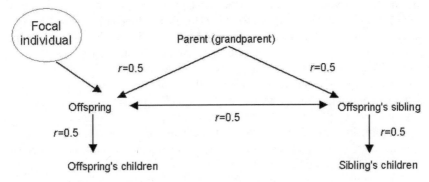

FIG. 2.1.   Multiplying along the arrows connecting two individuals gives the probability that they will share an allele by common descent. (A grandparent, A, is equally related to all his or her children, B and C, and to all his or her grandchildren, D and E. However, the focal individual, B, shares an allele with any of his or her children, D, with probability 0.5, and with any of his or her nieces and nephews, E, with probability 0.25. Thus, B is selected to desire an unequal share of A's resources.) From "The Theory of Evolution: Of What Value to Psychology?," by C. B. Crawford, 1989, *Journal of Comparative Psychology, 103*, p. 8. Copyright © 1989 by the American Psychological Association. Adapted with permission.

Recently Haig (1993, 2002) extended Trivers' thinking by considering three sets of genes that may have different interests: genes in the mother, maternally derived genes in the current child, and paternally derived genes in the current child. Because maternal genes have an equal stake in each child, they will be selected to transfer resources to children as a function of the children's likelihood of reproducing. Genes in the current child have a greater interest in the current child than in future children and will be selected to maximize transfer of resources to the current child. Some genes can be imprinted with information about their parental origin. This fact makes the situation more complicated if the mother has children from different fathers because paternally active genes in the current offspring have no stake in offspring fathered by different males. Haig provided arguments and evidence of how these conflicts have influenced the evolution of the female reproductive system and how they can lead to serious health problems for mothers.

Kinship plays a particularly important role in explaining the empirical data in chapter 9 on family violence by Wilson and Daly and Shackelford and Weekes-Shackelford's (chap. 11) work on child support. But the real significance of kinship is that it shifts the emphasis in evolutionary thinking from the level of the individual to the level of the allele and sheds light on many difficult problems.

RECIPROCITY

Because much behavior, both in animals and in humans, includes interactions between individuals that are not genetic kin, additional concepts are necessary for explaining the evolution of social behavior. Darwin recognized the importance of cooperation. However, it was Trivers (1971) who developed the modern theory of reciprocal altruism. Consider the example he used in developing his theory. Suppose someone is standing on a dock and sees a man fall into the water and begin to drown. The individual knows that the man is not a genetic relative. But the person finds a life preserver and by throwing it to the man, saves his life. Will natural selection favor such action across evolutionary time? If there is even a 1/1000 chance that the rescuer will fall in and drown in the effort to save the drowning man, then it would seem that natural selection should select for a preference for ignoring the individual in trouble. But suppose that there is a 1/20 chance that the roles will be reversed, and that sometime the rescuer will need to be saved from a watery death. If there is a greater than 1/50 chance that the individual saved will save the rescuer, then natural selection can select for the tendency to help the drowning individual even though he is not a genetic relative.

In the evolution of tendencies to act reciprocally, because the original helping acts must occur by chance, they would have to be acts of low cost for the donors and provide large benefits for the recipients, or natural selection would eliminate the tendency to perform them, and the system could not get started. Moreover, the roles of donor and recipient must frequently reverse. Finally, original recipients must be able to "recognize" the helper so they can reciprocate when the roles are reversed. These conditions suggest that reciprocal altruism is most likely to evolve in highly intelligent, closely integrated species. Humans and the higher primates come to mind.

Cheating, that is, accepting help when it is given, but not reciprocating when the roles are reversed, can undermine reciprocity. Trivers distinguished between two types of cheating. In *gross cheating*, the recipient does not reciprocate or reciprocates so little to the original donor that the benefits are significantly less than the cost of the original donor's act. For example: I am drowning, you find a life preserver, throw it to me, and pull me in. Later, you are drowning and I merely toss you the nearest twig. In *subtle cheating*, both parties reciprocate, but one party reciprocates somewhat less than the other. Both parties benefit, but one consistently benefits more than the other. For example, you and I have lunch once a week. When it is your turn to pay for lunch we dine at a nice restaurant, but when it is my turn to pay we dine at the sandwich shop. However, you may not want to cancel the arrangement because you may need a letter of reference from me in the future.

The great benefits received by individuals involved in a reciprocal system will provide strong selection for mechanisms for engaging in reciprocity, but the benefits obtained by gross, and especially, subtle cheating will select for mechanisms for giving back less than one receives. Trivers (1985) argued that because human reciprocity may span many years and involve thousands of interactions varying on many dimensions, computing the cost–benefit ratios that keep the reciprocal system running requires a complex and subtle psyche. Guilt, fairness, moralistic aggression, gratitude, and sympathy are just some of the feelings and emotions required to make human reciprocal altruism run. Many authors have expanded upon Trivers' original notions (Alexander, 1987; Krebs, 1987).

PROXIMATE MECHANISMS AND KIN RECOGNITION

The mathematical analysis of kinship and reciprocity theory is impressive and indicates that natural selection can be expected to have produced adaptations mediating both cooperation and conflict between genetically related and unrelated individuals. But would not a complicated set of behavioral or mental mechanisms be required to make it all happen? In the late 1980s, Cosmides and Tooby (1987) and Symons (1987) began forcefully arguing that an evolutionary approach cannot be agnostic about the nature of the proximate mechanisms that produce behavior. The result was the beginning of a new area within evolutionary studies. It is known as Darwinian, or evolutionary, psychology and is concerned with: the stresses that existed in ancestral environments, the proximate mechanisms that evolved to deal with those stresses, and the way those evolved mechanisms function in contemporary environments (Crawford & Anderson, 1989).

If social organisms have evolved the capacity to put their helping behavior where their alleles are, as Hamilton and Trivers assumed, they must possess some proximate mechanisms for kin recognition, and these should be of interest to Darwinian psychologists. Possible mechanisms for kin recognition include spatial distribution (treating individuals in a prescribed geographic area as kin), frequency of association (treating frequent associates as kin), phenotype matching (treating individuals similar to oneself or similar to those with whom one was raised as kin), and recognition alleles (innately treating individuals with a particular genetic marker as kin). They have received attention from both biologists (Holmes, 1986; Waldman, 1986) and psychologists (Daly & M. Wilson, 1996; G. R. Johnson, 1989; Porter, 1987; Salmon, 1998).

If small kinship groups were an important feature of human social structure during evolution, then one or more of the aforementioned kin discrimination mechanisms may have evolved and may still be influencing people's behavior. Understanding the mechanism(s) involved may be critical if there is a desire to change human behavior through social learning. For example, if spatial distribution or association evolved as mechanisms of human kin discrimination, then encouraging individuals of different ethnic groups to live together in the same geographic area may contribute to ethnic harmony. However, other kin discrimination mechanisms may prescribe different means for achieving ethnic harmony. If treating individuals similar to those with whom one was raised is a human kin discrimination mechanism, then ethnically integrating schools starting with preschools rather than high schools is more likely to lead to ethnic harmony. If treating individuals similar to oneself as kin was an aspect of kin discrimination among ancestors, then it may be necessary to encourage different ethnic groups to adopt similar accents, manners, customs, and clothing to increase ethnic harmony. Finally, if genetically produced signs evolved among ancestors to discriminate between kin and nonkin, then producing ethnic harmony may, indeed, be difficult because social learning is not involved.

Studies of the impact of the use of kin terminology in political speech (Johnson, McAndrew, & Harris, 1987; Salmon, 1998) suggest that such terms act to promote the illusion of solidarity and shared interests between the speechmaker and their audience. The use of kin terms in political rhetoric can act to produce support for the speechmaker and their views even when the pre-speech political views of the listener are actually in opposition to those of the speechmaker. This suggests that the manipulation of kin recognition systems can be used to foster (as well as destroy when used to create divisions) ethnic and social harmony. Research on the evolutionary significance of proximate mechanisms involved in kin discrimination, social exchange, and mate selection is developing rapidly (see Barkow, Cosmides, & Tooby, 1992, for a review of some of this work).

ADAPTATIONS AND THE BEHAVIOR OF INDIVIDUALS

An *adaptation* is an anatomical structure, a physiological process, or a behavior pattern that contributed to ancestral individuals' ability to survive and reproduce in competition with other members of their species (Williams, 1966; E. O. Wilson, 1975). The beaks of Darwin's finches, which can be used to characterize the different species of finches living on the Galapagos, provide the classic example of an adaptation. Biologists, who are frequently interested in species differences and how they were shaped through natural selection, often do not focus on how the concept of adaptation can be used to explain differences in behavior within a particular species. However, when the focus is on the behavior of a single species, as it is in the study of human behavior, the focus must be on how the concept of adaptation can be used to explain differences in behavior manifest by members of the same species. Consider several examples.

Williams and Nesse (1991) gave several examples of how adaptations can help an organism respond differently to differing circumstances. Fever appears to be the result of a specific regulatory mechanism that adjusts body temperature in response to the toxins of some bacteria. When fever is blocked by drugs such as aspirin, resistance to infection may be decreased. Similarly, the sequestering of iron in the liver, which reduces the iron content of the plasma by up to 20%, deprives some bacteria of a vital mineral and inhibits their spread through the body. In both cases, the adaptations adjust bodily functions in response to varying environmental conditions.

Consider a behavioral example in some detail. Figure 2.2 illustrates the mating strategy of the male scorpionfly. The strategy contains three mating tactics: (a) Males may obtain a dead insect, present it to a female, and copulate with her as she eats it; (b) they may generate a salivary mass, present it to the female, and copulate with her as she eats it; or (c) if they cannot obtain a dead insect or generate the salivary mass, then they may attempt a forced copulation (Thornhill, 1980). In a variety of experimental studies, Thornhill (1980) showed that all three tactics are available to all adult males, and it is success in male–male competition that determines the behavior employed to obtain a mating. In these examples, the putative adaptations respond to both external and internal environmental contingencies, producing differences in behavior that contributed to ancestral fitness.

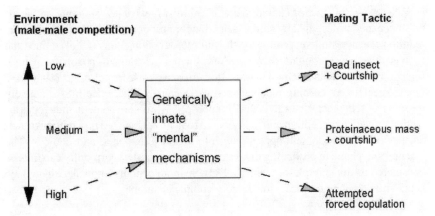

FIG. 2.2.   Mating tactics in scorpionflies (*Panorpa sp.*). (The level of male–male–male competition determines the reproductive tactic used. Heritability of the tactics is zero because all males have alleles for all tactics.) From "The Theory of Evolution: Of What Value to Psychology?," by C. B. Crawford, 1989, *Journal of Comparative Psychology, 103*, p. 15. Copyright © 1989 by the American Psychological Association. Adapted with permission.

Adaptations as Decision Makers

Adaptations can be understood in terms of processes for carrying out the cost–benefit analysis an ancestral organism required to survive its daily encounters with problems in its internal and external environment. The fever adaptation, for example, can be considered as a set of decision processes for dealing with certain kinds of invading bacteria, such as the rule: "If bacteria A, B, or C is invading the body, raise body temperature *X* degrees." Harmful bacteria may be destroyed if the body temperature is raised *X* degrees, which is beneficial to the individual. But the adaptation has costs as well benefits. Energy is required to raise the body temperature. Moreover, the rise in body temperature can damage other systems of the body if it is excessive and prolonged. Similarily, the three mating tactics of the male scorpionfly have costs as well as benefits. Even the strong dominant males, who obtain matings by presenting dead insects to females as nuptial gifts, risk broken legs and torn wings in the competition with other males for dead insects (Thornhill, 1980).

Thus, the working definition of an *adaptation* is "a set of genetically-coded decision processes that enabled ancestral organisms to carry out cost-benefit analyses in response to a specific set of environmental contingencies, and that organized the effector processes for dealing with those contingencies in such a way that gene(s) producing the decision processes would be reproduced better than alternate sets of genes" (Crawford, 1998).

When operating in the behavioral domain, think of sets of decision rules as "mental" mechanisms designed by natural selection for producing the different behaviors required for ancestral survival, growth, and reproduction. Buss (1999) coined the term *evolved psychological mechanisms* for mental mechanisms shaped by natural selection. These "innate school marms," to borrow a phrase from Lorenz (1966), are innate specialized learning mechanisms that organize experience into adaptively meaningful schemas. When activated by appropriate problem content, they focus attention, organize perception and memory, and call up specialized procedural knowledge that leads to domain-appropriate inferences, judgments, and choices. The "mental" mechanism producing the mating behaviors of the scorpionfly can thus be considered as an example of a simple Darwinian algorithm. Chomsky's language acquisition device provides a much more complex example.

Concurrent and Developmentally Contingent Tactics

The mating behavior of male scorpionflies is an example of a single mating strategy with *concurrently contingent tactics*, because the tactics employed depend on current environmental conditions. A strategy may also contain *developmentally contingent tactics*, or tactics that depend on external environmental conditions during development for their functioning (Crawford & Anderson, 1989). Song learning in some species of birds, which requires the song of an adult of the species to be heard during development, and language learning in humans, which also requires that information be obtained during development, provide examples of developmentally contingent tactics.

Current and Ancestral Environments and Fitness

Because ancestral and current environments may differ, adaptations or behaviors that contributed to ancestral fitness may no longer contribute to current fitness. Similarly, behaviors that may contribute to fitness now may not have contributed to it in the past. Suppose, for the sake of argument, that an adaptation for adjusting personal level of aggression to the current level of aggression observed in the environment occurred in both ancestral and current children. If the distribution of aggression seen on TV by children differs from the level of aggression that ancestral children would have seen, then the identical adaptations may produce quite different levels of aggressive behavior. Thus, from an evolutionary perspective, individuals from different cultures should not be expected to behave similarly, nor should individuals in the same culture be expected to always act uniformly.

Although a separation of gender roles, where men hunted and women gathered, may have contributed to ancestral fitness (Tooby & DeVore, 1987), such a separation may no longer contribute to fitness. Moreover, behaviors that contribute to the current fitness of at least some individuals, such as philosophic speculation or conducting scientific research, may not have contributed to ancestral fitness. This argument leads many to the conclusion that the study of reproductive fitness in current environments tells little about evolved adaptations (Crawford, 1993; Symons, 1989; Tooby & Cosmides, 1990).

The following distinctions may be helpful in clarifying the role of fitness in ancestral and current environments. A *beneficial effect* is an aspect of an adaptation that increases the probability that its carrier will have copies of its alleles represented in succeeding generations, whereas a *detrimental effect* is an aspect of an adaptation that reduces the probability that its carrier will have alleles represented in subsequent generations. If an adaptation's expected beneficial effects are not equal to its expected detrimental effects in a population, then natural selection may be occurring in that population and the adaptation may be evolving. A function is a beneficial effect that existed in an ancestral population, and hence, it can be said to be one of the causes of the evolution of the adaptation. The "thumb-finger" grip that enables people to manipulate the mouse on their computers (a beneficial effect) and that also enables them to inject dangerous drugs (a detrimental effect) impacts on their current reproductive fitness. Chipping stone tools may have been one of its beneficial effects in an ancestral environment, and hence one of its functions.

Note that if the environment has changed since an adaptation was shaped, the beneficial and detrimental effects in the current environment may not be identical to those in the ancestral environment. The beneficial and detrimental effects and the functions of an adaptation in an ancestral environment tell something about how that trait evolved and what problem(s) it evolved to solve.

The formation of an adaptation must be distinguished from how it is characterized in a current environment. An *adaptive trait*, such as using the mouse on the computer, is one that has at least one beneficial effect in a current environment. *Adaptiveness* is the degree to which an organism is able to live and reproduce in a given set of environments. *Adaptability* is the degree to which an organism is able to live and reproduce in varying environments. The panda has high adaptiveness in bamboo forests only, but the Norway rat has a high level of adaptability, as it thrives in many different environments. These terms help with understanding how a trait is related to survival, reproduction, and general functioning in a current environment.

NOVEL ENVIRONMENTS AND PROBLEMATIC BEHAVIOR

Figure 2.3 describes how adaptations function, both in the modern environment and the ancestral one. The particular example used is that of one mechanism for avoiding human brother–sister incest. Close inbreeding is detrimental to reproduction and survival because it brings deleterious recessive alleles, such as the allele causing phenylketoneuria, together in the same individuals. Natural selection has produced several different mechanisms in different species for reducing its likelihood. Intimate rearing of brothers and sisters during their first few years may reflect a mechanism humans evolved to help avoid it (Westermark, 1891). Evidence from boys and girls reared in the same children's houses in Israeli Kibbutzim and Chinese *sim pau* marriages, in which a genetically unrelated baby girl

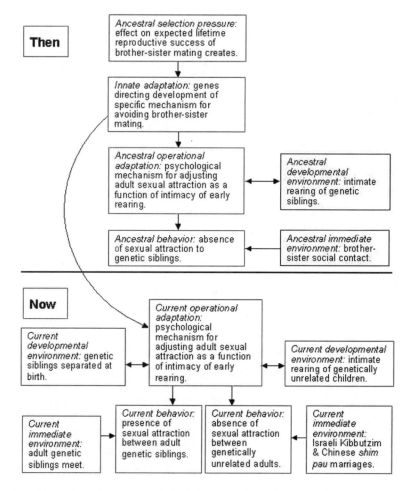

FIG. 2.3.   The evolutionary psychologist's perspective on how the evolved innate adaptation in conjunction with the developmental and immediate environments can produce different behaviors in ancestral and current environments. Note that the innate adaptation that prevented brother–sister incest in ancestral environments can produce either sexual attraction between genetic siblings or absence of sexual attraction between genetically unrelated individuals, depending on the conditions of rearing in the current environment. Because there is a clear distinction between ancestral and current environments, and between ancestral and current operational adaptations (although not between ancestral and current innate adaptations), ancestral and current behavior may differ considerably. Although ancestral behavior contributed to ancestral fitness, and hence the evolution of the innate adaptation, current behavior need not contribute to current fitness. From "The Future of Sociobiology: Counting Babies or Studying Proximate Mechanisms," by C. B. Crawford, 1993, *Trends in Evolution and Ecology, 8,* p. 185. Copyright © 1993 by Elsevier Science Publishers Ltd. Adapted with permission.

is adopted into a family at birth with the expectation that she will marry a son of the family at their sexual maturity, and sexual attraction between adult genetic siblings who were separated at birth provides support for the theory.

The bottom of the figure refers to the infinitesimal segment of evolutionary time of today (now) and the top to the environment of evolutionary adaptedness (then) (EEA; Bowlby, 1969), where the psychological tools that enable individuals to go about their daily business evolved. In the EEA, natural selection created the *innate adaptation*, the genotype that interacted with the *ancestral developmental environment*, to produce the *ancestral operational adaptation*, the psychological phenotype that responds to the immediate *environment* to produce *ancestral behavior*. The innate adaptation evolved because the behavior it produced contributed to reproductive success averaged across the time the organism and its ancestors lived in the EEA. However, it need not have contributed to reproductive success in any particular infinitesimal segment of evolutionary time, such as the present. For example, developmental conditions in one such segment may have been unusual preventing the adaptation from contributing to reproductive success.

In terms of incest avoidance, the benefits of avoiding brother–sister incest selected for one or more genes, now present in all humans, that enabled the development of psychological information-processing mechanisms for accessing the degree of genetic relationship between adults by accessing the degree of intimacy of their rearing during the first 3 or 4 years of life. This information was then used to help adjust the objects of adult sexual desire and would have helped prevent ancestral brother–sister incest.

Now consider two scenarios. A brother and sister are separated at birth and have no physical or social contact until they are adults. If they meet, they may be (and sometimes are) sexually attracted to each other (Bevc & Silverman, 2000) because their lack of intimate rearing indicates they are not genetically related. Now consider the intimate rearing of genetically unrelated children for the first few years of life as occurs in the children's houses of many Israeli Kibbutzim (Shepher, 1983) or in Chinese *shim pau* marriages (Wolf, 1995). In both cases, there is considerable evidence for the absence of sexual attraction between the genetically unrelated, and hence genetically benign, sexually partners. Note that in these scenarios the current behavior detracts from current reproductive success because the modern environment is quite different from the one in which the mechanism evolved.

GENETIC VARIATION AND NATURAL SELECTION

Suppose that identical twins that were separated at conception were reared in different environments, and because of the different environments their adult personalities and abilities differ greatly. One twin is extroverted and the other is introverted. One is aggressive and the other submissive. One is better at verbal reasoning and the other is better at quantitative reasoning. A common interpretation is that because the twins are genetically identical, genes are not involved in the production of these differences.

Return to Fig. 2.2, which describes scorpionfly mating, to help with the logic of this situation. Suppose that identical triplet scorpionflies are reared in environments differing in levels of male–male competition. Triplet A is reared in an environment high in male–male competition. Triplet B is reared in an environment where male–male competition is absent, and Triplet C is reared in a milieu with moderate male–male competition. How will their behaviors differ? Attempted forced copulation will be absent in the environment of Triplet B, which is free from competition, but it will be the usual tactic in the high competition environment of Triplet A. The proteinacious mass will be a frequent mating tactic in the moderate competition environment of Triplet C, but it will be rare in the low competition environment of Triplet B.

Because the three male scorpionflies are genetically identical, gene differences between them cannot be contributing to the differences in courtship behavior. But the genes that all three males have, and indeed the genes that every male scorpionfly has, contribute to the development of the behaviors that are seen. Although it is true that the environmental differences are producing the behavioral differences, and that genetic differences are not involved, the environmental differences are acting through the genetically innate information-processing mechanisms that all male scorpionflies possess (Crawford & Anderson, 1989). Hence, the genes that every male scorpionfly possesses are deeply involved in producing these different behaviors.

Although genetic variation is necessary for a trait to evolve by natural selection, from an evolutionary perspective it is not the main focus in the study of adaptation (Crawford & Anderson, 1989; Tooby & Cosmides, 1990). What is of interest is the correlation of the behavioral differences with fitness in the environment in which the trait evolved. Although the different tactics of male scorpionflies do not depend on genetic differences, variation in the tactics is correlated with environmental differences, and with fitness differences in those environments (Thornhill, 1980).

DEVELOPING EVOLUTIONARY EXPLANATIONS

Levels of Explanations

Those with an evolutionary orientation are usually interested in *ultimate*, or why, explanations rather than *proximate*, or how, explanations. Proximate explanations refer to the immediate factors, such as internal physiology and environmental stimuli, that produce a particular response. Ultimate explanations refer to the conditions of the biological, social, and physical environment that, on an evolutionary time scale, render certain traits adaptive and others nonadaptive (Mayr, 1961). Consider, for example, the question "Why do ground squirrels hibernate?" The proximate explanation is that hibernation comes about in the current environment because current climatic conditions trigger physiological mechanisms initiating hibernation. But the ultimate explanation is that it is climate, predator pressure, food supply, and so on, acting on an evolutionary time scale, that tell why squirrels have evolved to hibernate. Considering both levels of explanation may deepen understanding of the development and significance of a behavior. Consider in some detail the value of ultimate explanations.

RISK TAKING OR SENSATION SEEKING: THE ULTIMATE CAUSES

Males die off faster than females at all ages in most species because of disease, trauma and stress, accidents, and murder. Trivers (1985) provided convincing arguments against the notion that the unguarded male Y chromosome is the cause. Zuckerman's theory of sensation seeking (Zuckerman, Buchsbaum, & Murphy, 1980) could provide a proximate explanation. He found that measures of sensation seeking correlate with risk taking in a number of situations and are also related to a variety of behavioral variables, such as sexual experience, interest in new situations, experience with drugs, social dominance, sociability, playfulness, manic depressive tendencies, and psychopathy. Males score higher than females on measures of sensation seeking. Scores decline with age after age 16. Sensation seeking scores are also correlated with strength of initial orienting reflex, augmentation versus reduction of the average evoked brain potential, gonadal hormones and the enzyme monoamine oxidase. Moreover, many of the correlates of sensation seeking have moderate to high heritabilities.

Zuckerman and his colleagues argued that the bioamines, particularly the catecholamines, that may regulate the sensitivity of reward and activity centers in the limbic system play a central role in sensation seeking. Thus, depending on the level of analysis, gonadal hormones, catecholamines, or sensation seeking can be considered a proximate cause of the sex differences in mortality. But what are the ultimate causes of the excess in male over female mortality?

Darwin's theory of sexual selection can help explain sex differences in anatomy, physiology, and behavior. Can it help explain sensation seeking? In most species, females are a limiting resource for male reproduction, and hence males evolve tactics for competing for access to them.

In many species, natural selection favors traits that result in a reduction in survival prior to reproduction if those traits increase the reproductive success of those who do survive to mate. For example, diverting resources from growth of the immune system to risky behaviors of threat or aggression could increase the overall fitness of males if it reduced pre-reproductive male survival by one half, but more than doubled the reproductive success of those who survived. The risky behaviors that led Zuckerman et al. (1980) to postulate a trait of sensation seeking may have contributed to male reproductive success in ancestral populations.

What are the ultimate causes of the sex differences in sensation seeking? Males and females in sexually selected species invest in their offspring in different ways (Thornhill & Alcock, 1983). Females invest more than males in the construction of gametes and in postconception parental investment. These investments limit female reproductive success and are involved in shaping female reproductive adaptations involved in courtship, mating, and the rearing of offspring. Females in sexually selected species are often very selective in their choice of mates.

Males exchange effort and resources for mating (e.g., bride prices in humans and the nuptial gifts provided by some male insects). These exchanges limit their ability to obtain matings. They also invest in risky anatomy (organs of threat), physiology (testosterone impairs some aspects of the immune system), and behavioral displays that help them acquire matings, but that also limits their ability to obtain matings. From an evolutionary perspective, it is the risky male anatomy, physiology, and behavior that are the ultimate causes of the excess in male over female mortality and the sex differences in sensation seeking.

It should be possible to construct a model for predicting species differences in sensation seeking, risk taking, and differential mortality. Males of species characterized by relatively low post-zygotic male parental investment and relatively high costs of obtaining mates would be predicted to exhibit risky anatomy, physiology, and behavior and to suffer higher mortality than females. Psychologists might call them sensation seekers. As long as the animals were studied in their natural environment, such a model would require neither knowledge of the biochemistry or physiology of the species, nor constructs such as emotions, motivations, and drives. Instead, it would require information on differences between the sexes in investment in gametes, additional postzygotic parental investment, resources exchanged for a mating, and the elaboration of displays required for obtaining a mating.

Of what value are ultimate explanations to those interested in a single species, such as humans? A consideration of ultimate causation may help with gaining an understanding of the environmental factors that may alter a behavior, which can be used to choose independent variables for the development of within-species models of behavior; unraveling the causal sequence between environmental events and manifest behavior; and developing explanations with greater generality.

If it is assumed that members of the species have evolved a repertoire of concurrently and developmentally contingent behaviors for dealing with environmental contingencies, then it may be possible to use some part of evolutionary theory, such as sexual selection theory in the case of sensation seeking, to help identify crucial environmental variables for models explaining why different individuals behave differently.

Continue with the example of differential mortality and sensation seeking. Ancestral subordinate males who had difficulty attracting mates because they lacked social status and resources may have increased their fitness by increasing the riskiness of their behavior to obtain these attributes. Younger males, who had not yet acquired resources, physical size, social status, and reciprocal relationships with other members of their group, might have improved their fitness by engaging in risky behavior. If measures of sensation seeking had been given to such males, then they might have been expected to have attained relatively high scores on these measures. Thus an evolutionary perspective can be used to provide hypotheses about the independent variables that could be useful in explaining individual differences in sensation seeking. In particular, such hypotheses and research data could be useful in understanding and finding ways to deal with problems such as road racing and other forms of risk taking that claim the lives of both young men and bystanders.

A consideration of the ultimate causes of a behavior may help unravel the causal sequence of events between environmental contingencies and behavior. For example, sensation seeking may be a common element in behaviors males perform in attempts to achieve the social status and resources that were necessary for obtaining mates in ancestral environments. If this line of reasoning is followed, then gonadal hormones (rather than strength of initial orienting reflex, augmentation versus reduction of the average evolved brain potential, or monoamine oxidase) are likely to be an important proximate biological cause of sensation seeking. Moreover, the ultimate cause analysis further suggests that training in social and technical skills is more likely to be effective than drug therapy in changing behaviors related to risk taking and sensation seeking.

Many of those studying human behavior prefer explanations using proximate, empirically derived variables (Scarr, 1985). Sensation seeking, for example, is apparently a concept derived from the inspection and analysis of observed data. Although empirically derived concepts have an intuitive and commonsense appeal, and may function reasonably well as predictors within a particular context, they lack generality. If theories of behavior are to be developed that are not situation and population specific, then there must be constructs with greater generality. The natural sciences can call on theories such as classical mechanics, the theory of relativity, or the theory of evolution to guide the search for generality in explanations. The previous example illustrates how a consideration of both the proximate and ultimate causes of a behavior can lead to more general explanations and a deeper understanding of the behavior.

CONCLUSIONS

There are promises and limitations to the use of evolutionary psychology in the development of public and personal policy. Despite the embrace of Darwinian thought in the early part of this century, the past 75 years has seen a "de-biologising" of the study of human behavior. Neo-behaviorism, social learning theory, cognitive theory, modern psychoanalysis, and postmodernist explanations dominate, as well as politically liberal approaches to solving social problems. Little value is placed on ancestral history, human nature, or innate mental mechanisms in developing explanations for human behavior. And yet, without an understanding of why behavior developed, it seems unlikely that people can develop effective ways of dealing with aspects of human behavior that society finds undesirable.

REFERENCES

Alcock, J. (1993). *Animal behavior: An evolutionary approach* (5th ed.). Sunderland, MA: Sinauer Associates.

Alexander, R. D. (1987). *The biology of moral systems.* New York: Aldine de Gruyter.

Barkow, J., Cosmides, L., & Tooby, J. (1992). *The adapted mind: Evolutionary psychology and the generation of culture.* New York: Oxford University Press.

Bevc, I., & Silverman, I. (2000). Early separation and sibling incest: A test of the revised Westermark theory. *Evolution and Human Behavior, 21,* 151–161.

Bowlby, J. (1969). *Attachment.* New York: Basic Books.

Burnstein, E., Crandall, C., & Kitayama, S. (1994). Some neo-Darwinian decision rules for altruism: Weighting cues for inclusive fitness as a function of the biological importance of the decision. *Journal of Personality and Social Psychology, 67,* 773–789.

Buss, D. (1994). *The evolution of desire: Strategies of human mating.* New York: Basic Books.

Buss, D. (1999). *Evolutionary psychology: The new science of the mind.* Boston: Allyn and Bacon.

Cosmides, L. (1989). The logic of social exchange: Has natural selection shaped how humans reason? Studies with the Wason selection task. *Cognition, 31,* 187–276.

Cosmides, L., & Tooby, J. (1987). From evolution to behavior: Evolutionary psychology as the missing link. In J. Dupre (Ed.), *The latest on the best: Essays on evolution and optimality* (pp. 277–306). Cambridge, MA: MIT Press.

Crawford, C. (1984, August). Sex biased parental investment: Findings and frustrations. In *Human reproductive strategies: Empirical tests of evolutionary hypothesis.* Symposium conducted at the meeting of the Animal Behavior Society, Cheney, WA.

Crawford, C. (1993). The future of sociobiology: Counting babies or studying proximate mechanisms. *Trends in Evolution and Ecology, 8,* 183–186.

Crawford, C. B., & Anderson, J. L. (1989). Sociobiology: An environmentalist discipline? *American Psychologist, 44,* 1449–1459.

Crook, J. H., & Crook, S. J. (1988). Tibetan polyandry: Problems of adaptation and fitness. In L. Betzig, M. Borgerhoff Mulder, & P. Turke (Eds.), *Human reproductive behavior: A Darwinian perspective* (pp. 97–114). New York: Cambridge University Press.

Daly, M., & Wilson, M. (1980). Discriminative parental solicitude: A biological perspective. *Journal of Marriage and the Family, 42,* 277–288.

Daly, M., & Wilson, M. (1982). Whom are newborn babies said to resemble? *Ethology and Sociobiology, 3,* 69–78.

Daly, M., & Wilson, M. (1983). *Sex, evolution and behavior* (2nd ed.). Boston: Prindle, Weber & Schmidt.

Daly, M., & Wilson, M. (1996). Evolutionary psychology and marital conflict: The relevance of stepchildren. In D. M. Buss & N. Malamuth (Eds.), *Sex, power, conflict: Feminist and evolutionary perspectives* (pp. 9–28). New York: Oxford University Press.

Darwin, C. (1859). *On the origin of the species by means of natural selection or the preservation of favored races in the struggle for life.* London: John Murray.

Darwin, C. (1898). *The descent of man, and selection in relation to sex* (3rd ed.). New York: Appleton. (Original work published 1871)

de Catanzaro, D. (1991). Evolutionary limits to self-preservation. *Ethology and Sociobiology, 12,* 13–28.

Degler, C. (1991). *In search of human nature: The decline and revival of Darwinism in American social thought.* New York: Oxford University Press.

Eisenberg, N., & Miller, P. A. (1987). The relation of empathy to prosocial and related behaviors. *Psychological Bulletin, 101,* 91–119.

Fisher, R. A. (1930). *The genetical theory of natural selection* (2nd rev. ed.). New York: Dover.

Gould, S. J. (1982). *The panda's thumb: More reflections in natural history.* New York: Norton.

Haig, D. (1993). Genetic conflicts in human pregnancy. *Quarterly Review of Biology, 68,* 495–532.

Haig, D. (2002). *Geonomic imprinting and kinship.* New Brunswick, NJ: Rutgers University Press.

Hamilton, W. D. (1964). The genetical evolution of social behavior, I and II. *Journal of Theoretical Biology, 7*, 1–52.

Hamilton, W. D. (1971). Geometry of the selfish herd. *Journal of Theoretical Biology, 31*, 295–311.

Herrnstein, R. J., & Murray, C. (1994). *The bell curve: Intelligence and class structure in American life.* New York: The Free Press.

Hill, K., & Kaplan, H. (1988). Tradeoffs in male and female reproductive strategies among the Ache, parts 1 and 2. In L. Betzig, M. Borgerhoff Mulder, & P. Turke (Eds.), *Human reproductive behavior: A Darwinian perspective* (pp. 277–305). New York: Cambridge University Press.

Holmes, W. (1986). Kin recognition by phenotype matching in Belding's ground squirrels. *Animal Behavior, 34*, 38–47.

Johnson, G. R. (1989). The role of kin recognition mechanisms in patriotic socialization: Further reflections. *Politics and the Life Sciences, 8*, 62–69.

Johnson, J. L., McAndrew, F. T., & Harris, P. B. (1991). Sociobiology and the naming of adopted and natural children. *Ethology and Sociobiology, 12*, 365–375.

Kimura, D. (1987). Are men's and women's brains really different? *Canadian Psychology, 28*, 133–147.

Konishi, M. (1965). The role of auditory feedback in the control of vocalization in the white-crowned sparrow. *Zeitschrift für Tierpsychologie, 22*, 770–783.

Krebs, D. (1987). The challenge of altruism in biology and psychology. In C. Crawford, M. Smith, & D. Krebs (Eds.), *Sociobiology and psychology: Ideas, issues, and applications* (pp. 81–118). Hillsdale, NJ: Lawrence Erlbaum Associates.

LeBoeuf, B. J. (1974). Male–male competition and reproductive success in elephant seals. *American Zoologist, 14*, 163–176.

Lorenz, K. Z. (1966). *On aggression.* New York: Harcourt Brace Jovanovich.

Marler, P. (1984). Song learning: Innate species differences in the learning process. In P. Marler & H. Terrace (Eds.), *The biology of learning* (pp. 289–309). Berlin: Dahlem Konferenzen.

Maynard Smith, J. (1976). Group selection. *Quarterly Review of Biology, 51*, 277–283.

Mayr, E. (1961). Cause and effect in biology. *Science, 134*, 1501–1506.

McCullough, J. M., & Barton, E. Y. (1991). Relatedness and mortality risk during a crisis year: Plymouth colony, 1620–1621. *Ethology and Sociobiology, 12*, 195–209.

Miller, G. F. (2000). *The mating mind: How sexual choice shaped the evolution of human nature.* New York: Doubleday.

Orians, G. H., & Heerwagen, J. H. (1992). Evolved responses to landscapes. In J. Barkow, L. Cosmides, & J. Tooby (Eds.), *The adapted mind: Evolutionary psychology and the generation of culture* (pp. 555–579). New York: Oxford University Press.

Pinker, S. (2002). *The blank slate: The modern denial of human nature.* New York: Viking.

Plomin, R., Defries, J. C., & McLearn, G. E. (1980). *Behavioral genetics: A primer.* San Francisco: Freeman.

Porter, R. H. (1987). Kin recognition: Functions and mediating mechanisms. In C. B. Crawford, M. F. Smith, & D. Krebs (Eds.), *Sociobiology and psychology: Ideas, issues and applications* (pp. 175–205). Hillsdale, NJ: Lawrence Erlbaum Associates.

Ridley, M. (1993). *Evolution.* Oxford, England: Blackwell.

Salmon, C. A. (1998). The evocative nature of kin terminology in political rhetoric. *Politics and the Life Sciences, 17*, 51–57.

Scarr, S. (1985). Constructing psychology: Making facts and fables for our times. *American Psychologist, 40*, 499–512.

Shepher, J. (1983). *Incest, a biosocial view.* New York: Academic Press.

Sherman, P. W. (1977). Nepotism and the evolution of alarm calls. *Science, 197*, 1246–1253.

48   CRAWFORD AND SALMON

Sieff, D. F. (1990). Explaining biased sex ratios in human populations. *Current Anthropology, 31*, 25–48.

Silverman, I., & Eals, M. (1992). Sex differences in spatial abilities: Evolutionary theory and data. In J. Barkow, L. Cosmides, & J. Tooby (Eds.), *The adapted mind: Evolutionary psychology and the generation of culture* (pp. 533–549). New York: Oxford University Press.

Singh, D. (1993). Adaptive significance of female physical attractiveness: Role of waist to hip ratio. *Journal of Personality and Social Psychology, 65*, 293–307.

Sober, E. (1984). *The nature of selection.* Cambridge, MA: MIT Press.

Sober, E., & Wilson, D. S. (1998). *Unto others: The evolution and psychology of unselfish behavior.* Cambridge, MA: Harvard University Press.

Symons, D. (1987). If we're all Darwinians, what's the fuss about? In C. B. Crawford, M. F. Smith, & D. Krebs (Eds.), *Sociobiology and psychology: Ideas, issues, and applications* (pp. 121–146). Hillsdale, NJ: Lawrence Erlbaum Associates.

Symons, D. (1989). A critique of Darwinian anthropology. *Ethology and Sociobiology, 10*, 131–144.

Thornhill, R. (1980). Rape in *Panorpa* scorpionflies and a general rape hypothesis. *Animal Behavior, 28*, 52–59.

Thornhill, R., & Alcock, J. (1983). *The evolution of insect mating systems.* Cambridge, MA: Harvard University Press.

Thornhill, R., & Palmer, C. (2000). *A natural history of rape: Biological bases of sexual coercion.* Cambridge, MA: MIT Press.

Tooby, J., & Cosmides, L. (1990). The past explains the present: Emotional adaptations and the structure of ancestral environments. *Ethology and Sociobiology, 11*, 375–421.

Tooby, J., & DeVore, I. (1987). The reconstruction of hominid behavioral evolution using strategic modelling. In W. G. Kinzey (Ed.), *Primate models for the origin of human behavior* (pp. 183–237). New York: SUNY Press.

Trivers, R. L. (1971). The evolution of reciprocal altruism. *Quarterly Review of Biology, 46*, 35–57.

Trivers, R. L. (1974). Parent–offspring conflict. *American Zoologist, 14*, 249–264.

Trivers, R. L. (1985). *Social evolution.* Menlo Park, CA: Benjamin/Cummings.

Trivers, R. L., & Willard, D. E. (1973). Natural selection of parental ability to vary the sex ratio of offspring. *Science, 179*, 90–92.

Underwood, B., & Moore, B. (1982). Perspective-taking and altruism. *Psychological Bulletin, 91*, 143–173.

Waldman, B. (1986). Preference for unfamiliar siblings over familiar non-siblings in American toad (*Bufo americanus*) tadpoles. *Animal Behavior, 34*, 48–53.

Westermark, E. A. (1891). *The history of human marriage.* New York: Macmillan.

Williams, G. C. (1966). *Adaptation and natural selection: A critique of some current evolutionary thought.* Princeton, NJ: Princeton University Press.

Williams, G. C., & Nesse, R. (1991). The dawn of Darwinian medicine. *Quarterly Review of Biology, 66*, 1–22.

Wilson, E. O. (1975). *Sociobiology: The new synthesis.* Cambridge, MA: Harvard University Press.

Wilson, D. S., & Sober, E. (1994). Reintroducing group selection to the human behavioral sciences. *Behavioral and Brain Sciences, 17*, 585–608.

Wolf, A. (1995). *Sexual attraction and childhood association: A Chinese brief for Edward Westermark.* Stanford, CA: Stanford University Press.

Woolfenden, G. E., & Fitzpatrick, J. W. (1984). *The Florida scrub jay: Demography of a cooperative-breeding bird.* Princeton, NJ: Princeton University Press.

Wright, R. (1994). *The moral animal: Evolutionary psychology and everyday life.* New York: Pantheon.

Wynne-Edwards, V. C. (1962). *Animal dispersion in relation to social behavior.* Edinburgh, Scotland: Oliver & Boyd.

Zahavi, A. (1975). Mate selection—a selection for a handicap. *Journal of Theoretical Biology, 53,* 205–214.

Zahn-Waxler, C., Cummings, E. M., & Iannotta, R. (1986). *Altruism and aggression: Biological and social origins.* Cambridge, England: Cambridge University Press.

Zuckerman, M., Buchsbaum, M. S., & Murphy, D. L. (1980). Sensation seeking and its biological correlates. *Psychological Bulletin, 88,* 187–214.

Beyond Sociobiology: A Kinder and Gentler Evolutionary View of Human Nature

Maria G. Janicki
Douglas College

Be responsible, respectable,
Stable but gullible
Concerned and caring, help the helpless
But always remain ultimately selfish
—Lyrics from "Get the Balance Right," Martin L. Gore
© 1983 Grabbing Hands Music Ltd./EMI Publishing Ltd.

There is little argument that human beings are capable of performing kind, caring, helpful, and even heroic behaviors toward others. To the disapproval of some, evolutionary theorists often explain such helpful behaviors as being ultimately selfish. But behaviors that are considered ultimately selfish need not be selfish in the vernacular sense. For over 30 years, the existence of helpful behaviors among kin and non-kin (inclusive fitness and reciprocal altruism respectively) have been explained using theories from evolutionary biology. Because these theories are based on genetic selfishness, evolutionary theorists have been accused of providing an overly cynical depiction of human nature (for discussions, see Pinker, 2002, and Wright, 1994). This criticism was first directed at sociobiology, E. O. Wilson's (1978) term for the systematic study of animal and human social behavior using the principles of ethology, genetics, and evolutionary biology. Because much sociobiological research analyzes behavior in terms of how it maximizes individual fitness (reproductive success), sociobiology quickly became associated with a self-interested view of human nature. According to Frank (1991), this view is only a caricature of sociobiology. Frank suggested that "a closer look at sociobiology reveals that there is room for other interpretations, including the interpretation that some human behavior is genuinely noble" (p. 92). Since the 1970s, sociobiology has changed. It has bloomed and transformed into a number of specialized fields including evolutionary psychology, psychiatry, economics, and anthropology. Furthermore, in recent years, there has been an increasing amount of theory and research devoted to the evolution and nature of cooperative, helpful, and moral behaviors (Alexander, 1987; Axelrod, 1984; Caporael, Dawes, Orbell, & van de Kragt, 1989; de Waal, 1996; Frank, 1988; Krebs, 1998; Nesse, 1999; Tooby & Cosmides, 1996; Wright, 1994). These new ideas and research extend beyond the classic sociobiological theories of helping and altruism. There is a new focus on how individuals' behavioral traits or strategies benefit others, as well as themselves.

One of the purposes of this chapter is to demonstrate that viewing human nature through an evolutionary lens sheds light not only on the competitive dark side; it also illuminates the positive attributes and capabilities. Another purpose is to illustrate how theories of cooperative and helpful behavior have themselves evolved in recent years. I will first briefly review the classic evolutionary sociobiological theories of helpful behavior, namely, the theories of inclusive fitness and reciprocal altruism. Although invaluable as explanatory tools, these two theories have been criticized for being unable to account for all types of cooperative behaviors. Secondly, I will focus on some of the new evolutionary theories, particularly commitment models, which expose a gentler and kinder side of human nature. The new commitment theories provide a welcome expansion of the evolutionary understanding of close relationships such as friendships. I will also discuss some recent research that calls into question the assumption of human egoism and selfishness. Thirdly, I will discuss the interplay of culture and biology in the production of cooperative behavior. Public policies constitute cultural information that influences people's behavior. If one of the goals of public policy is to foster a cooperative society, then it is important to have a good understanding of the evolved capabilities for cooperative behavior in our species.

THE SELFISH GENE AND HUMAN NATURE

Natural selection is a process of differential reproduction. Within a population, individuals vary in their reproductive success. Genes that have the most positive effects on their bearer's reproductive success continue into future generations. Dawkins (1989) coined the term "selfish gene" to emphasize that the genes that further their own replication are those that are perpetuated in a species' gene pool. Behavioral traits and strategies that are products of natural selection were selected because these traits and strategies promoted their bearer's survival and reproductive success (i.e., biological fitness) better than alternative traits and strategies. The same is true for the evolved psychological mechanisms that underlie these behavioral adaptations. They would not be around today had they not yielded positive fitness effects throughout evolutionary history. When evolutionary theorists try to explain a behavior or mental process, their goal is to provide an ultimate cause. Ultimate causes explain why a particular trait evolved, that is, the function it served and how that function benefited fitness. Because genetic selfishness is inherent in all ultimate explanations, even tendencies to behave cooperatively and altruistically can be considered ultimately selfish.

Genetic selfishness has often been incorrectly equated with phenotypic selfishness. Frank (1988) referred to this viewpoint as the "self-interest model." The main assumption of this model is that individuals will act in ways that best satisfy their own interests, with little regard for the interests of others. There is little argument that genetic selfishness can translate into phenotypic selfishness, or what I have called "individual selfishness" (Janicki, 2000). It is incorrect, however, to conclude that individual selfishness is the only possible product of genetic selfishness (Gintis, 2001; Kenrick, 1991; Pinker, 2002). To do so is to confuse the products of natural selection with the process. As de Waal (1996, pp. 16–17) pointed out:

> why should we let the ruthlessness of natural selection distract from the wonders it has produced? Humans and other animals have been endowed with a capacity for genuine love, sympathy, and care—a fact that can and will one day be fully reconciled with the idea that genetic self-promotion drives the evolutionary process.

One of the products of the evolutionary process is altruistic behavior. Altruism, a behavior that confers a benefit to the fitness of the recipient while exacting a cost from the actor's fitness, was once considered paradoxical to evolutionary theory because of its frequent occurrences in humans and other animals. The puzzle of altruism was solved, to some extent, by the theories of inclusive fitness (Hamilton, 1964) and reciprocal altruism (Trivers, 1971). These theories are briefly explained in the next section. For more detailed discussions of these theories, see Axelrod (1984), Krebs (1987), and Trivers (1985).

THE ORIGINS OF HELPING BEHAVIOR

Kin-Directed Altruism

In 1964, W. D. Hamilton proposed a theory that explained the preponderance of altruistic behavior among close relatives. According to Hamilton's theory, an altruistic trait could be selected if individuals possessing it selectively helped those individuals who had a high likelihood of sharing that trait—those individuals being kin who share genes through common descent. The closer the relative, the higher degree of relatedness and the more likely one is to share a common gene. Hamilton expanded the concept of fitness to include not only the individuals' reproductive success (direct fitness), but also the influence they have on the reproductive success of relatives, multiplied by their degree of relatedness (indirect fitness). The term *inclusive fitness* refers to the combined direct and indirect fitness of an organism.

Hamilton's theory makes nepotism an integral part of human nature. The preferential treatment of relatives has been well documented. Evidence of kin-directed altruism has been found in the distribution of wealth in probated wills (M. S. Smith, Kish, & Crawford, 1987), in the helping patterns of American women (Essock-Vitale & McGuire, 1985), and in people's helping choices in hypothetical scenarios (Burnstein, Crandall, & Kitayama, 1994; Cunningham, 1983, as cited in Cunningham, 1986). Close kinship not only increases the likelihood of altruistic behavior, it also decreases the likelihood of malevolent behavior (Barber, 1994).

The psychological mechanisms that evolved for the purpose of directing help toward kin may also now direct help toward non-kin. It is unlikely that individuals evolved the ability to assess kinship through the conscious calculation of relatedness (Dawkins, 1979). Rather, decision rules likely evolved to direct help toward those who possessed characteristics that would have been a strong indicator of kinship in the ancestral environment. Several cues for kinship have been proposed, such as phenotypic similarity and frequency of interaction (Porter, 1987). It is possible that in the current environment, evolved mechanisms may direct helping toward non-kin who possess these kinship cues (e.g., friends). Furthermore, kinship terminology may be utilized to solicit helping from others (e.g., brother can you spare a dime?, join the sisterhood, etc.).

In summary, kinship and kinship cues may be powerful motivators of altruistic and cooperative behavior. The importance of kinship to social relationships is further discussed by Daly, Salmon, and Wilson (1997). They contended that this universal tendency is often overlooked by social scientists.

Reciprocal Altruism

An explanation of the evolution of altruism among non-kin was provided by Trivers' (1971) theory of reciprocal altruism. Reciprocal altruism is assumed to play a major role in social exchange—the everyday exchanges of goods, services, companionship, affection, and other commodities between friends, acquaintances, and others. In reciprocal altruism, partners take turns being the altruist. According to this theory, altruism will pay off if there is a high likelihood of reciprocation. Providing that the cost to the donor is less than the benefit to the recipient in each transaction, reciprocity will be profitable to both parties. The characteristics of the lives of early humans—living a long life, having a low dispersal rate, and living in small, mutually dependent, stable social groups—were favorable antecedents for the evolution of reciprocal altruism (Trivers, 1971). These conditions also favor the development of reciprocity systems in the present. For example, reciprocal relationships are more likely to develop in small towns where people know each other and interact on a regular basis, than in large cities where the high proportion of strangers makes it difficult to establish a reciprocal system and increases the opportunity for cheating.

Game theorists have used the Prisoner's Dilemma game to model the evolution of reciprocal systems (Axelrod, 1984; Axelrod & Hamilton, 1981). In this game, two players choose to either cooperate or defect, without knowing the choice of the other player. The scoring system gives the biggest payoff to the player who defects if the other player cooperates. The second best score is achieved if both players cooperate. Mutual defection produces a relatively low score for each player, whereas the lowest score is given to the player who cooperates when the other player defects. In a single round game, the best strategy is always to be selfish and to defect. In real life, however, much of human social behavior involves repeat interactions with familiar others.

To determine which strategy would be most successful if a series of games were played (iterated Prisoner's Dilemma), Axelrod (Axelrod & Hamilton, 1981; Axelrod, 1984) held two international tournaments that pitted a wide range of strategies against each other in a round robin tournament. In both competitions, the consistent winner was cooperative, not selfish. The winning strategy, Tit for Tat, closely mimics reciprocal altruism. The strategy uses two rules: Cooperate on the first turn; on the following turns, repeat what your partner has done on the previous turn. This strategy is advantageous for several reasons (Dawkins, 1989). It allows for cooperation to begin, it discriminates against cheaters, and it is capable of resuming cooperation if the partner who previously defected becomes cooperative. Using the computer tournaments as a model for the natural selection of cooperation, Axelrod demonstrated that cooperation can develop between two individuals if three conditions are met: Both expect to interact frequently in the future, there is no known time when these interactions will cease, partners do not value present outcomes much more than future ones, and discrimination against cheaters exists.

The success of the Tit for Tat strategy sheds light on the design of the cognitive processes required for maintaining reciprocal exchanges. As suggested by Cosmides and Tooby (1989, p. 84), "the natural selection process dictates that social exchange can evolve only if it is governed by a strategy that requires reciprocation and excludes or retaliates against cheaters." In their research, Cosmides and Tooby provided evidence of specialized mechanisms for cheater detection in social contracts (Cosmides, 1989; Cosmides & Tooby, 1992). Trivers (1971) also provided insight into the mental architecture regulating reciprocity. He proposed that the ability to feel guilt prevents people from cheating valuable exchange partners, or motivates them to make amends if they do cheat. He also proposed that moralistic aggression is an emotional response to being cheated by others. Betrayal by a trusted exchange partner should provoke the greatest amount of anger.

Whereas patterns of giving and receiving among kin may be at times unidirectional (e.g., parent to child), research has shown that relationships with non-kin tend to be reciprocal (Essock-Vitale & McGuire, 1985). Satisfaction is related to the amount of reciprocation in non-kin relationships (Rook, 1987), and the expectation of future reciprocation has been shown to be a motivator for helping (Kruger, 2003). Because reciprocity or social exchange is found in all cultures, it is considered to be a universal norm (Gouldner, 1960). Evolutionary biologists and psychologists, however, view reciprocity as more than a cultural phenomenon; they see it as an evolved specialized ability of the human mind.

BEYOND KINSHIP AND RECIPROCITY

Although the theories of inclusive fitness and reciprocal altruism have proved invaluable in understanding helpful and altruistic behavior, several evolutionary thinkers have begun to criticize the limitations of these theories (de Waal, 1996; Gintis, 2000; Nesse, 2002a; Tooby & Cosmides, 1996; Zahavi, 1995). The main thrust of these criticisms is that kin-directed and reciprocal altruism do not explain all forms of prosocial behavior. For example, people often help those who have never helped them before. Furthermore, both theories attempt to explain how a helpful behavior or behavioral strategy was selected to benefit the fitness of the actor. Advocates of the newer approaches contend that natural selection may have produced behavioral strategies that can produce truly unselfish behaviors. For example, both Frank (1988, 1991) and Nesse (1999, 2001b) emphasized the importance of emotional and behavioral adaptations for forming commitments to others (which may not initially be in one's best interest). In their study of friendship, Tooby and Cosmides (1996) encouraged the investigation of psychological mechanisms designed to provide benefits to others. The newer theories of cooperative behavior share at least one characteristic: an emphasis on the importance of being recognized as a cooperator or altruist. This characteristic is central to another key theory of cooperation, namely, indirect reciprocity.

Indirect Reciprocity

Alexander's (1987) model of indirect reciprocity provides another explanation of how cooperation could evolve among non-kin. Unlike Trivers' model of direct reciprocity, indirect reciprocity involves a helper being rewarded by a person other than the recipient. Helpful behavior is reciprocated indirectly either by those who witnessed or were told about the original helping act. An example of indirect reciprocity is the following: Arlene helps her elderly neighbor Jean with her grocery shopping. Another neighbor, Susan, observes, and later helps Arlene when she runs into car trouble. In systems of indirect reciprocity, reputation is very important because individuals who appear honest and helpful are seen as desirable exchange partners and are rewarded by others. Using computer simulations, Nowak and Sigmund (1998) demonstrated the viability of cooperative strategies that involve indirect reciprocity. An advantage of indirect reciprocity is that, unlike direct reciprocity, helping does not depend on the likelihood of two individuals interacting again in the future. This model extends beyond dyadic helping and contributes to our understanding of cooperative behavior within groups. Although Alexander (1987) provided an explanation of within-group cooperation, he made it clear that indirect reciprocity evolved because it ultimately served self-interests (i.e., it is not a group selection argument).

Similar to direct reciprocity, indirect reciprocity is vulnerable to cheaters. Individuals may use deception and possibly self-deception to feign altruistic behavior (Alexander, 1987). People's tendency to call attention to the sins of others, coupled with the tendency to obscure their own is at the root of hypocrisy and a profitable strategy (Wright, 1994). Deception is expected to be most prevalent among competitors, whereas individuals who share common interests (e.g., friends, spouses) are expected to restrain their deceptive tendencies (Alexander, 1987).

New ideas by evolutionary theorists are challenging the degree of selfishness purported to be inherent within systems of indirect reciprocity. Evolutionary theories of commitment, in particular, also feature reputation as a key motivator for altruistic behavior (Frank, 1988; Nesse, 2001a). However, unlike Alexander's (1987) selfish perspective, these new theorists believe systems similar to indirect reciprocity can yield truly altruistic behavior that may not always service self-interests. These theories are discussed next.

Commitment Theories

Theorists from several evolutionary disciplines have recently begun to explore the implications of commitment models (see Nesse, 2001a). Models of commitment were first developed by economists (Frank, 1988; Hirshleifer, 1987) as an alternative to the traditional self-interest models of economic behavior. According to Frank (1988, 1991) and Gintis (2001), self-interest models required revision because of their inability to predict or explain the behavior of participants engaging in economic games. One such game is the ultimatum game, in which one player is given a set amount of money to share with another player. Player 1 decides how much to give Player 2, and Player 2 decides whether to accept the offer. If Player 2 declines, both players receive nothing. Based on the self-interest model, the rational strategy for Player 1 is to offer one penny to Player 2, and for Player 2 to accept. When analyzing the strategies players do use, Guth, Schmittberger, and Schwarze (1982, as cited in Frank, 1991) found that Player 1 offers, on average, one third of the total amount to Player 2. Participants seemed to be motivated more by fairness than by self-interest. In another study, both players had their identities hidden from each other, and Player 1 was told that Player 2 would have to accept whatever offer was made (Kahneman, Knetsch, & Thaler, 1986, as cited in Frank, 1991). Even under these anonymous conditions, over three quarters of the participants made a fair offer to Player 2. Additional studies have found similar results (Gintis, 2001).

These research findings demonstrate that individuals' economic decisions can be quite irrational; participants choose to be fair rather than selfish. Frank (1988, 1991) argued that this irrational economic behavior stems from a suite of emotional responses that permit the formation of commitments. At this point, consider the following: What are commitments or commitment behaviors, and why are they important? These questions are answered next, and it becomes apparent that commitment behaviors are difficult to explain using the traditional evolutionary models of kin-directed and reciprocal altruism.

Nesse (2001b, p. 13) defined a commitment as "an act or signal that gives up options in order to influence someone's behavior by changing incentives or expectations." An example of a commitment is a marriage. When individuals enter into this legal commitment, they promise to stay with their spouse, in sickness and in health, good times and bad, and to give up the pursuit of any other mates. Of course, not all marriages work out this way, but the commitment of marriage, in principle, involves the giving up of some future (selfish) benefits in order to gain the benefits of this long-term relationship. Similarly, a tenant who signs a lease gives up the option to move in order to obtain the benefit of no rent increases (Nesse, 2001b). Commitments need not be legally binding. Friendships are an example. In order to enter into a committed relationship, one often has to demonstrate commitment by acting counter to self-interests. Furthermore, maintaining a committed relationship usually involves continuing to consider the interests of others (e.g., standing by a friend when times are tough).[1] Although such commitment behaviors are counter to selfish interests in the short term, the benefits of maintaining such relationships usually outweigh the costs. In committed relationships, individuals receive help when it is needed, not only when they can repay it. Help may be needed when they are least able to return it (e.g., during sickness). Individuals who rely only on direct reciprocity and are unable to commit to others have dim future prospects (Nesse, 1999). In summary, commitment strategies pay off in the long run, because people convince others that they would do things that are not in their best interests. In the social world, people who engage in commitment strategies are more successful than those who engage in rational self-interest strategies (Nesse, 2001b). Although commitment strategies may be ultimately selfish, they nonetheless can motivate truly altruistic behavior (Gintis, 2001; Nesse, 2001b).

Making a commitment involves taking a risk. If the human ability to form commitments evolved through natural selection (Frank, 2001; Nesse, 2001b), then human minds must possess psychological mechanisms specialized for avoiding the costs and reaping the benefits involved with forming commitments. How do individuals convince others of their true intentions to commit and yet avoid being deceived by the false intentions of others? Frank (1988, 1991) proposed that the capacity for displaying and discerning emotions is of paramount importance in this matter. In Frank's commitment model, emotions have two functions: to con-

---

[1]As is discussed later, commitments can be pledges to harm as well as to hurt. Both types involve behaving in ways that seem counter to self-interests in the short term.

vey reliable and honest signals of commitment to others, and to motivate an individual's own behavior. I consider each of these functions next.

The Role of Emotions in Commitments

Expressing Emotions.   Studies of the Prisoner's Dilemma game have shown that cooperative strategies can be very successful if individuals are able to distinguish the cooperators from the defectors, and to regulate their behavior accordingly (Frank, 1991). Using logical problems, Tooby and Cosmides (1989, 1992) showed that people are good at detecting cheaters using specialized cognitive reasoning skills. Another way to detect cheaters or deceivers is to read their emotional expressions. Emotions are expressed through the face and body, with facial expressions being the most complex. Although some of the muscles controlling facial expressions are under voluntary control, others are not. Genuine facial expressions usually involve some involuntary muscle movements and are very difficult, if not impossible, to fake. For example, the facial expression of sympathy involves the involuntary drawing up and together of the eyebrows. This facial configuration cannot be achieved voluntarily (Ekman, 1985, as cited in Frank, 2001). Frank proposed that the expression of sympathy is an honest indicator of commitment because an individual who feels sympathy in response to someone in distress is motivated to help.

Another important emotion is guilt. A person who is capable of strong guilt feelings will be less likely to cheat than those who feel little guilt, even when it is in his or her best interests to do so (Frank, 1991). People who display genuine emotional expressions of guilt indicate to others that they are a safe bet as exchange partners. Individuals will tend to avoid those who lack the ability to feel guilt or remorse at their own wrongdoings (e.g., with psychopaths being the most extreme case).

Facial expressions of positive emotions may also be used to identify and transmit signals that someone is cooperative and a good commitment partner. An authentic smile differs from a false one in that it involves a crinkling and furrowing of the skin at the outer corners of the eyes. The expression of this true smile, sometimes referred to as a Duchenne smile after the French anatomist who discovered it, has been positively correlated with subjective reports of positive emotions (Ekman, Davidson, & Friesen, 1990). Are sincere smiles also honest indicators of helpful and altruistic tendencies? In an interesting series of studies, Brown and his colleagues (Brown, Palameta, & Moore, 2003) had some success at distinguishing altruists from nonaltruists by observing their facial expressions. In their studies, the target individuals were videotaped while engaged in different kinds of activities (e.g., reading a story, playing a strategic game). In their analyses, Brown et al. (2003) discovered that the smile was a consistent cue to altruism.

Motivating Behavior.   Feelings of sympathy and guilt also serve to motivate cooperative behavior. Trivers (1971) first identified these emotions as critical features of a psychological system regulating reciprocal altruism. These emotions work equally in helping people maintain commitments. Guilt keeps people from harming relationships that provide benefits. As demonstrated by the studies conducted by Ketelaar and Au (2003), guilt also motivates cooperative behavior (also see Ketelaar, chap. 7 in this vol.). Sympathy motivates people to help when help is most needed. The tendency to feel sympathy and respond to someone in need may not be limited to humans. Although it is impossible to be sure of the emotional states of animals, de Waal (1996) offered several examples of primates and other mammals helping others who are in distress.

A cognitive process that can generate sympathy and lead to helping is empathy. Empathy refers to being able to take the other person's perspective and experience the same feelings, be they happy or sad. After conducting many related studies, Batson and his colleagues (Batson et al., 1981; Batson, 1990; Batson & Shaw, 1991) contended there is support for his hypothesis that empathy is a motivator of altruistic behavior. However, there is still some debate about the interpretation of his findings (e.g., see Kenrick, 1991; Krebs, 1991).

In summary, several evolutionary theorists have argued that the capacity to feel guilt and sympathy can both make people desirable relationship partners, and motivate them to behave altruistically toward others. This point is summed up nicely by de Waal (1996, p. 88), who stated that "Despite its fragility and selectivity, the capacity to care for others is the bedrock of our moral systems. It is the only capacity that does not fit the hedonic cage in which philosophers, psychologists, and biologists have tried to lock the human spirit."

The Dark Side of Commitment

Because of the focus of this chapter, only the positive and prosocial aspects of commitment theories have been discussed thus far. The capacity for commitment, however, may be directed toward harming as well as helping. In addition to the emotions of guilt and sympathy, Frank (1988, 1991) also discussed how feelings of vengeance and envy can be employed to demonstrate commitment to harm (vengeance) or to reject unfair treatment (envy). Similar to Trivers (1971) notion of moralistic aggression, feelings of vengeance may be stirred when an individual has been cheated or betrayed. Such feelings will be most intense after betrayal by a trusted partner or confidante (Shackelford & Buss, 1996). Similar to guilt and sympathy, feelings of vengeance serve as both motivators to action and signals to others. Vengeance motivates retaliation against the cheater or wrongdoer. Retaliating against others is often seen as irrational and inconsistent with a selfish perspective, as there may be little to gain, and high costs. Although retaliation itself is costly, Frank (1988, 1991) argued that having a reputation that you will retaliate against cheaters acts as a deterrent against future cheating.[2]

---

[2]A great deal of theory and research has explored the value of punishment in increasing within-group cooperation. For example, Gintis (2001) proposed that strong reciprocity, a behavioral tendency to cooperate with others and punish violators of group-beneficial norms, may have facilitated within-group cooperation. Boyd and Richerson (1992) explored how punishment may promote cooperation within a group. In their research, Price, Cosmides, and Tooby (2002) investigated punishment within groups and concluded that the primary motive is to deter free-riders (those who do not do their share) because they compromise the relative fitness of those who do engage in cooperative group activities.

Once individuals openly make a commitment, whether it be a vow of marriage or a threat to retaliate, the importance of reputation will require that some of those commitments be fulfilled even if they are costly to perform. As Nesse (2001b, p. 2) put it: "Before you know it, commitments lead people to do all kinds of things they would rather not do, whether this means carrying out spiteful threats or helping others who will never be able to reciprocate." People may not have to always carry out those pledges, but they must be prepared to do so in order to reap the benefits of those commitments.

Understanding the emotional factors that drive and regulate commitment improves the evolutionary understanding of many aspects of interpersonal relations including the special bonds of close friendships (Tooby & Cosmides, 1996), the importance of honor and face with respect to carrying out threats or promises (see Cohen & Vandello, 2001), and the steadfast adherence to religious beliefs and rituals (Irons, 2001, 1996). As the focus of this chapter is on the kinder side of human nature, I will now focus on a revised evolutionary understanding of close relationships.

Characteristics of Committed (Close) Relationships

Evolutionary theorists have only recently begun to examine how psychological mechanisms may operate differently in close and casual non-kin relationships. When examining the cooperative and altruistic behavior that often characterizes one's committed social relationships, it is easy to see that these behaviors are poorly explained by reciprocal altruism. Friendships, for example, are not based on Tit for Tat reciprocity. As Clark and her colleagues demonstrated in several studies, friends tend to help when help is needed or to please their friends, not because of expectations of immediate reciprocation (Clark, Mills, & Corcoran, 1989; Clark, Mills, & Powell, 1986). In committed relationships, individuals usually assume that their partner will eventually repay the help when it is needed. Offering immediate repayment is more characteristic of short-term or casual relationships. In these relationships, the future is uncertain and so debts for favors are often repaid promptly. For friends, however, immediate repayment may be viewed as offensive, perhaps because it conveys the message that the repaying partner does not expect the relationship to last (Shackelford & Buss, 1996).[3]

Being less concerned about immediate repayment from friends may indicate that the evolved mechanisms for detecting cheaters are relaxed when dealing with trusted individuals. Recent research has shown some support for this assertion. Cosmides, Tooby, Montaldi, and Thrall (1999) reported that people were less likely to activate cheater detection mechanisms in evaluating another person's behavior when they were given information that the person is honest than when they were not given this information.

---

[3]There are individual differences in the preferences regarding reciprocation. Individuals who are very concerned with balancing what is given and received within their relationships are considered to be high in exchange orientation (Murstein, Cerreto, & MacDonald, 1977). Those high in exchange orientation tend to be less satisfied in their close relationships (Buunk & Van Yperen, 1991; Murstein et al., 1977, 1987).

Although close relationships have been characterized by little concern over reciprocation (Clark et al., 1986, 1989), from an evolutionary perspective a complete lack of concern over reciprocity would have been maladaptive because it would have left individuals vulnerable to cheaters. Although immediate reciprocation may not be important, relationship partners likely do (perhaps unconsciously) keep track of relative inputs and outputs of each partner. Evidence for this tendency was found in my own research where individuals were asked to evaluate help or items they had exchanged in close relationships (Janicki, 2000). Individuals' ratings of the value of items or help they had given to their friends were positively correlated with ratings of the degree of upset at not being reciprocated. Also, ratings of the value of items received they had received from their friends were positively correlated with the upset at not reciprocating. Friends clearly seem to be attending (consciously or unconsciously) to the benefits and costs of their exchanges. Similar findings were found for relationships with romantic partners.

So although the occasional imbalance may be ignored, I expect a continuous pattern of helping a partner without receiving comparable or sufficient help in return will likely lead to the dissolution of the relationship. Even committed relationships, like marriages and friendships, may meet their demise for these reasons. There are, however, some exceptions. Committed partners will be less likely to end the relationship if the inability to return help is beyond the control of their partner (e.g., due to illness).

IS SELFISHNESS OVERESTIMATED?

The discussion thus far has attempted to introduce the reader to evolutionary theories that do not, as commonly assumed, view human nature as being consumed by brute selfishness. Although selfishness has had a role in evolutionary models, it is also a common assumption in many nonevolutionary ones. An egoist, self-serving view of humans has been long held by economists (see Gintis, 2001, for a review) as well as psychologists (see Batson, 1990, for a review), among other disciplines. In recent years, there has been an increase in empirical evidence showing that people do not behave as selfishly as expected. Could people be overestimating the degree of selfishness in human nature? The next section reviews some of the research that is relevant to this question.

As mentioned earlier, behavior that is counter to rational self-interests has been shown by players of economic games, including the ultimatum game (a game that involves the distribution of resources). In the Prisoner's Dilemma game, the best strategy to use in a one shot game is to defect. However, studies show that many people still choose to cooperate (Gintis, 2001). Whereas the most successful strategy in a series of Prisoner's Dilemma games was originally found to be Tit for Tat (Axelrod, 1984; Axelrod & Hamilton, 1981), recent computer simulations of the game have found that Tit for Tat can be succeeded by a nicer strategy that incorporates forgiveness (Nowak & Sigmund, 1992). The Generous Tit for Tat (GTT) strategy allows for "mistakes" of defection by other players. Unlike Tit for Tat, GTT will not result in unending defection if partners accidentally defect on their turn.

In my own research, a search for individual selfishness in social exchange produced unexpected results (Janicki, 1993, 2000). A series of studies investigated individuals' perceptions of actual exchanges (any form of giving or helping) they had with friends, relatives, romantic partners, and acquaintances. Two of the key variables that were investigated were individuals' ratings of the cost and value of what they had given and received. Based on a model of individual selfishness, it was predicted that individuals would overestimate the cost and value of what they had given, and underestimate what they had received (i.e., what others gave). It was expected that this "subtle-cheating bias" would have been adaptive because it would motivate individuals to repay less than what was actually required. I proposed that this bias could involve self-deception, as people might not realize they are subtly cheating others, and vehemently deny it if they were caught. Wright (1994) mentioned some similar ideas in his popular book about evolutionary psychology and morality. Wright suggested that self-serving biases in social accounting are "a corollary to the theory of reciprocal altruism" (p. 277). He further remarked that "humans seem unconsciously compelled to give a bit less than they get" (p. 277).

However, the research findings were opposite to my predictions. In five studies, individuals consistently indicated that the cost of what they gave to others was, on average, lower than the cost of what they received from others. In some studies, the value of what was received was rated higher than what was given. These findings are consistent with research conducted by McGuire (1993), who reported that participants perceived the costs and benefits of helping to be higher when taking the recipient's perspective than when taking the helper's point of view. In summary, no evidence was found for a selfish distortion of the perceived costs of giving to others (i.e., a subtle-cheating bias).

Another prediction I drew from the individual selfishness model was that people would be more concerned about getting reciprocated by others than about reciprocating others (Janicki, 1993). My findings were robust, but opposite to the original prediction. In all five of my studies (Janicki, 1993, 2000), participants reported a greater concern over repaying others than about being repaid. Although the data was entirely self-report, a social desirability explanation for the responses was ruled out because an analysis of the correlation between participants' responses and their scores on a social desirability measure found no relation (Janicki, 1993). A relatively high concern over repaying others has also been found by Sprecher (1998), in her study of dating couples. She gave participants measures to assess two types of exchange orientation: concern about giving back to others after receiving (wishing to not be over-benefited) and concern about receiving back after giving (wishing to not be under-benefited). Scores on the former measure tended to be higher than those on the latter.

From these findings I proposed that social exchange in relationships was based less on individual selfishness, and more on what I called cooperative selfishness—

the tendency for individuals to behave in ways that help others but also help themselves by maintaining relationships that are beneficial. From an evolutionary perspective, feeling upset at not reciprocating may provide at least two benefits. Feeling guilty and upset at not reciprocating helps ensure that a person does not do any harm to a valuable relationship. As Frank (1988) suggested, feelings like guilt may have evolved even though they may not help maximize self-interests, but because people prefer to form reciprocal relationships with those they know will get upset or feel guilty if they do wrong. Guilt about not repaying, as well as concern over repaying others, may help people control their tendency to cheat others (Trivers, 1971). Without such controls, reciprocal and long-term relationships could not develop.

A second benefit provided by the concern over reciprocating others is the avoidance of becoming indebted to others. Greenberg (1980) defined indebtedness as an aversive state that motivates the individual to reduce it. People may avoid becoming indebted by declining to accept help if they feel they will not be able to reciprocate (Greenberg & Shapiro, 1971). There is good reason to be motivated to avoid becoming indebted to others. Being owed gives individuals power over those who are in their debt, which can prove quite costly to the persons owing. Greenberg and Shapiro stated that one of the reasons indebtedness is so aversive is that it is a threat to the recipient's status, power, and freedom of action. Even though feelings of guilt, and concerns over reciprocating others, may benefit self-interests in the long run, these feelings nevertheless contribute to the kind side of human nature.

Scientists are not alone in maintaining a selfish view of people. Research has shown that the layperson also holds this view. A series of studies by Miller and Ratner (1998) demonstrated that people consistently overestimate the influence of self-interests on the attitudes and behaviors of others. In some of the studies, participants were asked to predict the decision making of those with a vested interest in a particular issue, compared to those without a vested interest. For example, participants were asked to estimate the proportion of smokers, compared to nonsmokers, who would support various antismoking regulations. The researchers compared these estimates to a survey of actual smokers and nonsmokers, and found that participants had overestimated the proportion of smokers who would be against the rules.

In summary, both behavioral specialists and the average person seem quick to conclude that people's behaviors will be dictated by self-interests. Although without question this does occur, assuming selfishness is a default motivation in all cases is inaccurate. This view may not only be inaccurate, it may also be damaging. Nesse (1999, 2001b) stressed the fact that individuals' beliefs about themselves influence their behaviors, which in turn influence the behaviors of others and society as a whole. Psychologists have clear evidence of self-fulfilling prophecies: untrue beliefs individuals have about others that cause them to act toward these people in ways that makes them (others) behave as expected. People who have an overly negative view of the world will tend to find their experiences conform to their expectations. For this reason, Nesse was concerned about the kind of theoretical views that are held about human nature. Viewing individuals (people and animals) more optimistically can draw much criticism, but it is a risk that several theorists are willing to take (de Waal, 1996; Frank, 1988; Nesse, 2001b).

THE ROLE OF CULTURE

The theories that have been discussed thus far examine how our evolved psychology contributes to the cooperative side of human nature. There is no question that culture also makes an important contribution. One of the fundamental lessons of social psychology is that an individual's behavior is strongly influenced by the real or imagined presence of others. Social norms are particularly relevant here. Social norms consist of cultural information that can be descriptive (what people tend to do) or injunctive (rules for acceptable behavior). People tend to follow social norms due to a combination of external (e.g., rewards and punishments from others) and internal factors (e.g., a desire to be liked and to act correctly). The influence of norms alone is an insufficient and incomplete explanation for whether or not cooperative behaviors are adopted (Krebs & Miller, 1985). The problem is that there may be more than one norm to choose from and not everyone follows the same norm. A better understanding of how individuals choose the norms or rules to which they adhere can be gained by turning to evolutionary theorists who have tackled this issue.

Like social psychologists, evolutionary theorists have investigated individuals' abilities to learn from and be influenced by their culture. Rather than viewing individuals as passive receptacles of their culture, evolutionary theorists posit that individuals possess information- processing mechanisms that direct the adoption of some, but not all, cultural information in ways that would have proven adaptive over evolutionary history (Boyd & Richerson, 1985; Flinn & Alexander, 1982; Richerson & Boyd, 1989; Tooby & Cosmides, 1992). For example, Flinn and Alexander (1982) proposed the existence of cognitive mechanisms that guide people to imitate successful individuals and to accept advice from individuals who care about their success. Boyd and Richerson (1985) further elaborated on social learning mechanisms, proposing that people tend to imitate the cultural traits that are used by those considered successful and admired (indirect biases), used by the majority (frequency dependent biases), and considered to be most suitable by the individual (direct biases).

Given individuals' propensity to adopt the ideas and behaviors of others, it is undeniable that the content of those ideas and behaviors will influence cooperative and uncooperative tendencies. There is much evidence that this occurs. For example, in collectivist cultures, individuals tend to be more helpful toward members of their group than are people in individualist cultures. However, people in collectivist cultures are less helpful toward outsiders or strangers than are people in noncollectivist cultures (P. B. Smith & Bond, 1998).

Cultural trends regarding cooperative behavior also change over time. For example, critics of modern culture often lament the fact that there is much less emphasis on manners and helpful behavior than there was in the past. For example, Covey (1989) did a literature review spanning 200 years on books written about finding success. For the first 150 years, most books focused on building a person's character. Valuable traits included integrity, humility, patience, justice, and so on. Books of etiquette and manners were also prolific during this time. These books not only discussed the correct way to set a table and introduce guests, but also the proper way to treat people, namely with politeness and courtesy. For example, Eichler (1946, p. 40) firmly stated that the fundamental rule of etiquette is "regard for the rights and feelings of others." Even well-known psychologists wrote about the importance of character (e.g., McDougall, 1927). Covey's (1989) literature search found a disheartening change in the most recent 50 years of books. Rather than advocating the development of character, the authors of most of these books recommended developing attitudes, communications skills, and social influence techniques in order to manipulate others. Wright (1994) also noted that self-help books of the past (e.g., from Darwin's era) featured instructions on improving character whereas those that are popular today encourage self-absorption. It seems obvious that the cultural information surrounding people not only reflects their feelings and attitudes, it also shapes them.[4]

What is the source of culture, in particular the norms or standards regarding cooperative behavior? For an in-depth analysis of the biological foundations of moral norms, please see Krebs and Janicki (2004). In brief, cultural ideas originate, are modified, and are transmitted by evolved minds. The evolutionary origins of cooperative behavior that have been discussed likely have some influence on the content of moral norms (e.g., help your relatives). Evolved predispositions, however, may not always be able to keep a tight leash on culture. Several theorists believe that culture evolution is a distinct but parallel process to biological evolution. Perceptions of the interconnectedness between cultural and biological evolution vary. At one extreme, Dawkins (1989) argued that cultural evolution has been completely uncoupled from biological evolution. According to Dawkins, cultural traits (which he called memes) that become popular and spread through the population do so merely because people find them psychologically appealing. They need not benefit a person's reproductive success. This process may lead to the adoption of cultural traits that are maladaptive.

Most evolutionary culture theorists take a less extreme position than Dawkins (1989) and argue that culture and genetic predispositions interact in a coevolutionary process (e.g., Boyd & Richerson, 1985; Durham, 1991). According to these theorists, evolved mechanisms that regulate the adoption of cultural traits will tend to serve evolved goals. Under certain conditions, however, the adoption of certain traits may prove maladaptive (Richerson & Boyd, 1989). This can occur when it is difficult to judge the merits of alternative cultural traits, and the default is

---

[4]For example, a recent advertisement in a men's magazine promoted a book that promised to show men how to "get all the sex without any commitment." I cannot help but wonder how such cultural messages shape people's behaviors toward others.

to rely on social learning. Compared to the ancestral environment, the modern world is characterized by innumerable and conflicting messages and behavioral models. Consequently, social learning may lead to the adoption of maladaptive behaviors. For example, individuals may use direct biases to imitate the behaviors and attitudes of popular media personalities. The behaviors of these personalities (e.g., music and movie stars) may not be adaptive for the individuals who imitate them. Depending on the characteristics of the most frequent behaviors or most salient role models, behaviors learned through these processes may vary in their degree of cooperativeness.[5]

The Freudian view of human nature depicted people as innately selfish creatures that required cultural training to become moral and civilized. The evolutionary perspective turns that view on its head. It stresses that people are born with genetic programs that make them capable of cooperative and moral behavior. The interaction of these programs with a person's cultural environment influences whether and how those behaviors are expressed. For example, when cooperative behavior is valued within a society, systems of indirect reciprocity may motivate individuals to maintain a reputation of being kind to others.

CONCLUSIONS

A main goal of this chapter was to demonstrate that taking an evolutionary approach to understanding human behavior can reveal not only ruthless selfishness, but also the capacity for altruism and kindness. The newer commitment models help explain why people may at times act irrationally against their own self-interests in ways that both help and harm others. Evolutionary theories of culture help explain how culture interacts with evolved psychology to produce cooperative or selfish behaviors.

Looking at current research revealed that beliefs about selfishness in human behavior may be overestimated by the scientist and layperson alike. Taking a more optimistic view of human nature may prove beneficial to individuals and society (Nesse, 2001b), but care must be taken not to commit the moralistic fallacy. The moralistic fallacy involves making the assumption that what ought to be, is (Crawford, chap. 1 in this vol.). It would be incorrect to assume that people are cooperative and good just because we would like them to be. We must rely on empirical evidence on which to draw these conclusions.

In this chapter, I have not had the opportunity to discuss all of the evolutionary theories that pertain to cooperative behaviors. A controversial and important model that should be mentioned is the modern version of group selection theory (Sober & D. S. Wilson, 1998). This model has been met with criticism by several evolutionary theorists (e.g., Maynard Smith, 1998) who are unconvinced that it improves on earlier gene selection models.

---

[5]Of course, it may not always be adaptive to behave cooperatively. In a hostile environment, selfishness may prove to be the best strategy.

Another new perspective that may prove to be fruitful is the integration of dynamical systems theory with evolutionary psychology (Kenrick, Li, & Butner, 2003). This perspective considers how the decisions that individuals make (e.g., to cooperate or defect) within a dynamic system influence those around them, which in turn affect the final outcome. Using simulations, Kenrick et al. (2003) demonstrated that the interaction of group dynamics with evolved psychologies can produce surprising results. These findings may lead to a greater understanding of how cooperative behaviors arise through gene–culture interactions.

Some people may find it difficult to believe that there is a gentle and kind side to human nature, when the news is filled with stories of war and other human tragedies. But these events do not contradict what has been discussed. They merely emphasize that evolved tendencies to be cooperative within our own groups can sometimes lead to hostility against other groups. It is ironic that the same psychological mechanisms that generate cooperative and helpful behavior can also produce animosity and aggression. In-group favoritism, as well as discrimination against out-group members, are well-studied cross-cultural phenomena that appear to be part of human nature (for an evolutionary interpretation, see Krebs & Denton, 1997). It is important to acknowledge and understand the workings of these perceptual biases because they can strongly influence the production of cooperative or aggressive behavior.

In conclusion, if individuals create public policies with the goal of increasing cooperative behavior, it is important that they take into consideration the design of the evolved mechanisms that produce helpful behavior. Understanding what makes people cooperate can facilitate the process of creating those policies and make those policies more effective. It is also worth considering that these policies contribute to the cultural information that shapes behavior. Finally, based on what has been discussed in this chapter, the automatic assumption that people will always be motivated by self-interests should be reconsidered.

REFERENCES

Alexander, R. D. (1987). *The biology of moral systems.* New York: Aldine de Gruyter.

Axelrod, R. (1984). *The evolution of cooperation.* New York: Basic Books.

Axelrod, R., & Hamilton, W. D. (1981). The evolution of cooperation. *Science, 211,* 1390–1396.

Barber, N. (1994). Machiavellianism and altruism: Effect of relatedness of target person on Machiavellian and helping attitudes. *Psychological Reports, 75,* 403–422.

Batson, C. D. (1990). How social an animal?: The human capacity for caring. American *Psychologist, 45,* 336–346.

Batson, C. D., Duncan, B. D., Ackerman, P., Buckley, T., & Birch, K. (1981). Is empathic emotion a source of altruistic motivation? *Journal of Personality and Social Psychology, 40,* 290–302.

Batson, C. D., & Shaw, L. L. (1991). Evidence for altruism: Toward a pluralism of prosocial motives. *Psychological Inquiry, 2*(2), 107–122.

Boyd, R., & Richerson, P. J. (1985). *Culture and the evolutionary process.* Chicago: University of Chicago Press.

Boyd, R., & Richerson, P. J. (1992). Punishment allow the evolution of cooperation (or anything else) in sizable groups. *Ethology and Sociobiology, 13*(3), 171–195.

Brown, W., Palameta, B., & Moore, C. (2003). Are there nonverbal cues to commitment? An exploratory study using the zero-acquaintance video presentation paradigm. *Evolutionary Psychology, 1*, 42–69.

Burnstein, E., Crandall, C., & Kitayama, S. (1994). Some neo-Darwinian decision rules for altruism: Weighting cues for inclusive fitness as a function of the biological importance of the decision. *Journal of Personality and Social Psychology, 67*(5), 773–789.

Buunk, B. P., & Van Yperen, N. W. (1991). Referential comparisons, relationship comparisons, and exchange orientation: Their relation to marital satisfaction. *Personality & Social Psychology Bulletin, 17*(6), 709–717.

Caporael, L. R., Dawes, R. M., Orbell, J. M., & van de Kragt, A. J. C. (1989). Selfishness examined. Cooperation in the absence of egoistic incentives. *Behavioral and Brain Sciences, 12*, 683–739.

Clark, M. S., Mills, J. R., & Corcoran, D. M. (1989). Keeping track of needs and inputs of friends and strangers. *Personality and Social Psychology Bulletin, 15*(4), 533–542.

Clark, M. S., Mills, J. R., & Powell, M. C. (1986). Keeping track of needs in communal and exchange relationships. *Journal of Personality and Social Psychology, 51*(2), 333–338.

Cohen, D., & Vandello, J. (2001) Honor and "faking" honorability. In R. M. Nesse (Ed.), *Evolution and the capacity for commitment* (pp. 163–185). New York: Russell Sage Foundation.

Cosmides, L. (1989). The logic of social exchange: Has natural selection shaped how humans reason? Studies with the Wason Selection Task. *Cognition, 31*, 187–276.

Cosmides, L., & Tooby, J. (1989). Evolutionary psychology and the generation of culture, Part II. Case Study: A computational theory of social exchange. *Ethology and Sociobiology, 10*, 51–97.

Cosmides, L., & Tooby, J. (1992). Cognitive adaptations for social exchange. In J. Barkow, L. Cosmides, & J. Tooby (Eds.), *The adapted mind: Evolutionary psychology and the generation of culture* (pp. 163–228). New York: Oxford University Press.

Cosmides, L., Tooby, J., Montaldi, A., & Thrall, N. (1999, June). *Character counts: Cheater detection is relaxed for honest individuals.* Paper presented at the Human Behavior and Evolution Society Annual Meeting, Salt Lake City, UT.

Covey, S. R. (1989). *The 7 habits of highly effective people.* New York: Simon & Shuster.

Cunningham, M. R. (1986). Levites and brother's keepers: A sociobiological perspective on social behavior. *Humboldt Journal of Social Relations, 13*(1&2), 35–67.

Daly, M., Salmon, C., & Wilson, M. (1997). Kinship: The conceptual hole in psychological studies of social cognition and close relationships. In J. A. Simpson & D. T. Kenrick (Eds.), *Evolutionary social psychology* (pp. 265–296). Hillsdale, NJ: Lawrence Erlbaum Associates.

Dawkins, R. (1979). Twelve misunderstandings of kin selection. *Zeitschrift für Tierpsychologie, 51*, 184–200.

Dawkins, R. (1989). *The selfish gene* (rev. ed.). Oxford, England: Oxford University Press.

de Waal, F. (1996). *Good natured.* Cambridge, MA: Harvard University Press.

Durham, W. H. (1991). *Coevolution: Genes, culture, and human diversity.* Stanford, CA: Stanford University Press.

Eichler, L. (1946). *The new book of etiquette* (rev. ed.). Garden City, NY: Garden City Publishing Company.

Ekman, P. (1985). *Telling lies: Clues to deceit in the marketplace, marriage, and politics.* New York: Norton.

Ekman, P., Davidson, R. J., & Friesen, W. V. (1990). The Duchenne smile: Emotional expression and brain physiology. *Journal of Personality and Social Psychology, 58*(2), 342–53.

Essock-Vitale, S. M., & McGuire, M. T. (1985). Women's lives viewed from an evolutionary perspective: II. Patterns of helping. *Ethology and Sociobiology, 6*, 155–173.

Flinn, M. V., & Alexander, R. D. (1982). Culture theory: The developing synthesis from biology. *Human Ecology, 10*, 383–400.

Frank, R. H. (1988). *Passions within reason. The strategic role of the emotions.* New York: Norton.

Frank, R. H. (1991). Economics. In M. Maxwell (Ed.), *The sociobiological imagination* (pp. 91–110). Albany: State University of New York Press.

Frank, R. H. (2001). Cooperation through emotional commitment. In R. M. Nesse (Ed.), *Evolution and the capacity for commitment* (pp. 57–76). New York: Russell Sage Foundation.

Gintis, H. (2001). Foreword: Beyond selfishness in modeling human behavior. In R. M. Nesse (Ed.), *Evolution and the capacity for commitment* (pp. xiii–xviii). New York: Russell Sage Foundation.

Gouldner, A. W. (1960). The norm of reciprocity: A preliminary statement. *American Sociological Review, 25*(2), 159–178.

Greenberg, M. S. (1980). A theory of indebtedness. In K. Gergen, M. S. Greenberg, & R. Willis (Eds.), *Social exchange: Advances in theory and research* (pp. 3–26). New York: Plenum Press.

Greenberg, M. S., & Shapiro, S. P. (1971). Indebtedness: An adverse aspect of asking for and receiving help. *Sociometry, 34*(2), 290–301.

Hamilton, W. D. (1964). The genetical evolution of social behavior: II. *Journal of Theoretical Biology, 7*, 17–52.

Hirshleifer, J. (1987). On the emotions as guarantors of threats and promises. In J. Dupré (Ed.), *The latest on the best: Essays on evolution and optimality* (pp. 307–326). Cambridge, MA: MIT Press.

Irons, W. (1996). In our own self image: The evolution of morality, deception, and religion. *Skeptic, 4*(2), 50–61.

Irons, W. (2001). Religion as a hard-to-fake sign of commitment. In R. M. Nesse (Ed.), *Evolution and the capacity for commitment* (pp. 310–309). New York: Russell Sage Foundation.

Janicki, M. G. (1993). *Evolutionary influences on social exchange: Cognitive biases in perception and recall.* Unpublished master's thesis, Simon Fraser University.

Janicki, M. G. (2000). *An investigation of the cognitions and perceptions concerning social exchange in various types of relationships.* Unpublished doctoral dissertation, Simon Fraser University.

Kenrick, D. (1991). Proximate altruism and ultimate selfishness. *Psychological Inquiry, 2*(2), 135–137.

Kenrick, D., Li, N. P., & Butner, J. (2003). Dynamical evolutionary psychology: Individual decision rules and emergent social norms. *Psychological Review, 110*(1), 3–28.

Ketelaar, T., & Au, W. T. (2003). The effects of guilty feelings on the behavior of uncooperative individuals in repeated social bargaining games: An affect-as-information interpretation of the role of emotion in social interaction. *Cognition & Emotion, 17*(3), 429–453.

Krebs, D. (1987). The challenge of altruism in biology and psychology. In C. Crawford, M. Smith, & D. Krebs (Eds.), *Sociobiology and psychology: Ideas, issues, and applications* (pp 81–118). Hillsdale, NJ: Lawrence Erlbaum Associates.

Krebs, D., & Denton, K. (1997). Social illusions and self-deception: The evolution of biases in person perception. In J. Simpson & D. Kenrick (Eds.), *Evolutionary social psychology.* Mahwah, NJ: Lawrence Erlbaum Associates.

Krebs, D. L. (1991). Altruism and egoism: A false dichotomy? *Psychological Inquiry, 2*(2), 137–139.

Krebs, D. L. (1998). The evolution of moral behaviors. In C. B. Crawford & D. L. Krebs (Eds.), *Handbook of evolutionary psychology: Ideas, issues, and applications* (pp. 337–368). Hillsdale, NJ: Lawrence Erlbaum Associates.

Krebs, D. L., & Janicki, M. G. (2004). Biological foundations of moral norms. In. M. Schaller & C. S. Crandall (Eds.), *The psychological foundations of culture* (pp. 125–148). Hillsdale, NJ: Lawrence Erlbaum Associates.

Krebs, D., & Miller, D. (1985). Altruism and aggression. In G. Lindzey & E. Aronson (Eds.), *Handbook of social psychology* (3rd ed., pp. 1–71). New York: Random House.

Kruger, D. J. (2003). Evolution and altruism: Combining psychological mediators with naturally selected tendencies. *Evolution and Human Behavior, 24*(2), 118–125.

Maynard Smith, J. (1998). The origin of altruism. *Nature, 393*, 639–640.

McDougall, W. (1927). *Character and the conduct of life.* London: Methuen.

McGuire, A. (1993, June). *Perceived costs and benefits of helping behaviours: Psychological extensions of evolutionary theorizing.* Paper presented at the Evolution and Human Sciences Conference at the London School of Economics.

Miller, D. T., & Ratner, R. K. (1998). The disparity between the actual and assumed power of self-interest. *Journal of Personality and Social Psychology, 74*(1), 53–62.

Murstein, B. I., Cerreto, M., & MacDonald, M. G. (1977). A theory and investigation of the effect of exchange-orientation on marriage and friendship. *Journal of Marriage and the Family,* 543–548.

Murstein, B. I., Wadlen, R., & Bond, C. F., Jr. (1987). The revised exchange-orientation scale. *Small Group Behavior, 18*(2), 212–223.

Nesse, R. M. (1999). The evolution of commitment and the origins of religion. *Science and Spirit, 10*(2), 32–33, 46.

Nesse, R. M. (Ed.). (2001a). *Evolution and the capacity for commitment.* New York: Russell Sage Foundation.

Nesse, R. M. (2001b). Natural selection and the capacity for subjective commitment. In R. M. Nesse (Ed.), *Evolution and the capacity for commitment* (pp. 1–44). New York: Russell Sage Foundation.

Nowak, M. A., & Sigmund, K. (1992). Tit for Tat in heterogeneous populations. *Nature, 355*, 250–253

Nowak, M. A., & Sigmund K. (1998) Evolution of indirect reciprocity by image scoring. *Nature, 393*, 573–577

Pinker, S. (2002). *The blank slate: The modern denial of human nature.* New York: Viking.

Porter, R. H. (1987). Kin recognition: Functions and mediating mechanisms. In C. Crawford, M. Smith, & D. Krebs (Eds.), *Sociobiology and psychology: Ideas, issues, and applications* (pp 175–203). Hillsdale, NJ: Lawrence Erlbaum Associates.

Price, M. E., Cosmides, L., & Tooby, J. (2002). Punishment as an anti-free rider psychological device. *Evolution and Human Behavior, 23*, 203–231.

Richerson, P. J., & Boyd, R. (1989). The role of evolved predispositions in cultural evolution. *Ethology & Sociobiology, 10*, 195–219.

Rook, K. S. (1987). Reciprocity of social exchange and social satisfaction among older women. *Journal of Personality and Social Psychology, 52*(1), 145–154.

Shackelford, T. K., & Buss, D. M. (1996). Betrayal in mateships, friendships, and coalitions. *Personality and Social Psychology Bulletin, 22*(11), 1151–1164.

Smith, M. S., Kish, B. J., & Crawford, C. B. (1987). Inheritance of wealth as human kin investment. *Ethology and Sociobiology, 8*, 171–182.

Smith, P. B., & Bond, N. H. (1998). *Social psychology across cultures* (2nd ed.). Boston: Allyn & Bacon.

Sober, E., & Wilson, D. S. (1998). *Unto others: The evolution and psychology of unselfish behavior.* Cambridge, MA: Harvard University Press.

Sprecher, S. (1998). The effect of exchange orientation on close relationships. *Social Psychology Quarterly, 61*(3), 220–231.

Tooby, J., & Cosmides, L. (1992). The psychological foundations of culture. In J. H. Barkow, L. Cosmides, & T. Tooby (Eds.), *The adapted mind: Evolutionary psychology and the generation of culture* (pp. 19–136). New York: Oxford University Press.

Tooby, J., & Cosmides, L. (1996). Friendship and the Banker's Paradox: Other pathways to the evolution of adaptations for altruism. *Proceedings of the British Academy, 88*, 119–143.

Trivers, R. (1971). The evolution of reciprocal altruism. *Quarterly Review of Biology, 46*, 35–57.

Trivers, R. (1985). *Social evolution.* Menlo Park, CA: The Benjamin/Cummings.

Wilson, E. O. (1978). *On human nature.* Cambridge, MA: Harvard University Press.

Wright, R. (1994). *The moral animal.* New York: Vintage.

Zahavi, A. (1995). Altruism as a handicap—The limitations of kin selection and reciprocity. *Journal of Avian Biology, 26*(1), 1–3.

4

Darwin and Evolutionary Moral Psychology

Harmon Holcomb
University of Kentucky

Humans exhibit ethical behavior by nature because their biological makeup determines the presence of the three necessary, and jointly sufficient, conditions for ethical
behavior. (a) the ability to anticipate the consequences of one's own actions; (b) the
ability to make value judgments; and (c) the ability to choose between alternative
courses of action. Ethical behavior came about in evolution not because it is adaptive
in itself, but as a necessary consequence of man's eminent intellectual abilities, which
are an attribute directly promoted by natural selection.   —(Ayala, 1995, p. 118)

I shall argue that evolutionary psychology undermines a strong and typical argument against sociobiological forays into ethics, namely, the one by the preemi-
nent evolutionary biologist Francisco Ayala quoted above (1995). Many people
hold variants on Ayala's views, which imply that a naturalistic, evolutionary study
of ethics is not possible beyond a few very general points about how ethical behavior originated (i.e., natural history). My method is to draw lessons from Darwin's
views in relation to evolutionary psychology for the relevance of evolution to three
questions: about the natural history of morality (descriptive ethics), moral norms
(prescriptive or normative ethics), and meta-ethics (philosophical ethics). I assume that evolutionary psychological studies should not be narrowly identified

with an innatist-adaptationist approach, but instead seek multidisciplinary integration of fields within psychology and adopt a multilevel biopsycho-sociocultural approach to human nature (Holcomb, 2002). Let me first contrast Ayala's basic approach with my own in a way that speaks to philosophical problems raised in Crawford's introduction to this volume.

Ayala asked and answered the three questions about the evolution of ethics as follows. In regard to natural history, is the capacity for ethics—the proclivity to judge human actions as either right or wrong—biologically determined? He answered, "Yes." The capacity for ethics is a necessary attribute of human nature. However, ethics is not an evolved adaptation; instead, it is a by-product of evolved intelligence. With regard to moral norms, are the systems or codes of ethical norms accepted by human beings biologically determined? He answered, "No." Moral norms are products of cultural evolution, not of biological evolution. So, this eminent evolutionist accepted that humans are ethical by nature and that ethical norms often lead to adaptive behavior due to the adaptive value of intelligence. He denied that ethical norms are sociocultural correlates of behaviors directly fostered by biological evolution. With regard to justification, do so-called sociobiological views of morality commit the naturalistic fallacy? He answered, "Yes." We commit the fallacy of inferring "what ought to be the case" from "what is the case," when we hold that evolution predisposes us to accept certain ethical norms, namely, those consistent with objectives induced by natural selection.

Thus, against the standard view held in common by sociobiologists and evolutionary psychologists, Ayala argued that (a) the capacity for morality is not an adaptation, just a by- product of general intelligence, which is an adaptation; (b) moral norms are products of cultural rather than biological evolution; and (c) evolutionary ethics fail to escape the naturalistic fallacy, despite their protestations to the contrary. The rebuttal to Ayala goes as follows. Contrary to (a), Darwin was right that the moral sense involves more than intelligence, namely, the social instincts and emotions. Contrary to (a) and (b), evolutionary psychology supplies empirical, theoretical, and conceptual reasons to posit an adaptive, universal morality acquisition device. It underlies variable moral norms and behaviors analogous to the way Chomsky's "universal grammar" underlies variable linguistic norms and behaviors. Contrary to (c), moral rules are grounded in human purposes, using evolution to add to and enhance understanding of morality's functions. This analysis opens up empirical inquiry in calling for a field of evolutionary moral psychology in descriptive ethics, avoids the "culturally versus biologically determined" fallacy that besets normative ethics, and identifies deeper issues behind the often superficial talk of the "naturalistic fallacy" in meta-ethics. The organization of this chapter into three sections corresponds to these arguments and rebuttals first about natural history, second about moral norms, and third about meta-ethics. Evolutionary psychology's success in establishing the study of function in psychology provides the basis for advocacy of a functionalist approach to each of these three dimensions of evolutionary ethics.

The main argument against evolutionary psychology and sociobiology has been a moral one: They necessarily reinforce immoral aspects of the status quo, or lead to immoral public policies and personal decisions, or lead to an amoral worldview. Instead, evolution (descriptively) helps with understanding why the status quo is what it is and why changes occur when they occur. It (proscriptively) has not led to newsworthy immoral public policies or personal decisions, and it (philosophically) elucidates the nature of the moral situation while not uniquely determining any particular ethic or conception of right and wrong. Generally, for almost any well-articulated evolutionary hypothesis, one can think of possible ways to make it useful or harmful in applying it, a sense in which science is value neutral, but whether an application leads to "good" or "bad" consequences often depends on prior moral or sociopolitical views, a sense in which science is value dependent. I argue that evolution informs moral psychology, which investigates moral views in everyday life (as Wright, 1994, did for Darwin), but without trying to "derive moral imperatives from evolution," as Ayala and critics assumed.

Because cultural variation often reflects ecological variation, the evolutionary psychological study of caring should be combined with the Darwinian anthropological study of the ecological contexts in which our evolved moral psyches operate. Consider the hunter-gathering lk! in Africa. They face continual scarcity of resources so severe that individual survival does not permit much caring for others. Their culture is the limiting case in which gaining minimal fitness turns off our morality acquisition device. Such cases show that Ayala not only failed to realize that purely intellectual decision making would not be moral without an underlying substrate of caring, he also failed to realize that the fact that morality's expression is culture bound does not remove it from the biological domain. Consider some contemporary examples.

Changes in social policies are intertwined with changes in moral norms. Recent cultural changes toward social equality are changing the opportunities that provide the range of options for evolved strategies to take. They are leading to men's greater concern with their looks and women's greater concern with work. These cultural changes are biological changes (i.e., changes in "the conditions of life" that change the effects of behaviors on fitness, its correlates, the constraints, and the behavioral options). New supposedly purely "cultural" moral policies against oppression of women fall into evolutionary categories (see Batten, 1992, for a feminist evolutionary ethic that sees "sexism versus feminism" as an episode in the evolution of men's control over women's reproduction and women's efforts to subvert that control).

Nepotism is an example of an outcome of an evolutionary constant (caring for our family) that we want to change. We can enact policies that interact with our evolved psychological mechanisms to either increase or decrease nepotism (or other traits). Using fitness-related cost–benefit analysis, we can make nepotism in various conditions either more beneficial or more costly to would-be nepotists. This is a real-life issue in states such as Kentucky, in which powerful county administrators suggest appointments of their kin to the few available high quality jobs. This volume provides an antidote to the stereotype that evolutionary hypotheses require a conservative political agenda (for a left-wing egalitarian evolutionary ethic, see Singer, 2000).

Yet our mission to improve public policies and personal decisions using evolutionary thinking does not touch the underlying philosophical aspect of this objection, namely, that by following evolutionary imperatives we will do immoral or amoral things. For instance, the best way to promote my fitness is to kill or dominate sexual rivals, as sexual selection theory implies, and kill or dominate all non-kin who are nonreciprocators, as kin selection theory and social exchange theory imply, if it is possible to get away with it, *ceteris paribus*. The fact that each individual makes compromises with others' evolved ends makes this an impractical option. Yet, any theory that implies that we engage in moral behavior only because cheating is too costly is not likely to be viewed as a theoretical basis for genuinely moral behavior and moral norms but only for prudential behavior and prudential norms. This philosophical point will motivate critics to write off this volume as well-intended suggestions about what we should do or ought to do that fail to recognize that the logic of evolutionary psychology itself leads to bad outcomes. Ironically, that vice can be turned into a virtue. Evolutionary psychology can be recognized as a legitimate tool of policy by those critics who think its claims false or unjustified, because theories do not have to be true to be useful in some domains (e.g., Newtonian theory helps in building satellites even though it is false as compared to Einstein's relativity theories, and many incompatible psychiatric theories help people to a similar degree). When evolutionary psychology delivers a pattern of useful results, people can ascribe them to nonevolutionary psychological or cultural means of effecting positive change, thereby including both advocates and critics.

Thus, even if evolutionary psychology proves practically useful when based on something like Crawford's chapter, his Table 1.1 (in this vol.), which correlates specialized versus generalized psychological mechanisms with the efficacy of sociopolitical and moral policies, can be viewed as yet a more subtle instance of the fallacy of inferring "ought" from "is." Why? It seems to commit him as a matter of the logic of his position, despite his protestations, to holding that evolution predisposes us to accept certain ethical norms: "Correct" versus "incorrect" beliefs about the nature of ancestrally evolved mental mechanisms (whether they are domain-general or domain-specialized) lead to "correct" versus "incorrect" decisions concerning public policies. He appeals to the consequence of promoting "well-being" rather than "fitness" as the goal of public policies and personal decisions, but that does not affect the fallacy.

To give a sense of these sort of naturalistic ethics, consider an example from a purely philosophical work where the purely philosophical reasoning itself provides an example of a distinction between philosophical ethics and evolutionary moral psychology. When using evolution to inform public policy, individuals need to know whether the policy is morally relevant or nonmoral. Ross long ago explicated the concept of (moral) right and wrong, contrary to Moore's utilitarianism, as encompassing far more than good and bad consequences of an action. The intention is not to endorse Ross' full intuitionist ethical theory, but to illustrate how evolution can be significant for moral theory (see Bradie, 1994; M. Nitecki & D. Nitecki, 1993; Thompson, 1995). The aim is to give depth to the view of the nature of the moral agent by illuminating the functionality of the moral agent as a social organism with an evolved adapted mind.

What is an objective basis for moral obligation in social relationships that includes good consequences but covers more obligations than acts of benevolence?

> In fact the theory of "ideal utilitarianism," if I may for brevity refer so to the theory of Professor Moore, seems to simplify unduly our relations to our fellows it says, in effect, that the only morally significant relation in which my neighbours stand to me is that of being possible beneficiaries of my action. They do stand in this relation to me, and this relation is morally significant. But they may also stand to me in the relation of promise to promiser, of creditor to debtor, of wife to husband, of child to parent, of friend to friend, of fellow countryman to fellow countryman, and the like; and each of these relations is the foundation of a prima facie duty, which is more or less incumbent on me according to the circumstances of the case. (Ross, 1930/1989, p. 554)

Evolutionists can help give a natural history of morality by identifying the psychological mechanisms specialized to handle the relation of wife to husband (involving sexual selection and evolved specialized psychological mechanisms such as sexual jealousy), child to parent (involving Darwinian natural selection and specialized psychological mechanisms involving parental manipulation and birth order), of friend to friend (involving reciprocal altruism), promisee to promiser and creditor to debtor (involving reciprocal altruism and social exchange in the sense of Cosmides and Tooby), and fellow countrymen to fellow countrymen (involving individual selection for group-living adaptations or group selection for group-beneficial adaptations). We are not trying to view every mental mechanism as an adaptation (vulgar adaptationism), but to understand the evolutionary status of our psychological mechanisms, whether they are direct adaptations, exaptations, correlated traits, by-products, and so forth. Moral reasoning is deontic (about permission, obligation, and prohibition) and our very ability to reason about what one may do, must do, and must not do has already been subjected to a history of selection pressures. Morality arises from these social relationships and reflects the different selection pressures affecting them.

How are moral personal decisions to be made?

> When I am in a situation, as perhaps I always am, in which more than one of these prima facie duties is incumbent on me, what I have to do is to study the situation as fully as I can until I form the considered opinion (it is never more) that in the circumstances one of them is more incumbent than any other, then I am bound to think that to do this prima facie duty is my duty sans phrase in the situation. (Ross, 1930/1989, p. 554)

Evolutionists can help inform moral norms by using the preceding evolutionary considerations to "study the situation as fully as I can." There are conflicts of interests between different parties in the situation that involve the impact of genetic nonidentity on what values promote ancestral fitness. Evolved *strategies* are conditional on various circumstances in their operation and thus sensitive to differences between ancestral and current environments. Such adaptive culturally variable and individually variable strategies lead to cost–benefit calculations of consequences on well-being and to values other than well-being such as reparations, gratitude, justice, self-improvement, honesty, respect, love, and so on. These evolutionary studies can combine information about traits that have an evolutionary past with traits that are new and have no evolutionary past ("purely cultural traits") to generate moral norms specific enough to guide personal decisions or general enough to guide public policy. We are not trying to derive moral norms from evolutionary imperatives alone (biological determinism), but are combining our antecedent nonevolutionary knowledge with our evolutionary knowledge to create a more fully informed emotionally sensitive (Irons, 1996) deontic ethic of human relations.

How can we give arguments in meta-ethics that fit our commonsense intuitions?

> The essential defect of the 'ideal utilitarian' theory is that it ignores, or at least does not do full justice to, the highly personal character of duty. If the only duty is to produce the maximum of good, the question who is to have the good-whether it is myself, or my benefactor, or a person to whom I have made a promise to confer that good on him, or a mere fellow man to whom I stand in no such special relation-should make no difference to my having a duty to produce that good. But we are all in fact sure that it makes as vast difference. (Ross, 1930/1989, p. 555)

Ross stated an intuition that most people share. An individual's obligations to self, parents, children, friend, reciprocator, or group-member differ in terms of just those differences in social relationship. Evolutionists can use this standard form of philosophical argument: Philosophical explications of concepts are judged by how well they create coherence between our general principles and our judgments about specific cases of applying those principles. Our judgments about whether I am obligated to do something in a specific case rest on intuitions, as arguments have to come to an end somewhere. To the extent that we accept moral principles because they fit our evolved moral intuitions, given that we have an evolved moral sensibility or morality acquisition device inherent in our minds, then our standard form of philosophical argument is a form of naturalistic philosophy, in which science is continuous with philosophy. That does not mean that we must accept our moral intuitions (nothing is absolute). We can identify from whence they came and decide to what extent we want to modify them in relation to principles in a dynamic dialectical interplay of revisions in our principles and intuitive/trained judgments in order to maintain reflective equilibrium. Intuitions play this role in philosophical theories that differ on whether a moral concept is fundamental or derived: deontology (duty-based), utilitarianism (utility-based), intuitionism (intuition-based), or virtue (virtue-based) ethics.

Given that this is "the decade of the brain," evolutionary psychology can buttress its evidence with neurological evidence. Various moral aptitudes are lost when specific areas of the brain are injured. Ayala's purely intellectualist view of morality would be falsified by evidence that these neural circuits are found not only on the left brain areas that process and store logical information, but also on the right brain areas that intuitively process contextual information inherent in recognizing faces of kin and non-kin differently. Assuming that our logical moral principles and intuitive moral relationship-based recognitions would be improved by engaging the left and right brain in moral learning, it is a short step to prescriptions that we should teach moral concepts both verbally and visually, discussing moral concepts from a combined thinking and feeling point of view (as in the feminist care ethic; Larabee, 1993).

The preceding example is not a final truth, but it does indicate that naturalistic moral psychology is possible. Ayala's three questions about natural history, moral norms, and meta-ethics can be addressed in a unified way informed by evolutionary psychology. The next section analyzes and rebuts each of Ayala's arguments in detail in relation to what can be added by Darwin himself.

NATURAL HISTORY OF MORAL CAPACITY: ADAPTATION OR BY-PRODUCT?

Ayala's most novel argument is about the character of human's evolved predisposition to engage in ethical behavior. Most traditional evolutionary accounts (e.g., those of Trivers, Wilson, Dawkins, Ruse, and Alexander) posit that altruistic and cooperative intentions are the bedrock of ethics and evolved as one of the human adaptations. Ayala emphasized that "products of evolution" are not restricted to "adaptations." All evolutionists know this; a key methodological issue is how to argue persuasively that something is a direct adaptation or a by-product in a particular case.

Ayala's argument, in brief, is as follows. Intelligence gives human beings the ability to anticipate the consequences of their own actions, the ability to make value judgments, and the ability to choose between alternative courses of action. My evaluation of Ayala's argument, in brief, is as follows. Contrary to Ayala's position, Darwin concluded that ethical capacity is not reducible to intelligence; it also involves social "instincts" and social emotions. De Waal (1996) provided empirical evidence for a continuity of adaptations underlying morality from chimpanzees to humans that supports and fills out Darwin's position using current natural selection theory. Mealey (1995) supplied an empirical counterexample to Ayala's position: Sociopaths are not intellectually handicapped but behave immorally or amorally, having a deficit of social emotions and moral conscience. For these and other reasons, Darwin was right. Even so, Ayala's point can be recast. Is ethical capacity an adaptation involving all three traits, as Pinker-style arguments suggest, or a by-product of those adaptations? These rival hypotheses over the locus of functional design deserve empirical study in evolutionary moral psychology.

Why Morality Is Not a By-Product of Intelligence Alone

Darwin (1871/1993a) anticipated Ayala's argument but did not draw Ayala's conclusion. Darwin did indeed have the concept of a by-product of intelligence, for which he used the term "incidental result": "If it be maintained that certain powers, such as self-consciousness, abstraction, & etc., are peculiar to man, it may well be that these are the incidental results of other highly-advanced intellectual faculties; and these again are mainly the result of the continued use of a highly developed language" (p. 330). Darwin also recognized that the capacity for ethics involves each of Ayala's three conditions, namely, anticipating consequences, making value judgments, and choosing actions that maximize value: "A moral being is one who is capable of comparing his past and future actions and motives—of approving of some and disapproving of others" (pp. 351–352). But Darwin did not reduce ethical capacity to intelligence; instead, he saw it as a consequence of both the social instincts, including emotions such as love and sympathy, and intelligence: "I have endeavored to show that the moral sense follows, firstly, from the enduring and always present nature of the social instincts, in which respect he agrees with the lower animals; and secondly, from his mental faculties being highly active and his impressions of past events extremely vivid, in which respects he differs from the lower animals" (pp. 351–352).

Darwin's view, I shall argue, is superior to Ayala's in several ways. First, Darwin's posited a concrete scenario in time, whereas Ayala only posited abstract necessary and sufficient conditions for the evolution of ethical capacity. If Darwin is right, then intelligence is necessary but insufficient for an ethical capacity. So, there should be cases in which Ayala's intellectual conditions are fulfilled but the behavior that results lacks an ethical dimension. Here is an everyday example: eating an ice cream cone. I anticipate the effects of eating ice cream; eating ice cream is aesthetically pleasing. I make a value judgment; I prefer what is aesthetically pleasing. I choose between alternative courses of action; I'll eat it rather than pass it by. Intuitively, there is nothing ethical about eating the ice cream cone, a "matter of taste." This counterexample is a reminder that there are values other than moral values (e.g., aesthetic value, economic value). Because reasoning about nonmoral values is insufficient for moral reasoning, Ayala's conditions are insufficient for moral capacity.

Consider how different conceptions of intelligence (or morality) make a difference to the issue. Sociobiologists advanced their conception of mentality as susceptibility to social learning. Evolutionary psychologists have a theory of social intelligence. If Ayala is right that ethics are a side effect of intelligence, and intelligence is susceptibility to social learning (Lumsden & Wilson, 1981, 1983) or else social intelligence is part of the adapted mind (Tooby & Cosmides, 1992), it follows that being a side effect of intelligence does involve social instincts. That would seem to reconcile Darwin's and Ayala's views.

At first sight, there does not seem to be a significant difference between Ayala's view that morality is a by-product of intelligence operating in social situations and the picture of morality as a dimension of social intelligence. However, the significant difference here is that Ayala's view is committed only to one domain-general cognitive mechanism (i.e., general intelligence is domain general), whereas the view that morality is an adaptation usually regards morality as a product of evolved domain-specific cognitive mechanisms (i.e., humans are moral beings not because they apply subject matter neutral reasoning to social situations but because moral thoughts, emotions, desires, and sensibilities utilize cognitions specific to the domain of moral social interactions).

Ayala wrote as if it is possible to drive a wedge between intelligence as an adaptation (and its by-product, morality) and other human adaptations, as evident from his decision not to discuss them in relation to morality. However, selection resulting in morality does not occur in isolation from other selection pressures; morality evolved as something built on a base of social, emotional, and cognitive adaptations. Evolutionary moral psychology can take as a fruitful point of departure the well-received empirical work of de Waal (1996) on the origins of right and wrong in chimpanzees. His main argument supports Darwin's position and yields the following conclusion:

> It is hard to imagine human morality without the following tendencies and capabilities found also in other species. Sympathy-related traits: attachment, succorance, and emotional contagion; learned adjustment to and special treatment of the disabled and injured; ability to trade places mentally with others (cognitive empathy). Norm-related traits: prescriptive social rules, internalization of rules and anticipation of punishment. Reciprocity: a concept of giving, trading, and revenge; moralistic aggression against violators of reciprocity rules. Getting Along: peacemaking and avoidance of conflict; community concern and maintenance of good relationships; accommodation of conflicting interests through negotiation. (p. 211)

De Waal's empirical work underscores the evolutionary postulate that the human mind evolved as an adaptation to group living, so that psychological capacities are adaptations to social life and ecological necessities, thereby uniting cognitive, social, and emotional aspects of morality that Darwin emphasized and Ayala overlooked. General conditions for the evolution of morality widespread in primates (de Waal, 1994, p. 32) include: group value, mutual aid, and the resolution of intra-group conflict through balancing individual and collective interests at a dyadic level (e.g., direct reciprocation of aid and reconciliation following fights) or higher social levels (e.g., community concern, care about good relationships between others, mediated reconciliation, peaceful arbitration of disputes). Human beings' moral systems also include appreciation of altruistic behavior on a group-wide basis and encouragement of contributions to the quality of the social environment. All these contribute to what Crawford termed "well-being." The functions of these moral tendencies are likely to be either directly selected adaptations or by-products of adaptations to such group-related conditions, as opposed to Ayala's account merely in terms of individuals.

In sum, Alexander (1986), de Waal (1982, 1996, 1999), and Sober and Wilson (1998) exemplified the sort of work that is creating a field of evolutionary moral psychology. This work taken as a whole supports and elaborates Darwin's view and undercuts Ayala's view: There are morality-specific adaptations—whether or not we define morality in a way that research into its animal origins identifies constituents of morality or preconditions for morality's emergence—and these psychological adaptations connect intellectual, social, and emotional aspects of human nature.

My third reason for favoring Darwin's position is that although Ayala accepted that intelligence is adaptive, he implausibly disallowed that compassion could be adaptive or that other psychological states inherent in having a moral conscience have been selected, whereas Darwin's scenario brings these into play from the start. Ayala (1995, p. 122) saw "no evidence that ethical behavior developed because it was adaptive in itself. I find it hard to see how evaluating certain actions as either good or evil (not just choosing some actions rather than others, or evaluating them with respect to their practical consequences) would promote the reproductive fitness of the evaluators." There is evidence that Ayala was ignoring or unaware of, for example, Alexander's well-known *Biology of Moral Systems* (1986). Ensuing work, de Waal, Wilson, and Sober filled out specific conditions for the evolution of a "moral sense" (see also Irons, 1996; Chisholm, 1999).

As for "evaluating does not promote fitness," the moral emotions of guilt and sympathy do activate behaviors. It is because Ayala implicitly defined morality in a way that severs it from behavior that he found it of no reproductive consequence, a verbal trick. He asserted that conscience does not contribute to reproductive success, and inferred without further ado that conscience is a by-product of intelligence alone. If such actions have an impact on reproductive success, and evaluative cognitions of right/wrong or good/bad are expressed using deontic reasoning (imperative or obligation-oriented language), moral capacity is a direct target of natural selection.

Ayala held that "humans evaluate their behavior as right or wrong, moral or immoral, as a consequence of their eminent intellectual capacities which include self-awareness and abstract thinking. These intellectual capacities are products of the evolutionary process, but they are distinctly human. Thus, I maintain that ethical behavior is not causally related to the social behavior of animals, including kin, and reciprocal altruism." Darwin's (1871/1993a, p. 119) position seems more plausible in the light of work by Alexander, de Waal, Wilson, and Sober, and so on. Human beings differ from the lower animals in virtue of these highly developed mental capacities, but are similar to them in virtue of the social instincts and emotions. These social and emotional adaptations did not disappear when human intelligence evolved (Griffiths, 2002), and so human intelligence is erected on (and perhaps co-evolved with) a base of social instincts and emotions rather than being separate from them. When consulting "moral conscience," individuals are consulting something that reflects both uniquely human traits, which involve human natural evolution and cultural evolution, but also traits they share as legacies of their hominid and primate ancestors (i.e., from the "environments of evolutionary adaptedness").

Sociopathy and Moral Conscience: An Example of Empirical Testing

What would a good empirical test of Ayala's versus Darwin's position be like? It would find a well-developed body of literature on human behavior that supplies a counterexample to Ayala by showing that some people have "normal intellectual capacity" as commonly understood but act immorally or amorally; if so, intellectual capacity is insufficient for moral capacity. The most telling empirical study of this sort is Mealey's widely known (1995) evolutionary study of sociopaths (also termed "psychopaths"). Sociopaths are not intellectually handicapped, yet they have a deficit of social emotions (love, shame, guilt, empathy, and remorse), lack a moral conscience, and exhibit manipulative and predatory antisocial behavior. Philosophical moral psychology adds detail to this counterexample (see Ci, 1991; Cleckly, 1976; Duff, 1977).

Mealey's hypothesis is that the personality and behavior of sociopaths are designed by natural selection as a successful life history strategy of social deception. Deception is common in animals. Sociopathy is a uniquely human form of an adaptive cheater strategy adopted when internal states and external circumstance put the human organism at fitness disadvantage when playing by the rules. Mealey used evolutionary game theory to suggest social policies for how to intervene in individual development or else increase the costs of sociopathy in order to decrease its prevalence. The issue for further empirical work is whether moral capacity is an adaptation or by-product of all three items: intelligence, sociality, and emotions.

Description and Prescription: Are Moral Norms Biologically Determined?

Ayala's (1992) argument on the question of whether moral norms are biologically determined is an exercise in line drawing typical of many critics of sociobiology. Ayala affirmed that it is the biological nature of Homo sapiens to make moral judgments, to accept ethical values, and to identify certain actions as either right or wrong. But he maintained that particular moral prescriptions are not determined by human biological nature; instead, they are "chosen by society or by individuals." He concluded that although ethical capacity is biologically determined, specific ethical norms are culturally determined and so specific ethical norms need not be adaptive even though intelligence makes people's actions generally, including moral actions, adaptive.

A hidden premise in this argument is that because morality is a by-product of human intelligence, the causation ("determination") of behavior differs in humans and animals. This inference rests on both the truth that humans are unique in that they act on the basis of reasoned choices as well as on the problematic assumption that reasons are causes. Evidently, the role of the by-product thesis for Ayala is to find a reason for holding that ethical norms are not biologically determined even though ethical capacity is biologically determined. This role evident in the hidden implication is that because actual norms are cultural, and therefore outside the domain of evolutionary study, the practical matter of choosing which norms people will live by is also cultural, and so also beyond the reach of biological evolutionary thought.

Evolutionary psychology helps to identify the confusions in these tacit assumptions: failure to distinguish a universal human mental predisposition for acquiring norms from the plethora of actual culturally variable norms, a false dichotomy between "biological" and "cultural," failure to see that by-products are subject to evolutionary explanation just as much as are direct adaptations, and a focus on causation to the exclusion of evolved functions.

Different peoples speak different languages and every normal human speaks some language, and so it may be inferred that the capacity for language is a universal part of human nature but specific languages are not. Similarly, different individuals and cultures have different moral norms and every normal human accepts some moral norms, and so it may be inferred that the capacity for ethics is a universal part of human nature but specific moral norms are not. No further argument is needed. So, the rest of the Ayala's argument about these two issues is moot.

The comparison between moral capacity and norms, on the one hand, and linguistic capacity and norms, on the other hand, is quite revealing. For moral norms to count as biologically determined, Ayala required that specific moral codes be universal. Obviously, they are not universal, and so he concluded that they are not biologically determined (in this sense). Here the movement from sociobiology to evolutionary psychology is fruitful. Following Pinker (1994, 1997), even though particular languages vary, there is a universal grammar. If the moral sense is like the linguistic sense, even though particular moral norms vary culturally, then analogous universal "grammar" for morality underlying culturally variable norms may be hypothesized. And some traits, such as mother-care and "do not kill group members," do appear to be pretty universal and are so because of obvious natural selection outcomes.

Contrary to Ayala's assumption, the by-product view does not eliminate the need for evolutionary research into specific variations in behavior. Here are two examples of practical importance: All people have a predisposition toward sexual jealousy in certain circumstances and toward aggression in certain circumstances, but only a few commit homicides and only a few commit rapes. Many specific, variable features of homicide were explained by Daly and Wilson (1988) with the assumption that sexual jealousy is an adaptation, and leaving open whether homicide is a by-product of direct selection for male aggression in various situations or a direct adaptation specific to situations in which murder increased fitness more than other forms of aggression. Jones (1999) refuted assumptions similar to Ayala's in suggesting legal prescriptions for an adaptation versus a by-product view of rape. Gender differences in moral decision making are expected from evolved gender differences (Buss, 1999; Mealey, 2000).

An evolved predisposition is directed toward domain-specific functionally specified types, not causally specified types. For instance, de Waal concluded his chapter on sympathy, saying that "one of the principal functions of morality seems to be to protect and nurture this caring capacity (the capacity to care for others), to guide its growth and expand its reach, so that it can effectively balance other human tendencies that need little encouragement" (1996, p. 88). Morality evolved to counteract preexisting tendencies, for example, toward aggression and sexual conquest that yield murder and rape (for evolution-based legal prescriptions on rape, see Jones, 1999). Paradigmatic morally wrong acts are "reasoned choices" with devastating impacts on the biological fitness on others and morally right acts are "reasoned choices" in contexts of care for others that protect necessities of their survival and reproduction.

Causation of behavior differs in animals and humans by virtue of human mind and culture. Ethical capacities and norms do serve evolved functions despite these differences, just as various traits in different nonhuman animal species serve evolved functions despite vast differences in the causation of their behaviors. Both sociobiology and evolutionary psychology have so far operated on a principle of silence on the way nature and nurture combine to cause behavior.

Ayala's presumption that "human behavior guided by norms is cultural, not biological" is common among critics; it is their dichotomy, not one typically held by evolutionary psychologists. This point is easily documented using the previous examples. In Daly and Wilson's terms (1988), "Natural selection is the inter-individual process that creates and organizes social responsiveness," and so evolutionary biology is essential to analyzing variable social and circumstantial influences on behavior (p. 296). In de Waal's (1999) terms, "The unexpected richness of a research program that integrates developmental, genetic, evolutionary and cultural approaches to a well-circumscribed phenomenon demonstrates the power of breaking down old barriers between disciplines" (p. 99).

In saying that moral codes are not biologically determined because they are culturally chosen and culturally variable, Ayala echoed a dichotomy between "biology" and "culture" that forgets about psychology. The aim of evolutionary psychology has been to provide the missing link. In principle, this missing link is needed, but the multilevel connections are often no better specified than in well-known examples from sociobiology. For instance, sociobiologists linked the moral code "incest is wrong" with inbreeding. They recounted Westermark's century-old finding (Kitcher, 1985), namely, that children growing up together lack sexual desire for each other later on, with his explanation of it as an evolved mechanism designed to prevent inbreeding. De Waal (1999) described the framework that supplants the nature–nurture dichotomy:

> The framework includes as developmental component (learned sexual aversion), an innate component (the effect of early familiarity), a cultural component (some cultures raise unrelated children together, others raise siblings of the opposite sex apart), a sound evolutionary reason (suppression of inbreeding) and direct parallels with animal behavior. On top of this comes the cultural taboo, which is unique to our species. (p. 99)

Still, the Westermark effect is a good example of what critics like Ayala say is missing: Culture is relevant in two ways in the quote about the framework. Evolutionary explanations do take account of culture, that is, in terms of behaviors—whether kin or non-kin children are raised together. Evolutionary psychology has not yet taken account of how a cultural taboo (e.g., moral norms about who may or may not have sex with, kill, or rape whom) connects with all the other levels.

There must be more clarity in the form of evolutionary explanation of moral prescriptions. For instance, attitudes toward the utilitarian principle might be explained according to the following scheme: Variations in people's attitude toward moral norms reflect variations in cultural and mental variables in ways that reflect evolutionary principles. Given that the moral norm X (e.g., the golden rule) arose in people with certain minds and culture, and such people are predisposed to accept or reject whatever norms have certain evolutionary functions (e.g., promoting various types of cooperation), those people are predicted from theoretical expectations based on a selection process (e.g., reciprocal altruism) to favor norm X over alternative norms just in case X better fulfills those evolutionary functions than do the alternatives. This defines an adaptive optimum, and of course would be developed using expectations about ancestral environments and current adaptive function, constraints on selection, and other standard moves. The whole story could be applied to other norms that arise, so that it explains the variability of the norms themselves rather than positing one norm for all humans. That is, we posit a deep universal moral grammar, not a universal moral norm, just as linguists posit a deep universal grammar, not a language. Sociobiologists and evolutionary psychologists do not try to derive a single unique moral norm "from biology," as Ayala assumed.

To posit a universal moral "grammar" is to posit something widespread in the species that constrains and enables humans to form fitness-relevant predispositions toward moral behaviors and moral norms. A universal grammar or moral grammar is to be thought of as a widespread language acquisition device or a widespread morality acquisition device. Now, a predisposition is to be defined as the condition of being disposed in advance. An evolved predisposition is a disposition for forming various dispositions in various circumstances, which are environmentally contingent on mental and cultural variables and reflect a repertoire of possible adaptive strategies. For example, Daly and Wilson (1988) identified as an adaptation the parental inclination to vary the love and solicitude offered a child according to certain specified circumstances. A predisposition is directed toward domain-specific, functionally specified types—strategies for achieving reproductive success that explain facts about human commonalities or individual differences, not toward causally specified targets that are universal, necessary attributes of the species. By distinguishing causes and functions, we can both agree with Ayala that the causation of behavior differs in animals and humans by virtue of human mind and culture and hold that distinctively human moral norms serve evolutionary functions.

Justification of Moral Norms and the Naturalistic Fallacy

According to standard analytic philosophy, questions of explanation are one thing, and questions of justification are another. Yet, when most people learn about human evolution, they say such things as: "What warrants ethical behavior, if humans are merely accidental products of history?" Such questions collapse normally distinct questions: (A) How could we explain the presence of ethics in our society in an evolutionary view? (B) How can we justify enforcing moral norms or construct a normative ethics that we live by? Explanation is run together with justification because the doubt is: If human nature is what evolutionists say it is—with morality, like other human features, being a means to the end of reproductive success—then how can humans be genuine moral agents? Wouldn't moral reasoning reduce to a rationalization for actions undertaken in our genetic self-interest? These misgivings alert us to the fact that every ethic presupposes a view of human nature.

Having been unable to solve problems posed by the naturalistic and moralistic fallacies, we should dissolve them, rejecting the way the problems are posed. This is pertinent because both evolutionists and their critics reject "is-ought" inferences as fallacious, but give us no positive account of how statements about what is and about what ought to be are conceptually related. My dissolution has a natural progression of key elements: a basic insight, a logical analysis of "is-ought" inferences, a model of discourse about science, an unsolved issue of limits on human nature imposed by human evolutionary past, and a methodology for practical Darwinism. The basic insight is that both fallacies depend on starting from too much of a separation of "is" from "ought" and then trying to bridge the gap with too tight an inference between "is" and "ought." Instead, "is" and "ought" interpenetrate in the first place, so no such (fallacious) bridge is needed. Empirical claims play a crucial role in moral arguments, sociopolitical or moral ideals have hidden empirical suppositions, as social constructivists emphasize (e.g., that we ought to maximize happiness for all affected by our actions presupposes that we all desire happiness). "Ought" implies "can" and limits to human nature provide limits to which moral policies we can adopt, where Crawford's link between domain-general mechanism and human malleability and between domain-specialized mechanisms and human limits are supposed to escape the charge of evolutionary determinism (which charges limits to what we can do that interfere with popular political agendas, again raising the issue of the biological determinism in the arena of psychological mechanisms). Sociopolitical and moral ideals have hidden empirical suppositions (e.g., the utopias and dystopias listed in Crawford's chapter 1 in this vol. suppose that human psychological mechanisms are typically domain general or domain specific, or a mixture of both). Moral and policy arguments rely on a mixture of empirical (factual) and moral (value) assumptions, for example, "In environmental condition X, people will become unhappy; we ought not perform specific acts or adopt moral rules that make people unhappy given their evolved and new psychological mechanisms, therefore we ought to prevent environmental condition X ceteris paribus." Premises paraded as purely empirical or purely scientific are often value laden and thus not subject to Hume's logical point. For instance, intelligence tests privilege efficient performance of certain tasks rather than others as indicators of intelligence, and these tasks are typically what it takes to function in a contingent set of sociocultural conditions.

The logical analysis is as follows. Hume was right that moral and policy conclusions cannot be inferred from purely empirical premises. Crawford is right that idealistic social reformers cannot validly infer that something is or can be the case just because we think it ought to be the case. But there is an obvious alternative to "is-therefore-ought" status quo rationalizations and "ought-therefore-is" wishful thinking. Moral and policy arguments rely on a mixture of empirical (factual) assumptions and moral (value) assumptions (e.g., If we release nuclear weapons, millions of humans will die; we ought not to do things that cause millions of humans to die; therefore, we ought not to release nuclear weapons). Moral theories do presuppose a theory of human nature. We value human life not just in this generation but in the next generation because natural selection operates by the criterion of reproductive success; it has "designed" human nature so that we care about future. Presuppositions are not inferences but substantive assumptions of people's reasoning; this point permits us to finesse Hume's "is-therefore-ought fallacy."

The human species, and human nature, is still evolving biologically, psychologically, and culturally. Evolutionary psychology can help determine which empirical assumptions to make and social reformers can help determine which sociopolitical and moral assumptions to make. As an ideal of discourse, I call for an end of the "two opposing camps" model of advocates and critics who charge each other with these fallacies, to be replaced by a "mutual engagement" model in which evolutionary psychologists and critics engage each other's guiding ideas seriously. Even to the extent that science and ethics constitute separate domains and ethical norms vary culturally and their content is underdetermined by our evolved psychological mechanisms, we can use arguments from one realm to help solve problems in the other realm (e.g., see Mealey, 2000, chap. 12 on sexual politics; see the issues of *Zygon: Journal of Religion and Science*, especially issues of March 1980, June 1980, June 1984, December 1987, December 1988, March 1991, March 1994, and December 1998). Although cultural transmission is a separate process from genetic transmission, different cultures impose different selective pressures on their members. In principle, we can change behavior by changing our cultures through cultural means that change existing selective pressures, thereby controlling which evolved psychological mechanisms are activated in various conditions to yield the desired thoughts, emotions, motivations, or development courses. We need more information on the proximate inputs that activate/deactivate evolved mechanisms in order for theory to guide practice in many domains, but we know enough without exact knowledge of these causal inputs to create policy and guide personal decisions in some domains (e.g., we know enough about the evolution of mate attraction and jealousy to construct a detailed "how-to" manual for getting mates and learning the risks that make long-term marriages fail).

The problem of evolutionary limits involves the substantive issue of how to found society on moral principles and yet be flexible enough to persist over evolutionary time. Scientists must be explicit about where value commitments enter into their arguments and social reformers who evaluate evolutionary psychology must be explicit about where presuppositions about evolved human nature enter into their arguments. Advocates of evolutionary psychology must engage ethical and policy inquiry, questioning their assumptions about which goals their policies and decisions fulfill, not just taking one for granted subject to sociopolitical critique. Critics of the field must engage scientific inquiry, questioning their assumptions about evolutionarily relevant social behavior, informed by current evolutionary research, not just assuming that, for example, no cognitive sex differences exist.

Evolutionary psychology can inform a naturalistic ethic that has limits. As to the limits, there can be goals that are not dictated by fitness strategies because the mission is to create a better world for ourselves as individuals, not to create the most fitness enhancing strategies. As to the ethic, even though we are not attempting to derive some moral ideal from facts about the natural world, we can derive moral norms from our understanding of the purposes of morality, and evolutionary psychology (a function-oriented science) can elucidate the proximate and ultimate functions of morality and the nature of the evolved moral agent. There is a tension inherent in morality. On the one hand, given its evolutionary past, morality is tied to life and death issues, to mating and family issues, and to group-cohesion issues because our domain-specialized morality acquisition device evolved by natural selection and that device would have been selected against if its average effect on its possessors was not to enhance their biological fitness. On the other hand, given the evolved self-consciousness of human persons, morality is tied to quality of life issues we decide for ourselves, to higher-order intentionality and critical reflection using domain-general reasoning, and to obligations and responsibilities we ascribe to ourselves and to others as unique individuals by virtue of our self-concepts and relationships to others that may bear little relevance to which actions raised our fitness in the past or present. A central aim of evolutionary moral psychology should be to study the connections and discontinuities between human nature considered in terms of traits selected for and against and the well-being of human individuals and groups using such combinations.

Consider a key insight for finessing the "naturalistic fallacy": Evolutionists should not try to derive moral norms from evolution; instead, we should derive them from our understanding of the purposes (functions) of morality, which includes both ordinary (nonevolutionary) facts as well as evolutionary facts. This "derivation" is not supposed to be a logical derivation, thereby escaping the charge that an "ought" statement is being invalidly deduced from an "is" statement. Instead, this derivation is an expression of who we are, which includes our human nature as the particular persons we are. Because evolutionary models that identify and explain human nature and individual differences are biopsychosocial models (they span biological, psychological, social, and cultural characteristics), the naturalistic ethical system is self-supporting, expressing our own understanding of ourselves as moral agents. Justification has to come to an end somewhere. There is no Archimedean point outside ourselves to which we can appeal to justify our most basic beliefs. In the end, we justify adhering to the moral norms we hold by explaining how it is that we, being who we are, are the sorts of creatures that use those norms to guide our lives (see Arnhart's naturalistic virtue ethic, 1992; M. Nitecki & D. Nitecki, 1993; Thompson, 1995).

When we do tackle the problem of how moral norms are to be justified using evolutionary moral psychology to inform our answer, evolutionists should not try to derive norms from evolution, but from our understanding of the purposes of morality, including what we can learn from science and nonscience about its purposes (treated as functions). Its proximate functions involve biological, psychological, and sociocultural variables. Its ultimate function is evolutionary: to pass on genes by means of strategies that are executed using these proximate variables. This evolutionary biopsychosocial model of right and wrong conduct uses evolution to add to and enhance pre-evolutionary understanding of morality's purposes. These purposes must be consistent with some of the "proximate goals" natural selection has instilled in human beings or else they would not fit human nature, a requirement of any naturalistic ethics in which "ought" implies "can."

Evolutionary moral psychology identifies numerous proximate goals of morality. For instance, one function may be to aid normal group members when conflicts arise between them and social deviants:

> In fact, however, moral sanctioning as a special kind of cooperative behavior would appear to provide reproductive advantages to group members in competition with the deviant. When greedy individuals or cheats or recidivist killers within the group are curbed, the rest of the group's members increase their fitness by denying to would-be upstarts special advantages such as multiple wives, a lion's share of subsistence, or a longer life span. If this analysis makes sense, then the individual capacity for cooperative egalitarian behavior benefits reproductive success. (Boehm, 1993, p. 249)

Not only do critics who give moral arguments against evolutionary psychology commit "the moralistic fallacy," they also ignore the ways evolutionary thinking relevant to morality can explain the egalitarianism they favor. In principle, specific functions of morality can be identified in relation to the four main tendencies and capacities de Waal identified: sympathy-related traits, norm-related traits, reciprocity, and getting along (the category moral injunctions and punishments promoting cooperation fall under). Individual cultural circumstances set and limit the options evolved moral agents have in manifesting their repertoire of evolved cognitive-social-emotional capacities in behavior according to norms.

Darwin's Normative Ethics

Which sort of normative ethics did Darwin espouse? He did not try to read morality" off of "nature." Instead, just as he declined to derive any conclusion about whether God exists from his theory of evolution by natural selection, he declined to derive any conclusion about the basis of right and wrong from that theory. This chapter suggests something similar, namely, distinguish evolutionary moral psychology (the science) from theories of right and wrong (philosophy). Open up a line of empirical inquiry in moral psychology that seeks the ways in which whatever view of human nature is presupposed in a given ethical philosophy relates to evolution. Our research question takes the form: For the ethical theory at hand, what does it presuppose about human nature and how could creatures who fit this ethical theory have evolved the sort of psyche called for in what that theory counts as "moral"? Consider some examples.

Consider Alchin's (1997) quick summary of utilitarianism: "First, ethics may be defined as certain behaviors or acts themselves. This view is commensurate with one major tradition in philosophy (consequentialism or utilitarianism) that views ethics in terms of concrete acts or consequences that either benefit or harm individuals (cause happiness or suffering)." There is textual evidence that Darwin was a utilitarian. He suggested, "As all men desire their own happiness, praise or blame is bestowed on actions and motives, according as they lead to this end; and as happiness is an essential part of the general good, the greatest-happiness principle indirectly serves as a nearly safe standard of right and wrong." (Darwin, 1871/1993a, p. 364). Evolutionary moral psychology can investigate the way moral norms and behavior tap into an evolved human nature that desires the happiness of oneself and of group members.

Was Darwin a deontologist? Consider Alchin's (1997) characterization of deontology:

> Second, ethics might be construed in terms of "conscience." It is not what we do that counts; it is why we do it—and the feelings, reasons, or motivations that we associate with our acts. This view parallels a second major tradition in philosophy (deontology) that emphasizes intent and moral choice rather than consequences alone.... Darwin was most interested in this aspect of morality, the impulse to help our fellow humans—or the moral sense, as he called it. In this view, ethical behavior results from ethical intentions and ethical societies are the collective results of individuals each acting ethically. (Alchin, 1997)

There is textual evidence that Darwin was committed to deontological (duty-based) ethics (e.g., in Darwin's attempt to reconstruct the evolutionary basis of how human faces express emotions. Darwin (1872/1993b) wrote about respect for others:

> With respect to real shame from moral delinquency, we can perceive why it is not guilt, but the thought that others think us guilty, which raises a blush. A man reflecting on a crime committed in solitude, and stung by his conscience, does not blush; yet he will blush under the vivid recollection of a detected fault, or of one committed in the presence of others, the degree of blushing being closely related to the feeling of regard for those who have detected, witnessed, or suspected fault. (p. 390)

Evolutionary moral psychology can investigate the way norms and behavior tap into an evolved human nature that internalizes rules commanding benevolence or aid to others (moral principles) given a prior fellow-feeling that drives people to take interest in one another (moral sentiments). For a guide to how a Kantian can incorporate evolution into deontological theorizing, see Rauscher (1997).

Both Darwin and Ayala saw morality as a product or by-product of thought about consequences in which decisions about what action to do are determined by the values placed on past actions present in memory and future actions chosen so as to maximize good. Due to the nature of the conditions of life, a group may find that a maxim holds no matter what the consequences in normal conditions (e.g., Do not kill your mate's lover—in most cases, there will be relatives who are enraged and the action will risk retaliation and thus lower your own fitness). So defining right and wrong in terms of consequences gives way to defining them intrinsically, with intrinsic worth reducible to worth constant as results vary. Hence, it may help the deontologist to understand, although the right may not be definable in terms of the good, why reason comes up with the "right" in the way it does. So, evolutionary psychology does not support utilitarianism over its competitors; in fact, it does not by itself favor any ethical theory, as the appearance of support is due to the bridge of principles that connect science and philosophical ethics, rather than the science itself.

My rational reconstruction of what Darwin is getting at is the following train of reasoning, using his utilitarianism as an example. Methodologically, the ultimate moral principle is to be rationally justified by considering the purpose of morality, which divides into proximate and ultimate functions. These functions are located in the fact that desires are rooted in the struggle for existence and morality is rooted in the fulfillment of individual desire. An individual's sense of happiness accompanies the fulfillment of his desire. Social relations reflect ways of fulfilling individual basic desire for our own happiness. The social purpose of morality is to facilitate these social relations. Indeed, the basis for morality lies in moral responsibility, which in turn lies in responsibilities incurred through social relations (e.g., as a mother, father, daughter, son, family member, friend, member of society). As long as the things that make us happy are the things that enhance their survival prospects, morality's ultimate function is to ensure that we survive as individuals who live in groups, not just individual happiness. The "moral" thing to do does not always bring the greatest happiness to the individual moral agent. Therefore, it is rational to hold that we should act so as to create the greatest overall balance of happiness over unhappiness for particular individuals in one's largest social group.

In sum, Darwin bypasses the problem of deriving "ought" from "is" by identifying the "foundation" of morality with the purpose of morality, and by locating the proximate functions of morality in the tasks for which the attributes of the evolved psyche were designed via their ultimate functions (which are the ways they contribute to the survival and reproduction of group-living individuals).

Following Darwin (and Mill), we justify particular moral norms in terms of some ultimate moral principle, which itself is justified by considering the proximate and ultimate purpose of morality, e.g. we should act so as to perpetuate the human species, so our norms should benefit our children and their descendents (a principle argued on evolutionary grounds by Hartung, 1995, 1996). Here is a sketch of how we do so. We act on our desires. Our actions involve evolved intellectual, emotional, and social predispositions. Being self-conscious organisms that live in groups, the history of gene-culture coevolution has led us by now to desire to act morally. Without an evolutionarily grounded principle "We ought to do what's best for future generations," there wouldn't be moral agents today; evolution is relevant to our core idea of morality, but we cannot derive moral truths from that core alone. We cannot assume that morality has been optimized by natural selection, and so can make arguments using these and other resources that morality should now serve other functions or serve the same functions in different ways. Evaluation of moral codes or human actions must take into account evolutionary knowledge, alongside all the other relevant considerations. Having decided that the totality of relevant considerations favor X over the alternatives, we act on X.

The twin key ingredients of a naturalistic approach to meta-ethics are functionality and responsibility (Ruse's, 1986, 1994, naturalistic approach includes functionality but ignores responsibility in reducing morality to moral sentiment.).

Moral obligations arise from an assent to the authority of moral feelings based on a judgment about the relationship of oneself to others or of oneself to one's group or of oneself to an out-group (Cordry, 1997). In individual psychological development, people realize that others are selves and that I am an "other" just as others are "selves." Moral feelings are social feelings. They are feelings about what it is good or bad to do in various social circumstances and relationships. Moral obligation arises when, given the felt values of certain social behaviors and the similarity of self and others, I assent to follow the guidelines implicitly in the felt values. Through this self-conscious choice good behaviors become right actions and bad behaviors become wrong actions. Moral obligations involve the choice to take up a responsibility in a way that is biological and psychological (social, intellectual, and emotional). So, there are two steps from moral feelings to moral obligations: The felt values are universalized and once universalized, as regulated by a moral ideal, they are assented to. Today equality is a moral ideal, but naturalists find other ideals according to cultural variations. So, no one moral ideal is inherent in human nature.

Moral obligations have an objective ground in the sense that any agent who recognizes the authority of moral ideals is bound by that act of recognition. Moral ideals are objective in a further sense, namely, they are universally aimed at and applicable, where universality presupposes a domain of individuals to which they are applicable. Over evolutionary history this domain has been from people's in-group to the whole of humanity, as evident in the world religions, and now even to some nonhuman animals. When any two moral agents interact, both expect there to be some ideals about behavior governing their interaction, and may differ in how far they expect themselves and others to live up to that ideal. Realizing that the particular norms they believe in might be less than ideal, then, due to the common goal of having a moral ideal, they have a basis for discussing ideals, arriving at shared ideals or even changing ideals.

In conclusion, the objective ground for morality is that moral obligations arise out of our evolved nature as social organisms with specialized morality acquisition devices and out of our ability to assert to them or dissent with them, both in terms of particular alleged obligations and ideals of responsibility. This inclusive and moderate evolutionary meta-ethic avoids both the "biological versus cultural determinism" fallacy and the "naturalistic" fallacy. It applies to reasoning using norms other than the greatest-happiness principle (i.e., any norm that fulfills the purposes of morality). Evolutionists should not try to derive moral norms from evolution alone, but from an understanding of the purposes of morality. For example, Fukuyama (2002, p. 115) takes this approach in deriving public policy for the biotechnology revolution: "is" and "ought" are bridged by the goals and ends human beings set for themselves, as "virtually every serious philosopher in the Western tradition since Plato and Aristotle" has maintained. The question of the purposes of morality—its proximate and ultimate functions at the individual, family, social, and cultural levels—is an empirical question that needs to be addressed. Regard moral behaviors, intentions, codes, principles, and even meta-ethical theories as "tapping into" evolved psychology. The aim to turn this metaphor ("tapping into") into a body of empirical and theoretical work using techniques and methods that meet scientific standards defines the new field of evolutionary moral psychology.

REFERENCES

Alchin, D. (1997, July). Teaching Darwin seriously: Addressing evolution and ethics. Paper presented to the *International Society for the History. Philosophy, and Social Studies of Biology.* Seattle, WA.

Alexander, R. D. (1986). *The biology of moral systems.* Hawthorne, NY: Aldine de Gruyter.

Arnhart, L. (1992). Feminism, primatology, and ethical naturalism (including roundtable commentaries and author's response). *Politics and the Life Sciences, 11,* 157–170.

Ayala, F. (1995). The difference of being human: Ethical behavior as an evolutionary by-product. In H. Rolston III (Ed.), *Biology, ethics, and the origins of life* (pp. 113–137). Boston: Jones and Bartlett.

Batten, M. (1992). *Sexual strategies: How females choose their mates.* New York: Tarcher/Putnam.

Boehm, C. (1993). Egalitarian behavior and reverse dominance hierarchy. *Current Anthropology, 34*(3), 227–254.

Bradie, M. (1994). *The secret chain: Evolution and ethics.* Albany, NY: SUNY Press.

Buss, D. (1999). *Evolutionary psychology: the new science of the mind.* Boston: Allyn & Bacon.

Chisholm, J. (1999). *Death, hope, and sex: Steps to and evolutionary ecology of mind and morality.* Cambridge, England: Cambridge University Press.

Ci, J. (1991). Conscience, sympathy and the foundation of morality. *American Philosophical Quarterly, 28*(1), 439–459.

Cleckley, H. (1976). *The mask of sanity.* St. Louis: Mosby.

Cordry, B. (1997). *The nature of the beast: On the significance of evolution for moral theory.* Unpublished paper, University of Kentucky.

Daly, M., & Wilson, M. (1988). *Homicide.* Hawthorne, NY: Aldine de Gruyter.

Darwin, C. (1993a). The descent of man, and selection in relation to sex. In D. M. Porter & P. W. Graham (Eds.), *The portable Darwin* (pp. 321–360). New York: Penguin. (Original work published 1871)

Darwin, C. (1993b). The expression of the emotions in man and animals. In D. M. Porter & P. W. Graham (Eds.), *The portable Darwin* (pp. 364–393). New York: Penguin. (Original work published 1872)

Duff, A. (1977). Psychopathy and moral understanding. *American Philosophical Quarterly, 14*(3), 189–200.

Fukuyama, F. (2002). *Our post-human future: Consequences of the biotechnology revolution.* New York: Picador.

Griffiths, P. (2002). From adaptive heuristic to phylogenetic perspective: some lessons from the evolutionary psychology of emotion. In H. Holcomb (Ed.), *Conceptual challenges in evolutionary psychology: Innovative research strategies* (pp. 309–325). New York: Kluwer Academic.

Hartung, J. (1995). Love thy neighbor: The evolution of in-group morality. *Skeptic, 3*(4), 86–99.

Hartung, J. (1996). Prospects for existence: Morality and genetic engineering. *Skeptic, 4*(2), 62–71.

Holcomb, H. (Ed.). (2002). *Conceptual challenges in evolutionary psychology: Innovative research strategies.* New York: Kluwer Academic.

Irons, W. (1996). The evolution of morality, deception, and religion. *Skeptic, 4*(2), 50–61.

Jones, O. D. (1999). Sex, culture, and the biology of rape: Toward explanation and prevention. *California Law Review,* 827–941.

Kitcher, P. (1985). *Vaulting ambition: Sociobiology and the quest for human nature.* Cambridge, MA: MIT Press.

Larabee, M. J. (Ed.). (1993). *An ethic of care: Feminist and interdisciplinary perspectives.* New York: Routledge.

Lumsden, C., & Wilson, E. O. (1981). *Genes, mind, and culture.* Cambridge, MA: Harvard University Press.

Lumsden, C., & Wilson, E. O. (1983). *Promethean fire: Reflections on the origin of mind.* Cambridge, MA: Harvard University Press.

Mealey, L. (1995). The sociobiology of psychopathy: An integrated model. *Behavioral and Brain Sciences, 18,* 523–599.

Mealey, L. (2000). *Sex differences: Developmental and evolutionary strategies.* New York: Academic Press.

Nitecki, M., & Nitecki, D. (1993). *Evolutionary ethics.* Albany, NY: SUNY Press.

Pinker, S. (1994). *The language instinct.* New York: Morrow.

Pinker, S. (1997). *How the mind works.* New York: Norton.

Rauscher, F. (1997). How a Kantian can accept evolutionary metaethics. *Biology & Philosophy, 12,* 303–326.

Ross, W. D. (1989). What makes right acts right? In J. Feinberg (Ed.), *Reason and Responsibility: Readings in some basic problems of philosophy* (7th ed., pp. 553–560). Belmont, CA: Wadsworth. (Original work published 1930)

Ruse, M. (1986). *Taking Darwin seriously.* Boston: Blackwell.

Ruse, M. (1994). Evolutionary ethics: A defense. In H. Rolston III (Ed.), *Biology, ethics, and the origins of life* (pp. 93–112). Boston: Jones & Bartlett.

Singer, P. (2000). *A Darwinian left.* New Haven, CT: Yale University Press.

Sober, E., & Wilson, D. S. (1998). *Unto others: The evolution and psychology of unselfish behavior.* Cambridge, MA: Harvard University Press.

Thompson, P. (Ed.). (1995). *Issues in evolutionary ethics.* Albany, NY: SUNY Press.

Tooby, J., & Cosmides, L. (1992). The psychological foundations of culture. In J. H. Barkow, L. Cosmides, & J. Tooby (Eds.), *The adapted mind* (pp. 19–136). New York: Oxford University Press.

de Waal, F. B. M. (1982). *Chimpanzee politics: Power and sex among apes.* London: Jonathan Cape.

de Waal, F. B. M. (1996). *Good natured: The origins of right and wrong in humans and other animals.* Cambridge, MA: Harvard University Press.

de Waal, F. B. M. (1999). The end of nature versus nurture. *Scientific American, 281,* 95–99.

Wright, R. (1994). *The moral animal: The new science of evolutionary psychology.* New York: Pantheon.

PART II

Cognitive and Affective Psychological Processes

❧

I n the first section, evolutionary psychology was conceptualized in terms of the problems and stresses human and primate ancestors encountered, the psychological mechanisms that natural selection shaped to deal with them, and the way those evolved mechanisms function in the current world. The purpose of this section is to provide an evolutionary perspective on some of the cognitive and affective processes involved in making public policy and private decisions.

Badcock (chap. 5) uses research on autism, in particular work that focuses on how mentalistic thinking (the ability to infer that other people experience mental states like our own) is deficient in autistics, to examine human mentalism (theory of mind) as an adaptation itself—one that may rely on particular skills such as gaze-monitoring and the interpretation of intention. Badcock situates the mind in place as the critical link between genes and human behavior.

Why humans possess a mind divided into the conscious and unconscious has been the focus of philosophers and some psychologists for hundreds of years. Evolutionary psychology would suggest that both conscious and unconscious information processing have been subject to natural selection. A process that renders information unconscious, such as self-deception, may have adaptive significance if it enhances the fitness of individuals engaging in it. Surbey (chap. 6) reviews the evidence supporting a functional view of self-deception and discusses the practical implications that further work may have for public and private policy.

No on would argue against the view that emotions play a central role in human affairs, whether those affairs are public or private. Chapter 7 by Ketelaar provides an overview of recent research on emotions with a focus on the role of emotions in moral judgments and in decision making, or strategic behavior in economic bargaining games. Game theory is used to look at how multiple paths can lead to the same outcome and how emotions influence which strategy is adopted. He illustrates how evolutionary psychology can provide a bridge between empirical literature on how emotions operate at the level of public and private behavior and the theoretical literature on emotions and rationality.

It has been argued that law is composed of two different types of rules: primary and secondary rules of obligation. Primary rules are pre-legal rules found in all human societies that are hypothesized to form the basis of social structure in nontechnological societies. Secondary rules are those legal rules that complement primary ones. They are relatively recent in origin and are not found in all cultures. Fiddick (chap. 8) reviews the psychological literature on primary rules of obligation from an evolutionary perspective and the resulting implications for secondary rules and legal theory.

Mentalism and Mechanism: The Twin Modes of Human Cognition

Christopher Badcock
London School of Economics

Much of the difficulty that people have had in the past with evolutionary approaches to human psychology and behavior arose from the tendency of 20th-century evolutionists to ignore the mind and concentrate wholly on genes and/or behavior. According to Williams (1985), one of the most important of 20th-century Darwinists:

> only confusion can arise from the use of an animal-mind concept in any explanatory role in biological studies of behaviour.... Mind may be self evident to most people, but I see only a remote possibility of its being made logically or empirically evident.... I feel intuitively that my daughter's horse has a mind. I am even more convinced that my daughter has. Neither conclusion is supported by reason or evidence. Only if it violates physical laws would mind be a factor that biologists would have to deal with.... There is no such evidence for mind as an entity that interferes with physical processes, and therefore there can be no physical or biological science of mind.... No kind of material reductionism can approach any mental phenomenon. (pp. 1, 21–22)

Williams concluded that the "solution to the non-objectivity of mind" is "to exclude mind from all biological discussion." Elsewhere, Williams castigated what he called "lubricious slides into discussions of pleasure and anxiety and other concepts proper to the mental domain" as nothing other than "flights of unreason" on the part of authors who "claim to have provided a physical explanation of mental phenomena" (Williams, 1996, p. 169).

Anti-mentalism was typical of most 20th-century Darwinists and students of animal behavior. Similar comments to those of Williams can be found in the work of the ethologists, Tinbergen (1907–1988) and Lorenz (1903–1989). These writers concentrated on observed behavior and mistrusted mental terms, which were often dismissed as "anthropomorphic" (i.e., committing the error of attributing human thoughts and feelings to animals). Such views have been perpetuated and popularized by their pupils, such as Dawkins (1995).

To this extent, evolutionary anti-mentalism resembled that of the behaviorist movement, which dominated mid-20th century academic psychology. Behaviorism derived its name from its dogmatic assertion that the mind was a "black box" that could not be opened and whose internal workings science could not speculate about. All that could be studied objectively was what went into it in the form of stimuli and what came out of it as observed behavior. Nothing else could be said. Behaviorism was the study of behavior, not of the mind—mindless psychology, if ever there was.

The result of such views was what might be called evolutionary, genetic, or ethological behaviorism: "explanations" of behavior that went directly from the evolutionary, genetic, or ethological factors proposed to the observed behavioral result. Such an approach neglected the mental level of explanation altogether, and at times left you wondering why organisms that have them have minds at all—so irrelevant did they seem to behavior. Where human beings were concerned, evolutionary, genetic, or ethological behaviorism prompted understandable protests that such an approach was "reductionistic" and diminished people to the status of mindless robots, controlled by their genes or evolutionary programming to act in ways essentially no different from the way in which an ant or an amoeba might behave.

THEORY OF MIND

Premack and Woodruff originated the term *theory of mind*, which describes the ability to infer that other people experience mental states like our own. They claim that such a capacity may properly be viewed as a theory because mental states are not directly observable, and can be used to make predictions about the behaviors of others (Premack & Woodruff, 1978).

Conversely, the inability to attribute such states to others that is seen in *autism* has been graphically described as "mindblindness." People with autism tend to be insensitive to other people's feelings, are poor at interpreting others' intentions, beliefs, and knowledge, and often fail to anticipate the reactions that other people will have to their behavior. They have difficulty dealing with misunderstandings, and are often unable to practice, detect, or understand deception. The result is that their behavior often seems bizarre, callous, or childish to others (Baron-Cohen & Howlin, 1993).

Experiments suggest that normal children acquire a theory of mind between age 3 and 5, but that autistic children are notably lacking in this respect. Studies show that autistic children do not differ from others in their ability to understand the functions of an internal organ like the heart. Nor are they deficient in their knowledge about the location of organs such as the liver or brain. However, whereas other children are able to understand that the brain has purely mental functions, autistic children tend to associate it only with behavioral functions, so that it appears that specifically mental, unobservable events are beyond their comprehension. As Baron-Cohen (1989) put it, "Lacking a theory of mind is in one sense akin to viewing the world as a behaviorist" (p. 580).

Today a great deal of evidence of many kinds has accumulated in support of the view that theory of mind deficits characterize autism (Baron-Cohen, Tager-Flusberg, & Cohen, 2000). Indeed, research has even begun to reveal the brain structures that might be involved. In a recent experiment using brain-imaging, 10 autistic and 10 normal subjects viewed animations of two moving triangles on a screen in three different conditions: moving randomly, moving in a goal-directed fashion (chasing, fighting), and moving interactively with implied intentions (coaxing, tricking). The last condition frequently elicited descriptions in terms of mental states that viewers attributed to the triangles. The autism group gave fewer and less accurate descriptions of these latter animations, but equally accurate descriptions of the other animations compared with the controls. While viewing animations that elicited mentalizing, in contrast to randomly moving shapes, the normal group showed increased activation in parts of the brain previously identified with theory of mind functions. The autism group showed less activation than the normal group in all these regions (Castelli, C. Frith, Happ, & U. Frith, 2002).

DIRECTION OF GAZE

From an evolutionary point of view, a plausible origin for theory of mind might be found in *direction of gaze*. Primates are typified by forward-rotated eyes, often to the extent that the visual axes of the eyes are practically parallel (as in the human case). The benefit of this is excellent stereoscopic vision, which would have served their ancestors well in the arboreal habitat in which primates almost certainly first evolved. However, the cost is a notable reduction in field of vision, particularly when compared with the almost panoramic view enjoyed by most mammals, whose visual fields normally overlap only a limited amount at the front, leaving only a small blind area behind the head. The result is that primates have become more social (and more vocal) so as to gain the advantage of many different pairs of eyes (Allman, 1999).

Primates have also compensated by becoming sensitive to the direction of gaze of others. This is particularly important because, not only can it tell a person where the others in the group are looking, it can also give useful clues about what they are seeing, their state of mind, and intentions. (Indeed, an analogy now exists in military technology: Radars function essentially like eyes, and like them can be directed. Rules of engagement in some recent conflicts have allowed pilots to interpret a lock-on to their aircraft by an enemy radar as hostile, and to react immediately rather than wait for the missile launch or gun attack that might be expected to follow.)

In other words, not only may direction of gaze have an important social dimension in primates like human beings, it also may have evolved as a critical and fundamental factor in primate sociality from the beginning. What might at first have seemed an aftereffect of social behavior, or a trivial detail in it, now begins to take on the appearance of a central, strategic social adaptation.

There is now good evidence that autistics are notably lacking in awareness of direction of gaze, and are poor at interpreting its psychological significance. If there is indeed a mental module specialized for gaze-monitoring as some have speculated, it appears to be defective in their case. However, there are also reasons for thinking that it could be overactive, or at least that some people may overinterpret its output. Here the best example is the delusion of being watched or spied on that is so typical of paranoia.

The most famous paranoiac in the psychiatric literature was Daniel Paul Schreber (1842–1911), a German high court judge who published an autobiographical account of his illness that was later the subject of a paper by Sigmund Freud (Freud, 1911; Schreber, 1903). Schreber included in it a section entitled "Direction of Gaze" long before the subject had been introduced into discussions of theory of mind (Schreber, 1903, chap. 18). According to Schreber, the sun was a living being who spoke to him in human language, or was the organ of a higher being lying behind it (Schreber, 1903, p. 47). Although impossible before his illness, during the course of it Schreber believed he could look at the sun without blinking—indeed, the sun's rays visibly paled before him when he did so (quoted by Freud, 1911, pp. 53–54; for evidence of similar findings in other cases, see Galaiena, 1976; Gerbaldo & Thaker, 1991).

Schreber also often railed at the sun, which at times he saw as God's eye, and paranoiacs are often morbidly sensitive to other people's direction of gaze to the extent of interpreting it as hostile and/or intrusive. Indeed, they sometimes feel they are being watched even when no one is there. Nowadays they often extend this naturally evolved sensitivity about direction of gaze to modern technological surrogates for it, and become similarly pathologically preoccupied with cameras, closed-circuit TV and ray- or radiation-producing mechanisms of many different kinds. Such delusions might fit nicely under another of Schreber's headings: "Egocentricity of the rays regarding my person" (Schreber, 1903, chap. 20). Indeed, Harry Stack Sullivan (1892–1949), a psychiatrist famed for treating schizophrenics, advised his colleagues to sit at the side of such a patient rather than facing them, never to look them in the eyes (which he found created suspicion), and to address them in the third person (personal communication from Andy Thompson, quoted with thanks by kind permission).

MENTALISM

Another deficit found in autism is an ability to judge and interpret others' intentions toward oneself: what Baron-Cohen called *intentionality detection*. Autistic people often fail to pick up cues directed at them in otherwise obvious and unmistakable ways, and are poor at interpreting body language or judging the implications of others' statements and behavior. Indeed, autistic children notably make pronoun-reversal errors, referring to themselves as "you" and their mothers as "I" or "me." However, language-impaired controls, such as sufferers from Down syndrome, do not make comparable errors, despite their poor speech competence (Baron-Cohen, 1989).

If autistics are deficient in this respect, then paranoiacs are notable in detecting intentions far too readily, and in overinterpreting their significance for themselves. Furthermore, this oversensitivity to intention can take two forms, depending on whether the intention is positive or negative. Positive overinterpretation of other's intentions underlies *erotomania*. In this case, the subject delusionally believes that others are attracted to, or are in love with, them. However, negative overvaluation of intention is much more common and seen in the delusions of persecution that are found in so many paranoiacs. Here, as usual, Schreber was no exception: "A conspiracy against me was brought to a head … its object was to contrive that … I should be handed over to a certain person in a particular manner … my soul was to be delivered up to him, but my body … was to be transformed into a female body, and as such surrendered to the person in question with a view to sexual abuse …" (Freud, 1911, p. 19). Indeed, Schreber's delusional system centered on a universal struggle of good against evil in which Schreber himself played a central Christ-like role as the persecuted savior of the human race.

Another autistic deficit is found in what Baron-Cohen called *shared attention mechanism*. Autistic people typically do not become involved in group conversations or activities because they usually fail to understand the element of collective psychological activity that is inevitably involved. Once again, paranoiacs are characteristically at the opposite extreme and are given to imagining concerted group activity often expressed as conspiracies against them, as the last quotation illustrates. To take another example, Schreber noticed that every time he needed to go himself, "some other person in my vicinity was sent (by having his nerves stimulated for that purpose) to the lavatory, in order to prevent me evacuating. This is a phenomenon which I have observed for years and upon such countless occasions—thousands of them—and with such regularity, as to exclude any possibility of its being attributable to chance" (Freud, 1911, p. 26).

Finally, autistic people are deficient in theory of mind: They fail to attribute mental states to others and to react to them accordingly. Here again, paranoia shows the opposite tendency. In Schreber's case, this was a readiness to attribute minds (what he actually called "bemiracled residues of former human souls") to birds and trees and generally to mentalize (he would have called it to "spiritualize") the whole world (Freud, 1911, p. 17). Hence the sun's rays were by turns the "nerves of God" or "God's spermatozoa." The entire universe became the stage for a spiritual drama centering on Schreber and his eventual redemption of the world through his transformation into a woman who would give birth to a new race of men (Schreber, 1903).

Adopting the modular view of the mind that has become popular with evolutionary psychology, Baron-Cohen summed up his approach by suggesting that autistics may have deficits in four particular modules (Baron-Cohen, 1995). Add to the previous argument that, if autistics are characterized by deficits in the mental modules listed here by Baron-Cohen, then paranoiacs might be regarded as characterized by their expression in excess:

- Eye direction detection (paranoid delusions of being watched)
- Intentionality detection (paranoid delusions of persecution/erotomania)
- Shared attention mechanism (paranoid delusions of conspiracy)
- Theory of mind mechanism (paranoid religious/mystical delusions)

Although currently fashionable with many evolutionary psychologists, modular thinking has it critics (even including one of its founders; Fodor, 2000). One limitation of the modular approach to the previous factors is that it suggests that each is a separate, discreet, all-or-nothing functioning subunit of the mind, with little overlap or possibility of variation. Nevertheless, this is not the only way to see it. Making the same point in different terms to Baron-Cohen's mental modules, it might be said that whereas autism was characteristically *hypo*-mentalistic (too little mentalistic thinking), paranoia was *hyper*-mentalistic (too much). This, in turn, would suggest that *mentalism*—the ability to attribute minds to others and to interpret and understand mental states—was not an all-or-nothing phenomenon of human psychology, but covered a continuum stretching from the extremes of hypo-mentalism in severe autism to hyper-mentalism in cases of paranoia like Schreber's.

Mentalism, then, is the language that human beings use to talk about their own behavior. It uses verbs like *think, feel, intend, believe, foresee, wish, know,* and *understand*; adjectives like *good, bad, moral, immoral, right, wrong, true, false, evil, criminal, human,* and *divine*; nouns like *mind, soul, spirit, motive, aim, desire, love, hate, justice,* and *desert.* Mentalism invokes conditions like consciousness, righteousness, redemption, knowledge, ignorance, obligation, and culpability, and enables its practitioners a unique ability to travel mentally through time in both directions: imaginatively into the future and retrospectively into the past (Suddendorf & Corballis, 1997).

Although not one of Baron-Cohen's defective modules, language is yet another mentalistic phenomenon that fits the hypo-/hyper-mentalistic pattern found in autism and paranoia. Words and the concepts they represent are clearly mentalistic—particularly when the concept is a purely abstract one, like mentalism itself. And even when a word represents an object that might rightly be seen as part of the physical world, the fact remains that the word representing it is an arbitrary mental construct imposed by linguistic tradition and mentalistic to that extent. Indeed, paranoiacs like Schreber are often given to coining neologisms, and his book is embellished with many elaborate pieces of inventive phraseology and word-elision whose precise meaning is wholly Schreberian.

Hearing voices is another classic symptom epitomized by Schreber, whose verbal mentalistic sensitivity was such that he could discern that souls in general and God in particular spoke the "basic language," a vigorous if somewhat antiquated German, characterized by its great wealth of euphemisms (Freud, 1911, p. 23). Autism, by contrast, is hypo-mentalistic in this respect also because a linguistic deficit is typical of the disorder, and verbal communication skills are usually severely impaired.

SEX, AUTISM, AND ENGINEERING

If there is indeed a continuum of mentalism, ranging from the hypo-mentalistic extreme represented by autism to the hyper-mentalistic one represented by paranoia, then recent research suggests that sex differences may also relate to it. Here the critical finding is that autism and the milder, less severe Asperger's syndrome, which seems to share many of the same mentalistic deficits, are more prevalent in males than females.

Although those who are diagnosed with autism and Asperger's syndrome have deficits in language development, social ability, and mentalism, they are notably better than average at spatial tasks. This finding is important, not only because it suggests that there may be pluses as well as minuses associated with hypo-mentalism, but because it ties in with what is already known about normal differences between the sexes where issues like language, social skills, and spatial ability are concerned.

Here, studies suggest average female superiority in language skills, social judgment, empathy and cooperation, perceptual speed (finding matching items), fine motor coordination, pretend play in childhood, and mathematical calculation. Male superiority is normally found in mathematical reasoning (especially geometry, logic: at the highest level male mathematicians outnumber females 13:1), embedded figure tasks, some (but not all) spatial skills, target-directed motor skills (irrespective of practice), navigation, and geography (boys always win the National Geography Bee, which tests children in grades four to eight on their knowledge of places around the world, and male college students can locate almost twice as many countries on an unlabeled map of the world as females) (Baron-Cohen, 2002; J. M. Dabbs & M. G. Dabbs, 2000; Kimura, 2000).

From birth, girls attend more to social stimuli, such as faces and voices than do boys, who have a preference to attend more to nonsocial, spatial stimuli, such as mobiles or traffic. Most girls develop language earlier than most boys, and normally girls develop social skills sooner than boys. However, babies with autism lack the innate preference for looking at faces rather than objects found normally in both sexes and shown, for example, in the readiness of older babies to return a smile. Here it may be significant that autistics process visual information about faces in the same part of the brain normally used for objects alone, rather than in the specialized face recognition and reaction region found in normal people (Pierce, Muller, Ambrose, Allen, & Courchesne, 2001).

Asperger's syndrome is sometimes called "the engineer's disorder" and authorities in the field comment that

> it is hard to find a clinical account of autism that does not involve the child being obsessed by some machine or another. Typical examples include extreme fascinations with electricity pylons, burglar alarms, vacuum cleaners, washing machines, video players, trains, planes and clocks.... Showing an apparently precocious mechanical understanding, whilst being relatively oblivious to their listener's level of interest, suggests that their folk physics might be outstripping their folk psychology in development. (Baron-Cohen, 2000, p. 75)

According to a recent survey of 919 families of children with autism or Asperger's syndrome which listed occupations of parents, fathers of children with autism or Asperger's were twice as often employed in engineering as were fathers in any of four control groups of children with Tourette's or Down syndrome. Another study of a mathematician, a physicist, and a computer scientist all diagnosed with Asperger's tested them against controls on folk physics and folk psychology (Reading Eyes Test). Although all three equaled control subjects' performance on sex judgments on the eye test, all scored more than one standard deviation below controls on folk psychology and more than one standard deviation above on folk physics (which is comparable to 85% of Asperger's subjects, who also score at or above this level). As the researchers commented, "These results strongly suggest that theory of mind (folk psychology) is independent of IQ, executive function and reasoning about the physical world ... and may therefore have its own unique evolutionary history." They concluded,

> There thus seems to be a small but statistically significant link between autism and engineering.... The current result might also help to explain why a condition like autism persists in the gene pool: the very same genes that lead an individual to have a child with autism can lead to superior functioning in the domain of folk physics. Engineering and related folk physics skills have transformed the way in which our species lives, without question for the better. Indeed, without such skills, Homo sapiens would still be pre-industrial. (Baron-Cohen, Wheelwright, Stone, & Rutherford, 1999, pp. 475–483)

Astonishing evidence of the link between autism and engineering can be found in Silicon Valley (Santa Clara County, CA). In 1993, there were 4,911 diagnosed cases of classic autism in Santa Clara County. In 1999, the figure passed 10,000 and, in 2001, there were 15,441 cases; seven new ones are added per day, and 85% are children. Given that employment in Silicon Valley is primarily in electronic engineering and computing, and that equal opportunity employment means that many children born there will have both parents in these industries, so-called *assortative mating* has been suggested as the most likely explanation. This is the idea that likes attract, and people tend to marry partners who have much in common with themselves. In other words, it looks as if mentalistic deficits in people with engineering skills are being compounded in their children by inheritance of these deficits from both parents. There is certainly strong evidence that autism and Asperger's syndrome are heritable disorders. For example, there is a 90% chance an identical twin of a sufferer will also be diagnosed autistic. The risk of second child being autistic if one is already rises from 1-in-500 to 1-in-20, while the risk for a third being autistic after two children already are diagnosed is 1-in-3 (Silberman, 2001).

MECHANISM

If gaze-monitoring and the attendant social sensitivities usually found most developed in females suggest an evolutionary origin for mentalism, then the throwing, tool using and fabricating skills associated with hunting suggest a parallel for what might be called *mechanism*. In other words, if mentalism is a noun equivalent for theory of mind or folk psychology, then mechanism as understood here would be an equivalent for "theory of bodies" or "folk physics" (Baron-Cohen, 1999).

The contrast between the false belief and false photo test is a telling illustration. Here the finding is that an autistic who sees an object moved without the knowledge of another person does not usually appreciate that other's ignorance of its new position—a clear mentalistic deficit (indeed, one that has been called the acid test of theory of mind; Wimmer & Perner, 1983). However, an autistic who sees an object moved after they have photographed it usually predicts where it will appear in the resulting photograph correctly. This can be seen as a compensating mechanistic competence to the extent that it involves a correct understanding of the optics of photography (Baron-Cohen, 2000).

An additional virtue of looking at things this way is that it avoids stigmatizing autistics as simply deficient and instead balances their mentalistic deficits against compensating cognitive skills, suggesting that their apparent mental retardation in one dimension might open up precocious development in another. Ten percent of autistics, but only 1% with other developmental deficits, show so-called *savant skills* (in other words, outstanding cognitive and memory ability found among more prevalent disability). Such talents are usually limited to music, art, math and calendar calculation, mechanical and spatial skills, and often feature astonishing memorization feats, and the combination of blindness, autism, and musical genius is unusually frequent (Treffert, 2001). For example, a pair of identical twin savants described by Sacks possessed calendar-calculating skills over an 80,000 year range; could not do simple arithmetic, but would calculate lengthy primes for fun; could instantly count the number of matches that fell out of a box; and could remember the weather and the important political events on every day of their adult lives while having little or no memory of more personal events (Sacks, 1995).

Hamilton (1936–2000, the originator of modern, "selfish gene" Darwinism) described himself as "almost idiot savant" (Hamilton, 2001, p. xxvii) and rated himself "fairly good at woodwork as at other handicrafts" to the extent of having carpentry as a "reserve life plan" in case his theory proved unpublishable (Hamilton, 1996, p. 26). Hamilton also conformed to the typical family of someone with autistic tendencies suggested earlier: His father was a well-known engineer (designer of the Callender-Hamilton bridge), and a geriatrician sister had engineering skills to the extent that she developed an improved pressure mattress for the treatment of bed sores (Bliss, 2001). Hamilton described himself as possessing "notably a trait approaching to autism about what most regard as the higher attributes of our species ... a person who ... believes he understands the human species in many ways better than anyone and yet who manifestly doesn't understand in any practical way how the human world works—neither how he himself fits in and nor, it seems, the conventions." He continued,

> It is known now how autists, for all that they cannot do in the way of human relationships, detect better out of confusing minimal sketches on paper the true, physical 3-D objects an artist worked from, than do ordinary un-handicapped socialites ... so may some kinds of autists, unaffected by all the propaganda they have failed to hear, see further into the true shapes that underlie social phenomena. (Hamilton, 2001, pp. xxvii–xxxi)

The significance of these comments is that Hamilton's insights were almost exclusively into the fundamental *mechanisms* of evolution: natural and sexual selection, population genetics, and Mendelian inheritance. Furthermore, it is these very mechanisms that arouse most resistance in the general public when they are invoked as explanations, causes, or foundations of human behavior. Such invocations typically attract denunciation as "reductionistic," "deterministic," "sexist," "racist," and so on. But what most of such reactions share in common is their mentalistic bias: They are offended by the claims of evolutionary and genetic explanation because they appear to impugn mentalistic agency—the belief that not only do people have minds, but that their minds and not their genes or evolved psychology determine their behavior.

Scientific insights also appear to question mentalistic states—especially consciousness, the quintessence of mentalism—because here, as elsewhere with mentalistic subjectivity, the facts now strongly suggest that consciousness is very much the last part of the mind to become aware of what people are doing (Libet, 1985). And it is now an irrefutable fact that the vast majority of what goes on in people's brains does so in total ignorance of their consciousness as such (LeDoux, 1996). This in turn casts doubt on the true nature of mental contents, such as beliefs, emotions, and intentions, and generally makes mentalistic subjectivity seem worryingly different from objective, scientific knowledge of the mechanisms of the brain and mind.

MENTAL CULTURE

According to the distinction suggested here, biological science describes the evolved genetic, neurophysiological, and psychological mechanisms underlying human thought, feeling, and behavior, whereas social and environmental factors determine the mentalistic subjectivity of human actors. What may be termed mental, or nonmaterial, culture can be seen to be both mentalistic in content and as arbitrary, or individually or socially determined, in nature. Indeed, the mentalistic aspects of culture are discussed next.

Etiquette, Social Conventions, and Language

Although language has been rightly described as an instinct from the mechanistic, evolved point of view (Pinker, 1994), here language is understood merely as a collection of arbitrary signs determined by cultural convention. And the same goes for etiquette: shaking hands or bowing, and eating with a fork rather than chop-sticks, are clearly also arbitrary, culturally determined conventions (what sociologists like Durkheim, 1982, called "social facts" and later structuralist social scientists applying the linguistic analogy would regard as *signifiers*; Lévi-Strauss, 1969).

Abstract and Conceptual Art, Literature, and Aesthetics

Recent research on the abstract art of Piet Mondrian (1872–1944), who claimed that elements of his compositions were critically placed for aesthetic effect, suggest that, on the contrary, subjects (experts included) are unable to pick real Mondrians from others randomly generated by computer (Taylor, 2002). Much so-called conceptual art appears to rely similarly on the mental attitude of the spectator more than it does on the intrinsic qualities of the object in question, and this is the reason I suggest that all such nonrepresentational, nonrealist art should be regarded as essentially mentalistic.

   The appreciation of literature relies fundamentally on mentalistic skills, and particularly on theory of mind to represent reality by purely representational and figurative means. Aesthetic values in general are highly subjective. Beauty notoriously lies in the eye—or perhaps the *mind*—of the beholder, and what one person regards as "artistic" or aesthetically pleasing may just as easily seem ugly or prosaic to another. (For example, painted depictions of nudes are usually regarded as art, whereas photographic depictions of the same models could just as easily be seen as examples of erotica—or even pornography.)

Religion, Superstition, and Ethics

As mentioned earlier, Schreber interpreted his delusions as religious and mystical insights into reality, and to the extent that all theological thinking presupposes the existence of supernatural beings and a psychic or spiritual dimension to the human mind, it could similarly be viewed as hyper-mentalistic. Indeed, such an approach readily suggests an intriguing new evolutionary insight into religion. According to this way of looking at it, theory of mind originally evolved to facilitate purely psychological interpersonal interactions in primeval societies. However, in the absence of the more mechanistic, scientific understanding of the physical world that was not to evolve until recently, existing mentalistic adaptations were applied to the universe as a whole, transferring concepts like agency, intention, culpability, and prescience to deities, demons, and supernatural entities of all kinds. As a result, reality as a whole—and not just social reality—became peopled with mental agents who could be influenced in ways analogous to those in which ordinary humans could be: through supplication (prayer), generosity (sacrifice), or contrition (penance). In this way, personal needs, failings, and frustrations beyond the remedy of mere mortals could be redressed, and a mentalistic pre-adaptation set the scene for the evolution of religion, magic, and superstition as independent cognitive systems.

Historically and socially, morality and religion are closely associated, and the routine tendency to name, blame, and shame leaves little doubt that an ability to make and manipulate moral concepts such as justice, virtue, and culpability are of enormous importance in attempts to influence the behavior of others by purely mental means (witness the frequency with which purely intellectual disagreements can lead to accusations of the "wickedness" or "immorality" of who or what is being criticized; McKie & Thorpe, 2002).

Law, Political Authority, and Ideology

There is also a close affinity between ethics and law, particularly when the latter has a religious or scriptural basis as it does for example in Judaism or Islam. But all legal codes are mentalistic to the extent that they can, and typically do, lead to legal argument and contestation (e.g., in the conduct of trials). Compare this situation with that of laws as they are understood in natural science to see how different legal principles are from scientific ones. It is not possible, for example, to advocate the repeal of the second law of thermodynamics in the same way as any other human law, or dispute Mendelian inheritance in the same way that someone might challenge a will.

As for political authority, Weber (1968) argued that political power can be legitimated in three fundamental ways: either by tradition, by legal-rational rules, or by a leader's charisma. To the extent that traditional authority relies on memory and a respect for precedent, that bureaucratic authority relies on reasoned justification, and that charismatic authority relies on subjective appreciation of it by those over whom it is exercised, all three ultimately rest on psychological factors that are mentalistic in the sense intended here. Indeed, legitimacy is itself a wholly mentalistic and ultimately subjective factor as can readily be seen where it becomes controversial. For example, in terrorism/freedom struggles, one person's illegitimate terrorist outrage is another's justified attack on repressive authority. Where ideology is concerned, no one will need to be convinced that the appeal of political ideologies lies in the arguments used to justify them, the emotions that they arouse, and in other mentalistic factors on which they rely, such as the personalities of political leaders or the beliefs of their followers.

MATERIAL CULTURE

In contrast to mental culture, what might be termed material culture (the kinds of things studied by cultural anthropologists) reflects mechanistic cognition, rather than mentalism.

Mathematics and Calendar Calculation

Even though systems of mathematical notation and the base number for counting systems may vary culturally, mathematical principles (e.g., Pythagoras' theorem, or numbers like pi) remain true irrespective of culture or circumstance. And mathematical logic and numerical expression remain fundamental to mechanistic thinking wherever it is systematically applied in the sciences, technology, or engineering.

Calendrical calculation is a particularly notable application in many cultures, and can often be embodied in objects characteristic of material culture such as written records, buildings, or religious artifacts. And already pointed out, calendrical calculation is also a prime expertise of savants, many of whom are autistic.

Representational and Utilitarian Art and Architecture

Savant syndrome can also be expressed in outstanding artistic talent, but here the output, be it drawing, painting, sculpture, or modeling, is characteristically realistic, rather than abstract or conceptual. Indeed, this is often how savant's artistic skills are first recognized: Even as children they show technical competence in representing things in their art that goes far beyond what is normal for their age. To the extent that realistic art relies on objectivity rather than subjectivity, it may be seen as mechanistic in the sense intended here rather than mentalistic. Indeed, according to a provocative theory recently put forward by David Hockney and others, many artists who achieved highly realistic results relied on mirrors and lenses to project images that could then be copied. To this extent, such techniques could be seen as anticipating photography, with which they shared many technical details resulting from a common reliance on the principles of optics and the physical qualities of the reflecting or refracting medium that was used, such as focal length or refractive index (Hockney, 2001; Steadman, 2001).

In utilitarian art such as ceramics, joinery, or glass blowing, the link with technology and mechanical skill is self-evident, and in architecture the mechanistic basis is more evident still. Buildings are, after all, ultimately a question of engineering in whatever materials may be used, and although glass, wood, stone, brick, and concrete remain the most common, today materials employed in more conventional engineering such as metal, plastics, or composites are also increasingly used in architecture along with the engineering principles they make possible, such as cantilevers, pivots, tensioning, and damping.

Science, Technology, and Engineering

Having already made the point about science, technology, and engineering being the epitome of mechanistic as opposed to mentalistic cognition, there is one thing to add. As applied to human behavior, the result of such thinking is not simply hypo-mentalistic, but actually anti-mentalistic, as suggested at the beginning. Its effect is to reduce human beings to the status of unthinking, biologically determined robots without the many mentalistic attributes listed that humans rightly think make them exceptional: etiquette, social conventions, and language; abstract and conceptual art, literature, and aesthetics; religion, superstition, and ethics; law, politics, and ideology.

CONCLUSIONS: THE NATURALISTIC AND MORALISTIC FALLACIES REVISITED

Crawford (chap. 1) contrasts *the naturalistic fallacy*—what exists is what ought to be, or facts should dictate values—with *the moralistic fallacy*—what ought to be is what exists, or values should dictate facts. However, the argument set out here suggests an intriguing new way of resolving the issue, and of doing justice to both sides of the argument about fact and value.

According to this way of looking at it, what is fallacious about both is their common overstepping of the boundaries between what I have termed mentalistic and mechanistic cognition. The moralistic fallacy mentalizes facts by confusing a purely psychological factor (moral evaluation, wholly justifiable in its proper, human context) with objective realities outside and beyond human subjectivity. It uses the mentalistic verb "ought" in a context to which it does not apply. The naturalistic fallacy, conversely, objectifies mental, human subjectivity by treating it as if it were continuous with the natural world. To use the jargon of cognitive science, both erroneously portray domain-specific systems of representation as domain-general. But, in reality, values can only be applied to human subjectivity, and facts belong to the separate world of objective reality.

The mistake made by these fallacies with regard to the two modes of cognition distinguished here could be compared to someone expecting a spreadsheet program to play music on their computer, or an e-mail program to produce graphics. No one today expects a single piece of software to be able to do everything that can be done on a computer, and the same applies according to my argument to the human brain. Yet, up until the present, the assumption that has been generally made is that the human mind is equipped to comprehend any kind of reality using essentially the same basic cognitive skills and processes. Although external influences on cognition in the form of political, social, and economic biases were exhaustively catalogued in the 19th and 20th centuries, the existence of internal, biological, brain-based biases was largely ignored. But as this chapter has argued, today the situation is quite different, and recent research into autism, theory of mind, and normal sex differences in cognition has transformed the situation entirely. Indeed, now it seems completely naive to think that there is only one mode of human cognition and just a single means by which people comprehend reality.

Consider a surgeon operating on a patient. The surgeon treats the patient as an unconscious, material object on which the surgery is performed, rather as a mechanic might approach a piece of machinery that needed fixing. (Here autistic tendencies would not matter. Indeed, to the extent that they helped the surgeon be detached and objective in operating on a patient, they might actually be beneficial.) But in a clinical interview, the same surgeon would treat the same patient as a conscious subject, for example, in negotiating a drug regime or postoperative care. In such contexts as this, the surgeon is obliged to respect the patient's real freedom to choose, for example, in agreeing or not agreeing to take medication or exercise in circumstances where, unlike the situation on the operating table, the surgeon does not have the power to enforce compliance on an unfeeling object. (And in such circumstances of persuasion, mentalistic skills would definitely pay off, whereas autistic tendencies would be a serious handicap.) Clearly, both the mechanistic approach to surgery and the mentalistic one to the clinical interview are appropriate and correct, and no one would criticize a surgeon for either. On the contrary, a surgeon who insisted that the patient should be conscious and choose for themselves each and every procedure during surgery would probably have as few patients as one who treated patients in interviews as if they were inert, unconscious bodies on an operating table!

Much the same applies to mentalistic and mechanistic cognition. Each has its appropriate context. Essentially, what has been proposed here is that values of an ethical, aesthetic, political, legal, or religious kind have a proper place in mentalistic cognition, which is rightly applied in the humanities; is voluntaristic in its mode of explanation; relates peculiarly to psychological subjectivity; is the basis of mental culture; and is particularistic in the sense that mental life is individually or socially determined and culturally relative. Material facts, on the other hand, relate to mechanistic cognition, which is properly applied in technology and the sciences; is deterministic in its mode of explanation; relates peculiarly to physical objectivity; is the basis of material culture; and is universalistic in the sense that scientific and technological truths are equally valid in all cultural contexts.

This chapter has attempted to show that the fact/value problem is part of this much larger picture and finds new and unexpected insights in the study of autism and paranoia, as well as in normal sex differences in cognition. Essentially, this chapter has argued that human cognition employs two distinct, noncommensurate and in many ways incompatible modes, each appropriate and reliable in its specific domain, but prone to fallacious or unreliable outputs if employed in the other. If it has been successful in clarifying the differences between mentalism and mechanism, for want of better terms, hopefully a contribution—however small—has been made toward avoiding any future confusion between them.

One virtue of this way of looking at things is that it would discourage religious, political, and moral credulity, bigotry, and fanaticism of all kinds by cutting mentalism down to size, so to speak. This is because all such reactions are quintessentially mentalistic, and according to this analysis, mentalism is just another human adaptation: the psychological equivalent of something like striding bipedalism, rather than some God-given, specially created or necessarily evolved spiritual superiority. (To use one of the few good analogies in another species, mentalism might be viewed as a means of communication and interaction as peculiar to the human species and as quaint in its symbolism as the waggle-dance is to bees.)

Seeing culture as essentially mentalistic would also reduce literary and artistic snobbery and elitism, and would help to counter emotive, phobic, and irrational reactions to scientific and technological innovation. Finally, understanding and accepting the mentalistic deficits of mechanistic thinking would also help to limit social exclusion, prejudice, and misunderstanding of autistics of all kinds. Indeed, such a change in attitude might confer a new and special esteem on those who, like William Hamilton, have arguably contributed the most of lasting worth to the human species as a whole through their work in engineering, technology, and science.

ACKNOWLEDGMENTS

The author wishes to thank Simon Baron-Cohen, Charles Crawford, Robert Kruszynski, Alex Monto, Bob Robbins, Thomas Suddendorf, and J. Anderson Thomson Jr. for their helpful comments and suggestions.

REFERENCES

Allman, J. (1999). *Evolving brains.* New York: Scientific American Library.

Baron-Cohen, S. (1989). Are autistic children "behaviorists"? An examination of their mental-physical and appearance-reality distinctions. *Journal of Autism and Developmental Disorders, 19*, 579–600.

Baron-Cohen, S. (1995). *Mindblindness: An essay on autism and theory of mind.* Cambridge, MA: MIT Press.

Baron-Cohen, S. (1999). The extreme male-brain theory of autism. In H. Tager-Flusberg (Ed.), *Neurodevelopmental disorders* (pp. 401–429). Cambridge, MA: MIT Press.

Baron-Cohen, S. (2000). Autism: Deficits in folk psychology exist alongside superiority in folk physics. In S. Baron-Cohen, H. Tager-Flusberg, & D. J. Cohen (Eds.), *Understanding other minds* (pp. 73–82). Oxford, England: Oxford University Press.

Baron-Cohen, S. (2002). The extreme male brain theory of autism. *Trends in Cognitive Science, 6*, 248–254.

Baron-Cohen, S., & Howlin, P. (1993). The theory of mind deficit in autism: some questions for teaching and diagnosis. In S. Baron-Cohen, H. Tager-Flusberg, & D. J. Cohen (Eds.), *Understanding other minds* (pp. 466–480). Oxford, England: Oxford University Press.

Baron-Cohen, S., Tager-Flusberg, H., & Cohen, D. J. (Eds.). (2000). *Understanding other minds.* Oxford, England: Oxford University Press.

Baron-Cohen, S., Wheelwright, S., Stone, V., & Rutherford, M. (1999). A mathematician, a physicist and a computer scientist with Asperger syndrome: Performance on folk psychology and folk physics tests. *Neurocase, 5*, 475–483.

Bliss, M. R. (2001, September). *In memory of Bill Hamilton: Hazards of modern medicine.* Paper presented at the Origin of HIV and Emerging Persistent Viruses, Accademia Nazionale dei Lincei, Rome.

Castelli, F., Frith, C., Happ, F., & Frith, U. (2002). Autism, Asperger syndrome and brain mechanisms for the attribution of mental states to animated shapes. *Brain, 125*, 1839–1849.

Dabbs, J. M., & Dabbs, M. G. (2000). *Heroes, rogues and lovers: Testosterone and behavior.* New York: McGraw-Hill.

Dawkins, R. (1995). Reply to Lucy Sullivan. *Philosophical transactions of the Royal Society B, 349*, 212–224.

Durkheim, É. (1982). *The rules of sociological method and selected texts on sociology and its method* (W. D. Halls, Trans.). London: Macmillan.

Fodor, J. (2000). *The mind doesn't work that way: The scope and limits of computational psychology.* Cambridge, Massachusetts: MIT Press.

Freud, S. (1911). Psycho-analytic notes on an autobiographical account of a case of paranoia. In J. Strachey, A. Freud, A. Strachey, & A. Tyson (Eds.), *The standard edition of the complete psychological works of Sigmund Freud* (Vol. 12, pp. 1–82). London: Hogarth.

Galaiena, M. L. (1976). Solar retinopathy. *American Journal of Opthalmology, 8*(3), 304–306.

Gerbaldo, H., & Thaker, G. (1991). Photophilic and photophobic behavior in patients with schizophrenia and depression. *Canadian Journal of Psychiatry, 36*(9), 677–679.

Hamilton, W. D. (1996). *Narrow roads of Gene Land* (Vol. 1). Oxford, England: Freeman/Spektrum.

Hamilton, W. D. (2001). *Narrow roads of Gene Land: Vol. 2. The evolution of sex.* Oxford, England: Freeman/Spektrum.

Hockney, D. (2001). *Secret knowledge: Rediscovering the lost techniques of the old masters.* London: Thames & Hudson.

Kimura, D. (2000). *Sex and cognition.* Cambridge, MA: MIT Press.

LeDoux, J. (1996). *The emotional brain: The mysterious underpinnings of emotional life.* New York: Simon & Schuster.

Lévi-Strauss, C. (1969). *The elementary structures of kinship.* Boston: Beacon.

Libet, B. (1985). Unconscious cerebral initiative and the role of conscious will in voluntary action. *The Behavioral and Brain Sciences, 8*, 529–566.

McKie, R., & Thorpe, V. (2002, September 22). Raging boffins. *The Observer.*

Pierce, K., Muller, R. A., Ambrose, J., Allen, G., & Courchesne, E. (2001). Face processing occurs outside the fusiform "face area" in autism: Evidence from function MRI. *Brain, 124*, 1337–1353.

Pinker, S. (1994). *The language instinct: The new science of language and mind.* London: Allen Lane.

Premack, D., & Woodruff, G. (1978). Does the chimpanzee have a theory of mind? *Behavioral and Brain Sciences, 1*(4), 515–526.

Sacks, O. (1995). *An anthropologist on Mars: Seven paradoxical tales.* London: Picador.

Schreber, D. P. (1903). *Denkwürdigkeiten eines nervenkranken* [Memoirs of my nervous illness]. (I. Macalpine & R. A. Hunter, Trans.). Leipzig: Oswald Wusse.

Silberman, S. (2001, December). The geek syndrome. *Wired, 9.*

Steadman, P. (2001). *Vermeer's camera: Uncovering the truth behind the masterpieces.* Oxford, England: Oxford University Press.

Suddendorf, T., & Corballis, M. C. (1997). Mental time travel and the evolution of the human mind. *Genetic, Social, and General Psychology Monographs, 123*(2), 133–167.

Taylor, R. (2002). Spotlight on visual language: Do Piet Mondrian's beliefs about aesthetic appeal of this art stand up to scrutiny? *Nature, 415*, 961.

Treffert, D. A. (2001). Savant syndrome: "Special faculties" extraordinaire. *Psychiatry Times*, 20–21.

Weber, M. (1968). *Economy and society: An outline of interpretive sociology* (E. Fischoff, Trans.). New York: Bedminster.

Williams, G. (1985). A defense of reductionism in evolutionary biology. In R. Dawkins & M. Ridley (Eds.), *Oxford surveys in evolutionary biology* (pp. 1–27). Oxford, England: Oxford University Press.

Williams, G. C. (1996). *Plan and purpose in nature.* London: Weidenfeld & Nicolson.

Wimmer, H., & Perner, J. (1983). Beliefs about beliefs: Representation and constraining function of wrong beliefs in young children's understanding of deception. *Cognition, 13*, 103–128.

6

Self-Deception: Helping and Hindering Personal and Public Decision Making

Michele K. Surbey
James Cook University

Our world is largely illusory. We view life through a multifaceted prism constructed by our sensory and perceptual systems, and the cognitive architectures of our minds. Our interpretations of the physical world are constrained by our evolved sensory and perceptual capacities, the so-called *umwelt*. Hence, our record of the physical world is improvised and lacking complete fidelity, but sufficient for successfully negotiating our environment. The illusory countenance of the physical world extends into our mental lives. Our conscious experience and assessment of our inner and social worlds are colored and biased by psychological mechanisms selected during the Pleistocene for a life of dependent sociality and problem solving. Although acutely tuned to concrete dangers, humans are a generally optimistic species (Weinstein, 1980). The prism casts an undoubtedly rosy hue, as certain threatening aspects of the landscape are glossed over or ignored. People put aside worry, walk hand in hand with whom might otherwise be their enemy, give without necessarily receiving, and look forward to a better future while facing a certain death. Other times, the prism focuses sharply on what is crucial. Human beings are a reasoning species whose logical calculations must be both expedient and based on available, although often incomplete, information. Thus, people employ many mental shortcuts, rules of thumb, or "heuristics" in making sense of the world (Fiske & Taylor, 1991; Kahneman, Slovic, & Tversky, 1982).

A subset of these rose-colored, cognitively expedient mental mechanisms underlying human sociality and penetrating reasoning skills is the focus of this chapter. Of particular interest are those mechanisms uniquely contributing to the illusory quality of our world by enabling people to conceal information from themselves. Trivers (2000) described self-deception as the "active misrepresentation of reality to the conscious mind" (p. 114). Rather than being a unitary process, however, "self-deception" appears to encompass a number of mechanisms producing distortions of reality, including repression, denial, and positive illusions or the self-enhancing biases. These mechanisms constitute a subconscious level of processing that sometimes plays an unrecognized role in the daily decision making and lives of individuals. They influence how individuals perceive themselves, the characteristics they attribute to others, and, hence, their social interactions with them. These mechanisms may enhance mental and physical health or produce pathology and maladaptive behaviors. They also affect people's perceptions and interactions within community, national, and global contexts. Self-deception manifested at a public or political level can have widespread, sometimes catastrophic, implications.

Although the focus here is on unconscious processes, the possession of self-awareness and consciousness is generally considered a cornerstone in human evolution. It is not known why brain expansion occurred (see Badcock, 2000; Cartwright, 2000, for alternative views), but consciousness appears to have arisen in conjunction with encephalization in the hominid line. The growth of the neocortex is associated with increased intelligence or problem-solving ability, much of which involves the conscious and intentional processing of information. There appear to be numerous benefits to rationalism, in thinking about one's own and another's thoughts, and in consciously working through problems and remembering solutions. However, consciousness is not without costs and there are limits to its benefits. For example, the greater our intelligence and insight, the more vivid our awareness of the unpleasant, frightening aspects of reality. Complete awareness of reality and one's own fate could be both paralyzing and self-defeating. Peterson (1997) aptly noted that "as our capacity for consciousness evolved, so did a corresponding capacity to turn it off" (p. 186). Presumably, both conscious and unconscious processes have been subject to selection and it is perhaps their unique coexistence in our species that defines us. Moreover, there is an interplay between the levels of consciousness, a fact made famous by Freud (1938), and it is this interplay that further distinguishes humans and entreats explanation. The following pages review a selection of the evidence for the dissociation and exchange of information between levels of consciousness, and discuss their potential functional value in the human species. In addition, I consider how knowledge of such processes might better inform people's own individual decisions, as well as those occurring at the level of organizations or groups.

CONCEPT AND MEASURE OF SELF-DECEPTION

Self-deception has been both narrowly and broadly construed. Gur and Sackeim (1979) defined self-deception as the process whereby two contradictory beliefs are held at different levels of consciousness, with the act deciding which belief is held in consciousness being a motivated act. They demonstrated this process employing a voice recognition task where participants were asked to identify several recorded voices as either their own or belonging to someone else, while their galvanic skin response (GSR) was recorded. GSR reactivity is greatest when individuals hear their own voice and reduced in response to another's voice. Motivational state was manipulated by preexposing participants to the experience of doing well (success) or poorly (failure) on an intelligence test. Gur and Sackeim expected that success would enhance self-regard and dispose participants to misidentify others' voices as their own, whereas failure would reduce self-regard, and increase the tendency to misidentify one's voice as belonging to another. Self-report results from the voice recognition task confirmed these predictions. However, although failure in the pretreatment task resulted in a decrease in conscious recognition of one's voice, GSR recordings indicated recognition at a physiological level. Gur and Sackeim suggested that the discrepancy between self-report responses and GSR readings was indicative of self-deception.

In addition, Sackeim and Gur (1978) developed a paper-and-pencil test, the Self-Deception Questionnaire (SDQ), whose scores were associated with the inconsistency in physiological arousal and self-report described earlier. The SDQ consists of 20 psychologically threatening, but generally true, items such as "Have you ever doubted your sexual adequacy?" Consistent denial of the relevance of the items indicates self-deception. Scores on the SDQ are highly intercorrelated with scores on related measures, such as the Byrne Repression-Sensitization Scale, Weinberger's Repressive Coping Scale, and Miller's Monitoring and Blunting Scale (Turvey & Salovey, 1993–1994). Self-deception is often used synonymously with the terms *repression* or *denial* and this seems justified as these processes appear to be conceptually and psychometrically similar, and play a comparable role in modulating negative thoughts (Nesse & Lloyd, 1992). Scores on the SDQ are also positively related to Paulhus' Self-Deception Subscale of the Balanced Inventory of Desired Responding (BIDR) (Turvey & Salovey, 1993–1994). Paulus' latest version of the BIDR (1991), the Paulus Deception Scales (PDS, 1998), consists of two uncorrelated subscales: Self-Deceptive Enhancement (SDE)—the unintentional tendency to give positively biased self-descriptions, and Impression Management (IM)—the conscious tendency to create a positive impression of oneself for others. The SDE has become another commonly used measure of self-deception presumably un-contaminated by other-deception.

Within social cognition, self-deception is defined more broadly as the unintentional, unconscious tendency to view oneself or one's situation in an unrealistically positive way (Robinson & Ryff, 1999) or, alternatively, as "the systematic motivated avoidance of threatening or unpleasant information about the self" (Baumeister & Cairns, 1992, p. 851). Human beings tend to view themselves, their worlds, close friends, and relatives in a biased, overly positive way, referred to as positive illusions (Taylor, 1989). Over a decade ago, Fiske and Taylor (1991) referred to such self-enhancing or self-serving biases as having a "self-deceptive quality," but now they are considered to be a type of self-deception, a perspective endorsed here. Mele (1997) rejected Gur and Sackeim's (1979) view of self-deception for depending on an impossible state of mind and proposed that cognitive biases, such as selective attention and the confirmation bias, account for many instances of self-deception without involving the paradoxical situation of holding two opposing beliefs at the same time. A large number of instruments, primarily paper-and-pencil tests, exist to measure biased forms of reasoning, including the self-enhancing biases (see Fiske & Taylor, 1991).

At first glance, positive illusions or the self-enhancing biases may seem quite unlike the processes of repression, or what Gur and Sackeim (1979) referred to as self-deception. Yet all are in the service of concealing information from consciousness and result in distortions of reality. Viewing life with a positive slant is self-deceptive in that negative events and possibilities are downplayed. There is a focus on one aspect of reality while another aspect, although perceived at another level, is effectively ignored in consciousness. Take, for example, people's responses to the classic question posed about a glass of water half-filled with water: Is the glass half-*full* or half-*empty*? (Fig. 6.1). Whereas the question is metaphorical, tapping one's view of life, concrete responses to it illustrate the perceptual biases underlying illusions. Focusing on the fullness of the glass, or on what is there, rather than what is missing would represent a positive bias. A negative bias would involve noting how much

FIG. 6.1. Is the glass half-*full* or half-*empty*?

more the glass could be filled, or how much water is missing from a full glass. The reality is that the glass is half-*filled*, or equally empty and full. Therefore, someone who says the glass is half-*full* still perceives that the glass is not filled to capacity, yet ignores that perception and focuses on the *fullness* of the glass. Because maintaining a positive illusion necessitates ignoring another aspect of reality or relegating it to the unconscious, holding a positive illusion is not dissimilar to Gur and Sackeim's (1979) definition of self-deception, although it may not produce the same kind of sympathetic arousal/self-report incongruity. It may be detectable, however, by methods, such as *f*MRI, that are capable of recording the activation of different neurological networks. Therefore, although certainly Mele (1997) was correct that some forms of self-deception result from cognitive biases, he was perhaps interpreting Gur and Sackeim's view of self-deception too literally and dispensing with it unnecessarily (Barnden, 1997). Different conceptualizations and measures of self-deception likely tap the existence of a number of processes by which information can become concealed from consciousness or exist on more than one level of consciousness (see Krebs, Ward, & Racine, 1997). In other words, there are likely various forms of self-deception, with assorted neurological bases, different proximate and ultimate etiologies, and diverse functions.

PRESENCE AND FUNCTIONAL VALUE
OF SELF-DECEPTIVE MECHANISMS

Within the personality, clinical, social psychology, and neuropsychology literatures there is considerable evidence for the existence of unconscious processes, such as self-deception. *Why* humans process and store information at the level of the unconscious can only be explicated in light of the forces shaping human beings during our evolutionary history. Self-deceptive mechanisms are most likely to be invoked when a situation is ambiguous, where concrete information is lacking, and when motivations are high or the matter important versus trivial (Taylor & Brown, 1988). Whereas motivations tend to be viewed as proximate causes, presumably some motivations are the result of millions of years of selection. Where self-deception has enhanced fitness in our evolutionary past, humans will be motivated to self-deceive. The following sections review the potential forms and adaptive functions of self-deceptive mechanisms and consider what evolutionary forces, including natural selection, sexual selection, parent–offspring conflict, kin selection, reciprocal altruism, and intragenomic conflict could have produced these processes (see summary in Table 6.1).

Reducing Cognitive Load and Increased Processing Efficiency

People engage in many activities of which they are not conscious. Their hearts beat on, their digestive and metabolic systems churn away, they blink when a puff of air hits their eyes, and they ovulate and produce sperm without ever having to think about it. Humans possess inadequate cognitive resources to be consciously aware of

TABLE 6.1

Potential Functions of Self-Deceptive Mechanisms and the Selection Pressures or Processes Operating on Them

Function	Selection Pressure(s) or Processes Involved
Reduction of cognitive load	Natural selection to limit the costs of consciousness (e.g., elimination of distractions, provision of parallel pathways providing economical support for other processes, such as memory and learning)
Assisting deception and competition	Natural selection to avoid detection of deception and to acquire and maintain competitive edge. Sexual selection, if employed in intra-sexual competition
Promoting family bonds	Natural or kin selection to establish harmonious family relationships, moderate parent–offspring conflict and sibling rivalry, acquire mates and maintain mating relationships. Sexual selection, if adaptive mechanisms sexually differentiated.
Facilitation of reciprocal altruism	Natural selection to reap benefits of mutual cooperation with non-kin.
Maintenance of mental and physical health	Natural selection for perseverance in adversity and motivation to take action toward fitness-enhancing goals (e.g., locating a new food source or a mate, engaging in parental care or cooperation)
Sequestering of threatening thoughts and memories	Natural selection to eliminate thoughts and memories that might impede taking action toward fitness-enhancing goals

all such activities. As it is, the human brain is a very expensive organ to run, using 20% of all energy expended, while comprising only 2% of total body weight. Although neural messages, such as those from a touch sensor on the finger, take only a few milliseconds to reach the brain, such signals take many times longer (500 milliseconds) to register in consciousness, suggesting significantly greater processing occurs in conscious thought (see Trivers, 2000). Consciousness is costly and not to be wasted on functions that could be more economically handled by other means. Thus, for example, the peripheral nervous system is functionally divided, resulting in habitual "vegetative" activities occurring automatically and unconsciously along a separate neural pathway than those involved in voluntary activities (the autonomic vs. somatic). For a significant saving, some information is processed and responses generated at the level of the spinal cord. When information is processed by the central nervous system, especially the cortex, it is processed selectively; making the most of sometimes sparse information and handling at times an overwhelming amount of information. Consciousness is a porthole into a sea of unconscious activities. And, like an angler regulates his quarry, consciousness controls or manipulates certain aspects of subconscious processing. But due to their sheer volume and the relative costliness of consciousness, only some processes can be viewed and governed in this way, resulting in information remaining at, or sometimes being shunted to subconscious levels, submerged from view.

The unconscious seems to be a place for keeping information that is well known and need not be continually revisited. *Automatic processing* refers to the initiation of an activity that is then carried out without conscious awareness (Logan, 1980). Many activities begin as a result of conscious or *controlled processing*, and through conscious rehearsal some responses begin to occur automatically. When individuals first start driving or learn a new route, they consciously think of every turn involved. However, over time, they begin to drive familiar routes as if on "automatic pilot," arriving at their destination without consciously remembering exactly how they got there. An unusual occurrence along the route, say a dog running out into the road, could jar drivers back into conscious awareness and action, but automatic processing generally serves to shunt habitual behaviors and thoughts to the subconscious as a means of reducing cognitive load.

At other times, the unconscious appears to support conscious processes by providing economical parallel pathways for processing information. *Implicit memory* involves the unconscious acquiring of information that is later recalled or recognized. *Implicit learning* results in the learning of a task or increased performance on a task without conscious awareness of the learning process (Lewandowsky, Dunn, & Kirsner, 1989). The ability to learn is an important adaptation and together implicit learning and memory reduce the cognitive energy required to learn. In so far as they involve the possession of implicit versus explicit knowledge, these processes are an example of a dissociation between thoughts held in consciousness and the unconscious.

People are constantly bombarded with information from the environment, but limited in their ability to deal with it all consciously. Many biases in thinking are the result of limitations on the human ability to process information and a reliance on cognitive shortcuts or "heuristics." These are "fast and frugal" algorithms generally pretty successful in providing answers under conditions of limited time, information, or computational capacity (Gigerenzer & Goldstein, 1996; Gigerenzer, Todd, & the ABC Research Group, 1999). They usually produce the right decision in a fitting context with little effort, and so are an efficient means of dealing with a complex world. As types of biased information processing, the self-enhancing biases, together with the other mechanisms of self-deception (e.g., denial and repression) appear to eliminate threatening thoughts from consciousness, thus providing more energy for maintenance activities, as well as those that might productively serve to reduce the threat. Therefore, the unconscious is also a destination for information that might be overwhelming or distracting, or otherwise interfere with people's daily conscious functioning.

Self-Deception in the Aid of Deception, Cheating, and Competition

Because an organism's fitness generally depends on encoding and interpreting reality with reasonable accuracy, Wallace (1973) suggested that individuals could increase their relative fitness by causing others to misinterpret the environment, reducing the others' fitness. Human beings may have a special knack for manipulating information to their advantage so as to cause others to misconstrue reality. In addition to self-awareness, people have conscious awareness of the thoughts, perspectives, and motives of others. This awareness, termed *theory of mind*, develops by the fourth year of life, before which children do not understand that others can be led to believe a false belief. Theory of mind permits individuals to deceive others by anticipating their thoughts and behaviors and altering their perceptions of reality. But it also enables them to suspect or detect deception in others through the assessment of possible motives underlying their actions.

Trivers (1976, 1985) proposed that where misleading or deceiving others has fitness benefits, the primary function of self-deception is the successful deception of others. He suggested that there exists a coevolutionary struggle between the deceiver and the deceived: As deception increases in frequency, it intensifies selection for detection, and as detection spreads, it intensifies selection for further deceit. Self-deception renders the deception being practiced unconscious, thus eliminating the subtle signs of guilty self-knowledge, which could alert the potentially deceived to the deceiver's self-interest (Trivers, 1985). Individuals are generally more effective at deceiving others if they are themselves unaware of the deceit. As the character George Costanza, in the television comedy "Seinfeld," offered in explanation for his unscrupulous behavior, "It isn't a lie, if you believe it." Where deceit has fitness benefits, selection for other-deception selects for lying to oneself, or self-deception.

The conditions in which deceit and, presumably, self-deceit are most likely to occur include those where resources are in demand or competition is intense, and where recipients are nonrelatives (Trivers, 1985; Wallace, 1973). Where resources are limited, deceiving other individuals about where these can be located could increase the deceiver's relative fitness (Wallace, 1973) and hiding this deception through self-deception would increase its effectiveness. When the competition is for access to territories, hierarchies, or mates, as commonly occurs among males, self-deception could improve one's competitive edge. Trivers (1985) described how adult male chimpanzees engaged in aggressive displays typically make themselves appear larger, through pilo-erection, as a means of intimidating their opponents. Males who bluff or deceive their opponents by appearing larger, more motivated, and more confident than they actually are can be fairly successful in such competitions. In human beings, where conscious awareness of one's insecurities may prove to be handicaps in competitive situations, self-deception could serve to heighten an individual's perceived self-confidence and self-esteem. Starek and Keating (1991) examined the relation between scores on the SDQ and success in athletic competitions and found that swimmers who qualified for a national championship engaged in more self-deception than swimmers not qualifying. They proposed that self-deception improved motivation and performance among competitive swimmers by reducing stress and bolstering confidence. Self-deception might additionally increase success in competitions by repressing an individual's knowledge of the self-interests and abilities of a competitor. If competitors were completely aware of each others' determination or ability to win a particular competition, they might never have the confidence to compete against one another. Wrangham (1999) suggested that self-deception, particularly positive illusions, could be useful in group aggression, such as warfare, by enhancing the performance of combatants through the suppression of negative thoughts or feelings. Like Trivers (1985), Wrangham suggested that self-deception could increase success at war by enabling one competitor to bluff the other, possibly even winning the battle before it has begun if the other side retreats. Taken to an extreme level, however, self-deception could increase confidence beyond the warring parties' actual capabilities and result in people being led into battles that they cannot possibly win (Wrangham, 1999).

A Balm for Family Bonds

Whereas self-deception may have originated as an aid to other-deception and competition, it may also play a functional role in cooperation. Self-deception may be benevolent, not to aid deceit, but in facilitating strategies that require short-term sacrifice for the maintenance of long-term relationships (Alexander, 1987; Nesse & Lloyd, 1992). Although genetic kin share a high proportion of genes, their fitness interests are only partially overlapping. Where family members engage in long-term cooperative interactions with mutual fitness benefits (e.g., the sharing of resources, shelter, and domestic tasks) and the rearing of offspring, psychological mechanisms reducing constant conflict between kin would have been subject to kin selection. In family environments, self-deception could serve as a balm, smoothing over conflicts and promoting attachments.

Humans have a longer stage of juvenile dependency (childhood) than other mammals (Tanner, 1962). During the period of dependency, the optimal adaptive strategy of any offspring is to maximize the amount of investment (e.g., food, nurturing, protection) received from parents. Parents, however, are selected to apportion their investment according to what division would provide the greatest fitness benefits to themselves. The resulting parent–offspring conflict may be manifested at physiological, behavioral, and psychological levels (Haig, 1993; Trivers, 1974). According to Slavin (1985), children repress their own self-interests when they conflict with parental interests, whereas those that are acceptable to the parent and maintain family cohesiveness emerge in a child's consciousness. This results in closer parent–child relationships and heightened parental investment (Slavin, 1985). A second defense mechanism, identification, aligns parental and offspring views thus reducing conflict, and may also be useful in accruing additional investment through favoritism. There is a tendency for parents to feel closer to children who are most like them and, for example, to grieve more intensely for them than for children who are dissimilar (Littlefield & Rushton, 1986). Although children's use of the defense mechanisms may reduce parent–offspring conflict, parents who are themselves self-deceived into providing extended care to offspring will have higher fitness than those not subject to self-deception (Lockard, 1978). Through the use of self-deceptive mechanisms, a child's self-interest may be submerged during the period of dependence, yet remain intact and accessible for guiding behavior in later stages of life when parental investment is no longer crucial to offspring fitness. Slavin (1985) suggested that "failures" of repression occurring during adolescence reflect the reemergence of self-interest as independence is gained and individuals are able to pursue their own fitness interests through the production of their own offspring.

Self-deceptive mechanisms may also serve to mitigate sibling rivalry, a product of parent-offspring conflict. Employing hypothetical scenarios based on the Prisoner's Dilemma game as a measure of cooperation, Surbey and McNally (1997) contrasted people's intentions to cooperate with siblings versus nonrelated friends. They found that people intended to cooperate more with siblings than with friends, where the benefits of cooperating resulted in maintaining amicable relationships with a sibling and pleasing and complying with parents' wishes. More importantly, cooperation was positively tied to scores on the SDQ: The higher the level of self-deception, the greater the intentions to cooperate. Thus, the ability to self-deceive was associated with heightened intentions to cooperate with siblings.

Self-deceptive mechanisms likely play a role in mate attraction, selection, and retention. Trivers (1972) suggested that males would have heightened mating success if they could deceive females into thinking they were high quality mates. Where self-deception aided this deception, it may have been subject to sexual selection. By boosting a man's confidence and self-esteem and suppressing his faults and fears, self-deception could lead to greater attractiveness to the opposite sex. Linton and Wiener (2001) found that among single men, high levels of self-deception were related to a greater number of potential conceptions. In addition to a role in mate attraction, self-deception may help maintain romantic relationships once they have been formed. Whereas romantic partners do not share genes, they do have overlapping fitness interests when it comes to producing offspring and providing parental care. By inhibiting impulses to cheat and instilling belief in the positive qualities of a partner, self-deception may promote relationship stability and cooperation in the rearing of offspring (Nesse, 1990). Within romantic partnerships there is a tendency to idealize the relationship and reframe the imperfections of a partner in the best possible light (Murray & Holmes, 1994, 1997; Newman, 1999). This process appears to involve the same three types of illusions employed to sustain individual positive self-images described by Taylor and Brown (1988, discussed in a later section). Murray and Holmes (1997) found that people tended to rate their partners higher than other individuals on a number of characteristics (overly positive partner images), felt they had more control over potential problems in the relationship (illusion of control), and expected a better outcome for their relationship compared with the average relationship (unrealistic optimism). Holding such positive relationship illusions is a positive predictor of the stability of a relationship, whereas the lack of such positive illusions or attributing negative qualities to a partner signifies a poor prognosis. For example,

Bradbury and Fincham (1990) conducted an extensive review of the association between marital satisfaction and spousal attributions. They found that where marriages were troubled and spouses dissatisfied there was a preponderance of attributions resulting in partners being perceived as harboring negative, selfish intentions. Moreover, longitudinal, experimental, and clinical evidence suggested that such attributions influence marital satisfaction and not vice versa. This suggests that successful, happy marriages are maintained by attributions resulting in partners continually being seen in a positive light. Apart from the positive illusions, other measures of self-deception have been found to be related to the nature of romantic relationships.

Loving and Agnew (2001) constructed a measure of socially desirable responding in relationships, the Inventory of Desirable Responding in Relationships (IDRR), that was similar to the BIDR. It contained two subscales: Relationship Self-Deception (REL–SD) and Relationship Impression-Management (REL–IM). Loving and Agnew (2001) found that REL–SD was positively related to measures of commitment, satisfaction, investment, and dyadic adjustment among romantic couples. Surbey and Sullivan (2003) examined adults' levels of self-deception (using the SDQ), repression, and intended cooperation in hypothetical situations with a spouse or a neighbor. They found that intentions to cooperate were greater with hypothetical spouses than neighbors, and in situations where the cooperative behavior would benefit children. High levels of self-deception and repression were related to heightened intentions to cooperate.

Facilitating Reciprocal Altruism and Social Alliances with Non-kin

Whereas "selfish" strategies promote fitness in many competitive situations between non-kin, in others mutual cooperation or reciprocal altruism results in a net increase in fitness for both parties involved. The iterated Prisoner's Dilemma (PD) game paradigm has been employed as a model for the evolution of reciprocal altruism under these conditions (Axelrod, 1984). Each trial of the game represents an opportunity for an individual to cooperate with another or defect, with the payoff, or "fitness reward," dependent on the choice made by the other player. On any single trial, defection by a player when the other cooperates will earn the first player the highest reward (T) but cooperating when a partner defects results in receiving the lowest possible return (S). The payoffs occurring in the other conditions are intermediate, with the payoff for mutual cooperation (R) being higher than that for mutual defection (P). Under these conditions, where $T > R > P > S$, high levels of defection are expected in one-trial games. However, over many trials or iterations, where mutual cooperation (R) results in the highest fitness for both parties, $R > (S + T)/2$, high levels of cooperation are predicted. Therefore, the iterated PD is a model of how cooperation might evolve in social relationships with non-kin, where both parties have an ongoing relationship and are likely to engage in future interactions (Axelrod, 1980). Frank, Gilovich, and Regan (1993) showed that when given time to assess the other player in one-shot

PDs, individuals are reasonably accurate at predicting whether they will cooperate or defect. Alexander (1987) suggested that self-deception may enable individuals to appear cooperative, by suppressing selfish motives, and consequently elicit cooperation in others.

In addition, Nesse and Lloyd (1992) suggested that self-deception may facilitate cooperation through the repression of the selfish thoughts and motives of others. This ability would be important in the Tit for Tat solution to the PD, where payoffs for both partners are optimized over many iterations (Axelrod, 1980). The first rule of the Tit for Tat strategy is to always cooperate on the first move. However, it is not clear how cooperation could be initiated when, in one-trial games, the best option is to defect. This could occur if players began the game "optimistically" by assuming their partners will cooperate. By removing from conscious awareness the very real possibility that the other player might defect, self-deception may promote optimism and cooperation on the first turn. Findings that high levels of self-deception, as measured by the SDQ, predict heightened intentions to cooperate in PD games support this possibility (Surbey & McNally, 1997; Surbey & Rankin, 2001; Surbey & Sullivan, 2003). In addition, engaging in positive illusions, especially the illusion of control, appears to enhance cooperation on one-shot PD games (Morris, Sim, & Girotto, 1998; see further discussion in a later section). The Tit for Tat strategy is retaliatory in that defections are punished by a subsequent defection. However, it is also a forgiving strategy and once a cooperative alliance is established, forgiveness of a partner's occasional defection may be facilitated by self-deception (Alexander, 1975). An individual may self-deceive about the transgression of a friend and attribute a personal slight to a misunderstanding instead of regarding it as a defection, even if the transgression was indeed a result of the latter. Therefore, the ability to self-deceive may play multiple roles in cooperating with non-kin (see summary in Table 6.2). Those lacking in self-deception, or who are constantly aware of their own and another's selfish motives, may find it difficult to trust others, and initiate or maintain cooperation. Surbey and Rankin (2001) found that individuals with highly Machiavellian or narcissist personalities had low levels of self-deception and displayed reduced intentions to cooperate in hypothetical situations based on the PD game payoff matrix. Machiavellianism is a trait associated with the selfish manipulation and exploitation of others—the antithesis of reciprocal altruism.

Maintenance of Mental and Physical Health

It has been argued that highly accurate perceptions of the world and the self are necessary for mental health. In the early years of social cognition, people were seen as systematically gathering and processing information so as to arrive at logical and accurate inferences and decisions (see Taylor & Brown, 1988). It became quickly evident that information processing does not proceed in this way at all and is instead highly selective, and rife with shortcuts and biases (e.g., Fiske & Taylor, 1991; Kahneman et al., 1982). If this is the case, then an accurate portrayal of real-

TABLE 6.2
Potential Self-Deceptive Mechanisms Influencing Choice to Cooperate or Defect in a Two-Person Prisoner's Dilemma Game

Choice	
Cooperate	**Defect**
Repression of own selfish motives	Driven by own selfish motives
Repression of another's selfish motives to defect	Awareness of another's selfish motives to defect
Optimistic bias that another will cooperate	Pessimistic bias that another will defect
Illusion of control—cooperating will cause another to cooperate	No illusion of control—cooperating will not affect another person's choice
Attributions of another's transgressions (defections) to a neutral cause	Attributions of another's transgressions (defections) to selfish intent

ity cannot be the key to mental health because nobody engages in this type of processing. People consistently focus on positive, while ignoring unpleasant, information about themselves and the world. Positive illusions appear to promote mental health by allowing individuals to remain productive in the face of adversity, to care for others, and to be reasonably happy with their lives, although they may be less than ideal (Taylor & Brown, 1988). Krebs and Denton (1997) argued that positive illusions, while fostering mental health, concurrently promote fitness-enhancing behaviors. According to Taylor and Brown (1988), there are three general types of positive illusions: overly positive self-images, unrealistic optimism about the future, and an exaggerated sense of ability to control fate.

Overly Positive Self-Images. Due to the nature of genetic inheritance and exposure to suboptimal environmental conditions, most individuals are not perfect phenotypically and many exhibit faults and undesirable traits. However, if asked to compare themselves to others on an attribute or skill, such as intelligence or driving ability, most people tend to view themselves as above average or better off than other people (Taylor, 1989; Taylor & Brown, 1988). Trivers (2000) suggested that there has been selection for mechanisms to suppress the expression of negative phenotypic traits. Self-deception, in the form of positively biased views of oneself, could be considered a type of psychological suppression of one's negative phenotypic traits. In a similar vein, Krebs and Denton (1997) suggested that selection has resulted in the processing of social information in ways that result in people deceiving themselves about their own worth as well as the worth of others. Generally, people view themselves and their friends and relatives as more worthy than they view individuals from out-groups (Krebs & Denton, 1997). There appear to be quite a number of self-serving attributional biases, self-handicapping strategies, excuse-making tactics, and downward comparisons facilitating these positive illusions (see Fiske & Taylor, 1991, for an overview). Individuals with high scores on other measures of self-deception, such as the SDQ and SDE, have higher levels of self-esteem and make greater use of self-enhancing techniques to maintain a positive self-image and increase productivity on tasks than low self-deceivers (Johnson, 1995; Paulhus & Reid, 1991).

Unrealistic Optimism About the Future.   Kafka's gloomy statement "There is hope, but not for us" is, luckily, not a typical human sentiment regarding our imagined futures. Instead, people tend to think overly optimistically about the future, a phenomenon termed *unrealistic optimism* (Weinstein, 1980). In particular, people expect more positive outcomes for themselves than for others. "There is hope, especially for me" is a widespread illusion. Hence, the human ability to imagine and anticipate the future appears to be complemented by a tendency to see the future as rosy. Imagine what life would be like if, instead, people spent their days envisioning all the bad luck and unhappiness about to come their way and contemplating their eventual deterioration and demise. In a detailed examination of unrealistic optimism, Robinson and Ryff (1999) found that high levels of self-deception, as measured by the SDE, uniquely predicted higher expectations of future happiness. The optimism about the future, engendered by positive illusions, produces perseverance and results in people not giving up their goals (Krebs & Denton, 1997). Imagining that the future will be rosier than the past produces hope and a striving to make it so, a self-fulfilling prophecy. When goals include those with fitness-enhancing capabilities, such as finding a better food source or acquiring a mate, this results in selection for positively biased expectations.

An Exaggerated Sense of Personal Control.   Albeit limited, the human ability to control the environment is supplemented by the illusion that we can control fate far beyond that which is possible. People tend to overestimate the control they have over events that they can influence (Miller & Ross, 1975) as well as over chance events (Crocker, 1982). The illusion of control could enhance fitness by encouraging individuals to attempt goals they might not otherwise. Additionally, the corresponding illusion that we can control other's behavior may facilitate cooperation. Morris and colleagues (1998) found that one strategy employed in the two-person iterated Prisoner's Dilemma game is based on the notion that how one plays will influence how the other person plays. Thus if I cooperate, this will *cause* the other person to cooperate, whereas if I defect this will result in the other person defecting. Therefore, the illusion of control could play a role in reciprocal altruism by motivating both parties to cooperate in anticipation of the other following suit.

If the tendency to hold positive illusions is associated with mental health, then abnormal levels of self-deception or the self-enhancing biases would be expected to be associated with mental illness. Beck (1967) noted that depressives engage in a number of cognitive distortions resulting in overly negative self and worldviews. For example, depressed individuals do not exhibit the illusion of control

(Abramson & Alloy, 1981; Alloy, Abramson, & Viscuci, 1981) and instead perseverate about their inability to control their lives. A negative relationship between scores on the SDQ and the Beck Depression Inventory indicates that depressives exhibit reduced levels of self-deception (Beck, 1967; Roth & Ingram, 1985; Sackeim, 1983). The lack of self-serving attributional biases or a breakdown of self-deception may be a defining characteristic of depression.

In addition to promoting mental health, positive illusions may also play a constructive role in physical health. A well-known observation in behavioral medicine is that denial is an effective coping strategy when faced with a life-threatening illness and may prolong life, whereas depression hastens mortality. Self-deception may also be advantageous in less serious conditions, as demonstrated by Cohen and Lazarus (1973) in a study examining coping styles in patients recovering from hernia, gall bladder, and thyroid surgery. They found that patients who were the most "vigilant," in terms of focusing on their symptoms and condition, took longer to recover and experienced more complications than those who used avoidant coping styles, which included downplaying and denying the extent of their illness. Since then there has been considerable documentation of the positive value of positive illusions on recovery from cancer and in the optimal functioning of the immune system (see Taylor & Brown, 1988, for a review of some of these findings). Whereas some self-deception may enhance recovery, Werhun and Cox (2000) found that people scoring highly on repression and self-deception and with low levels of anxiety sensitivity tend to avoid seeking medical care and do not deal effectively with their condition to the detriment of their physical health. In addition, although the inhibition of emotional responses achieved by self-deception may have psychological benefits, the concurrent and continuous activation of the sympathetic nervous system can have detrimental effects on a number of organs, the immune system, and blood pressure in the long term (Rutledge, Linden, & Davies, 2000).

Support for Taylor and Brown's (1988) argument that self-deception or positive illusions contribute to positive mental health has been accumulating, but it has also been challenged and there is some evidence to the contrary (Colvin & Block, 1994). Under some conditions, self-deception is associated with maladaptive behaviors and outcomes. Baumeister (1989) and Taylor and Brown (1988) suggested that there are optimal levels of positive illusions or self-deception (Baumeister, 1989). It makes sense that an optimal level of self-deception has been selected in order to strike a balance between seeing reality accurately, but preserving a positive view of self and the world. Therefore, mild positive illusions or moderate levels of self-deception would be beneficial, but unfettered positive illusions or the inability to self-deceive would be associated with pathology and poor behavioral outcomes.

Sequestering of Threatening Thoughts and Memories

When subjected to adverse circumstances people tend to have negative feelings and emotions: fear, pain, disillusionment, unhappiness. Whereas deception involves manipulating others' knowledge, feelings, and behavior, self-deception involves deceiving oneself in order to manipulate one's own feelings (Silver, Sabini, & Miceli, 1989). When negative emotions are experienced, individuals may be motivated to self-deceive and avoid or repress these emotions. Self-deception is negatively related to anxiety symptoms, self-reports of negative emotion, and anger (Flett, Blankstein, Pliner, & Bator, 1988; Sackeim & Gur, 1978). Similarly, unrealistic optimism and self-rated anxiety are negatively associated (Dewberry, Ing, James, Nixon, & Richardson, 1990). Presumably, the suppression of negative affect under stressful conditions would reduce cognitive load and enable continued pursuit of individuals' goals.

In addition to reducing negative affect, self-deceptive mechanisms might also serve to suppress recollection of a traumatic event and keep it from intruding into conscious thought. Nachson (2001) reconceptualized the recovered memory–false memory debate in terms of deception and self-deception on the part of victim, therapist, and perpetrator. Supporters of the recovered memory position suggest that repression or self-deception could result in a memory of abuse being submerged, until recovered years later under therapy. However, some purported recalled instances of abuse have turned out to be the result of fabrication or suggestion during therapy. Part of the debate revolves around whether true self-deception, normal memory loss, or actual deception has occurred and how these three alternative explanations can be judicially distinguished. A similar quandary arises in dealing with potential perpetrators, some who vehemently deny the abuse when it really has occurred, others who admit to abuse that has not taken place.

Nachson (2001) suggested that both victim and perpetrator of childhood sexual abuse may self-deceive to keep the traumatic event out of consciousness and preserve a positive view of self. In addition, victims may engage in self-deception in order to maintain a positive view of the perpetrator, who is often a relative or known to the victim. When sexual abuse is known to have occurred, victims who are later found to be unaware of it or who deny that it occurred are considered to have self-deceived. Because many abusers are parents or guardians, repression of the memory of the abuse could serve to preserve the facade of a normal loving parent–child relationship for the child (Nachson, 2001), and facilitate the continuation of parental investment. On the other hand, the perpetrator of child sexual abuse, while denying having committed a crime, might self-deceive through a reframing of the experience. Many child molesters report that the abused child wanted the sexual relationship. Wright and Schneider (1999) suggested that this may be a true belief, rather than an outright lie. Through processes, such as selective attention and the confirmation bias, an initial question about whether a child is sexually interested in them may eventually become a belief. For example, a molester may begin selectively attending to information consistent with the possibility that a child wishes a sexual relationship as well as interpret otherwise neutral information as further support. Abusers thus come to feel that they did not do anything that the child did not wish. According to Wright and Schneider (1999), the most effective therapy for perpetrators of child sexual abuse involves working through their decision-making processes and exposing the biased thinking that brought them to the act of molestation.

NEUROLOGICAL SUBSTRATES AND SUBROUTINES UNDERLYING SELF-DECEPTION

By its very nature, self-deception has been difficult to study directly, with sceptics oftentimes relegating the topic to the worlds of mystery and parapsychology. However, the mechanisms underlying self-deception may be identical or akin to those involved in other well-known cognitive and perceptual processes. Moreover, advanced EEG, PET, and fMRI methodologies promise to enable direct identification of the different neural structures or subroutines of the brain involved in conscious versus unconscious processing. A number of clinical conditions or syndromes, including blindsight, split-brain phenomena, alien hand, prosopagnosia, and anosognosia (unawareness of neurological deficits) provide evidence for the existence of separate neural circuitry for conscious and unconscious thoughts (see reviews in Badcock, 2000; Krebs, Denton, & Higgins, 1988; Lockard & Mateer, 1988). For example, *blindsight* is a phenomenon that occurs when the primary visual cortex is damaged, resulting in a complete lack of conscious perceptions of visual information (Weiskrantz, 1986). Individuals with blindsight can successfully negotiate their environments and avoid objects without conscious vision because other neural pathways from the retina to the cortex exist, processing information silently, unconsciously, and coordinating it with motor activity. *Prosopagnosia* is the inability to recognize familiar faces in the absence of major cognitive, sensory, or intellectual impairments (Nachson, 1999). Studies utilizing physiological methods (e.g., GSR and eye movements) to tap unconscious recognition reveal that, in contrast to their verbal reports, prospagnosic patients recognize faces at an unconscious level (see Nachson, 1999, for a review). One model of prosopagnosia suggests that there are two visual pathways (ventral and dorsal) from the subcortical limbic system to areas of the visual cortex associated with overt or covert face recognition. When the ventral pathway is impaired but the other intact, covert recognition occurs without overt recognition (Nachson, 1999). This results in a situation whereby an individual does not report knowledge, although that knowledge exists at an unconscious level, thus satisfying one of Gur and Sackeim's (1979) conditions for ascribing self-deception.

Phenomena such as blindsight and prosopagnosia suggest that there are at least two distinct areas of the brain, or a "dissociation" between different parts, responsible for processing the same information at both conscious and unconscious levels (Nachson, 1999). Where information is crucial to survival, such neural redundancies could act as back-up systems. Where consciousness only patrols one of multiple tracts of information flow, and this tract is severed, processing still occurs, just not consciously. The result is a particular type of self-deception that could be manifested in clinical, as well as nonclinical, situations. Why some neural tracts came to be invigilated by consciousness, while others remained subconscious, is not clear. One suggestion is that *intragenomic conflict* is responsible for the creation of neural tracts processing at different levels of consciousness (Badcock, 2000; Trivers, 1997, 2000; Trivers & Burt, 1999). Intragenomic conflict refers to competition between different portions of the genome, including mitochondrial DNA and DNA of maternal and paternal origin. Alleles of maternal and paternal origin appear to be imprinted and are only expressed in individuals if they are of a particular parental origin, a phenomenon referred to as *genomic imprinting* or parent-specific gene expression (Ohlsson, 1999). Under some conditions (e.g., where siblings have different fathers, or where groups are typified by male-dispersal) maternally and paternally imprinted genes have disparate fitness interests (Haig, 2000). Moreover, these imprinted genes appear to control the development and actions of different body tissues, including brain tissues. For example, the neocortex appears to derive largely from the expression of maternal genes, whereas the limbic system, especially the hypothalamus, appears to be under paternal control (Haig, 2000; Trivers, 2000). The limbic system controls emotions, drives, and appetites, and is involved in memory and learning. The neocortex is the center of the intellect and serves as an interface between environmental conditions and individual needs. The differential expression of paternal and maternal genes in different brain tissues could produce a divided mind or "multiple selves," or a "parliament of the mind" (Haig, 2000). Moreover, where brain or other tissues are the site of antagonism between maternally and paternally imprinted genes, a biased, self-serving information flow might be expected between them, a type of "selves deception" (Trivers, 2000). Thus intragenomic conflict could produce some forms of self-deception and their underlying neurological substrates (Badcock, 2000; Trivers, 2000). The neocortex, largely under the influence of maternally imprinted genes, likely moderates kin social interactions and altruism, in part by suppressing the demands of the limbic system whose appetites and interests are largely driven by paternally derived genes (Badcock, 2000; Haig, 2000; Trivers, 2000). It is even possible that encephalization is the result of an arms race between maternally and paternally imprinted genes, with the cortex expanding to suppress the interests of subcortical systems (Badcock, 2000). The suppression of subcortical systems by cortical processes may constitute yet another form of self-deception.

Although some conscious and unconscious processes may involve entirely different and separate neural substrates, creating a divided mind, some forms of self-deception might be related to the activation or inhibition of alternate subroutines in intimately entwined neural circuits. Lateral inhibition, which is the inhibition of certain circuits by others at the same level of processing (Martindale, 1991), may be one candidate. In one sense, self-deception involves people lying to themselves. George Costanza's statement "It isn't a lie, if you believe it" reflects the folk wisdom that if people tell themselves a lie often enough, eventually they come to believe it. Is there any evidence suggesting that this can happen or is this just a convenient excuse for con artists? Anderson and Green (2001) found that when people consciously attempt to keep a thought out of consciousness, the thought or memory becomes increasingly resistant to recall. They employed a series of retrieval tasks in which participants were first presented with unrelated word pairs, with the right-hand member of each pair serving as a retrieval cue for the other word (e.g., ordeal—roach). Then the cue word was presented alone and participants were asked to either recall and repeat (think about) the associated word or to not think about or repeat the word and attempt to keep its memory from entering consciousness. To determine if keeping a memory from awareness reduced its ability to be retrieved, participants were asked to recall the associated words when again presented with the cue words alone. Impairment of retrieval increased with the number of suppression trials. Anderson and Green (2001) suggested that this resulted from an executive process inhibiting memories intentionally kept out of consciousness. Based on previous studies of the location of related inhibitory processes, they deduced that the think/no-think task recruits a network of cells in at least three cortical regions that operate through the inhibition of other cortical processes. Anderson and Green (2001) further noted that frequent encounters with cues to unwanted thoughts may paradoxically reduce the ability to recall the thought. Therefore, although the suppression of unwanted thoughts or memories is initially intentional, the inhibition may be sustained for a long time without further conscious intention. These findings might shed light on how memories of childhood sexual abuse could be repressed, with exposure to the perpetrator or other cues serving to maintain the repression for many years. A related observation is that people often engage in purposeful self-deception or as Newman (1999) suggested "People talk themselves into things" (p. 62). They make a commitment to an action or decision, and then determined to strengthen that commitment, attempt to convince themselves that their decision was the appropriate one. By constantly ignoring the possibility that it was not the right decision, and focusing on the evidence suggesting that it was, they may come to believe that their decision was indeed appropriate. They lose sight (and memory) of evidence to the contrary and effectively engage in self-deception.

ACKNOWLEDGING SELF-DECEPTION: PERSONAL INSIGHT, APPLICATIONS, AND PUBLIC POLICY

Every day individuals make judgments and decisions that are not entirely rational or based on formal principles of logic. However, rules, laws, and public policies are based on the model of the "reasonable man." They appeal to our illusion that humans are rational beings in conscious control of their destiny and sometimes neglect those processes occurring unconsciously and perhaps not so easily controlled through rational thought. Hence, the blind adoption and following of such policies may actually inhibit the development of those qualities that we prize as distinctly human: forgiveness, optimism, altruism, charity. A greater understanding of how the interplay between the levels of consciousness affects social behavior and mental health could increase personal insight, inform public policy, and have numerous practical applications.

Personal Insight and Applications

When individuals make a decision, inference, or judgment, they often do so in a biased and self-serving way (Newman, 1999). This is not intentional, but the joint result of our tendency to self-deceive and the mental shortcuts people use when evidence is incomplete or ambiguous. As argued in earlier sections, the use of self-deceptive mechanisms at a personal level can be advantageous in the pursuit of goals (including fitness enhancing goals) and in the maintenance of mental health. The general populace would probably not find the notion that self-deception is beneficial out of line with their thinking. Folk wisdom suggests that sometimes it is better not to dwell on the negative aspects of life, that people should try to put these out of their minds. During a recent telephone conversation, my older sister inquired about the topic of this chapter. After hearing that the topic was "self-deception," she thought for a second and, although a layperson unfamiliar with the evolutionary or social psychological literatures, said, "Oh, self-deception—we (referring to the members of her household) think that sometimes it is a very good thing.... We often tell each other to engage in a little denial." With this response, I surmised that my rather "academic" summary of the chapter was quite unnecessary and moved on to the next topic of conversation.

The human tendency toward biased information processing and concealing information from ourselves can be advantageous and fitness-enhancing, but under some conditions it is not. In these situations, being aware of our illusions and tendencies to self-deceive can help guard against their negative consequences. For example, whereas some self-deception may be useful in forming and maintaining romantic relationships, extremely high levels of self-deception may result in individuals staying in unbalanced, even abusive, relationships. Individuals (usually women) sometimes remain in unhealthy relationships far beyond what many people would consider tolerable, until a crisis occurs that makes the unsound nature of the relationship suddenly apparent. When individuals in relationships are isolated, or keep information about the negative qualities of the relationship to themselves—which women tend to do more than men (Loving & Agnew, 2001)—then corroborating evidence that the relationship is unhealthy may not be present. In contrast, in public circumstances where threatening feedback or negative circumstances cannot easily be ignored and people are concerned about how they are viewed by others, they may be less likely to be blinded by self-deception (Baumeister & Cairns, 1992). Although people are biased toward idealizing their relationships, ignoring partners' poor behavior, and making excuses for them, when enough evidence to the contrary finally builds up, the romance is over. Newman (1999) noted the very public example of the different ways in which Woody Allen and Mia Farrow's relationship was described before and after their break-up. Before the break-up, Lax (1991, as cited in Newman, 1999) described their relationship as strong with no end in sight. However, following the break-up, and after it became evident that Allan was having an affair with one of Mia's adopted daughters, Farrow (1997, as cited in Newman, 1999) described Allan as a controlling and abusive man.

In perceiving others who are not close friends or are members of outgroups, self-deception can sometimes lead to a rush to judgment (Krebs & Denton, 1997). There is a large literature regarding how people make dispositional inferences about others and their self-serving nature. For example, people tend to overestimate the importance of dispositional factors and underestimate the importance of situational factors when it comes to making inferences about others (Ross, 1977). However, when it comes to themselves, situational explanations prevail. So if someone else is poor or unemployed, it is because they are lazy or stupid. However, if we ourselves are poor or unemployed, it is because we have not been given the appropriate opportunities to succeed. In addition, people tend to make inferences about others that correspond to the behavior they exhibit (Gilbert & Jones, 1986) and the behaviors directed toward them. If someone behaving honestly is observed being monitored by someone else, they are perceived as more dishonest than the average person (D. T. Miller, personal communication, March 15, 2003). For example, if someone is stopped and searched for shoplifted property, then they must have done something to have provoked the search. Mindfulness of our tendencies to make such rash judgments could help guard against unjust attributions.

Human beings are pretty good at avoiding concrete risks, but when risks are abstract or involve a calculus of odds and incomplete facts, self-deception may result in individuals taking unnecessary risks or engaging in acts harmful to themselves as well as others. The maintenance of unhealthy practices, such as smoking or eating excess fat, engages a number of mechanisms including denial and the biased processing of information about the health risks involved. Trivers and Newton (1982) conducted a detailed analysis of the cockpit tapes of Air Florida's Flight 90 that crashed shortly after take-off, killing 78 people. Their analysis suggests that the pilot engaged in self-deception when he ignored the instrument readings that were alarming the co-pilot. The co-pilot appeared to be more realistically attuned to the dangers than the pilot, but was unable to make a sufficiently strong case to the pilot to abort the take-off while it was still possible.

An awareness of the functions of the self-deceptive mechanisms, and the conditions under which they are invoked, may be useful in the treatment of mental illness. Two specific therapies often employed in treating depression, cognitive behavior therapy (CBT) and rational-emotive behavior therapy (REBT), are aimed at identifying and modifying cognitive distortions to more closely fit reality (Beck, 1967; DeRubeis & Beck, 1988; Dobson, 1988). However, to the extent that positive illusions enhance mental health, the focus on reality prescribed by the cognitive-based therapies could unwittingly counteract their general benefits (Kinney, 2000). Therefore, Kinney (2000) suggested that the cognitive change produced by CBT should be biased to contain a self-deceptive component, rather than altered to fit more closely with reality. Sackeim (1983) suggested that if lack of self-deception is a crucial characteristic of depression, then therapies attempting to increase people's insight would be misplaced. Depressives possess too much insight and they would probably benefit more from therapies that focus less on reality and more on producing positive distortions or altering processing strategies (Roth & Ingram, 1985). According to Anderson and Green's (2001) findings, not thinking about negative thoughts, even if they are consonant with reality, could be a better means of positively restructuring consciousness rather than constantly rehashing negative cognitions as a means of coping with them.

Collective Self-Deception and Public Policy

Although positive illusions or self-deception may have benefits or adaptive consequences for an individual, self-deception on the part of a collective or group of people may be catastrophic (Goleman, 1989). In groups, people's positive biases often become magnified, as others share individual illusions of control, superiority, and positive views of the future. Group-held illusions may lull individuals into a state of unfounded security and inaction. As group members people face little contradictory evidence to their views that they are fine, the world is fine, and everything will turn out in the end. For example, as a species, humans face a number of global perils, including the loss of the ozone layer, destruction of specialized ecosystems (e.g., tropical rain forests), and the possibility of a nuclear or biological war. Yet most people carry out their daily activities as if these perils do not exist. It seems that the broader the peril, or the more abstract or distant it is, the less an impact it has on people's thoughts or behaviors. Ambiguous, abstract perils do not stir us to action to avoid them. Goleman (1989) suggested that one way to shake people from this state of collective self-deception, is to use their illusions of control to convince them that they can make a difference if they take action. Another way is to increase the saliency of the danger of inaction so that the reality of the peril can no longer be denied.

Trivers (2000) suggested that self-deception at the level of organizations has played a role in a number of more circumscribed, modern disasters. According to Trivers (2000), the disastrous loss of *Challenger*, about two decades ago, occurred as a result of "organizational self-deception." Using rather convoluted logic and faulty statistical arguments, the safety unit of NASA apparently underrepresented the chances of the shuttle's O-rings being damaged (the cause of the disaster) and overrepresented the safety of the flight. This created an illusion of safety for the other units of NASA, which was apparently accepted without further review. If a review had been conducted, the potential for disaster would have been readily apparent (see Trivers, 2000). An analysis of the 2003 NASA shuttle disaster, the break-up of *Columbia* on reentry, is not yet complete, but one possibility is that officials downplayed the significance of damage to insulation tiles on one wing during take-off. Denial of this potential danger would have eclipsed any efforts to rescue the crew with another ship.

Whereas spiralling collective and organizational self-deception may have deleterious outcomes, the dampening of normal levels of self-deception in individuals as a result of institutional and public policies could also have negative collective consequences. In Prisoner's Dilemma games, if one player suspects the other may defect or cheat, then the best option is to defect, or not cooperate to avoid being exploited (Axelrod, 1984). Cosmides and Tooby (1992) purported that "cheater detection" mechanisms have evolved and when triggered help individuals avoid cooperating with those who would take the benefits of their cooperation without reciprocating. If it is assumed that social cooperation depends on the repression of the possibility of defection by others, then government or media campaigns constantly emphasizing cheating by others (e.g., tax evasion, theft, speeding, shoplifting, scams) could have the opposite effect intended. For example, young men forced to contemplate the consequences of dangerous driving increase, rather than decrease, their risky, unlawful behavior (Taubman-Ben Ari, 2000). Consciously thinking about or being made aware of the possibility that another individual may be a cheater may reduce a person's ability to self-deceive or repress thoughts about another's selfish motives. Making people continually aware of their own and others' selfish motives by emphasizing these in an excessive system of rules intended to catch cheaters, may actually reduce levels of self-deception and thus cooperation. Cooperating in a sea of defectors is a maladaptive, costly strategy.

Policymakers are not oblivious to the effects of priming cheater detection mechanisms (although that is not how they would refer to such circumstances), but this awareness is not always helpful. Recently, a local shopkeeper was ordered by the municipal council to remove the security bars from his shop windows. The council's rationale was that they created the impression that the area was crime-ridden and would deter shoppers from the area (or prime their cheater detection mechanisms). The shopkeeper's attempts to fight this order, his failure to do so, and his eventual compliance with the order were publicized by the local television station. Ironically, within a few days of removing the bars, his shop was broken into and burgled, while the store's security camera captured everything on tape. Although the council members had displayed some insight regarding the impression created by the bars, the risk of displaying vulnerability when there are cheaters in our midst escaped attention. As a result, the hapless shopkeeper became the unwitting and unwilling "sucker" for an opportunistic and news-savvy cheat. Reciprocal altruism is partially maintained by the possibility of retaliation should someone defect (Axelrod, 1984; Machalek & Cohen, 1991). Therefore, policies that imply the means to catch and punish cheaters are in place, but that do not create the impression that cheaters are everywhere, might produce maximum levels of law-abidingness and cooperation.

CONCLUSIONS

The prism through which we view life produces many areas of sharp clarity, but others remain opaque or blurred, sometimes hidden from view. According to Schneider (2001), reality is fuzzy. There is fuzziness in our knowledge of and interpretations of reality (Schneider, 2001). The mechanisms of self-deception described in this chapter are a component of the fuzzy logic applied to the world in order to survive it and they add a rosy gloss to people's perceptions of reality. In so far as it results from the limitations of consciousness and is a means, under some conditions, to protect us from consciousness, the human ability to self-deceive is not coincidental. The self-deceptive mechanisms have potentially arisen as the outcome of a number of selective forces: natural selection for cognitive efficiency, maintenance of a positive outlook and hope in adversity, concealment of threatening thoughts that could limit adaptive responding, the ability to form mutually beneficial social alliances; kin selection for smooth family relationships; and sexual selection for success in mate selection and retention. Some forms of self-deception appear to be related to the existence of different brain structures or tracts devoted to either the conscious or unconscious processing of information. Others possibly arise from executive functions such as the lateral inhibition of cortical processes. The view advanced here is that the self-deceptive mechanisms reflect evolved functional dissociations between the levels of consciousness. At moderate levels, self-deception promotes mental health and effective coping with environmental demands. At extremely low or high levels, individual or collective self-deception may have detrimental consequences. In order to make the most of the human condition, albeit fuzzily construed, individuals and policymakers would do well to be aware of the existence, powers, and pitfalls of our ability to self-deceive.

REFERENCES

Abramson, L. Y., & Alloy, L. B. (1981). Depression, non-depression, and cognitive illusions: A reply to Schwartz. *Journal of Experimental Psychology, 110,* 436–447.

Alexander, R. D. (1975). The search for a general theory of behavior. *Behaviour Science, 20,* 77–100.

Alexander, R. D. (1987). *The biology of moral systems.* New York: Aldine.

Alloy, L. B., Abramson, L. Y., & Viscusi, D. (1981). Induced mood and the illusion of control. *Journal of Personality and Social Psychology, 41,* 1129–1140.

Anderson, M. C., & Green, C. (2001). Suppressing unwanted memories by executive control. *Nature, 410,* 366–369.

Axelrod, R. (1980). Effective choice in the prisoner's dilemma. *Journal of Conflict Resolution, 24,* 379–403.

Axelrod, R. (1984). *The evolution of cooperation.* New York: Basic Books.

Badcock, C. (2000). *Evolutionary psychology: A critical introduction.* Oxford, England: Polity.

Barnden, J. A. (1997). Deceived by metaphor. *Behavioral and Brain Sciences, 20,* 105–106.

Baumeister, R. F. (1989). The optimal margin of illusion. *Journal of Social and Clinical Psychology, 8,* 176–189.

Baumeister, R. F., & Cairns, K. J. (1992). Repression and self-presentation: When audiences interfere with self-deceptive strategies. *Journal of Personality and Social Psychology, 62,* 851–862.

Beck, A. T. (1967). *Depression: Clinical, experimental, and theoretical perspectives.* New York: Harper & Row.

Bradbury, T. N., & Fincham, F. D. (1990). Attributions in marriage: Review and critique. *Psychological Bulletin, 107,* 3–33.

Cartwright, J. (2000). *Evolution and human behaviour.* London: Macmillan.

Cohen, F., & Lazarus, R. S. (1973). Active coping processes, coping dispositions, and recovery from surgery. *Psychosomatic Medicine, 35*, 375–389.

Colvin, C. R., & Block, J. (1994). Do positive illusions foster mental health? An examination of the Taylor and Brown formulation. *Psychological Bulletin, 116*, 3–20.

Cosmides, L., & Tooby, J. (1992). Cognitive adaptations for social exchange. In J. Barkow, L. Cosmides, & J. Tooby (Eds.), *The adapted mind* (pp. 163–228). New York: Oxford University Press.

Crocker, J. (1982). Biased questions in judgment of covariation studies. *Personality and Social Psychology Bulletin, 8*, 214–220.

DeRubeis, R. J., & Beck, A. T. (1988). Cognitive therapy. In K. S. Dobson (Ed.), *Handbook of cognitive behavioural therapies* (pp. 307–356). New York: Guilford.

Dewberry, C., Ing, M., James, S., Nixon, M., & Richardson, P. (1990). Anxiety and unrealistic optimism. *Journal of Social Psychology, 130*, 151–156.

Dobson, K. S. (Ed.). (1988). *Handbook of cognitive behavioral therapies.* New York: Guilford.

Fiske, S. T., & Taylor, S. E. (1991). *Social cognition* (2nd ed.). New York: McGraw-Hill.

Flett, G. L., Blankstein, K. R., Pliner, P., & Bator, C. (1988). Impression management and self-deception components of appraised emotional experience. *British Journal of Social Psychology, 27*, 67–77.

Frank, R. H., Gilovich, T., & Regan, D. T. (1993). The evolution of one-shot cooperation: An experiment. *Ethology and Sociobiology, 14*, 247–256.

Freud, S. (1938). *The basic writings of Sigmund Freud.* New York: Random House.

Gigerenzer, G., & Goldstein, D. G. (1996). Reasoning the fast and frugal way: Models of bounded rationality. *Psychological Review, 103*, 650–669.

Gigerenzer, G., Todd, P. M., & the ABC Research Group. (1999). *Simple heuristics that make us smart.* Oxford, England: Oxford University Press.

Gilbert, D. T., & Jones, E. E. (1986). Perceiver-induced constraint: Interpretations of self-generated reality. *Journal of Personality and Social Psychology, 50*, 269–280.

Goleman, D. J. (1989). What is negative about positive illusions?: When benefits for the individual harm the collective. *Journal of Social and Clinical Psychology, 8*, 190–197.

Gur, R. C., & Sackeim, H. A. (1979). Self-deception: A concept in search of a phenomenon. *Journal of Personality and Social Psychology, 37*, 147–169.

Haig, D. (1993). Genetic conflicts in human pregnancy. *Quarterly Review of Biology, 68*, 495–532.

Haig, D. (2000). Genomic imprinting, sex-biased dispersal and social behavior. In D. LeCroy & P. Moller (Eds.), *Annals of the New York Academy of Sciences: Vol. 907. Evolutionary perspectives on human reproductive behavior* (pp. 149–163). New York: New York Academy of Sciences.

Johnson, E. A. (1995). Self-deceptive coping: Adaptive only in ambiguous contexts. *Journal of Personality, 63* ,759–791.

Kahneman, D., Slovic, P., & Tversky, A. (Eds.). (1982). *Judgment under uncertainty: Heuristics and biases.* Cambridge, England: Cambridge University Press.

Kinney, A. (2000). Positive illusions of well-being and irrationality: Implications for rational-emotive behavior therapy. *Journal of Contemporary Psychotherapy, 30*, 401–415.

Krebs, D., & Denton, K. (1997). Social illusions and self-deception: The evolution of biases in person perception. In J. A. Simpson & D. T. Kendrick (Eds.), *Evolutionary social psychology* (pp. 21–47). Hillsdale, NJ: Lawrence Erlbaum Associates.

Krebs, D., Denton, K., & Higgins, N. C. (1988). On the evolution of self-knowledge and self-deception. In K. B. MacDonald (Ed.), *Sociobiological perspectives on human development* (pp. 103–139). New York: Springer-Verlag,

Krebs, D., Ward, J., & Racine, T. (1997). The many faces of self-deception. *Behavioral and Brain Sciences, 20*, 119.

Lewandowsky, S., Dunn, J. C., & Kirsner, K. (1989). *Implicit memory: Theoretical issues.* Hillsdale, NJ: Lawrence Erlbaum Associates.

Linton, D. K., & Wiener, N. I. (2001). Personality and potential conceptions: Mating success in a modern Western male sample. *Personality and Individual Differences, 31,* 675–688.

Littlefield, C. H., & Rushton, J. P. (1986). When a child dies: The sociobiology of bereavement. *Journal of Personality and Social Psychology, 51,* 797–802.

Lockard, J. S. (1978). Speculations on the adaptive significance of cognition and consciousness in nonhuman species. *Brain and Behavioral Sciences, 4,* 583–584.

Lockard, J. S., & Mateer, C. A. (1988). Neural bases of self-deception. In J. S. Lockard & D. L. Paulhus (Eds.), *Self-deception: An adaptive mechanism?* (pp. 23–39). Englewood Cliffs, NJ: Prentice-Hall.

Logan, G. D. (1980). Attention and automaticity in Stroop and primary tasks: Theory and data. *Cognitive Psychology, 12,* 523–553.

Loving, T. J., & Agnew, C. R. (2001). Socially desirable responding in close relationships: A dual-component approach and measure. *Journal of Social and Personal Relationships, 18,* 551–574.

Machalek, R., & Cohen, L. E. (1991). The nature of crime: Is cheating necessary for cooperation? *Human Nature, 2,* 215–233.

Martindale, C. (1991). *Cognitive psychology: A neural network approach.* Pacific Grove, CA: Brooks/Cole.

Mele, A. R. (1997). Real self-deception. *Behavioral and Brain Sciences, 20,* 91–136.

Miller, D. T., & Ross, M. (1975). Self-serving biases in attribution of causality: Fact or fiction? *Psychological Bulletin, 82,* 213–225.

Morris, M. W., Sim, D. L. H., & Girotto, V. (1998). Distinguishing sources of cooperation in the one-round Prisoner's Dilemma: Evidence for cooperative decisions based on the illusion of control. *Journal of Experimental Social Psychology, 34,* 494–512.

Murray, S. L., & Holmes, J. G. (1994). Story-telling in close relationships: The construction of confidence. *Personality and Social Psychology Bulletin, 19,* 668–676.

Murray, S. L., & Holmes, J. G. (1997). A leap of faith?: Positive illusions in romantic relationships. *Personality and Social Psychology Bulletin, 23,* 586–604.

Nachson, I. (1999). Self-deception in neurological syndromes. *Journal of Mind and Behavior, 20,* 117–132.

Nachson, I. (2001). Truthfulness, deception and self-deception in recovering true and false memories of child sexual abuse. *International Review of Victimology, 8,* 1–18.

Nesse, R., & Lloyd, A. (1992). The evolution of psychodynamic mechanisms. In J. Barkow, L. Cosmides, & J. Tooby (Eds.) *The adapted mind* (pp. 601–624). New York: Oxford University Press.

Nesse, R. M. (1990). The evolutionary functions of repression and the ego defenses. *Journal of the American Academy of Psychoanalysis, 18,* 260–285.

Newman, L. S. (1999). Motivated cognition and self-deception. *Psychological Inquiry, 1,* 59–63.

Ohlsson, R. (Ed.). (1999). *Genomic imprinting: An interdisciplinary approach.* Heidelberg: Springer.

Paulhus, D. L. (1991). Measurement and control of response bias. In. J. P. Robinson, P. R. Shaver, & L. S. Wrightman (Eds.), *Measures of personality and social psychological attitudes* (Vol. 1, pp. 17–59). San Diego: Academic Press.

Paulhus, D. L. (1998). *Paulus Deception Scales: The Balanced Inventory of Desirable Responding-7. User's manual.* Toronto: Multi-Health Systems.

Paulhus, D. L., & Reid, D. B. (1991). Enhancement and denial in socially desirable responding. *Journal of Personality and Social Psychology, 60,* 307–317.

Peterson, C. (1997). *Psychology: A biosocial approach* (2nd ed.). New York: Longman.

Robinson, M. D., & Ryff, C. D. (1999). The role of self-deception in perceptions of past, present, and future happiness. *Personality and Social Psychology Bulletin, 5,* 595–606.

Ross, L. (1977). The intuitive psychologist and his shortcomings: Distortions in the attribution process. In L. Berkowitz (Ed.), *Advances in experimental social psychology* (Vol. 10, pp. 173–220). New York: Academic Press.

Roth, D. L., & Ingram, R. E. (1985). Factors in the Self-Deception Questionnaire: Associations with depression. *Journal of Personality and Social Psychology, 48*, 243–251.

Rutledge, T., Linden, W., & Davies, R. F. (2000). Psychological response styles and cardiovascular health: Confound or independent risk factor? *Health Psychology, 19*, 441–451.

Sackeim, H. A. (1983). Self-deception, self-esteem, and depression: The adaptive value of lying to oneself. In J. Masling (Ed.), *Empirical studies of psychoanalytic theories* (Vol. 1, pp. 101–157). Hillsdale, NJ: Analytic Press.

Sackeim, H. A., & Gur, R. C. (1978). Self-deception, self-confrontation and consciousness. In G. E. Schwartz & D. Shapiro (Eds.), *Consciousness and self-regulation, advances in research and theory* (Vol. 2, pp. 139–197). New York: Plenum.

Schneider, S. L. (2001). In search of realistic optimism: Meaning, knowledge, and warm fuzziness. *American Psychologist, 56*, 250–263.

Silver, M., Sabini, J., & Miceli, M. (1989). On knowing self-deception. *Journal for the Theory of Social Behaviour, 19*, 213–227.

Slavin, M. O. (1985). The origins of psychic conflict and the adaptive functions of repression: An evolutionary biological view. *Psychoanalysis and Contemporary Thought, 8*, 407–440.

Starek, J. E., & Keating, C. F. (1991). Self-deception and its relationship to success in competition. *Basic and Applied Social Psychology, 12*, 145–155.

Surbey, M. K., & McNally, J. J. (1997). Self-deception as a mediator of cooperation and defection in varying social contexts described in the iterated Prisoner's Dilemma. *Evolution and Human Behavior, 18*, 417–435.

Surbey, M. K., & Rankin, A. (2001, June). *Inter-relationships among Machiavellianism, narcissism, and self-deception in predicting levels of cooperation in the Prisoner's Dilemma Game.* Paper presented at the annual meeting of the Human Behavior and Evolution Society, London.

Surbey, M. K., & Sullivan, M. S. (2003). *Self-deception and repression predict intentions to cooperate with hypothetical spouses and neighbours in Prisoner's Dilemma-like games.* Manuscript submitted for publication.

Tanner, J. M. (1962). *Growth at adolescence* (2nd ed.). Oxford, England: Blackwell.

Taubman-Ben Ari, O. (2000). The effect of reminders of death on reckless driving: A terror management perspective. *Current Directions in Psychological Science, 9*, 196–197.

Taylor, S. E, (1989). *Positive illusions: Creative self-deception and the healthy mind.* New York: Basic Books.

Taylor, S. E., & Brown, J. D. (1988). Illusion and well-being: A social psychological perspective on mental health. *Psychological Bulletin, 103*, 193–210.

Trivers, R. L. (1972). Parental investment and sexual selection. In B. Campbell (Ed.), *Sexual selection and the descent of man 1871–1971* (pp. 136–179). Chicago: Aldine.

Trivers, R. L. (1974). Parent–offspring conflict. *American Zoologist, 14*, 247–262.

Trivers, R. L. (1976). Foreword. In R. Dawkins, *The selfish gene* (pp. v–vii). New York: Oxford University Press.

Trivers, R. L. (1985). *Social evolution.* Menlo Park, CA: Benjamin/Cummins.

Trivers, R. L. (1997). Genetic basis of intra-psychic conflict. In N. Segal, G. E. Weisfeld, & C. C. Weisfeld (Eds.), *Uniting psychology and biology: Integrative perspectives on human development* (pp. 385–395). Washington, DC: American Psychological Association.

Trivers, R. L. (2000). The elements of a scientific theory of self-deception. In D. LeCroy & P. Moller (Eds.), *Annals of the New York Academy of Sciences: Vol. 907. Evolutionary perspectives on human reproductive behavior* (pp. 114–131). New York: New York Academy of Sciences.

Trivers, R. L., & Burt, A. (1999). Kinship and genomic imprinting. In R. Ohlsson (Ed.), *Genomic imprinting: An interdisciplinary approach* (pp. 1–23). Heidelberg: Springer.

Trivers, R. L., & Newton, H. P. (1982). The crash of Flight 90: Doomed by self-deception? *Science Digest, 66–67,* 111.

Turvey, C., & Salovey, P. (1993–1994) Measures of repression: Converging on the same construct? *Imagination, Cognition and Personality, 13,* 279–289.

Wallace, B. (1973). Misinformation, fitness, and selection. *The American Naturalist, 107,* 1–7.

Weinstein, N. D. (1980). Unrealistic optimism about future life events. *Journal of Personality and Social Psychology, 39,* 806–820.

Weiskrantz, L. (1986). *Blindsight: A case study and implications.* Oxford, England: Oxford University Press.

Werhun, C. D., & Cox, B. J. (2000). Levels of anxiety sensitivity in relation to repressive and self-deceptive coping styles. *Journal of Anxiety Disorders, 13,* 601–609.

Wrangham, R. (1999). Is military incompetence adaptive? *Evolution and Human Behavior, 20,* 3–17.

Wright, R. C., & Schneider, S. L. (1999). Motivated self-deception in child molesters. *Journal of Child Sexual Abuse, 8,* 89–111.

Ancestral Emotions, Current Decisions: Using Evolutionary Game Theory to Explore the Role of Emotions in Decision Making

Timothy Ketelaar
New Mexico State University

I f there was only one best strategy for every real-world decision problem, policy making would be easy. Policymakers could simply dispatch game theorists to model each decision problem as a strategic game and then locate the one strategy that leads to the greatest payoff. The task of policymakers would then be to determine how best to implement these singularly best strategies in the real world. Unfortunately, we do not live in such a world. Instead we live in a complex and noisy world where many different strategies (not just one) can succeed and where numerous other strategies are fraught with peril. Fortunately, evolutionary game theory can provide us with valuable tools for identifying strategies that might fare well in these sorts of environments. The current chapter explores how several of these game theoretic tools—the folk theorem and the concept of frequency dependent selection—can help decision theorists and policy makers to appreciate that there are often multiple paths to success in many real-world decision problems. Along these lines, it is proposed that the concept of emotion will be particularly useful to decision theorists and policymakers who wish to understand why not all strategists adopt the same strategy.

For several decades it was commonly assumed that the most successful tactics to employ in repeated interactions, such as the iterated Prisoner's Dilemma, were strategies that embodied cold-hearted self-interest. More recently, attention has focused on the claim that "nicer" strategies such as Tit-for-Tat cooperation—and its theoretical cousin reciprocal altruism—are more successful tactics in these situations. The current chapter uses insights from evolutionary game theory to explore why these strategies are not as common as one might predict. There are at least two reasons why one would expect that not all members of the population will adopt a particular strategy (e.g., Tit-for-Tat), despite clear evidence that this strategy is superior to many alternatives. First, it turns out that, contrary to popular belief, Tit-for-Tat is not the singularly "best" strategy in indefinitely repeated social interactions such as the repeated Prisoner's Dilemma. In this regard, the *folk theorem* from game theory can be used to identify conditions under which a multitude of equilibrium strategies (rather than just one) can exist in many social dilemmas that are repeated indefinitely. Second, individual differences in emotion can spawn a plethora of strategies ranging from the detached and ruthless pursuit of immediate self-interest to the more kindhearted use of cooperative tactics. Speculation about the possible role of emotions in decision making has a long history, dating back at least as far as A. Smith's (1759/2000) *Theory of Moral Sentiments* and emerging more recently in the theoretical writings of Trivers (1971, 1985), Hirschleifer (1987, 2001), and Frank (1988, 2001). Using an evolutionary approach, this chapter argues that these two aspects of decision making—the folk theorem and emotional influences on strategic behavior—may be conceptually intertwined. In particular, the evolutionary process of frequency dependent selection is explored as a possible basis for the stable coexistence of multiple emotion-based strategies in the same population.

FROM NASH TO AXELROD: THE FOLK THEOREM AND THE REPEATED PRISONER'S DILEMMA

In *The Theory of Games and Economic Behavior* (1944), von Neumann and Morgenstern introduced a new approach to decision making known as game theory. In game theory, social interactions were depicted as multiperson games in which the outcome depended not just on the strategy an individual adopted, but also on the strategy choice of their rival (Von Neumann & Morgenstern, 1944). Game theory depicted social interactions as games, not to trivialize them, but rather to formalize how it is possible to think strategically about complex, real-world decisions. At the onset of the cold war, for example, game theory allowed policymakers to characterize complex decision scenarios such as nuclear deterrence and the arms race in terms of just three components: players, strategies, and the payoffs that resulted from each player's strategy choice. A major breakthrough in game theory came in 1951 when a young mathematician named John Nash proved how there exists at least one solution, or "equilibrium point," for a large class of decision problems modeled by game theory (see Kuhn & Nasar, 2002, for a review of Nash's contributions). These so-called Nash Equilibria represent an individual's best response to the strategy options available to them and their rival in the context of a particular strategic game. A rational player who has identified an equilibrium strategy would, by definition, *not* be motivated to unilaterally switch to a different strategy (Nash, 1951).

Given that game theory allowed equilibrium strategies to be identified for a wide range of scenarios, some theorists began to wonder whether human decision makers would actually choose an equilibrium strategy when confronted with an actual social dilemma. For instance, even before Nash had published his paper on the equilibrium concept, two of his colleagues at the RAND Corporation, economists Merrill Flood and Melvin Dresher, devised a strategy game with the explicit goal of determining whether people would play this game in the manner that Von Neumann–Morgenstern–Nash would predict (Poundstone, 1992). The rest as they say, is history. When Flood and Dresher designed this simple two-person, two-choice game, which later became known as the Prisoner's Dilemma, they had no idea that this game would become the social sciences' iconic image of the conflict between individual and collective self-interest (Poundstone, 1992; Ridley, 1996).

Several decades after Flood and Dresher first inquired about whether humans actually behave in accord with economic theory, game theoreticians had turned their attention to many other intriguing questions. Yet interest in the Prisoner's dilemma remained as strong as ever, due in large part to an unusual Prisoner's Dilemma tournament hosted by a young political scientist (Poundstone, 1992). I refer, of course, to Robert Axelrod's computer simulation of a Prisoner's Dilemma tournament (Axelrod, 1980a, 1980b, 1984). Although the specific conclusions of Axelrod's tournament have often been grossly misunderstood, his work helped to draw attention to the complexities involved in identifying successful strategies in repeated games. Binmore (1998, p. 320) noted: "His achievement was to pioneer the evolutionary approach to the problem of how equilibria are selected." In particular, Axelrod's tournament provoked social scientists to reject the then common assumption that the only strategies that could successfully evolve in a repeated social dilemma were those that embodied ruthless noncooperation. Axelrod's work showed that nice guys can indeed finish first (see Ridley, 1996). Before discussing the results of Axelrod's tournament and how they relate to the role of emotion in strategic decision making, it will be useful to briefly review the game theoretic structure of the Prisoner's Dilemma, including its role in understanding the so-called folk theorem.

Game Theory and the Prisoner's Dilemma

Discovering a good strategy for the classic Prisoner's Dilemma is rather straight-forward because the game tree for this social dilemma is quite simple, consisting of just two players, two strategy choices (cooperate or defect), and four possible sets of payoff outcomes that must be considered (see Fig. 7.1). It quickly becomes obvious that the best outcome occurs if individuals choose to defect when their rival chooses to cooperate (the so-called temptation to defect). Because the payoffs are symmetric for the two players, the worst outcome occurs if one player chooses to cooperate and their rival chooses to defect (the so-called sucker's payoff). A player can quickly identify that defection is the best strategy in the Prisoner's Dilemma because the expected payoff for defection (the average of the two defection outcomes: mutual defection and temptation to defect) is higher than the expected payoff for cooperation (the average of the two cooperation outcomes: mutual cooperation and the sucker's payoff). Defection is the equilibrium strategy for the classic Prisoner's Dilemma game because a rational player would not be motivated to unilaterally switch to cooperation.

Discovering the best strategy for a single shot game, where each player encounters the other only once, is relatively straightforward, but what about an iterated Prisoner's Dilemma that lasts many rounds? By contrast with a single shot game, it turns out that repeated games often allow for a vast number of successful strategies (not just defection). This point applies not only to the repeated Prisoner's Dilemma, but to a great number of indefinitely repeated games. In fact, the existence

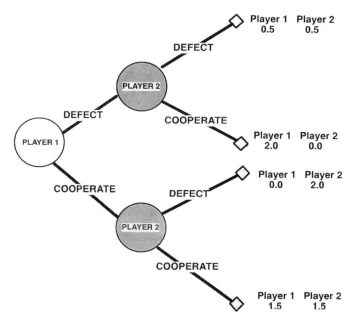

FIG. 7.1.   The game tree for the classic Prisoner's Dilemma.

of multiple equilibrium strategies in indefinitely repeated games has been so widely appreciated that it goes by the label "the folk theorem" (see Binmore, 1998; Fundenberg & Tirole, 2000).

The Folk Theorem

Although the technical definition of the *folk theorem* is clearly beyond the scope of the current chapter, its basic logic can be stated quite simply (see Binmore, 1998; Fundenberg & Tirole, 2000; Lomborg, 1996; Rasmussen, 1994). The reason that there exists a vast number of successful tactics (and not just one best strategy) in an indefinitely repeated game has to do with the simple fact that indefinitely repeated games can allow many different strategies to meet the requirements of a Nash equilibrium. Consider, for example, two players engaged in an indefinitely repeated Prisoner's Dilemma. If each player *repeatedly* selects their "best" strategy for the single shot game (i.e., defection), they both end up in an endless cycle of mutual defections. This sets up an incentive for both players to coordinate on *any* alternative strategy that results in a more profitable outcome than continuous defection. One simple way to motivate an opponent to locate such an alternative strategy and to stick to it (recall the temptation to defect) is to threaten to defect for the remainder of the game if the opponent deviates even once from the proposed alternative strategy (see Binmore, 1998; Lomborg, 1996). Defecting for the remainder of the game essentially holds the opponent perpetually to a much lower set of payoffs (e.g., mutual defection or the sucker's payoff) than could be obtained by simply sticking with the proposed alternative strategy (in this case cooperation). Under the veil of a credible threat of unrelenting punishment for deviating, no rational player would be motivated to unilaterally switch from the proposed alternative strategy. As a result, when the threat of such punishment is credible, almost any proposed strategy that results in a higher payoff than unrelenting punishment can be considered a Nash equilibrium (Binmore, 1998; Fundenberg & Tirole, 2000). This, in essence, is the folk theorem.

Economists have labored hard to develop the mathematical basis of this folk theorem (see Fundenberg & Tirole, 2000; Rasmussen, 1994). With all due apologies to those economists, it is possible to illustrate how the folk theorem leads to a multitude of equilibrium strategies by considering a rather contrived, nonmathematical, example. Consider a repeated Prisoner's Dilemma between two fictitious characters, Dr. Strangelove and Captain Mandrake. In this hypothetical example, Dr. Strangelove claims to possess a nuclear bomb and he is willing to use it if his demands are not met. Dr. Strangelove's demands are rather straightforward: "Cooperate with me for the remainder of the game, or else." More specifically, "If you deviate from the strategy of cooperation, even once, I'll blow you up with my nuclear bomb!" If Dr. Strangelove's threat is credible, and Captain Mandrake is a rational strategist, then Captain Mandrake would be expected to cooperate (he won't deviate and get himself blown up). Now imagine that both strategists, Dr. Strangelove and Captain Mandrake, each possess a bomb and each have made the same credible threat: Cooperate or else! Assuming that the threat of nuclear obliteration is equivalent to an unrelenting punishment (for deviating), sticking with the proposed strategy (cooperation) is now a Nash equilibrium because no rational player would be motivated to unilaterally switch to any other strategy. However, cooperation is not the only equilibrium strategy in this scenario. Suppose, for example, that both Dr. Strangelove and Captain Mandrake have made a slightly different, but equally threatening, demand: "Alternate between cooperate and defect for the remainder of the game, or else!" Under the veil of a credible threat of nuclear demise, no rational player would be motivated to unilaterally switch from this *new* proposed strategy (i.e., alternating between cooperate and defect). In fact, provided that the threat of punishment for deviating is sufficiently large and credible, almost any proposed strategy could become a Nash equilibrium. In the indefinitely repeated Prisoner's Dilemma, the threat of unrelenting punishment is, of course, typically manifest in the form of permanently lower payoffs, rather than nuclear devastation. Nonetheless, if each strategist possesses not a bomb, but rather a credible threat of defecting for the remainder of the game (contingent on the other player deviating from the proposed strategy), then no rational player would be motivated to unilaterally switch from the proposed strategy whatever that strategy may be (assuming, of course, that the proposed strategy has a better payoff than would be achieved by the unrelenting punishment).

An underlying assumption of the folk theorem is that the threat of unrelenting punishment must be credible. Indefinitely repeated games often satisfy this condition simply by virtue of their being repeated (rather than single shot) games and because their ending (i.e., last round of play) is, by definition, unknown (thus, the label "indefinitely" repeated). A threat of unrelenting punishment is hardly convincing in a single shot game because—nuclear weapons excepted—a threat of unrelenting defection cannot be carried out once the game ends. An opponent is either going to defect just once or not at all; unrelenting punishment in the form of a continuous sequence of defections is simply not possible in the single shot game. Similarly, if both players know when the game is going to end, then they would still be motivated to defect on the last round because the last round is essentially a single shot game and the threat of punishment no longer applies. Backward induction would then lead a rational strategist to defect on the second to last round as well, because they already know how they would ideally behave on the last round (they would defect). Similarly, if it would be best to defect on the last *two* rounds, then they would be motivated to defect on the third to last round, the fourth to last round, and so on. It is in this sense that it is possible to show mathematically that if the threat of unrelenting punishment is sufficiently large and credible and the probability that the game will be played indefinitely is large enough, then there exists a multitude of strategies that meet the requirements of a Nash equilibrium (Fundenberg & Tirole, 2000).

In developing game theory, Von Neumann and Morgenstern assumed that a rational player would first consider all possible courses of action before selecting a "best" strategy. However, as the folk theorem clearly suggests, indefinitely repeated games open up a Pandora's box for the strategist who is attempting to locate a singularly "best" strategy among a multitude of plausible alternatives (Binmore, 1998). It turns out that even the apparently simple task of searching through all possible courses of action (to locate all of the equilibrium strategies) is often much more complex than it would appear at first glance. This is the case because the number of branches that must be searched in any reasonably complex game tree (in order to locate and evaluate the final outcomes) grows exponentially as the number of rounds increases (see Koller, Megiddo, & von Stengel, 1996; Koller & Pfeffer, 1997; Shannon, 1950; also Ketelaar & Todd, 2001). The seemingly undemanding game of tic-tac-toe, for example, consists of a vast game tree containing at least 15, 120 different outcomes (Dixit & Skeath, 1999), and even a relatively simple repeated Prisoner's Dilemma game involving just 20 rounds of play would entail constructing a game tree with over 1 million different branches (Ketelaar & Todd, 2001; Koller et al., 1996; Koller & Pfeffer, 1997). Rather than evaluating all possible courses of action, an alternative method for identifying good strategies would be to conduct a tournament consisting of computer programs where each program represents a different strategy for playing the indefinitely repeated game. "Good" strategies could then be identified simply by observing which programs (strategies) perform well in this tournament. This is precisely what Robert Axelrod did.

Axelrod's Tournament

The "competitors" in Axelrod's tournament were computer programs submitted by experts from psychology, political science, game theory, economics, sociology, and mathematics (Axelrod, 1984). These programs took the form of decision rules, each specifying a complete plan of action for a "player" in the iterated Prisoner's Dilemma. The programs included such strategies as "random," which cooperated or defected with equal probability and a rather spiteful strategy named "FRIED-MAN" that cooperated every round until its opponent defected; thereafter, it defected for the remainder of the game.

Axelrod's tournament was essentially a series of three simulated Prisoner's dilemma tournaments (see Axelrod, 1984). The first tournament consisted of a competition among 14 different computer programs in a game lasting exactly 200 moves. Each program (strategy) competed in a series of five pair-wise contests against every other strategy, including its twin and random. By contrast with the first tournament, the second tournament consisted of 63 computer programs. Although no strategy in the first tournament was explicitly designed to exploit the fact that the game ended on the 200th move, the format of the second tournament was modified in order to avoid possible end game effects. Specifically, the probability that the game ended on any given move was set at $p = .00346$. This resulted in each pair of strategies being matched against every other strategy in a total of five games that lasted, on average, 151 moves (see Axelrod, 1980b). Axelrod's third and final tournament consisted of a reanalysis of the results of this second tournament. This reanalysis aimed to simulate a "survival of the fittest" competition in which over time it could be observed which strategies waxed and waned in terms of their relative frequency of occurrence in the larger population of strategies. This was accomplished by interpreting "the average payoff received by a particular strategy as proportional to that individual's expected number of offspring" in the next generation (Axelrod, 1980b, p. 398). In this way, a strategy that performed well against all other strategies in the first round would be better represented in the next generation, and so on.

Today most social scientists know the answer to the question of which strategy "won" the three tournaments; the "declared" victor was a deceptively simple strategy known as Tit-for-Tat. Tit-for-Tat (TFT) was submitted by psychologist Anatol Rappaport and consisted of the following simple rule:

> Cooperate on the first move, on all subsequent moves copy what your opponent did on the preceding move.

Although TFT did *not* win every pair-wise contest in which it was entered, it did manage to win the first tournament by scoring an average of 504 points per game (see Axelrod, 1980a). The second best strategy earned 500 points, the third best earned 486, and the worst strategy (random) earned just 276 points. As a useful benchmark, consider that scores in this tournament could range from 1,000 (for repeatedly earning the "temptation to defect" payoff), to zero points (for repeated earning the "sucker's payoff") with 600 points being awarded to any strategy that could sustain a state of mutual cooperation across all 200 rounds. A similar outcome transpired in the second tournament in which TFT competed against 62 strategies, many of which were designed with knowledge of the results of the first tournament. Again, although TFT did not win every pair-wise contest, it managed to outscore the next best strategy by 12 points (see Axelrod, 1980b, for a detailed account). In Axelrod's third tournament, in which he simulated a "survival of the fittest" competition, an interesting result emerged. By 500 generations, 96% of the population was comprised of just 11 strategies from the initial set of 63. After 1,000 generations, Tit-for-Tat was the most numerous strategy, occupying 14.5 % of the population, followed by the second and third place strategies, which comprised 13.9% and 13.1 % of the population, respectively.

Despite TFT's success in these computer tournaments, Axelrod (1980a, 1980b) did not conclude that TFT was the only good strategy in the repeated Prisoner's Dilemma. Instead, Axelrod (1984 p. 15) asserted that "in the Prisoner's Dilemma, the strategy that works best depends directly on what strategy the other player is using and, in particular, on whether this strategy leaves room for the development of mutual cooperation." Contrary to Axelrod's original conclusions, many social scientists today arrive at a very different verdict regarding Axelrod's tournament, a verdict that suggests that many are unaware of the implications of the folk theorem in regard to indefinitely repeated games. As some game-thereoticians (Hirschleifer & Martinez Coll, 1988, p. 369) noted: "Qualifying statements do appear from time to time in Axelrod's work. But the dramatic image of the tournaments, in which TIT-FOR-TAT as David slew assorted Goliaths, apparently caught the fancy of a number of commentators who went on to make rather extreme claims on behalf of TIT-FOR-TAT as the sole or main source of social cooperation." Although Axelrod's work showed that Tit-for-Tat reciprocity could be a successful strategy in the repeated Prisoner's Dilemma, the folk theorem serves as a reminder that there exists a vast number of potentially successful tactics (and not just one best strategy) in indefinitely repeated games (see Binmore, 1998; Fundenberg & Tirole, 2000; Lomborg, 1996; Rasmussen, 1994).

Tit-for-Tat Reciprocity Meets the Folk Theorem

Game theorists have long lamented on how the complex problem of strategy choice in indefinitely repeated games is often treated by social scientists as if the folk theorem did not exist and that there was just one best strategy in the form of Tit-for-Tat reciprocity (see Hirshleifer, 1999). One reason why TFT has risen to a level of such prominence in the minds of social scientists has to do with the reasonable degree of fit between TFT and a mechanism for sustaining cooperation known as reciprocal altruism. The concept of reciprocal altruism was born a full decade before Axelrod's tournaments when Trivers (1971) demonstrated how natural selection could sustain cooperation between two genetically unrelated individuals. Reciprocal altruism is essentially the equivalent of a social contract in which one individual bestows a benefit on a second individual with the expectation of being repaid (by the recipient) at some later date. Triver's demonstrated that as long as the *eventual* benefit to the individual who provided the aid was greater than the cost of this initial act of cooperation, neither individual had an incentive to defect from this reciprocal Tit-for-Tat exchange. Consistent with the folk theorem, the work of Triver's (and later Axelrod) provides support for the existence of alternative pathways to success (other than strict noncooperation) in indefinitely repeated games. Yet, as Binmore (1998, p. 315, emphasis in original) dutifully noted:

> The folk theorem was largely ignored by scholars outside economics for more than twenty years. Only with Triver's coining of the term *reciprocal altruism* did its message begin to enjoy widespread currency. But it was the later publication of Axelrod's *Evolution of Cooperation* that really put the folk theorem on the map. Unfortunately, much of what has been said about the tit-for-tat paradigm is overblown or mistaken. Worse still, the popularity that the paradigm enjoys has obscured the important fact that there are many more ways of supporting a social contract than by naive pairwise reciprocation.

One of the more promising candidates for an alternative pathway to strategic success involves the role of emotions as psychological mechanisms that commit the individual to a course of action that, although successful in the long haul, may not be in their immediate self-interest (Hirshleifer, 1987, 2001). It is not often appreciated, for example, that over one third of Triver's (1971) path-breaking paper on *reciprocal altruism* was devoted to a discussion of the role of *emotions* in cooperative exchanges. Trivers (1971, p. 50) pointed out, "It seems plausible, furthermore, that the emotion of guilt has been selected for in humans partly in order to motivate the cheater to compensate his misdeed and to behave reciprocally in the future, and thus to prevent the rupture of reciprocal relationships." It turns out that theorizing about the impact of emotions (e.g., guilt) on cooperative behavior has a long history in the social sciences, dating back to Adam Smith's (1759/2000) *Theory of Moral Sentiments*.

HOW EMOTIONS IMPACT ON STRATEGY CHOICE: ADAM SMITH'S THEORY OF MORAL SENTIMENTS

> The man who acts according to the rules of perfect prudence, of strict justice, and of proper benevolence, may be said to be perfectly virtuous. But the most perfect knowledge of those rules will not alone enable him to act in this manner; *his own passions are very apt to mislead him—sometimes to drive him, and sometimes to seduce him, to violate all the rules which he himself, in all his sober and cool hours, approves of.* (Adam Smith, 1759/2000, p. 349, emphasis added)

By arguing that moral passions motivate individuals to make choices that sometimes conflict with their immediate self-interests, Adam Smith (1759/2000) was among the first modern scholars to offer an explanation for why people do not always behave in accord with apparently well-established rules for behavior. Game theorists today are much less interested in understanding how moral passions divert individuals from the path of "perfect prudence" and "strict justice." Instead, they are far more interested in understanding why individuals so often ignore the lure of immediate payoffs associated with ruthlessly self-interested behavior (Frank, 1988, 2001; Hirschliefer, 1987, 2001). In this regard, Adam Smith's theory is as relevant today as ever.

Smith's (1759) *Theory of Moral Sentiments* espoused a decidedly Epicurean view of human nature in which pleasure and pain were the root source of an individual's decision to follow or violate the established rules of proper social behavior. Interestingly, Smith argued that the "pleasures and pains of the mind" exert a far greater influence on behavior than the actual bodily experience of these hedonic states. By this Smith meant that individuals typically experience much greater happiness from the mental states that give rise to pleasure (fantasy, reminiscence) than from the actual physical experience of such events. Smith (1759/2000, p. 432, emphasis added) contended that "when we enjoy the greatest pleasure, we shall always find that the bodily sensation, *the sensation of the present instant, makes but a small part of our happiness*, that our enjoyment chiefly arises either from the cheerful recollection of the past, or the still more joyous anticipation of the future, and that *the mind always contributes by much the largest share of the entertainment*." Similarly, Smith claimed that individuals typically suffer more pain from the recollection of a terrible experience or the dread of some horrible future event than from the actual immediate physical sensations produced in these situations.

By emphasizing the psychological component of emotion (over their physical aspects), Adam Smith's theory is consistent with much of the social psychology literature on emotion and judgment. In particular, research in the social cognitive tradition has demonstrated that the influence of emotion on judgment depends on a variety of *cognitive factors* specific to each emotion (Clore, Schwarz, & Conway, 1994; Lerner & Keltner, 2001; Rozin, Lowery, Imada, & Haidt, 1999). For example, in a recent study of the effects of emotion on risk perception, Lerner and Keltner (2001) showed that angry individuals (compared to fearful individuals) tend to appraise future events as more probable. These effects are consistent with the different cognitive structures associated with these two emotions; anger invariably involves a sense of certainty, whereas fear is defined by a mental state of uncertainty (Smith & Ellsworth, 1985). Smith's theory appears to be at odds, however, with at least one currently popular model of emotion, Demasio's (1994) *somatic marker hypothesis*. The *Somatic Marker Hypothesis* posits that individuals experience emotions primarily in terms of somatic states (e.g., that sensation in the pit of your stomach when you are nervous) rather than in terms of mental states or cognitions. Demasio (1994) argued that these somatic states function, much like a car's dashboard warning lights, to alert us to pay heed to some particular aspect of the environment. By contrast, Adam Smith proposed that mental states (not their somatic representations) provide a much greater inducement for behavior. Following Smith, why put the information on the somatic dashboard when it can be wired directly into the decision engine, the mind?

Although game theorists have conducted relatively few empirical studies to explore the link between emotion and strategic behavior in repeated games, psychologists have conducted extensive research on the link between social-moral emotions (e.g., guilt) and pro-social behavior in general. Research on the development of the social-moral emotions, for example, suggests that children who are predisposed to feeling guilty display their guilt by spontaneously offering assistance to others (Chapman, Zahn-Waxler, Cooperman, & Iannotie, 1987; Estrada- Hollenbeck & Heatherton, 1998). Other research suggests that engaging in guilt-provoking behaviors (e.g., accidentally destroying someone's camera) leads to greater helping behavior in subsequent interactions with an unrelated third party (Cialdini, Darby, & Vincent, 1973; Cunningham, Steinberg, & Grev, 1980; Isen, Clark, & Schwartz, 1976; Isen & Simmonds, 1978; J. W. Regan, 1971; D. T. Regan, Williams, & Sparling, 1972). Finally, there is evidence that the absence of moral sentiments is associated with a corresponding reduction in pro-social behavior (see Demasio, 1994, for a review of the neuropsychological evidence). A defining characteristic of sociopaths, for example, is their "apparent lack of sincere social emotions" (Mealey, 1995, p. 524). According to one researcher, these individuals comprise only 5% of the adult population yet account for more than 50% of all criminal acts (Mealey, 1995).

Adam Smith Meets Robert Frank:
A Theory of Emotional Commitments

Although the Prisoner's Dilemma has traditionally been used to model the conflict between individual and collective self-interest, economist Robert Frank (1988) used this two-person game to illustrate the role of moral sentiments in an entirely different, but equally important, conflict. In his book, *Passions within Reason*, Frank (1988) showed how the moral sentiments discussed by Adam Smith could, in principle, solve the conflict between immediate and long-term self-interest. Consistent with Hirschleifer's (1987) formal analysis of these issues, Frank referred to these sorts of conflicts as "commitment problems." Commitment problems arise whenever immediate incentives run contrary to one's long-term interests. The dieter, for example, faces the immediate attraction of a piece of cake, weighed against the long-term cost of gaining weight. Diners in a restaurant face the immediate benefit of not leaving a tip, weighed against the potential long-term damage to their reputation for being stingy. The key "problem" of commitment problems centers on the fact that the psychological reward mechanism produces a representation of an individual's circumstances that displays the short-term benefits *right now* (see Frank, 1988, pp. 76–80). The activation of this reward mechanism can be an attractive lure for behavior that is not in their long-term best interest. Consider married individuals who face the immediate attraction of an extramarital liaison, balanced by the long-term threat to their marital stability.

Using the Prisoner's Dilemma as an example, Frank argued that moral sentiments could explain why we live in a world where some individuals shirk the immediate payoff associated with defection in favor of more cooperative strategies. Frank (1988) observed that the moral sentiments:

> can and do compete with feelings that spring from rational calculations about material payoffs.... Consider, for example, a person capable of strong guilt feelings. This person will not cheat even when it is in her material interests to do so. The reason is not that she fears getting caught but that she simply does not *want* to cheat. Her aversion to feelings of guilt effectively alters the payoffs she faces. (p. 53)

According to Frank, if an individual experiences feelings of guilt while contemplating cheating, then this feeling state can serve as a potent counterweight to the immediate payoffs that could be reaped from this strategy. Because these feelings coincide with the activation of the reward mechanism, the individual has two concurrent sources of information that can be taken into account when deciding how to behave. One source of information (from the immediate reward mechanism) informs the individual about the *immediate* consequences of a given strategy and the second source (from moral sentiments such as guilt) informs the individual about the *future* (in this case negative) consequences of that very same strategy choice.

In this manner, Frank (1988; see also Hirschleifer, 1987) proposed that moral sentiments function as commitment devices, mechanisms that provoke individuals to make binding commitments to strategies that maximize their long-term payoffs, even at the expense of sometimes shirking short-term rewards. Decision theorists have yet to empirically test Frank's model in the realm of emotion, preferring instead to focus on understanding how temporal discounting—in principle—could explain the specious attractiveness of short-term rewards (see Herrnstein, 1970; Loewenstein, 1987). Nonetheless, subjecting Frank's translation of Adam Smith to empirical test would be relatively straightforward. A central implication of Frank's model, that guilt feelings provoke commitment to more cooperative strategies, could be tested simply by examining whether individuals who experience guilt feelings while considering "defection" in the Prisoner's Dilemma are more likely to forgo this initially attractive strategy in favor of alternative (more cooperative) strategies. This is precisely the direction that has been pursued in several recent studies of guilt and strategy choice.

Empirical Support for Frank's Commitment Model: The Impact of Guilt in Repeated Games

In two studies involving repeated social bargaining games, Ketelaar & Au (2003) explored whether guilt was associated with higher levels of cooperation. Following Frank (1988), they predicted that feelings of guilt would provoke individuals to shift their attention away from initially attractive strategies (e.g., defection) and toward other (more cooperative) strategies. Although there have been numerous studies of guilt and cooperation in the social psychology literature (Cialdini et al., 1973; Isen et al., 1976), very few of these studies have actually measured guilty feelings or explored the possible "informative functions" of these feeling states in relation to strategy choice in a game theoretic context. In this regard, Ketelaar and Au (2003) employed a game theoretic framework to test Frank's ideas in two studies of guilt and strategy choice. The first study examined the effects of a laboratory "guilt" induction on strategy choice in the repeated Prisoner's Dilemma and a second study utilized a more naturalistic setting to examine the impact of "online" guilt feelings in a repeated ultimatum game.

In an indefinitely repeated Prisoner's Dilemma, Ketelaar and Au (2003) observed that individuals who were experimentally manipulated into a guilty mood displayed significantly higher levels of cooperation (53% cooperative responses) compared to individuals in a neutral mood control condition (39% cooperation). This study was modeled on Isen et al.'s (1976) influential research on negative affect and cooperation. College students were randomly assigned to either a guilty or neutral mood induction and then asked to make behavioral choices (cooperate or defect) in two sets of 40 rounds of a repeated Prisoner's Dilemma. Consistent with Triver's (1971) views on emotion in reciprocal exchanges, the results revealed that the largest effects of the guilt manipulation were seen among those individuals who tended to defect in the earlier rounds of the Prisoner's Dilemma. In other words, individuals who had previously defected appeared to be most motivated by feelings of guilt to "compensate" for their earlier misdeeds by behaving more cooperatively in the later rounds (see Ketelaar & Au, 2003). Although these findings were consistent with the view that guilt provokes increased cooperation, this study suffered from the same criticisms that have applied to Isen's earlier work (see Ketelaar & Au, 2003). Specifically, the presence or absence of guilt feelings was experimentally manipulated, thus it was not clear whether in more naturalistic settings all individuals would be equally likely to have experienced guilt after defection. In other words, this study left open the possibility that there exists individual differences in the capacity to experience moral sentiments, individual differences that could have an impact on strategy choices.

In a second study, Ketelaar and Au (2003) followed up on their Prisoner Dilemma experiment by exploring whether naturally occurring feelings of guilt could affect the fairness of monetary *ultimatums* in a two-person decision scenario known as the repeated ultimatum game. The ultimatum game is a two person game in which one individual is asked to make a proposal on how to split a sum of money. The second individual has the task of either accepting or refusing the offer. If the offer is accepted, then the money is split as proposed. If the offer is rejected, then neither party receives any money. Given the commonly observed propensity of individuals to propose fair divisions of the money in ultimatum games (see Thaler, 1992), Ketelaar and Au constrained the selection of possible offers such that it was impossible for an individual to propose a completely fair (50/50) split of the money. Specifically, they instructed participants that the task was to divide $19 *into whole dollar increments.*[1] Participants then engaged in this task twice over the course of one week. Self-reports of a variety of emotions, including guilty feelings, were confidentially recorded for each participant immediately following each round of negotiation. Of primary interest was whether individuals who made unfair offers during the first round of negotiation (i.e., proposing to give more money to themselves than to their partner), and felt *guilty* about it, would propose more generous offers one week later during round two.

Ketelaar and Au observed that the tendency to report feelings of guilt varied as a function of the type of offer that the individual made during the first round of negotiation. Moreover, individual differences in the propensity to feel guilty were predictive of strategic behavior in the second round of negotiation. Not surprising, none of the individuals who proposed a generous offer in round one reported feelings of guilt, whereas over one half (57%) of the individuals who made a selfish offer in round one reported such feelings. More important, the fairness of the monetary ultimatums proposed in the second round of negotiation differed significantly as a function of whether or not the individual reported guilt feelings in the first round. Ketelaar and Au observed that the vast majority of individuals (91%) who reported feeling guilty after making a selfish offer, later gave a generous offer in the second round. By comparison, only 22% of the individuals who reported no feelings of guilt after making a similarly selfish offer[2] ended up proposing a generous offer in the second round.

---

[1]Given the odd number of dollars to be divided ($19), the possible divisions of money ranged from extremely *generous* proposals ($0 for me, $19 for you) to extremely *selfish* proposals ($19 for me, $0 for you), but could never be completely fair (i.e., a 50/50 split).

[2]There was no difference in the size of the offers given by guilty feeling and nonguilty feeling individuals during the first round and all offers proposed during the first round were accepted. Both groups had median offers of $9 to their partner; thus, this effect could not be attributed to individuals who felt guilty after a selfish offer in the first round having proposed a substantially more selfish offer than those individuals who reported no guilt (see Ketelaar & Au, 2003).

So, why doesn't everyone who behaves selfishly in the ultimatum game feel guilty? Adam Smith (1759/2000) argued that individual differences in the tendency to experience moral sentiments, such as guilt, could be attributed to individual differences in the capacity to exercise "self-command" over these emotions. According to Smith (1759/2000), the individual who could endure the proper amount of guilt after a transgression, or could restrain feelings of anger after suffering an insult, could be said to possess the moral virtues of fortitude and temperance, respectively. Yet, the folk theorem is a reminder that self-command in the form of fortitude and temperance is not the only pathway to success in a repeated social dilemma. In this final section, I argue that evolutionary game theory may be useful in understanding both why not all strategists adopt the same strategy and why not all strategists experience feelings of guilt when pursuing noncooperative behavior. In particular, I utilize the concept of frequency dependent selection to explore the possibility that individual differences in emotion can account for individual differences in strategies in repeated social dilemmas.

Adam Smith Meets the Folk Theorem:
Emotions as Frequency Dependent Strategies in Social Games

It seems plausible that individual differences in the capacity to experience moral sentiments could translate into stable individual differences in the strategies that individuals employ. Recall that Frank (1988) argued that the individual who was prone to feelings of guilt might not defect, even when it was in their material interest to do so. In this regard, it is not unreasonable to assume that individuals who are prone to feeling guilty (when they consider defection) would tend to pursue somewhat different outcomes in social games than their less guilt-prone counterparts. In the social psychology literature, individual differences in the types of outcomes that individuals prefer are dubbed "social motives" (Au & Kwong, in press; Messick & McClintock, 1968; Van Lange, Otten, DeBruin, & Joireman, 1997).

Social motives are typically assessed by presenting individuals with a series of matrices known as "decomposed games" (see Fig. 7.2). Each decomposed game contains a different payoff distribution and individuals are instructed to select the particular distribution that they would most prefer to see realized. This methodology typically reveals three broad classes of social motivation referred to as Cooperators, Individualists, and Competitors (Au & Kwong, in press; Van Lange et al., 1997; Van Lange & Visser, 1999). *Cooperators* correspond to individuals who routinely prefer outcomes that maximize joint payoffs between participants (see Fig. 7.2). *Individualists*, by contrast, routinely prefer outcomes that maximize their own payoffs with little regard for the payoffs that others receive, whereas *Competitors* are individuals who typically choose outcomes that maximize their relative advantage over their rival. In contrast to individualists, competitors are concerned with their opponent's outcomes and they actively strive to maximize the difference between their payoff and that of their rival, even if this means accepting an outcome that is not the very best that they could achieve otherwise (see Fig. 7.2).

	Cooperator	Individualist	Competitor
You get	480	540	480
Other gets	480	280	80

You get	400	500	400
Other gets	400	200	0

FIG. 7.2.   Sample matrices of payoff distributions for decomposed games.

Social motives as measured by decomposed games are predictive of behavior in social bargaining games such as the Prisoner's Dilemma (see Au & Kwong, in press; Van Lange et al., 1997, for reviews). Not surprising, empirical studies show that cooperators tend to cooperate more than individualists who, in turn, tend to play more cooperatively than competitors. Moreover, social motives are also predictive of whether (and how) an individual responds to noncooperation on the part of their opponent. Cooperators and individualists tend to adopt a strategy reminiscent of Tit-for-Tat, where they are initially rather cooperative until their partner fails to exhibit pro-social behavior, in which case they then switch to noncooperative behavior (Kelley & Stahelski, 1970; Van Lange & Visser, 1999). The behavior of competitors, on the other hand, appears to be much less contingent on the behavior of their opponent. Competitors tend to play noncooperatively regardless of what their rival is doing. That is, competitors appear less willing to engage in cooperative behavior even when there are strong incentives for doing so (e.g., when they encounter a strategy such as Tit-for-Tat that explicitly punishes noncooperation).

Why are several different varieties of social motive (and not just one) routinely observed in the adult population? Before exploring the possibility that individual differences in emotion might underlie these individual differences in social motives, the next section briefly reviews the evolutionary conditions under which several different social motives (rather than just one) could be maintained in the same population.

Frequency Dependent Selection of Social Motives: Lomborg's (1996) Nucleus and Shield

Evolutionary pressures need not invariably drive the entire population to adopt a single strategy, such as defection or Tit-for-Tat. In this regard, evolutionarily, game theorists have used the concept of frequency dependent selection to describe conditions under which natural selection could support the stable coexistence of a mix of different strategies in the same population. Frequency dependent selection occurs whenever the success of a strategy depends on the relative frequency of other strategies in the same population (Maynard Smith, 1982). The stable 50:50 sex ratio is a classic example of frequency dependent selection in action. In the case of the two sexes, the success of each strategy (male, female) depends on the relatively frequency of the other strategy in the same population. When one sex becomes more common, it can be shown that the evolutionary payoff for being a member of the rarer sex increases accordingly (Maynard Smith, 1982). As a result, natural selection will begin to favor members of the more rare sex because they will tend to have higher reproductive success. Over time, this process of frequency dependent selection will lead to an increase in the relative frequency of the more rare strategy until some sort of equilibrium is reached. At this equilibrium point, neither strategy benefits from increasing (or decreasing) its relative frequency in the population. For humans, this equilibrium corresponds to an approximately 50:50 sex ratio. Frequency dependent selection can, of course, explain how multiple strategies (not just two) can be maintained in the same population so long as the success of each strategy depends on the relative frequency of other strategies.

Computer simulation studies suggest that frequency dependent selection can be a potent force in determining the structure of the population that emerges over evolutionary time (Lomborg, 1996). In this regard, Lomborg (1996) conducted a series of simulations of the repeated Prisoner's Dilemma in which he built on Axelrod's (1984) original computer tournament. Rather than starting with a diverse set of strategies (as was the case in Axelrod's original tournament), Lomborg's simulations began with all individuals adopting the very same strategy: defection. Lomborg then modeled a noisy world[3] in which this initial population was allowed to evolve via a combination of mutation (modeled by small random changes in strategies), as well as "evolutionary" processes such as innovation and imitation (see Lomborg, 1996, for a detailed account). Lomborg's simulations differed from Axelrod's original tournament in that Lomborg's tournaments allowed as many as 32,768 possible strategies to compete[4] (compared to Axelrod's original set of just 63) and incorporated vastly more agents (an initial population > 1 million compared to Axelrod's initial population of only 63 agents). Other differences included the use of a vast number of generations (100,000 to 300,000 generations compared to just 1000 in Axelrod's original tournament) and a

---

[3]Noise was modeled in these simulations as two types of error: (a) *misimplementations* in which one player makes the mistake of failing to correctly implement the intended strategy (e.g., defecting when the intention was to cooperate and visa versa) and (b) *misperceptions* in which one player behaves as intended, but the other player mistakenly believes that a different choice was made (e.g., falsely believing that an opponent defected when the individual in fact, cooperated, and vice versa).

[4]For technical reasons, Lomborg (1996) restricted his simulations to just 20 coexisting strategies, but because these strategies were allowed to "evolve" via mutation, error, learning, and innovation, the exact composition of these 20 strategies varied over the course of a given simulation run.

format that allowed for simultaneous (rather than a strictly pair-wise) competition among a multitude of strategies.

Lomborg's (1996) simulations revealed that cooperative strategies not only emerged from this pool of initially uncooperative strategies, but they eventually came to occupy a significant portion of a "meta-stable[5]" population structure. This relatively stable structure represented over 60% of the population after 300,000 generations and consisted of variations on just two strategy clusters that Lomborg referred to as the "Nucleus" and "Shield." Although the exact constituents of these clusters varied over time, the *Nucleus* consisted mainly of strategies that exhibited nearly continuous cooperation, despite the noisy and changing environment in which they found themselves. The *Shield*, by contrast, was comprised of a relatively diverse set of "cautious cooperators" who maintained a high level of cooperation with the nucleus (and with themselves), but were also quite successful in repelling aggressive invaders (Lomborg, 1996). The remainder of the population consisted of a relatively diverse set of strategies, including a relatively small number of aggressive noncooperators.

Two processes—variation and imitation[6]—appeared to be responsible for the *emergence* of new strategies (including cooperation) in these simulated worlds that were initially comprised of only defectors (Lomborg, 1996). However, once new strategies emerged, their *maintenance* as relatively stable features of the population (if this occurred at all) appeared to be due to a process of frequency dependent selection. The success of the strategies that comprised the "shield," for example, appeared to be dependent on their ability to maintain a high degree of cooperation with a substantial number of cooperative nucleus strategies. The success of the cooperative strategies in the nucleus depended, in turn, on there being relatively few aggressive noncooperators in the population. Lomborg (1996) found that a significant increase in the number of aggressive noncooperators in the population could cause the relatively stable nucleus-shield structure to collapse. It turned out, paradoxically, that the central obstacle to the maintenance of a cooperative nucleus was the problem of keeping out strategies that were "too nice." If these "too nice" strategies entered the population in significant

---

[5]Although this population structure was not evolutionarily stable in the sense of Maynard Smith's (1982) term, this structure tended to survive as a relatively stable population structure except when aggressive invaders managed to gain a sizable foothold in the population, in which case the nucleus-shield structure tended to collapse.

[6]Variation was modeled in Lomborg's simulation by creating small random changes (innovations) in existing strategies every fourth generation (see Lomborg, 1996). Imitation, on the other hand, was modeled by two different processes. First, Lomborg set the parameters of the model such that .02 % of the population (approximate 200 to 2,000 agents) would adopt any new innovation as soon as it emerged. Second, at the end of each generation a random fraction of the strategies compared their payoffs to a randomly chosen strategy. If the strategy scored fewer points than the randomly chosen strategy, it would switch to that strategy; otherwise the strategy stayed the same. In this environment, new strategies could accumulate over time because the successful innovations were more likely to be imitated. As a result of these dual processes of variation and imitation, cooperative strategies could gain a tentative foothold in this initial population of all defectors.

numbers, they created an environment in which aggressive invaders could thrive. This was the case because aggressive invaders gained points by exploiting these strategies, including the "nice" cooperators located in the nucleus. However, once the shield strategies became established in the population, it was rather difficult (but not impossible) for these aggressive noncooperators to destabilize the nucleus-shield structure. Lomborg (1996, p. 298) noted, "Although it is easy for an innovation to exploit the nucleus, meta-stability works because it is impossible to simultaneously exploit the shield or even do tolerably well against some segment of it." The inability of aggressive noncooperators to compete successfully against the shield strategies—coupled with their relatively poor performance when competing with other noncooperators—often resulted in a frequency dependent population dynamic where the extremely noncooperative strategies tended to comprise only a small portion of the population relative to the more cooperative strategies in the nucleus and shield (Lomborg, 1996).

Lomborg's (1996) findings suggest that in a noisy and changing environment evolutionary selection pressures can generate a frequency dependent population structure consisting of two clusters of relatively cooperative strategists (the nucleus and shield) and a third, much smaller, set of relatively diverse strategies that includes aggressive noncooperators. In Lomborg's simulations, the largest of these clusters (approximately 43% of the population) consisted of highly cooperative strategies. The second largest cluster (the shield) represented approximately 18% of the population and consisted of strategies that, although quite cooperative, appeared to function primarily as a defense against the relatively smaller number of aggressive noncooperators (Lomborg, 1996). The similarities between Lomborg's findings and the known distributions of social motives in the human population are quite intriguing. For example, in a recent review of 47 studies that employed the decomposed game methodology, Au and Kwong (in press) found that just three clusters of social motives accounted for approximately 87% of the adult population. The largest of these clusters represented approximately 46% of the population and consisted of *cooperative* strategists. The second largest cluster consisted of *individualists* who comprised approximately 25% of the population and the smallest cluster consisted of highly noncooperative *competitors* who represented just 13% of the population. Despite the tendency for the percentage of cooperative strategists in the adult population to increase slightly with age, the relative frequencies of these three social motives appears to be quite stable over time with a ratio of approximately 4:2:1 of cooperators, individualists and competitors (see Van Lange et al., 1997). By comparison, Lomborg's (1996) simulations observed a similar ratio in which there were nearly twice as many cooperators in the nucleus as there were cautious strategists in the shield, and where highly aggressive noncooperators represented only a small fraction of the entire population.

EMOTIONS AS STRATEGIES IN SOCIAL GAMES?

Future research might investigate whether behavior in repeated social interactions (e.g., those modeled by the iterated Prisoner's Dilemma) can be predicted or understood not only in terms of game-theoretic concepts (e.g., the folk theorem, Nash equilibria, etc.), but also in terms of individual differences in emotions. One wonders, for example, whether individual differences in emotion could give rise to a nucleus-like cluster of cooperative strategists or a shield-like set of more cautious cooperators analogous to those found in Lomborg's (1996) simulations. One interesting possibility would be to explore whether the propensity to experience guilt feelings (or other sorts of emotions) are trait-like dispositions that are not only stable across time, but are also predictive of strategic behavior in repeated social interactions. In particular, it might be useful to investigate whether the propensity to experience certain moral sentiments, such as guilt feelings, correspond to different varieties of "moral virtues" or social motives that are evolutionarily distributed in the population in a manner suggested by Lomborg's (1996) simulations. Mealey (1995, p. 524, emphasis added) noted that "as long as evolutionary pressures for emotions as reliable communication and commitment devices leading to long-term cooperative strategies coexist with counter pressures for cheating, deception, and 'rational' short-term selfishness, a mixture of phenotypes will result, such that *some sort of statistical equilibrium will be approached.*" Frequency dependent selection is precisely the sort of evolutionary process that is capable of maintaining such a "statistical equilibrium" among several distinct emotion-based phenotypes in the same population. If this is the case, then it might be useful to determine whether emotional signals (or the lack thereof) can be used to identify which individuals correspond to the nucleus of continuous cooperators, the shield of more cautious cooperators, or the aggressive non-cooperators who lie at the periphery of the population.

Another intriguing speculation is that there exists certain individuals in the population who tend to experience a certain amount of schadenfreude-like[7] pleasure from punishing free-riders and noncooperators (see Price, Tooby, & Cosmides, 2001 for a discussion of the role of punitive sentiments in social interactions). Such individuals, if they exist, might be analogous to Lomborg's (1996) shield strategists in the sense that they possess an emotional predisposition (e.g., schadenfreude, contempt) to punish noncooperators in a manner that essentially functions to protect the nucleus of unconditional cooperators with whom they share a frequency dependent symbiosis. Although the human population may not necessarily be comprised of just two clusters of strategists (a nucleus of continuous cooperators and a protective shield of more punitive strategists), game theoretic analyses of strategic interactions (including computer simulations) are consistent with two findings that are repeatedly observed in empirical studies of human cooperation: First, apparently not all members of the population adopt the same strategy and, second, the largest cluster of strategists does in fact appear to be a nucleus of highly cooperative

---

[7]*Schadenfreude* is a German term that refers, roughly, to the experience of positive emotions while observing the demise of an opponent or rival.

individuals. Future research might empirically investigate what role, if any, emotions play in the relatively stable coexistence of these different strategies in the same population.

IMPLICATIONS FOR PUBLIC POLICY

Emotions play a central role in human affairs both public and private. Policy-makers must take into account "emotional exuberance" in the stock markets, road rage on the highways, and people who adopt emotional commitments to strategies that do not appear to be in their immediate self-interest. Despite the rather obvious intrusion of these passions into everyday decision making, it is somewhat surprising to observe that the concept "emotion" is so rarely incorporated into public policy decisions or theoretical models of personal decision making. When it comes to formal game-theoretic accounts of rational decision making, it is not uncommon to observe that the role of emotion is theoretically explored, but then empirically ignored. As a result, relatively little is known about the *empirical* validity of the rich array of theoretically plausible models of how emotions, in principle, might function in strategic decision contexts (e.g., deSousa, 1987; Elster, 1991; Frank, 1988; Hirschleifer, 1987; Nesse, 1990; Nesse & Williams, 1994; Price et al., 2002; Tooby & Cosmides, 1990).

There is reason to be optimistic, however, that future research in the game theoretic tradition might incorporate a more *empirical* approach that includes an examination of the possible role of emotions in public and private decision making. Such optimism stems from the observation that emotional dispositions can be easily assessed via self-reported subjective mental states or through more objective behavioral indices such as facial expressions. One advantage to exploring emotions as predictors of behavior in strategic interactions is that such an approach avoids the obvious problem of circularity that often confronts researchers who use measures of social motives to predict behavior. Because social motives are typically defined as tendencies to prefer particular outcomes in decomposed games, it is not surprising to then observe that individuals with cooperative motives behave cooperatively, whereas individuals with less cooperative motives tend to behave less cooperatively. Whereas it is informative to know that these social motives are relatively stable trait-like dispositions (Van Lange et al., 1997), it remains for future research to discern the actual psychological mechanisms underlying these individually different preferences for outcomes. In this regard, investigating the link between emotions and social motives may prove useful.

This chapter began with a reminder that identifying an effective public policy is often quite difficult precisely because many of the decision scenarios encountered actually support the stable coexistence of several successful strategies, rather than just one. We then reviewed how game theoretic concepts such as frequency dependent selection and the folk theorem can inform policymakers and decision analysts about the conditions under which several different strategies can succeed in the very same population. Unfortunately, these concepts (frequency dependent selection, the folk theorem) say relatively little about the actual psychological mechanisms that give rise to these individually different strategies. In this regard, it was argued that emotion theory might provide a nice compliment to game theory. When combined with game theoretic insights, emotion theories (e.g., Smith's, 1759/2000, theory of moral sentiments or Frank's, 1988, theory of emotional commitments) can provide valuable insights into why not everyone adopts the same strategy in social interactions that take the form of indefinitely repeated games. If these emotion theories can be successfully integrated with game theory, policymakers and decision theorists might obtain a clearer understanding of why the human population is not comprised solely of individuals with cooperative motives, but instead appears to reflect a mix of strategists ranging from those who display a detached and ruthless pursuit of immediate self-interest to those who tend toward more kindhearted acts of cooperation.

ACKNOWLEDGMENTS

This chapter benefited from helpful comments from Deborah Alonzo, Winton Au, Gregg Bromgard, Charles Crawford, Catherine Salmon, and David Trafimow.

REFERENCES

Au, W. T., & Kwong, J. Y. Y. (in press). Measurement and effects of social value orientation in social dilemmas: A review. In R. Suleieman, D. V. Budescu, I. Fischer, & D. Messick (Eds.), *Contemporary psychological research on social dilemmas.* Cambridge, England: Cambridge University Press.

Axelrod, R. (1980a). Effective choice in the Prisoner's Dilemma. *Journal of Conflict Resolution, 24,* 3–25.

Axelrod, R. (1980b). More effective choice in the Prisoner's Dilemma. *Journal of Conflict Resolution, 24,* 379–403.

Axelrod, R. (1984). *The evolution of cooperation.* New York: Basic Books.

Binmore, K. (1998). *Game theory and the social contract: Vol. 2. Just playing.* Cambridge, MA: MIT Press.

Chapman, M., Zahn-Waxler, C., Cooperman, G., & Iannotie, R. (1987). Empathy and responsibility in the motivation of children's helping. *Developmental Psychology, 23,* 140–145.

Cialdini, R. B., Darby, B. L., & Vincent, J. E. (1973). Transgression and altruism: A case for hedonism. *Journal of Experimental Social Psychology, 9,* 502–516.

Clore, G. L., Schwarz, N., & Conway, M. (1994). Affective causes and consequences of social information processing. In R. S. Wyer & T. Srull (Eds.), *The handbook of social cognition* (2nd ed., pp. 323–417). Hillsdale, NJ: Lawrence Erlbaum Associates.

Cunningham, M. R., Steinberg, J., & Grev, R. (1980). Wanting to and having to help: Separate motivations for positive mood and guilt-induced helping. *Journal of Personality and Social Psychology, 38,* 181–192.

Demasio, A. R. (1994). *Descartes' error: Emotion, reason and the human brain.* New York: Grosset/Putnam.

deSousa, R. (1987). *The rationality of emotion.* Cambridge, MA: MIT Press.

Dixit, A., & Skeath, S. (1999). *Games of strategy.* New York: Norton.

Elster, J. (1995). Rationality and the emotions. *The Economic Journal, 116,* 1386–1397.

Estrada-Hollenbeck, M., & Heatherton, T. F. (1998). Avoiding and alleviating guilt through prosocial behavior. In J. Bybee (Ed.), *Guilt and children* (pp. 215–231). New York: Academic Press.

Frank, R. H. (1988). *Passions within reason: The strategic role of the emotions.* New York: Norton.

Frank, R. H. (2001). Cooperation through emotional commitment. In R. M. Nesse (Ed.), *Evolution and the capacity for commitment* (pp. 57–76). New York: Russell Sage Foundation.

Fundenberg, D., & Tirole, J. (2000). *Game theory.* Cambridge, MA: MIT Press.

Hirshleifer, J. (1987). On the emotions as guarantors of threats and promises. In J. Dupré (Ed.), *The latest on the best: Essays on evolution and optimality* (pp. 307–326). Boston: MIT Press.

Hirshleifer, J. (1999). There are many evolutionary pathways to cooperation. *Journal of Bioeconomics, 1,* 73–93.

Hirshleifer, J. (2001). Game-theoretic interpretations of commitment. In R. M. Nesse (Ed.), *Evolution and the capacity for commitment* (pp. 77–92). New York: Russell Sage Foundation.

Hirschleifer, J., & Martinez Coll, J. C. (1988). What strategies can support the evolutionary emergence of cooperation? *Journal of Conflict Resolution, 32,* 367–398.

Hirschleifer, J., & Martinez Coll, J. C. (1991). The limits of reciprocity. *Rationality and Society, 3,* 35–64.

Isen, A. M., Clark, M. S., & Schwartz, M. F. (1976). Duration of the effect of good mood on helping: "Footprints on the sand of time." *Journal of Personality and Social Psychology, 34,* 385–393.

Isen, A. M., & Simmonds, S. F. (1978). The effect of feeling good on a helping task that is incompatible with good mood. *Social Psychology, 41,* 346–349.

Kelley, H. H., & Stahelski, A. J. (1970). Social interaction basis of cooperators and competitor's beliefs about others. *Journal of Personality and Social Psychology, 16,* 66–91.

Ketelaar, T., & Au, W. T. (2003). The effects of guilty feelings on the behavior of uncooperative individuals in repeated social bargaining games: An affect-as-information interpretation of the role of emotion in social interaction. *Cognition & Emotion, 17,* 429–453.

Ketelaar, T., & Todd, P. (2001). Framing our thoughts: Ecological rationality as evolutionary psychology's answer to the frame problem. In H. R. Holcomb, III (Ed.), *Conceptual challenges in evolutionary psychology* (pp. 179–211). Dordrecht: Kluwer Academic.

Koller, D., Megiddo, N., & von Stengel, B. (1996). Efficient computation of equilibria for extensive two-person games. *Games and Economic Behavior, 14,* 247–259.

Koller, D., & Pfeffer, A. (1997). Representations and solutions for game-theoretic problems. *Artificial Intelligence, 94,* 167–215.

Kuhn, H. W., & Nasar, S. (Eds.). (2002). *The essential John Nash.* Princeton, NJ: Princeton University Press.

Lerner, J., & Keltner, D. (2001). Fear, anger, and risk. *Journal of Personality and Social Psychology, 81,* 146–159.

Loewenstein, G. (1987). Anticipation and the valuation of delayed consumption. *Economic Journal, 97,* 666–684.

Lomborg, B. (1996). Nucleus and shield: The evolution of social structure in the iterated Prisoner's Dilemma. *American Sociological Review, 61,* 278–307,

Maynard Smith, J. (1982). *Evolution and the theory of games.* Cambridge, England: Cambridge University Press.

Mealey, L. (1995). The sociobiology of sociopathy: An integrated evolutionary model. *Behavioral and Brain Sciences, 18,* 523–599.

Messick, D. M., & McClintock, C. G. (1968). Motivational bases of choice in experiments. *Journal of Experimental Social Psychology, 4,* 1–25.

Nash, J. (1951). Non-cooperative games. *Annals of Mathematics, 54,* 286–295.

Nesse, R. (1990). Evolutionary explanations of emotions. *Human Nature, 1*, 261–289.

Nesse, R., & Williams, G. (1994). *Why we get sick: The new science of Darwinian medicine.* New York: Times Books.

Poundstone, W. (1992). *Prisoner's dilemma: John von Neumann, game theory, and the puzzle of the bomb.* New York: Anchor.

Price, M. E., Tooby, J., & Cosmides, L. (2001). Punitive sentiment as an anti-free rider psychological device. *Evolution and Human Behavior, 23*, 203–231.

Rasmussen, E. (1994). *Games and information: An introduction to game theory* (2nd ed.). Cambridge, MA: Blackwell.

Regan, J. W. (1971). Guilt, perceived injustice, and altruistic behavior. *Journal of Personality and Social Psychology, 18*, 124–132.

Regan, D. T., Williams, M., & Sparling, S. (1972). Voluntary expiation of guilt: A field experiment. *Journal of Personality and Social Psychology, 24*, 42–45.

Ridley, M. (1996). *The origins of virtue: Human instincts and the evolution of cooperation.* New York: Penguin Putnam.

Rozin, P., Lowery, L., Imada, S., & Haidt, J. (1999). The CAD triad hypothesis: A mapping between three moral emotions (contempt, anger, disgust) and three moral codes (community, autonomy, divinity). *Journal of Personality and Social Psychology, 76*, 574–586.

Shannon, C. E. (1950). Programming a computer to play Chess. *Philosophical Magazine, 41*, 256–275.

Smith, A. (1759/2000). *The theory of moral sentiments.* New York: Prometheus Books.

Smith, C. A., & Ellsworth, P. C. (1985). Patterns of cognitive appraisal in emotion. *Journal of Personality and Social Psychology, 48*, 813–838.

Thaler, R. H. (1992). *The winner's curse: Paradoxes and anomalies of economic life.* Princeton, NJ: Princeton University Press.

Tooby, J., & Cosmides, L. (1990). The past explains the present: Emotional adaptations and the structure of ancestral environments." *Ethology and Sociobiology, 11*, 375–424.

Trivers, R. L. (1971). The evolution of reciprocal altruism. *Quarterly Review of Biology, 46*, 35–57.

Trivers, R. (1985). *Social evolution.* Menlo Park, CA: Benjamin/Cummings.

Van Lange, P. A. M., & Visser, K. (1999). Locomotion in social dilemmas: How people adapt to cooperative, tit-for-tat, and noncooperative partners. *Journal of Personality and Social Psychology, 77*, 762–773.

Van Lange, P. A. M., Otten, W., DeBruin, E. M. N., & Joireman, J. A. (1997). Development of prosocial, individualistic, and competitive orientations: Theory and preliminary evidence. *Journal of Personality and Social Psychology, 73*, 733–746.

Von Neuman, J., & Morgenstern, O. (1944). *The theory of games and economic behavior.* Princeton, NJ: Princeton University Press.

Natural Law
and Natural Selection:
Deontic Reasoning as Part
of Evolved Human Nature

Laurence Fiddick
ESRC Centre for Economic Learning and Social Evolution

The application of evolutionary psychology, with its emphasis on a universal human nature, to natural law legal analyses, which seek to ground human laws in human nature, would appear to be an obvious practical extension of the former. Indeed, evolutionary psychological research on deontic reasoning speaks directly to questions of intuitive conceptions of rights and duties that may conceivably guide legal reasoning. Evolutionary psychology can, therefore, buttress theories of natural law at one of their weakest points by providing scientifically credible foundations for the basic concepts of the approach: rights, duties, human nature, and so on that have often appeared metaphysically suspect. The fit between evolutionary psychology and natural law is far from perfect however. Besides simply lending scientific credence to natural law theories' conceptual framework, evolutionary investigations of deontic reasoning also raise questions about the adequacy of that framework. This chapter reviews the psychological literature in detail, exploring the convergences and divergences with jurisprudence in an effort to reach a balanced assessment of the support evolutionary theorizing has to offer natural law theories.

HUMAN NATURE IN NATURAL LAW
AND EVOLUTIONARY PSYCHOLOGY

Natural law has a venerable history, being traced back at least as far as Plato and Aristotle and finding important advocates through history such as Aquinas and Locke. Natural law theories propose that legal systems are based on prior conceptions of right and/or duty that are part of our human nature, bestowed on us by God or as part of our species' essential characteristics. It is the view that law is an elaboration of morality or at least ought to conform to moral principle. Opposed to natural law theory is the view, known as legal positivism, that law is a matter of social convention. Legal positivism has an equally ancient pedigree stretching back to the Sophists and finds mainstream support within modern Anglo-American legal scholarship. According to the legal positivists, legal rights and duties are founded, not in a prior framework of social norms, but in acts of social agreement or political coercion. Legal positivists do not necessarily deny the existence of prior social norms, they just question whether these underlie laws of society: Laws are the product of social construction and not a reflection of essential human nature.

Anyone familiar with the debate over sociobiology and evolutionary psychology in the social sciences will easily recognize the parallels with the natural law–legal positivism debate in law. In the social sciences, evolutionary analyses of human thought and behavior have been contrasted with what Tooby and Cosmides (1992) called the "standard social science model," which is the view that the human mind and culture are boundlessly variable social constructions: Anthropology studies the socially constructed, cultural content that shapes individuals' lives, whereas psychology studies the generalized learning mechanisms that make the acquisition of this content possible. Evolutionary psychologists, on the other hand, have attempted to resurrect the notion of a universal human nature, arguing that a large degree of mental content is built-in by natural selection and it is this evolved mental structure that broadly shapes human cultures. Besides confronting a common foe in social constructivism, evolutionary psychology can potentially put natural law on a stronger scientific footing by giving a thoroughly materialistic account of human nature.

By combining the modern computational theory of mind with the theory of evolution through natural selection, evolutionary psychology naturalizes human nature in two respects. First, the computational theory of mind (see Pinker, 1997)—the theory that mental processes can be viewed as computations over mental representations—provides a completely materialistic theory of thought. Although the theory may eventually prove to be an inadequate account of human intelligence, the existence of working computational devices like modern computers demonstrates the ontological plausibility of theories proposing to explain human thought in terms of mental representations and the computational transformations thereof. Second, by invoking natural selection as the artificer, evolutionary psychology provides an equally materialistic account of the origins of human thought. Human nature, according to evolutionary psychology, is not imprinted by the hand of God, but is the end product of the natural selection favoring ever more efficient and effective designs for reproduction and survival, regardless of whether the object in question is the human hand or the human mind. Moreover, human nature is universal to all humans, owing to our common heritage as a species. Human nature naturalized in this way appears more ontologically sound to modern sensibilities than earlier appeals to divine creation or, failing that, to remaining silent. Despite the obvious parallels between evolutionary psychology and natural law theory, this chapter argues that the picture is more complicated when evolutionary investigations of deontic reasoning, the domain of thought with the greatest relevance to law, are considered.

THE PSYCHOLOGY OF DEONTIC REASONING

Deontic reasoning is reasoning about *permission*, *obligation*, and *prohibition*: what one *may*, *must* and *must not* do, respectively. It is reasoning about acts, not facts: whether or not a particular action conforms to or violates a rule and not whether a description of the world is true or entailed by other descriptive statements. The relevance of deontic reasoning to legal reasoning is straightforward. As a system of rules that constrain and guide action, law constitutes a special class of deontic rules. Legal reasoning is a form of deontic reasoning. Likewise, moral rules are deontic rules. The deontic domain, more generally, is the superordinate category that includes both legal rules and moral rules, regardless of any overlap there may be between these two subdomains.

Deontic Reasoning in the Moral Development Literature

Deontic reasoning has been extensively studied in two separate psychological literatures: the moral reasoning literature and the cognitive reasoning literature. The focus of the moral reasoning literature, as the name implies, has been on moral rules, but it is also a literature that is heavily developmental. Earlier investigations of moral development by Piaget (1932/1999) and Kohlberg (1981, 1984) appeared to suggest that full moral competence was an ability that developed in adolescence, if at all, with a considerable body of research seeming to suggest that entire cultures (Shweder, Mahapatra, & Miller, 1987) and females (Gilligan, 1982) were delayed in their moral development according to the Piagetian/Kohlbergian framework. Findings such as these lend little support for a universal human nature. However, Piaget and Kohlberg's analyses of moral competence have been criticized as being biased against both non-Western cultures (Shweder, 1982b; Shweder et al., 1987) and females (Gilligan, 1982). These charges of bias provide little comfort to the defenders of human nature for they presuppose important cultural and sex-related differences in moral reasoning. However, the problems posed by Piaget and Kohlberg's research are more apparent than real because the cross-cultural and sex-related differences are to some extent a methodological artifact. What children and non- Western adults lack is not reasoned moral intuitions, but an inclination or ability to express those intuitions in the manner of a moral philosopher as demanded by Piaget and Kohlberg's methodology (Shweder, 1982a). When children's sociomoral competence is probed in a different manner, by questioning their implicit knowledge of distinctions between different domains of action, they display much earlier competence, both cross-culturally and across both sexes.

Instead of treating sociomoral competence as an undifferentiated ability that develops uniformly and in stages as Piaget and Kohlberg did, advocates of the "domain theory" of moral development have sought indirect evidence for children's moral knowledge by posing questions designed to elicit contrasting judgments of rules and violations in different domains of action. Turiel and his colleagues (see Turiel, 1998, or Smetana, 1995a, for a review of this literature) proposed that there are three distinct domains of action: the moral domain, the social conventional domain, and the psychological domain. In the moral domain, social actions are regulated by prescriptions that are "obligatory, universally applicable (in that they apply to everyone in individual circumstances), impersonal (in that they are not based on personal preferences), and determined by criteria other than agreement, consensus, or institutional convention" (Smetana, 1995a, p. 86). Other social actions fall within the domain of the social conventional. The rules governing actions in this domain are "arbitrary and agreed-on behavioral uniformities that structure interactions within social systems" (Smetana, 1995a, p. 87). Actions in the psychological domain are nonsocial and primarily have consequences for the self. The psychological domain includes both personal and prudential acts.

According to the domain theory of moral reasoning, both children and adults reason about acts falling within different domains in characteristically distinct ways. There is considerable evidence that adults and even young children make distinctions between rules regulating actions in different domains. Children and adults give domain-specific reasons for rules (e.g., Nucci, 1981; Nucci & Weber, 1995; Song, Smetana, & Sang, 1987; Turiel, 1983). For example, children tend to cite issues of welfare or fairness as justifications for moral rules, but instead tend to cite social agreement/coordination and prevailing customs/rules as justifications for social conventions (Nucci, Camino, & Sapiro, 1996; Song et al., 1987). Children and adults judge the permissibility of rule violations in a domain-specific manner (e.g., Nucci, 1981; Nucci et al., 1996; Nucci & Weber, 1995; Song et al., 1987; Tisak, 1993; Tisak & Turiel, 1984, 1988; Turiel, 1983). For example, children tend to believe that moral rules should never be violated and apply to all peoples, while social conventional rules may sometimes be legitimately violated and need not be followed by different social groups (Nucci et al., 1996; Song et al., 1987). Children and adults evaluate the seriousness of rule violations in a domain-specific manner (e.g., Nucci, 1981; Smetana & Bitz, 1996; Song et al., 1987;

Tisak, 1993; Tisak & Turiel, 1984, 1988; Turiel, 1983). For example, children judge violations of moral rules to be more serious than violations of social conventional or prudential rules, even when they are matched for degree of harm (Tisak, 1993; Tisak & Turiel, 1984, 1988). Children and adults judge the legitimacy of intervention in a domain-specific manner (e.g., Nucci et al., 1996; Nucci & Weber, 1995; Smetana, 1995b; Smetana & Asquith, 1994; Smetana & Bitz, 1996). For example, adolescents believe that parents and teachers have legitimate authority to regulate actions in the moral, conventional, and prudential domains, but not in the personal domain—although they sometimes disagree about what acts fall within what domain (Smetana & Asquith, 1994; Smetana & Bitz, 1996). One notable exception to these findings are psychopaths, who are unable to distinguish between moral rules and social conventional rules (Blair, 1995). But, given that psychopathy is probably an abnormal developmental outcome, this exception is entirely consistent with the proposal that deontic reasoning is a reliably developing component of human nature. The recent literature on moral reasoning, therefore, provides wide empirical support for the early emergence of multifaceted distinctions between different domains of social reasoning, but more importantly for present concerns, there is much greater cross-cultural and cross-sex consistency in these patterns of reasoning (though see Miller, Bersoff, & Harwood, 1990).

Deontic Reasoning in the Cognitive Reasoning Literature

Deontic reasoning has also been investigated independently in the cognitive reasoning literature. A large amount of the interest in deontic rules in this literature stems from the facilitatory effect that such rules have on performance on the Wason selection task. In the Wason selection task (Wason, 1968), participants are given a conditional rule that is said to apply to four cards containing information pertaining to the rule (see Fig. 8.1). The participants' task is to determine which of the four cards they would need to turn over to determine whether the rule has been violated. A conditional of the form: *If P then Q*, is violated in situations in which *P* is true and *Q* is false, instances of *P & not-Q*. The seemingly straightforward solution is to investigate situations in which *P* is true and situations in which *Q* is false in order to detect any possible instances of *P & not-Q*. On the selection task, this would require turning over cards with the information *P* or *not-Q*. The remarkable thing about the task is that, despite its apparent simplicity, it is notoriously difficult for people to solve correctly. Typically, fewer than 10% of participants give the logically correct solution to the task (see Evans, Newstead, & Byrne, 1993, for a review).

When deontic conditionals are employed, performance on the task increases substantially (e.g., Cheng & Holyoak, 1985; Cosmides, 1989; Gigerenzer & Hug, 1992; Girotto, Blaye, & Farioli, 1989; Griggs & Cox, 1982; Manktelow & Over, 1992). For example, when Griggs and Cox (1982, exp. 3) gave participants a version of the selection task employing the rule, *If a person is drinking beer, then the person must be over 19 years of age* (see Fig. 8.2), 70% solved it correctly, whereas not a single participant correctly solved an abstract, descriptive version of the task

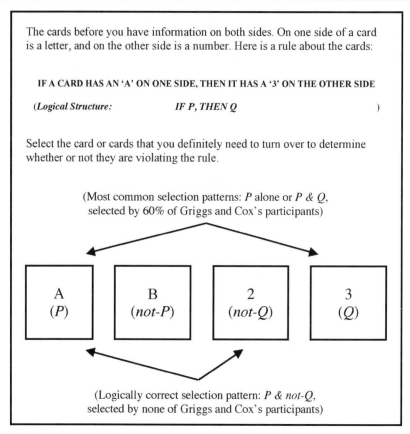

The cards before you have information on both sides. On one side of a card is a letter, and on the other side is a number. Here is a rule about the cards:

IF A CARD HAS AN 'A' ON ONE SIDE, THEN IT HAS A '3' ON THE OTHER SIDE

(*Logical Structure:*   *IF P, THEN Q*   )

Select the card or cards that you definitely need to turn over to determine whether or not they are violating the rule.

(Most common selection patterns: *P* alone or *P & Q*, selected by 60% of Griggs and Cox's participants)

| A | B | 2 | 3 |
| (*P*) | (*not-P*) | (*not-Q*) | (*Q*) |

(Logically correct selection pattern: *P & not-Q*, selected by none of Griggs and Cox's participants)

FIG. 8.1.   Descriptive selection task. Adapted from Griggs and Cox, 1982.

employing the rule, *If a card has an "A" on one side, then it has a "3" on the other side*. The drinking age rule is a conditional obligation of the form: *If P then Must Q*. It is also a fairly familiar rule, especially when compared with the abstract letter and numbers rule. It was this familiarity that Griggs and Cox initially thought accounted for improved performance. However, subsequent experiments have shown rather conclusively that it is the deontic nature of the rule and not its familiarity that influences participants' performance (Cheng & Holyoak, 1985; Cosmides, 1989). For example, studies show that people are able to solve deontic versions of the selection task employing such exotic rules as, *If a man eats cassava root, then he must have a tattoo on his face*, while simultaneously being unable to solve nondeontic versions of the task employing mundane rules such as, *If a person goes into Boston, then he takes the subway* (Cosmides, 1989).

   The experimental evidence further suggests that people are competent at reasoning about both obligation and permission. Where a conditional obligation is a rule of the form, *If P then Must Q*, a conditional permission is a rule of the form, *If P*

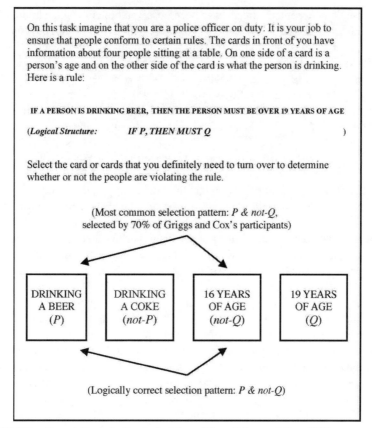

On this task imagine that you are a police officer on duty. It is your job to ensure that people conform to certain rules. The cards in front of you have information about four people sitting at a table. On one side of a card is a person's age and on the other side of the card is what the person is drinking. Here is a rule:

IF A PERSON IS DRINKING BEER, THEN THE PERSON MUST BE OVER 19 YEARS OF AGE

(Logical Structure: ***IF P, THEN MUST Q***   )

Select the card or cards that you definitely need to turn over to determine whether or not the people are violating the rule.

(Most common selection pattern: *P & not-Q*,
selected by 70% of Griggs and Cox's participants)

| DRINKING A BEER (P) | DRINKING A COKE (not-P) | 16 YEARS OF AGE (not-Q) | 19 YEARS OF AGE (Q) |

(Logically correct selection pattern: *P & not-Q*)

FIG. 8.2.   Prescriptive selection task. Adapted from Griggs and Cox, 1982.

then May Q. According to classical logic, these rules are logically identical, *If P then Q*, because classical logic does not accord any special status to the deontic terms *must* and *may*. Hence, from the perspective of classical logic people ought to select the *P* and *not-Q* cards regardless of whether the rule is an obligation or a permission. These two different types of rule are distinguished within deontic logic such that whereas *P & not-Q* is a violation of the conditional obligation, *not-P & Q* is a violation of the conditional permission. On versions of the selection task employing "switched" deontic rules (i.e., permissions as opposed to obligations; e.g., Cosmides, 1989) and "switched perspectives" where the focus is on one party's right (permission) as opposed to the other party's duty (obligation; e.g., Gigerenzer & Hug, 1992; Holyoak & Cheng, 1995; Manktelow & Over, 1991; Politzer & Nguyen-Xuan, 1992), people select the deontically appropriate *not-P* and *Q* cards. This suggests both that people are competent at making appropriate distinctions between permissions and obligations and they are not simply solving the task "logically."

These deontic content effects have been observed both in young children (e.g., Cummins, 1996b; Harris & Nuñez, 1996; Harris, Nuñez, & Brett, 2001; Nuñez & Harris, 1998) and cross-culturally, both in Western cultures (e.g., Cheng & Holyoak, 1985; Cosmides, 1989; Johnson-Laird, P. Legrenzi, & M. Legrenzi, 1972) and non-Western cultures (e.g., Cheng & Holyoak, 1985; Harris et al., 2001; Sugiyama, Tooby, & Cosmides, 2002). Sugiyama et al. (2002) even found these effects in preliterate, Amazonian hunter-horticulturalists. Hence, the cognitive literature also provides evidence of a universal, early-emerging deontic competence.

THE EVOLUTION OF DEONTIC REASONING

Two largely independent psychological literatures suggest that humans possess a universal and early emerging deontic competence. This raises the question: Where did it come from? This is not a question that the recent literature on moral development has devoted much attention to. In the Piagetian/Kohlbergian framework, this question was not as pressing because the level of competence postulated for young children was minimal, but domain theorists have proposed and found a more complex understanding of the social world at an early age. One obvious line of explanation for this deontic competence, or any reliably developing functional trait of some complexity, is natural selection (Dawkins, 1986) and it is within the cognitive literature that evolutionary theorizing about the adaptive function of deontic reasoning has been most prominent. Cummins (1996a, 1996b), for example, drew attention to the fact that humans, like most primates, have long lived within structured social environments in which behavior is highly constrained through a complex set of implicit social norms governing access to resources such as food and mates. In such a normative environment, the ability to easily and accurately assess which actions are permitted, obligated, and prohibited would have been favored by natural selection. This ability, Cummins argued, is achieved by the use of an innate deontic competence comprised of the ability to mentally represent and reason about deontic concepts.

Fiddick et al. (2000) argued that this may be too coarse a grain of analysis. The adaptive problems that need to be solved may have been more specific, at least with respect to the natural history of *Homo sapiens*. Given the expanded role of social cooperation in human societies and the hazards associated with humans' equally elaborated technological abilities, it could be argued that there were sufficient and divergent selection pressures for the evolution of distinct social and precautionary reasoning abilities. Deontic reasoning might best be viewed as the product of a collection of more domain-specific abilities, whereas in Cummins' view a more general deontic reasoning ability is the hypothesized adaptation.

The majority opinion within the cognitive reasoning literature clearly sides with Cummins' view that deontic reasoning is an undifferentiated ability (e.g., Cheng & Holyoak, 1985, 1989; Girotto et al., 1989; Manktelow & Over, 1990, 1991, 1995; Oaksford & Chater, 1994; Sperber, Cara, & Girotto, 1995). Yet, it is at odds with the moral reasoning literature where a clear distinction is made between social and nonsocial prudential rules (Smetana, 1995a). The moral reasoning literature would appear to accord better with Fiddick et al.'s more domain-specific proposal.

The empirical support for these two proposals would appear to hang on the relative merits of these two contrasting literatures. Does one literature or the other have a better grasp of deontic reasoning and what sense can be made of this discrepancy? It has been argued that the discrepancy between these two literatures is in part explained by cognitive reasoning researchers' reliance on a single task, the Wason selection task, suggesting a serious empirical weakness with the cognitive literature (Fiddick, 2004).

Given the selection task's history as a test of logical reasoning, cognitive psychologists routinely ignore the content of participants' selections, choosing instead to characterize performance according to an abstract logical assignment of the cards they select. Logically, participants may make identical selections even though the content of those selections may vary wildly. It is as though researchers equated responses on two questionnaires not on the basis of the questions' and answers' content, but on the basis of whether participants selected option A, B, C, or D. Although this may seem like a ridiculous strategy for comparing performance on questionnaires where the response options are merely a methodological convenience, it is more tempting to do so on the selection task where the response options are theoretically significant given that one is studying logical reasoning. However, placing so much weight on a logical characterization of performance is particularly dubious for deontic versions of the selection task given that most cognitive psychologists have long since abandoned the hypothesis that participants are reasoning logically on such versions of the task (Evans, 2002).

In contrast to the cognitive literature on deontic reasoning, a wider variety of methods have been employed in the moral reasoning literature. Moreover, the methods employed in the moral reasoning literature were designed specifically for studying deontic reasoning and not logical reasoning as was the selection task. When the methods of the moral reasoning literature are applied to the materials from the selection task literature, a more consistent pattern of results emerges in which participants make systematic distinctions between different classes of deontic rules (Fiddick, 2004). For example, in the moral reasoning literature, Rozin, Lowery, Imada, and Haidt (1999) presented experimental evidence suggesting that violations of different moral codes are associated with different emotional reactions. Adapting the methods that they used to the scenarios employed in the selection task literature, Fiddick (2004, exp. 2) observed a similar dissociation between different classes of deontic rules, despite the fact that the rules all elicited comparable performance on the selection task. Namely, violations of social contract rules were associated with angry reactions while violations of precautions were associated with fearful reactions. The permissibility of social contract and precaution rule violations were also evaluated differently and contrasting reasons were given for following such rules (Fiddick, 2004, exp. 1). Hence, the same pattern of domain-specific reasoning found in the moral reasoning literature was replicated with the materials of the cognitive reasoning literature when different methods were employed. Given that the similarity in selection task performance between different types of deontic rules appears to be artifactual, the weight of empirical evidence would appear to favor a more domain-specific analysis of deontic reasoning.

Multiple Adaptations for Deontic Reasoning

Tooby and Cosmides (1992) argued that the human mind is composed of a collection of mental adaptations, each specially designed by natural selection to solve a specific adaptive problem. The reasons for this are twofold: the computational power of domain-specific processes and the functional incompatibility of optimal solutions to different problems.

Artificial intelligence researchers make a distinction between weak and strong methods (Newell & Simon, 1972). Weak methods apply across a wide range of problems, but are inferentially weak. Strong methods, which employ a considerable amount of domain knowledge, are restricted in their application, but inferentially powerful (although they may be quite simple computationally; see Gigerenzer, Todd, and the ABC Research Group, 1999). For example, novices attempting to solve a problem will usually employ weak methods that have general applicability, whereas people with expertise for solving the problem typically have a considerable amount of domain knowledge that allows them to employ content-specific strong methods (Newell & Simon, 1972). Given the effectiveness and efficiency of strong methods, natural selection should favor the evolution of strong methods as solutions to ancestral problems where there are significant fitness dividends to be paid.

Furthermore, it is often the case that the optimal solution to one problem is functionally incompatible with the optimal solution to a second problem. For example, the design requirements for cold food storage are incompatible with those for cooking the food. Hence, a device that is optimally designed for the former is poorly designed for the latter. When the solutions to two adaptive problems are functionally incompatible in this way, natural selection should favor the evolution of two distinct mechanisms (Sherry & Schacter, 1987). Hence, generality without functional incompatibility and a loss of computational power can be achieved through the evolution of more, not fewer, domain-specific mechanisms—the so-called Swiss-army knife model of human mental adaptations (Tooby & Cosmides, 1992).

Deontic reasoning provides an excellent showcase for this model of human nature. At a more general level, different mechanisms might be expected for handling deontic reasoning as applied to social rules and directives for avoiding physical hazards. Hence, Cosmides, Tooby, and their colleagues (Cosmides, 1989; Cosmides & Tooby, 1989, 1992; Fiddick, Cosmides, & Tooby, 2000; Stone, Cosmides, Tooby, Kroll, & Knight, 2002) proposed that deontic reasoning is more specialized. It can be further subdivided into distinct subdomains of reasoning mapping onto different adaptive problems, namely, social exchange and hazard management. These cognitive adaptations support, but not exhaustively, those patterns of reasoning that are typically classified as deontic.

The Adaptive Problem of Social Exchange

The social world and the physical world impose different computational demands on an organism. Dennett (1987) argued that people possess several different strategies for predicting the behavior of objects (e.g., the physical stance and the intentional stance). The appropriateness of adopting any one strategy depends on the behavioral complexity of the object being dealt with. The physical stance assumes the lowest degree of behavioral complexity. Knowledge of the physical situation and the laws of physics, regardless of whether this is folk or scientific knowledge, are combined to predict the relatively simple law-like behavior of an object. As a predictive strategy, the physical stance works fairly well for midsized, rigid objects. At a higher order of complexity, the behavior of objects such as humans is not so easily predicted by the their physics alone, but instead is heavily influenced both by their internal organization and the way that they process information from the environment. When predicting a person's behavior, it is not sufficient to know that the person weighs so many kilograms and is traveling at a specific speed. His behavior, assuming that he is not falling from a building, will be much more complicated and better understood by postulating that he is rationally pursuing a goal on the basis of beliefs that are likely to be held by him. This strategy of imputing beliefs, desires, and rationality in order to predict the behavior of complexly organized systems is what Dennett called the intentional stance.

There is considerable psychological evidence that these cognitive strategies are reliably developing components of the human mind. Cognitive developmental research suggests that even very young infants expect solid, rigid objects to behave in ways suggested by classical mechanics (A. Brown, 1990; Leslie, 1994; Spelke, 1990), whereas infants also show an understanding of purposes and desires (Cassidy, 1998; Repacholi & Gopnik, 1997) and 3- to 4-year-old children can successfully infer others' behavior on the basis of their beliefs (Baron-Cohen, 1995; Leslie, 1994; Wimmer & Perner, 1983). Furthermore, studies of autism suggest that these competences are psychologically dissociable: People with autism show specific impairments in their understanding of intentional states (Baron-Cohen, 1995). Hence, there is evidence for distinct, reliably developing competencies that bear a considerable resemblance to Dennett's physical stance and intentional stance.

Reasoning about social interactions and hazards draw differentially on these comprehension strategies. The social world of higher primates has been likened to a game of chess (Humphrey, 1984) in which decisions are made, in part, in reaction to the decisions of an opponent. Although the rules and the purpose of the game are clear and simple, the outcome of this process of move and countermove is highly unpredictable at the outset. Beyond simply knowing the rules of the game that constrain play, a skilled player needs to be able to monitor the current state of play and this will crucially involve monitoring an opponent's own understanding of the current state of play, neither of which can be inferred in advance from the rules. In order to succeed in social games, such as coalition formation, mating, and so on, our ancestors needed to adopt the intentional stance, and so, Baron-Cohen (1995) argued, a set of cognitive adaptations embodying the intentional stance evolved, including a theory of mind module (ToMM) that forms representations of others' mental states.

One comparatively simple game of social chess is social exchange—reciprocal cooperation for mutual benefit (see Cosmides & Tooby, 1989, 1992). The decision players have to make is simple: Cooperate at some cost to themselves or do not cooperate and suffer no cost. Additionally, if their partner decides to cooperate, then they receive the benefit of their cooperation. "Gains in trade" can potentially be made whenever the benefit individuals derive from their partner's cooperation outweighs the costs they pay for cooperating themselves. Yet, these gains are difficult to realize because, although both parties stand to benefit by mutual cooperation, they each would be better off not cooperating, either cheating a cooperative partner or avoiding being cheated by an uncooperative partner. One way out of this impasse is the punishment/exclusion of cheaters in subsequent rounds of the game (Axelrod, 1984; Axelrod & Hamilton, 1981; Trivers, 1971). However, this is only part of the solution, because in order for cooperation to ever pay under this model, there has to be a sufficient number of cooperators in the environment in the first place and this cannot be assumed in the initial stages of a trait's evolution when it is a rare mutant. It is here that the intentional stance helps to get things off the ground.

In species living in a social environment of any complexity, the actions of an individual's conspecifics will invariably have fitness consequences for themself. Some actions will be beneficial; some will be harmful. The mix of fitness consequences may be entirely random or even heavily biased toward negative fitness consequences. The adaptive problem in this context is to tip the balance away from the negative and toward the positive (see Rothstein & Pierotti, 1988). A simple means to achieve a more favorable balance is for individuals to reward conspecifics for benefiting themselves and to punish them for harming themselves, thereby shaping conspecifics's behavior to be more beneficial and less harmful. There is a catch, however. Individuals need to know what their opponents consider beneficial and harmful in order to reward and punish them appropriately. It is here that the intentional stance pays its dues (Tooby & Cosmides, 1996). If individuals can appropriately model the beliefs and desires of their conspecifics, they can find a double coincidence of needs on which to base an exchange, greatly expanding the range of cooperative possibilities. Consider the case of cleaning fish, for example. Here cooperation is possible because the cleaner fish and the fish that are cleaned have a coincidence of needs in which both parties benefit—the cleaner fish get a meal of parasites and the fish that are cleaned are rid of their parasites. However, the cooperative arrangement is highly restricted to this one act on the part of the cleaner fish. Unable to model what the other party values, both are locked into a narrowly constrained system of cooperation that natural selection happened into by chance. In adopting the intentional stance, individuals can participate in cooperative interactions more flexibly by rewarding others based on a model of their current needs/desires. Furthermore, if these partners also possess the hypothesized ToMM, then they can figure out that an act of kindness was not simply random, but was contingent on the benefits they bestowed on the first individual, greatly contracting the learning process. Hence, a mental mechanism like ToMM is likely to play a crucial role in the flexible social exchange in which humans engage.

Although cheater-detection, the ability to detect and punish cheaters, is not sufficient for the establishment of social exchange, it is a necessary component for the evolution of such cooperation all the same (Axelrod, 1984; Axelrod & Hamilton, 1981; Trivers, 1971). Consequently, Cosmides and Tooby (1989, 1992; Cosmides, 1989) proposed that a critical component of a cognitive adaptation for social exchange is a "look for cheaters" algorithm that directs attention to potential cheaters. The evidence for this mental mechanism is supplied by studies conducted on the Wason selection task. An offer to engage in social exchange can be phrased as a social contract rule of the form: *If you take the benefit, then you must meet the requirement* (i.e., *If I benefit you, then you must benefit me*). Cosmides (1989) observed that most of the rules that had reliably elicited correct performance on the selection task were such social contracts, and not deontic rules more generally. The deontic content effect, she argued, can best be explained by the hypothesized "look for cheaters" algorithm. In the absence of a rationed benefit, individuals breaking a rule are not cheating and so the "look for cheaters" algorithm should not be activated. To test this, Cosmides (1989) devised parallel social contract and nonsocial contract versions of the selection task employing the same rule. The critical difference between the two versions of the task was whether the rule regulated access to a rationed benefit; it did in the case of the social contracts. The results supported Cosmides' proposal with 65% to 80% of participants successfully solving the social contract versions of the task, but only 0% to 40% of participants successfully solving the nonsocial contract versions, even though they employed the same rule. Although Cosmides' methods and interpretation of the results have been criticized (e.g., in addition to manipulating presence of a benefit, she manipulated the prescriptive/descriptive nature of the rule, see Cheng & Holyoak, 1989, for this and other criticisms), the effect has been replicated in subsequent experiments that have controlled for the purported methodological flaws (e.g., Barrett, 1999; Manktelow & Over, 1992; Platt & Griggs, 1993).

Defenders of more domain-general explanations of the deontic content effect were quick to point out that social contracts alone are not the only sort of rule that reliably elicit correct performance on the selection task. People also routinely solve precautionary versions of the selection task correctly, despite the fact that they typically do not involve a rationed benefit. For example, Manktelow and Over (1990) had participants solve a version of the selection task employing the rule: *If you clean up spilt blood, then you must wear rubber gloves.* They specifically designed the rule so that it could not be construed as regulating access to a rationed benefit, and yet 69% of the participants in their study solved the task correctly. Numerous precautionary versions of the selection task have been studied and routinely they elicit a large percentage of correct performance even though these rules are rather difficult to interpret as social contracts (hazards are usually not viewed as rationed benefits).

Precautions, or prudential obligations, are rules of the form: *If the hazard exists, then take the protective measure.* In the moral reasoning literature, prudential matters are often treated as though they are nondeontic—personal matters that people can choose to abide by or not, with no external constrain on anyone's actions (e.g., Barbieri, 1993; Nucci et al., 1996; Tisak, 1993; Tisak & Turiel, 1984). However, the physical environment itself imposes constraints, especially in conjunction with an ingrained preference to avoid unnecessary harm. People *ought* to avoid injury to themselves, even if this is not a sociomoral imperative. To suggest that prudential rules fail to be deontic because they specify acts that individuals "ought" to do in some weaker, nonmoral sense (cf. Dworkin, 1978, "The model of rules II") is to conflate the moral with the deontic—morality is just a subset of the deontic.[1] Hence, in the selection task literature, rules regulating behavior in hazardous situations are regularly treated as deontic rules and critics of Cosmides and Tooby's cheater-detection proposal have claimed that their theory is too narrow in its focus: People are not just competent at detecting cheaters, they are competent at deontic reasoning more generally (e.g., Cheng & Holyoak, 1989; Girotto et al., 1989; Manktelow & Over, 1990, 1995; Politzer & Nguyen-Xuan, 1992). However, this criticism ignores the fact that there are versions of the Wason selection task, employing bona fide deontic rules, that fail to elicit correct performance (e.g., Cosmides, 1989, exps. 5, 8, nonsocial contract permission; Manktelow & Over, 1990, bingo and politics scenarios; 1992, weak preference scenario). Instead, the general pattern of results suggests that precautions, like social contracts, tap into a different and distinct subdomain of reasoning.

The Adaptive Problem of Hazard Management

Hazards represent an obvious threat to the fitness of any organism. Hazards come in a variety of different forms: falling rocks, poisonous snakes, heavy machinery, pathogens, and so forth. Whether or not all hazards can be managed by a single set of cognitive adaptations is an open question, but it would seem reasonable to assume that most hazards do, nonetheless, impose a different set of computational demands than social exchange. Some hazards are social, such as threats issued by a conspecific, but it might be speculated that these are handled by specialized rea-

---

[1]It is worth noting here that when Fiddick (2004) had participants judge the permissibility of violating a precautionary rule, the judgments elicited matched the domain theorists' definition of a moral obligation. Namely, participants thought that people should adhere to the rule even if an authority figure or social consensus deemed it okay to violate the rule and participants thought the rule should be universally obeyed, even if the rule had never been explicitly formulated. Yet, despite the overlap with moral obligations, participants did not think that conformity to the rule was a moral matter.

soning processes of their own (Tooby & Cosmides, 1989). Many more hazards are inherently nonsocial and even in cases where the predatory behavior of conspecifics is involved (e.g., theft), it is questionable whether many of these interactions should be considered *social*. Hence, avoiding hazards draws more broadly on inferences made via the physical stance or more specialized inference procedures for dealing artifacts, animals, and contamination.

The role of intent, in particular, highlights the differences between social exchange and hazard management. When individuals make an offer to engage in a cooperative exchange, an important consideration in deciding whether or not to accept the person's offer is an assessment of whether he *intends* to honor his side of the bargain. If the conclusion is that he does not, it is unlikely that the offer will be accepted. When deciding whether to accept precautionary advice, it is necessary to ask whether the hazard really does exist and whether the proposed protection will work. Intent is not an issue, what are important are the physical and biological contingencies of the situation.

Even after a violation has occurred, intent exerts a differential influence on reasoning about social contracts and precautions. Intent is an important mitigating factor when judging the violation of a social contract. If two people have a deal whereby they reciprocate driving each other to the airport to avoid the cost of parking their car, then it makes a difference whether individuals violate the agreement because their car broke down or because they chose to stay at home and watch a football game instead. People tend to feel that an accidental violation, when unforeseen, is excusable, whereas an intentional violation is not. However, if a mother tells her child to wear an oven mitt when taking something hot out of the oven, it makes little difference whether the child forgot the rule and accidentally reached in to grab a pan or whether the child intentionally disobeyed the mother's rule and grabbed the pan. Either way, the child gets burned and that is what is relevant in this case.

The differential influence of actor intent can also be demonstrated on the selection task. For example, Fiddick (2004, exp. 3) presented people with four different versions of the selection task. Two versions of the task employed social contracts and two employed precautions. Within each content domain, actor intent was independently manipulated: The rule was either violated intentionally or accidentally. Although actor intent had no influence on performance on the precaution versions of the task, performance on the social contract versions of the task was selectively impaired in the accidental violation condition.

As already noted, unlike many nonhuman systems of reciprocity where the items of exchange are fixed, the "benefits" exchanged in human systems of reciprocity are often based on a particular individual's needs or desires. Hence, in order to determine whether any one party has illicitly benefited, it is often necessary to model the desires of that person in order to determine whether that person did indeed perceive the item of exchange to be a benefit—drawing once again on ToMM's ability to form representations of others' mental states. This highlights the importance of social perspective to cheater detection, yet another dimension in which reasoning about social exchange ought to differ from reasoning about hazards.

Recall the switched perspective effect that we referred to earlier in the discussion of deontic versions of the selection task. Gigerenzer and Hug (1992) observed that participants in their experiment could be made to select either the *P* and *not-Q* cards or the *not-P* and *Q* cards, depending on the perspective that they were cued to adopt. Social exchanges are inherently social, the interaction of two parties with diverging interests, and hence Gigerenzer and Hug argued that in many social exchanges there are *bilateral cheating options* where one or the other party to the exchange can cheat. The adaptive problem is for individuals to detect the cheating of their partner, not themselves, so participants cued into the perspective of one party should seek to find evidence of cheating by their partner resulting in a complementary pattern of selection task performance. This is indeed what they found.

Hazards typically are not social, so even though a precautionary rule may relate the actions of two parties, there is no reason to expect any principled difference in reasoning as a function of *social* perspective. The hazard objectively exists or it does not, it is not a matter of personal desires, but a factual matter (see Fiddick, 2004, exp. 1). Hence, there is no reason to expect any difference in reasoning performance across perspectives on the hazard—all parties should perceive the same objective facts of the matter and reason in a similar fashion. Fiddick (2000) tested this analysis of the perspective switching effect by designing parallel social contract and precaution versions of the selection task and manipulating the perspective that participants were cued to adopt. Although the perspective manipulation had an effect on performance of the social contract versions of the task, the same manipulation had no influence on performance of the precaution versions of the task.

These findings are further reinforced by the striking case of R. M. (see Stone et al., 2002). R.M. is a neurological patient who suffered bilateral damage to his orbitofrontal cortex, amygdala, and anterior temporal cortex. As a result, R. M. has significant difficulties with social intelligence, including a marked impairment in his ability to recognize and reason about others' mental states. Stone and her colleagues gave R. M. a battery of social contract and precaution versions of the Wason selection task. Where normal participants and brain-damaged controls had no difficulty solving either the social contract or precaution versions of the selection task, with performance on both versions of the task being nearly identical, R. M. was specifically impaired in his performance on the social contract versions of the task (i.e., specifically those versions of the task that are hypothesized to tap social intelligence). There were practically no performance differences between R. M. and normal participants on the precaution problems. When considering both the moral developmental evidence for domain distinctions and the selection task studies reviewed in this section, there are multiple converging lines of evidence supporting the proposed multiple adaptation account of deontic reasoning.

THE IMPLICATIONS OF MULTIPLE, EVOLVED DEONTIC ADAPTATIONS FOR NATURAL LAW THEORY

Domain-specificity

The experimental evidence reviewed in the preceding sections supports the proposal that humans have evolved, deontic reasoning abilities: a collection of abilities, not a single mechanism, that are specialized for reasoning about specific domains of action. Although the focus has been on two hypothesized cognitive adaptations in particular, a cognitive adaptation for social exchange and a cognitive adaptation for hazard management, there is little reason to believe that these mechanisms exhaust the range of evolved deontic reasoning mechanisms. Bugental (2000), for example, argued that humans possess evolved psychological mechanisms for reasoning about a variety of social domains, some of which, such as hierarchical relations (see Cummins, 1996a, 199b) or in-group sharing (Hiraishi & Hasegawa, 2001), may involve deontic intuitions as well. This suggests that rights and duties are best not viewed in the abstract, independent of the particular domain of application. There may be no "common ground" that underlies deontic and, by implication, legal reasoning (Sayre-McCord, 1986) and this has clear implications for law.

There is a strong intellectual tradition within our culture to view correct reasoning as based on a coherent assimilation of all the available information (Gigerenzer et al. 1999) and this vision of rationality finds its legal expression in Dworkin's (1978, "Hard Cases") influential model of adjudication. Dworkin described the ideal judge, Hercules, "a lawyer of superhuman skill, learning, patience and acumen." When deciding how to rule in hard cases (i.e., where the law is indeterminate), Dworkin argued that Hercules "must construct a scheme of abstract and concrete principles that provides a coherent justification for all common law precedents and, so far as these are to be justified on principle, constitutional and statutory provisions as well" (pp. 116–117). Of course, Dworkin may only be suggesting that judges consider all of the law that is *relevant* to the case at hand and relevance may be significantly constrained by domain boundaries. However, it is debatable whether Dworkin has this narrower agenda in mind given that he proposed that Hercules "must construct … a constitutional theory; since he is Hercules we may suppose that he can develop a full political theory that justifies the constitution as a whole" (p. 106). Dworkin would appear to be arguing that the law should be logically consistent through and through, but does this make sense if deontic rules are not a unified phenomenon?

Lawyers have traditionally made distinctions between different domains of law: criminal law, contract law, and the law of torts, for example. Is this simply a matter of tradition or is there an underlying psychological reason for law being so divided? Might criminal law, contract law, and the law of torts map, roughly, onto different adaptive domains such as morality, social exchange and hazard management, respectively, and if it did what implications would this have for the role of actor intent in contract law and the law of torts? Should different legal standards/

principles apply regarding intent when actor intent differentially influences people's reasoning about social contracts and precautions?

What is at issue are competing visions of rationality. On the one hand, there is unbounded rationality, the prevailing cultural norm, which favors content-blind norms: generality and consistency; and, on the other hand, there is bounded rationality, which favors content-dependent norms: specify and ecological correspondence (Gigerenzer et al., 1999). The model of deontic reasoning presented here exemplifies bounded rationality and a theory of natural law based on this model might well propose that law is likewise boundedly rational, with different ecologically based subdomains of law naturally constrained by different principles.

This suggests a more casuistical approach to legal reasoning. Casuistry undeniably has a bad reputation, perhaps deservedly so, but casuistry with scientifically informed boundaries may be less susceptible to abuse. Jonsen and Toulmin (1988) argued that a casuistical approach to moral/legal matters is more likely to generate a broad base of social consensus than an approach based on the consistent application of a general moral theory (i.e., unbounded rationality). Consensus in the casuistical approach rests in the fact that there is a fairly large set of cases for which there is general agreement about the rights and duties at hand. Conflicts only tend to arise in the relatively fewer hard cases. One might speculate that what differentiates between the easy and hard cases is the degree to which they fall under evolved domains of reasoning: The easy cases are those that are paradigmatic of evolved subdomains of deontic reasoning, generating the most consensus due to shared human nature, whereas the hard cases are those that cross domain boundaries or are evolutionarily novel.

Nonmoral Norms

The chapter has largely bypassed the question of whether and to what extent the domains carved out by moral reasoning researchers overlap the domains carved out by evolutionary psychologists, leaving several questions unanswered. Does morality, for example, map onto an evolved reasoning competence? Many evolutionists have argued that moral sense may be the product of natural selection (see Krebs, chap. 15 in this vol.). There is no reason to assume that natural law based on evolved human nature would necessarily be the law of the jungle—nature red in tooth and claw. Nevertheless, whereas natural law theorists have often attempted to ground law in the moral side of human nature, morality is not required to provide a naturalized account of rights, duties, and human nature. This raises the possibility of a natural law theory that is nonmoral in nature.

Morality often performs a double duty in natural law theories: It suggests the substance of the law and it supplies its legitimacy. However, the substance and legitimacy of law need not coincide. Theories of law based on the model of a social contract, for example, can accommodate a range of substantive differences in legal systems that are legitimated by the explicit or implicit consent of community members. Typically, it is the legal positivists who argue that the substance of the law is free to vary, but might a natural law theory based in part on nonmoral norms argue the same?

Natural law theories are often contrasted with legal positivism on an implicit and unwarranted premise: namely, that social conventions are in some way unnatural and alien to human nature. Although the gap between God-given morality and human artifice may look large from a theological perspective, the gap between human artifice and the comparative absence of such in other species is just as impressive from an evolutionary perspective. Social conventions are not simply a matter of historical chance, nor are they inevitable, but require a mind that is capable of forging and reasoning about conventions. As the experimental evidence reviewed suggests, this is an ability that even human children possess and, yet, it is largely absent in other species. Social convention is part of human nature. However, if our model of deontic reasoning is correct, then social convention is only one part of human nature. Other sides of human nature, such as prudential reasoning or possibly an evolved moral sense, are not conventional.

The real contentious issues in legal theory are the contentful ones. Whether or not the ability to form social conventions is a part of human nature, conventions are, at least with respect to their content, somewhat arbitrary, and it is this arbitrariness or lack thereof that concerns legal theorists. Is slavery inherently wrong, or has it *arbitrarily* been outlawed as a matter of social convention? What the present analysis of deontic reasoning suggests is that such questions should not be answered in overly general terms. For example, it should not be concluded that if prohibitions against slavery are not simply a matter of social convention, then law *in general* is nonconventional. Such general conclusions are not warranted if there are distinct normative subdomains. People may wish to prohibit slavery on moral grounds while simultaneously and without contradiction arbitrary permit or prohibit nonmoral acts on conventional grounds. In this way, our model of deontic reasoning may accommodate elements of both natural law theory and legal positivism.

The domain-specificity of deontic reasoning and the existence of nonmoral norms are not inherently problematic for natural law theories. Instead, they suggest the character that a natural law theory might assume if it were more scientifically informed. What is potentially more problematic in trying to derive a natural law theory from evolutionary psychology is the historical dimension of evolutionary analyses.

Deontic Intuition as a Historical Product

Unlike most typical natural law theories, evolutionary psychology does not view human nature as an essential property of our species. It is a historical product and shaped in important ways by our species history. Perhaps the theory that best fits the natural history of our species is that laid out by Hart (1994). Human beings' evolved deontic reasoning capacities can be thought of as supplying humans with what Hart (1994) called primary rules of obligation. Subsequent discussions of

Hart's views often suggest that Hart was talking about a subset of codified laws when he talked about primary rules of obligation, but this is not the sense a reader gets when reading Hart's actual discussion of such rules. Instead Hart's conception of primary rules (pp. 91–92) seemed to match D. Brown's (1991, p. 138) description of the core of law common to all cultures:

> [All human cultures] have law, at least in the sense of rules of membership in perpetual social units and in the sense of rights and obligations attached to persons or other statuses.... They have sanctions for infractions, and these sanctions include removal of offenders from the social unit—whether by expulsion, incarceration, ostracism, or execution. They punish (or otherwise censure or condemn) acts that threaten the group or are alleged to do so.

This is no more than the informal rules that have been described as moral rules, social conventions, precautions, and so on—rules that normal human adults can grasp by virtue of their evolved deontic competencies.

The problem with our evolved deontic reasoning capacities, and hence primary rules of obligation, is that they were designed by natural selection for use in ancestral, not contemporary, environments. Evolution through natural selection is a historical process. The universal and characteristic features of a species are the end product of a slow process of refinement that shapes the species to the selective and stable demands of its environment. Any moderately complex adaptation will require hundreds of generations of mutation and selection with evolutionary advances potentially lagging far behind changes in the environment, regardless of the present fitness consequences. As a result, modern adaptations are best viewed as the solutions to ancestral problems. For many species, this evolutionary lag is of little consequence because present environments are in many respects comparable to past environments in terms of the challenges facing member organisms. This is less the case with humans and especially so with respect to deontic rules.

Modern humans live in vastly more complex social worlds than our ancestors did. Not only is the scale of modern society greatly expanded, but so too has the degree of social/labor specialization. Where ancestral humans lived in small, face-to-face societies in which many members of the community were kin, modern humans tend to live isolated and anonymously among millions. Deontic reasoning mechanisms were designed by natural selection for living in a considerably different world than exists today. This raises the concern that deontic intuitions and informal evolved means of regulating social relations may be inadequate for coping with the modern world. As Hart (1994, p. 92) described the situation: "It is plain that only a small community closely knit by ties of kinship, common sentiment, and belief, and placed in a stable environment, could live successfully by such a regime of unofficial rules. In any other conditions such a simple form of social control must prove defective and will require supplementation in different ways." Hart captured the difficulty facing a natural law theorist seeking to ground law in evolved human nature—unadorned, evolved human nature may not be ideally suited to the modern world.

This is probably putting the case against human beings' natural abilities a little too strongly, for people do in fact cope in the modern world. Per capita levels of homicide, for example, are far lower in modern societies than they were in prehistoric or even premodern times (Daly & Wilson, 1988), so clearly it is not terribly difficult to regulate social behavior in the modern world. Moreover, the psychological processes used to comprehend and engage the ancestral world probably play an important role in structuring the existing cultural environment, such that the cultures people experience are themselves partially a reflection of evolved human nature (Tooby & Cosmides, 1992).

Still, many aspects of the modern world are evolutionarily novel and human's evolved abilities are not solely responsible for modern functioning. Only some abilities are adaptations. Reading, to cite one example, is a very useful cultural innovation. Undoubtedly, it is a cultural elaboration of an evolved ability to communicate via spoken languages (Pinker, 1994). However, there is more to reading than the mechanisms underlying spoken language. Modern legal systems are probably like reading: cultural elaborations of an evolved ability, deontic intuitions.

One of the features of cultural elaborations is that they are not universal. They must be learned. Unlike spoken language, which is found in every known human culture, there are entire cultures that lack a written language (Pinker, 1994). Likewise, there are individuals who are illiterate. The same is true of law. There are both cultures that lack modern legal systems (in the sense of Hart's secondary rules of obligation) and even within modern legal systems there are individuals, perhaps even the majority of the population, that are not fully competent in the use of the system. It takes years of specialized training in order to practice law, just as it takes years of specialized training in order to be able to read. From a psychological point of view, this suggests that two types of legal theory may be required: one that accounts for the lay reasoning and one that accounts for professional reasoning.

Not only may lay and professional reasoning differ, but there may also be individual and cultural differences in the way evolutionarily novel acts are interpreted. Consider an example from the selection task literature. How can drinking age restrictions be interpreted: *If a person is drinking beer, then the person must be over 19 years of age* (Griggs & Cox, 1982)? Cosmides (1989) argued that being permitted to drink alcohol is a rationed benefit such that this rule is a social contract (i.e., falls within the domain of social exchange). Yet, an argument could also be made that the rule is precautionary in nature (i.e., it protects vulnerable members of society from the harms of alcohol). Others, less concerned about drinkers' self-inflicted harm and more concerned about the potential harm to others from drunk driving, might even view this as a moral rule. Each of these interpretations is sensitive to evolutionarily novel and culturally variable factors. A Muslim who views the consumption of alcohol as a sin is not likely to view permission to drink alcohol as a rationed benefit. Likewise, the potential for self-inflicted harm is also evolutionarily novel and culturally variable. Before distillation was invented, it was more difficult to consume harmful doses of alcohol. Indeed, in lower concentrations alcoholic beverages may have even been beneficial as a safe source of water. Moreover, the potential for alcohol-induced harm to others has been greatly enhanced by further cultural innovations such as cars and guns. As this example illustrates, a single rule can be viewed either as a social contract, precaution, or moral rule, depending on the specific cultural circumstances and which aspects are emphasized—despite the fact that there might be universal agreement about the nature of social contracts, precautions, and moral rules more abstractly.

An evolved, universal human nature provides no guarantee that a universal consensus can be reached on matters of law—even ignoring situations in which individual interests might conflict. Just as a monolingual, English speaker is at a loss understanding Japanese—despite the existence of universal, evolved language mechanisms—considerable cultural exegesis is required in order to determine which elements of our evolutionary endowment are being invoked and elaborated in the legal system of a particular culture (or in the legal reasoning of an individual for that matter). This is not to say that legal reasoning will be endlessly variable, the product of historical, but nonevolutionary, contingency. Instead it suggests, as cultural psychologists are coming to realize (Rozin, 2000), that most cultural variation, legal systems included, will fall within a restricted subset of patterns (modes of construal) that are supplied by evolved human nature.

Jurisprudence is no less complicated than deontic reasoning (perhaps, in part, because the former is a reflection of the latter). Our treatment of legal theory is inevitably incomplete like our treatment of the psychology deontic reasoning. Still, even in this brief review, certain patterns and overlaps have emerged. Both evolutionary psychologists and legal theorists have an interest in human nature that is potentially complementary. Psychologists have an interest in discovering the objective features of human nature, and lawyers have an interest in using those discoveries to shape the law. An evolutionary perspective on deontic reasoning suggests that is it bounded, both historically and in scope, providing support for both natural law theorists and legal positivists, but also constraining direction of legal theorizing at the same time. As evolutionary studies of deontic reasoning develop, they will undoubtedly yield more points of contact from which lawyers can benefit.

REFERENCES

Axelrod, R. (1984). *The evolution of cooperation.* New York: Basic Books.

Axelrod, R., & Hamilton, W. (1981). The evolution of cooperation. *Science, 211*, 1390–1396.

Barbieri, M. (1993). Important variables in reasoning about social rules. *International Journal of Behavioral Development, 16*, 589–607.

Baron-Cohen, S. (1995). *Mindblindness: An essay on autism and theory of mind.* Cambridge, MA: MIT Press.

Barrett, H. C. (1999, June). *Guilty minds: How perceived intent, incentive, and ability to cheat influence social contract reasoning.* Paper presented at the annual meeting of the Human Behavior and Evolution Society, Salt Lake City, UT.

Blair, R. J. R. (1995). A cognitive developmental approach to morality: Investigating the psychopath. *Cognition, 57*, 1–29.

Brown, A. (1990). Domain-specific principles affect learning and transfer in children. *Cognitive Science, 14*, 107–133.

Brown, D. (1991). *Human universals*. Philadelphia: Temple University Press.

Bugental, D. (2000). Acquisition of the algorithms of social life: A domain-based approach. *Psychological Bulletin, 126*, 187–219.

Cassidy, K. W. (1998). Three- and four-year-old children's ability to use desire- and belief-based reasoning. *Cognition, 66*, B1–B11.

Cheng, P., & Holyoak, K. (1985). Pragmatic reasoning schemas. *Cognitive Psychology, 17*, 391–416.

Cheng, P., & Holyoak, K. (1989). On the natural selection of reasoning theories. *Cognition, 33*, 285–313.

Cosmides, L. (1989). The logic of social exchange: Has natural selection shaped how humans reason? Studies with the Wason selection task. *Cognition, 31*, 187–276.

Cosmides, L., & Tooby, J. (1989). Evolutionary psychology and the generation of culture, part II. Case study: A computational theory of social exchange. *Ethology and Sociobiology, 10*, 51–97.

Cosmides, L., & Tooby, J. (1992). Cognitive adaptations for social exchange. In J. Barkow, L. Cosmides, & J. Tooby (Eds.), *The adapted mind* (pp. 163–228). New York: Oxford University Press.

Cummins, D. D. (1996a). Dominance hierarchies and the evolution of human reasoning. *Minds and Machines, 6*, 463–480.

Cummins, D. D. (1996b). Evidence for the innateness of deontic reasoning. *Mind & Language, 11*, 160–190.

Cummins, D. D. (1996c). Evidence of deontic reasoning in 3- and 4-year-olds. *Memory & Cognition, 24*, 823–829.

Daly, M., & Wilson, M. (1988). *Homicide*. New York: Aldine de Gruyter.

Dawkins, R. (1986). *The blind watchmaker.* Harlow, England: Longman Scientific & Technical.

Dennett, D. (1987). *The intentional stance*. Cambridge, MA: MIT Press.

Dworkin, R. (1978). *Taking rights seriously*. Cambridge, MA: Harvard University Press.

Evans, J. St. B. T. (2002). Logic and human reasoning: An assessment of the deduction paradigm. *Psychological Bulletin, 128*, 978–996.

Evans, J. St. B. T., Newstead, S., & Byrne, R. (1993). *Human reasoning: The psychology of deduction*. Hillsdale, NJ: Lawrence Erlbaum Associates.

Fiddick, L. (2000, June). *Are rights and duties complementary and interdefined? Further evidence for separate domains of reasoning.* Poster presented at the Human Behavior and Evolution Society meeting, Amherst, MA.

Fiddick, L. (2004). Domains of deontic reasoning: Resolving the discrepancy between the cognitive and moral reasoning literatures. *Quarterly Journal of Experimental Psychology, 57A*.

Fiddick, L., Cosmides, L., & Tooby, J. (2000). No interpretation without representation: The role of domain-specific representations and inferences in the Wason selection task. *Cognition, 77*, 1–79.

Gigerenzer, G., & Hug, K. (1992). Domain specific reasoning: Social contracts, cheating, and perspective change. *Cognition, 43*, 127–171.

Gigerenzer, G., Todd, P., & the ABC Research Group. (1999). *Simple heuristics that make us smart*. Oxford, England: Oxford University Press.

Gilligan, C. (1982). *In a different voice: Psychological theory and women's development*. Cambridge, MA: Harvard University Press.

Girotto, V., Blaye, A., & Farioli, F. (1989). A reason to reason: Pragmatic basis of children's search for counterexamples. *Cahiers de Psychologie Cognitive, 9*, 297–321.

Griggs, R., & Cox, J. (1982). The elusive thematic-materials effect in Wason's selection task. *British Journal of Psychology, 73*, 407–420.

Harris, P., & Nuñez, M. (1996). Understanding of permission rules by preschool children. *Child Development, 67*, 1572–1591.

Harris, P., Nuñez, M., & Brett, C. (2001). Let's swap: Early understanding of social exchange by British and Nepali children. *Memory & Cognition, 29*, 757–764.

Hart, H. L. A. (1994). *The concept of law* (2nd ed.). New York: Oxford University Press.

Hiraishi, K., & Hasegawa, T. (2001). Sharing-rule and detection of free-riders in cooperative groups: Evolutionarily important deontic reasoning in the Wason selection task. *Thinking and Reasoning, 7*, 255–294.

Holyoak, K., & Cheng, P. (1995). Pragmatic reasoning with a point of view. *Thinking and Reasoning, 1*, 289–313.

Humphrey, N. (1984). *Consciousness regained.* New York: Oxford University Press.

Johnson-Laird, P., Legrenzi, P., & Legrenzi, M. (1972). Reasoning and a sense of reality. *British Journal of Psychology, 63*, 395–400.

Jonsen, A., & Toulmin, S. (1988). *The abuse of casuistry.* Berkeley, CA: University of California Press.

Kohlberg, L. (1981). *The philosophy of moral development: Moral stages and the idea of justice.* San Francisco: Harper & Row.

Kohlberg, L. (1984). *The psychology of moral development: The nature and validity of moral stages.* San Francisco: Harper & Row.

Leslie, A. M. (1994). ToMM, ToBy, and Agency: Core architecture and domain specificity. In L. Hirschfeld & S. Gelman (Eds.), *Mapping the mind: Domain specificity in cognition and culture* (pp. 119–148). New York: Cambridge University Press.

Manktelow, K., & Over, D. (1990). Deontic thought and the selection task. In K. Gilhooly, M. Keane, R. Logie, & G. Erdos (Eds.), *Lines of thought: Reflections of the psychology of thinking* (pp. 153–164). London: Wiley.

Manktelow, K., & Over, D. (1991). Social roles and utilities in reasoning with deontic conditionals. *Cognition, 39*, 85–105.

Manktelow, K., & Over, D. (1992). Utility and deontic reasoning: Some comments on Johnson-Laird and Byrne. *Cognition, 43*, 183–188.

Manktelow, K., & Over, D. (1995). Deontic reasoning. In S. Newstead, & J. St. B. T. Evans (Eds.), *Perspectives on thinking and reasoning: Essays in honour of Peter Wason* (pp. 91–114). Hove, England: Lawrence Erlbaum Associates.

Miller, J., Bersoff, D., & Harwood, R. (1990). Perceptions of social responsibilities in India and in the United States: Moral imperatives or personal decisions? *Journal of Personality & Social Psychology, 58*, 33–47.

Newell A., & Simon, H. A. (1972). *Human problem solving.* Englewood Cliffs, NJ: Prentice-Hall.

Nucci, L. (1981). Conceptions of personal issues: A domain distinct from moral or societal concepts. *Child Development, 52*, 114–121.

Nucci, L., Camino, C., & Sapiro, C. (1996). Social class effects on northeastern Brazilian children's conceptions of areas of personal choice and social regulation. *Child Development, 67*, 1223–1242.

Nucci, L., & Weber, E. (1995). Social interactions in the home and the development of young children's conceptions of the personal. *Child Development, 66*, 1438–1452.

Nuñez, M., & Harris, P. (1998). Psychological and deontic concepts: Separate domains or intimate connection? *Mind & Language, 13*, 153–170.

Oaksford, M., & Chater, N. (1994). A rational analysis of the selection task as optimal data selection. *Psychological Review, 101*, 608–631.

Piaget, J. (1999/1932). *The moral judgment of the child.* London: Routledge.

Pinker, S. (1994). *The language instinct.* New York: Morrow.

Pinker, S. (1997). *How the mind works.* New York: Norton.

Platt, R., & Griggs, R. (1993). Darwinian algorithms and the Wason selection task: A factor analysis of social contract selection task problems. *Cognition, 48*, 163–192.

Politzer, G., & Nguyen-Xuan, A. (1992). Reasoning about promises and warnings: Darwinian algorithms, mental models, relevance judgments or pragmatic schemas? *Quarterly Journal of Experimental Psychology, 44A*, 401–421.

Repacholi, B., & Gopnik, A. (1997). Early reasoning about desires: Evidence from 14- and 18-month-olds. *Developmental Psychology, 33*, 12–21.

Rothstein, S., & Pierotti, R. (1988). Distinctions among reciprocal altruism, kin selection, and cooperation and a model for the initial evolution of beneficent behavior. *Ethology & Sociobiology, 9*, 189–209.

Rozin, P. (2000). Evolution and adaptation in the understanding of behavior, culture and mind. *American Behavioral Scientist, 43*, 970–986.

Rozin, P., Lowery, L., Imada, S., & Haidt, J. (1999). The CAD triad hypothesis: A mapping between three moral emotions (contempt, anger, disgust) and three moral codes (community, autonomy, divinity). *Journal of Personality and Social Psychology, 76*, 574–586.

Sayre-McCord, G. (1986). Deontic logic and the priority of moral theory. *Nous, 20*, 179–197.

Sherry, D., & Schacter, D. (1987). The evolution of multiple memory systems. *Psychological Review, 94*, 439–454.

Shweder, R. (1982a). Beyond self-constructed knowledge: The study of culture and morality. *Merrill-Palmer Quarterly, 28*, 41–69.

Shweder, R. (1982b). Liberalism as destiny: Review of Kohlberg (1981). *Contemporary Psychology, 27*, 421–424.

Shweder, R., Mahapatra, M., & Miller, J. (1987). Culture and moral development. In J. Kagan & S. Lamb (Eds.), *The emergence of moral concepts in early childhood* (pp. 1–83). Chicago: University of Chicago Press.

Smetana, J. (1995a). Morality in context: Abstractions, ambiguities and applications. *Annals of Child Development, 10*, 83–130.

Smetana, J. (1995b). Parenting styles and conceptions of parental authority during adolescence. *Child Development, 66*, 299–316.

Smetana, J., & Asquith, P. (1994). Adolescents' and parents' conceptions of parental authority and personal autonomy. *Child Development, 65*, 1147–1162.

Smetana, J., & Bitz, B. (1996). Adolescents' conceptions of teachers' authority and their relations to rule violations in school. *Child Development, 67*, 1153–1172.

Song, M., Smetana, J., & Sang, Y. K. (1987). Korean children's conceptions of moral and conventional transgressions. *Developmental Psychology, 23*, 577–582.

Spelke, E. S. (1990). Principles of object perception. *Cognitive Science, 14*, 29–56.

Sperber, D., Cara, F., & Girotto, V. (1995). Relevance theory explains the selection task. *Cognition, 57*, 31–95.

Stone, V., Cosmides, L., Tooby, J., Kroll, N., & Knight, R. (2002). Selective impairment of reasoning about social exchange in a patient with bilateral limbic system damage. *Proceedings of the National Academy of Sciences, 99*, 11531–11536.

Sugiyama, L., Tooby, J., & Cosmides, L. (2002). Cross-cultural evidence of cognitive adaptations for social exchange among the Shiwiar of Ecuadorian Amazonia. *Proceedings of the National Academy of Sciences, 99*, 11537–11542.

Tisak, M. (1993). Preschool children's judgments of moral and personal events involving physical harm and property damage. *Merrill-Palmer Quarterly, 39*, 375–390.

Tisak, M., & Turiel, E. (1984). Children's conceptions of moral and prudential rules. *Child Development, 55*, 1030–1039.

Tisak, M., & Turiel, E. (1988). Variation in seriousness of transgressions and children's moral and conventional concepts. *Developmental Psychology, 24*, 352–357.

Tooby, J., & Cosmides, L. (1989, August). *The logic of threat.* Paper presented at the annual meeting of the Human Behavior and Evolution Society in Evanston, IL.

Tooby, J., & Cosmides, L. (1992). The psychological foundations of culture. In J. Barkow, L. Cosmides, & J. Tooby (Eds.), *The adapted mind: Evolutionary psychology and the generation of culture* (pp. 19–136). New York: Oxford University Press.

Tooby, J., & Cosmides, L. (1996). Friendship and the bankers's paradox: Other pathways to the evolution of adaptations for altruism. In W. G. Runciman, J. Maynard Smith, & R. I. M. Dunbar (Eds.), *Evolution of social behaviour patterns in primates and man: A joint discussion meeting of the Royal Society and the British Academy* (pp. 119–143). New York: Oxford University Press.

Trivers, R. (1971). The evolution of reciprocal altruism. *Quarterly Review of Biology, 46*, 35–57.

Turiel, E. (1983). *The development of social knowledge: Morality and convention.* Cambridge, England: Cambridge University Press.

Turiel, E. (1998). The development of morality. In W. Damon (Ed.), *Handbook of child psychology* (Vol. 3, 5th ed., pp. 863–932). New York: Wiley.

Wason, P. (1968). Reasoning about a rule. *Quarterly Journal of Experimental Psychology, 20*, 273–281.

Wimmer, H., & Perner, J. (1983). Beliefs about beliefs: Representation and constraining function of wrong beliefs in young children's understanding of deception. *Cognition, 13*, 103–128.

PART III

Real-World Applications

The authors in this section build on the material in the first two sections of the book in discussing how evolutionary psychology can be helpful in making public policy and private decisions.

Families are often viewed as a solidarity unit, joined by a commonality of interest rooted in the fact that family members' (relatives by blood and marriage) fitness is promoted by the reproductive success of their common kin. In chapter 9, Wilson and Daly suggest that the solidarity of mates can be threatened by a number of interacting factors. They focus on the relevance of these factors to the epidemiology of family violence.

In chapter 10, Salmon outlines the evolutionary rationale for sex differences with regard to some aspects of sexuality, focusing in particular on sex differences in preferences for erotic genres, namely pornography and the romance novel. The controversy over the pornography industry is discussed with regard to its possible impacts on men and women.

Shackelford and Weekes-Shackelford (chap. 11) present an evolutionary psychological analysis of the failure of men in the Western world to pay child support following divorce or dissolution of the relationship between the child's father and mother. They address several hypotheses toward why men so frequently fail to pay, as well as why women are sometimes reluctant to file charges against a spouse who has failed to provide support. They also address ways in which an evolutionary perspective can inform efforts to successfully collect child support from fathers.

Life history traits are psychological and phenotypic features that are associated with an individual's allocation of time, energy, and risk taking to reproduction and survival. May studies indicate that developmental correlates of uncertain or short adult survival lead to allocation to current reproduction, rather than to survival and delayed reproduction. Thornhill and Palmer (chap. 12) suggest that rape proneness in men may be a type of reproductive allocation cued by uncertain and/or brief future prospects. The implications of this perspective for reducing rape, as well as male criminal and delinquent behavior in general, are discussed.

The status of women in the workplace is usually analyzed according to a model claiming men and women are inherently similar, differing only in reproductive function and physical strength. The "glass ceiling," the "gender gap," and occupational segregation are attributed to external forces such as social conditioning and discrimination. Evolutionary theory suggests that the human mind is not sexually monomorphic and that sex differences in tempermental and cognitive traits will often lead the two sexes along different occupational paths. Browne (chap. 13) points out the failure of antidiscrimination laws to achieve workplace equality across the board and suggests that a deeper understanding of sex differences in occupational outcomes is required to develop a mature public policy perspective.

Psychopathy is a condition associated with persistent antisocial conduct beginning early in life. Psychopaths are of particular concern because they are more likely to reoffend and to reoffend violently than nonpsychopathic offenders. In chapter 14, Barr and Quinsey note that it is currently unclear whether psychopathy is a pathology of a life history strategy. Evidence that psychopathy is a life history strategy includes its high heritability, analyses showing they are a discrete class of individuals, that a number of psychopathic traits seem to confer fitness benefits, and the finding of relatively few neurodevelopmental abnormalities among highly psychopathic offenders. The implications of the view of psychopathy for identifying proximal causes and possible intervention are considered.

Krebs (chap. 15) focuses on the evolutionary processes that create moral dispositions, how these dispositions are contingent on contextual cues, and why they are in competition with more selfish and immoral urges. Krebs also considers the implications of these natural inclinations for public policies concerning socialization and social control, arguing that the key to maximizing morality is to structure social systems in ways that activate the evolved mechanisms that give rise to moral behaviors and increase the benefits of behaving morally.

In the final chapter, Robins provides a commentary on the previous chapters, giving a political perspective on the psychological ones presented.

Marital Cooperation
and Conflict

ॐ

Margo Wilson
Martin Daly
McMaster University

L aws and policies are instituted to regulate the pursuit of individual self-interest in situations in which people's interests may conflict. A theory of what those interests are, and of where they are likely to conflict, is a *theory of human nature*. It follows that all notions about what sorts of laws and policies would be effective and just are predicated upon theories of human nature, and more specifically of the nature of the human psyche: fundamental desires, social inference processes, specific susceptibilities to developmental influences, and so forth. However, the theories of human nature that inform legislative and policy debates are often implicit and unexamined, which is unfortunate because they are not always sound. Because psychological and social scientists are in the business of making models of human nature explicit, in order to test their validity, both the theories and the discoveries of psychological and social science can be relevant to the deliberations of legal scholars and policymakers. Moreover, because the human psyche is undoubtedly a product of the evolutionary process, consideration of how that process works can be a valuable guide in the pursuit of better models of the nature of the human psyche.

Psychologists who lack an evolutionary perspective sometimes misunderstand the evolutionary approach as unduly reductionistic, simplistic, and deterministic, with no place for human deliberation and agency. In fact, these complaints have no more applicability to evolutionary psychology than to psychological science in general. The evolutionary thinking that guides the development of our research questions and hypotheses treats people and other creatures as active agents with intricately structured information-processing abilities and self-interests, responding to ecological and demographic cues in ways that can be understood as having evolved to contribute to adaptive outcomes in ancestral environments.

In this chapter, we explore some implications of research findings concerning marital conflict, discoveries that were inspired by taking an evolutionary theoretical approach to understanding marital relationships and their characteristic conflicts. We trust that readers will not misunderstand us as advocates of the "naturalistic fallacy" (the belief that to provide a naturalistic explanation is to justify a behavior or practice). Rather, we suggest that an evolutionarily informed view of marital relationships and of the protagonists' perceptions, emotions, motives, and priorities may be useful in anticipating how particular social and economic conditions, laws, and policies are likely to be received by various segments of the populace.

FAMILY LAW REFORMS CAN PRODUCE UNINTENDED CONSEQUENCES

Policies that are designed to address one problem often create others. Although the issue is seldom articulated in this way, policymakers constantly face the question of whether proposed changes are likely to be considered unjust by certain segments of the population, perhaps to such a degree as to inspire noncompliance and a more general contempt for law and policy, and of whether proposed changes will create incentives for behavior that the policymakers deem undesirable.

When policymakers' implicit assumptions about human nature are unfounded, the risk that these unwanted consequences will be serious and that the policy will be a failure is exacerbated. We discuss here two examples from the domain of family law, both involving child support obligations, first in situations of uncertain paternity and secondly in situations of substitute parenthood. Both are cases where it seems to us that legislative missteps might have been avoided if decision makers had possessed a sounder evolution-based theory of the human mind.

Delict Versus Descent as Rationales for Imposing Child Support Obligations

According to Sass (1977), two major legal theories have been proffered as justifications for the imposition of a child support obligation on a reluctant putative father who is not married to the child's mother. (A "legal theory" is not analogous to a theory in science. The latter is, at least ideally, subject to disconfirmation by factual discovery, whereas a legal theory is a justificatory argument whose virtues and flaws are not subject to empirical test.) The first of these alternative legal theories is the *theory of delict*, whereby the father's liability arises from his (illicit) sexual access to the mother. The second is the *theory of descent*, whereby the father's liability is based on his genetic relationship with the child.

The theory of delict, as characterized by Sass and others, would seem to imply shared liability among all men who, by virtue of sexual access to the mother, had an opportunity to have sired the child, including even those known not to have done so. But in fact, such a line of reasoning is seldom if ever advanced; in practice, shared liability is proposed as a resolution in cases with unresolved paternity doubt. At various times, for example, the laws of Denmark, Norway, and France have all adopted ostensibly delictual constructions of the duty of support: A possibility that a man could be the sire warranted a support obligation without further assessment of whether he was in fact the sire. This sexual liability was imposed on all men who could have been the possible sire, unless the woman was a prostitute or otherwise sexually debauched, and in several legal decisions, justices have imposed such responsibility on several men at once (Sass 1977). But although such laws and rulings have been argued to be delictual in their reasoning, in that the obligation derives from the fact of illicit intercourse, it is noteworthy that there is almost always some unresolved doubt about paternity, and that judges who attempt to close the matter against future reversals of their decision are more concerned with judicial closure and limiting use of the courts than with ensuring that all those who enjoyed sexual access should pay. Moreover, the parties to such proceedings regularly protest that the imposition of obligation on one who is not the father would constitute an injustice, implicitly rejecting the principle that delict per se could constitute a principled basis for decisions. (There is the interesting case of multiple paternity obligations among some of the indigenous peoples of South America [Beckerman & Valentine, 2002], and it would be interesting to know more about the relatedness of the putative fathers to the children and the benefits and costs of child support.)

Arguably, the point at issue in the delictual legal theories has never ceased to be paternity, rather than mere sexual access, and the distinction between these laws and those that are more clearly descent based is simply one of standards of proof (Wilson, 1987). The implication is that legal decision makers, commentators, and principals all generally subscribe to the theory of descent. But why? Why should anyone think it fairer that obligations should be allocated on the basis of the chance victory of one man's sperm over others in the race to the egg, rather than on the seemingly more principled basis of moral choices and behavior?

Evolutionary theory provides a rationale for considering the existence and well-being of a child to constitute a benefit to its genetic parents, and for then interpreting the majority view that descent-based liability is fair, whereas delict-based liability is not, as a reflection of an intuitive recognition of that benefit. He who sires a child and escapes all obligation is viewed negatively, as a free-rider on the efforts of others, even if he is unaware of the child's existence and derives no pleasure from it. He has "gotten away with" something, but what? It cannot be mere illicit sexual pleasure, or else delictual constructions of support obligations would be widely considered just. They are not, and where they have been tried, they have been resisted and flouted until replaced by a descent-based rule (Sass, 1977). We infer that children are widely but implicitly perceived as constituting an intrinsic benefit to their genetic parents, over and above any pleasure had in conceiving them, and over and above any material and social benefits they may provide to whomever occupies a parental role.

Homo sapiens is a biparental species, in which males make regular and apparently essential investments in the welfare of children. Natural selection must always have favored those male minds that preferentially directed those investments to their own genetic offspring rather than to the children of rivals. Of course, men (like males in many other biparental species) often shirk their obligations, even to children they believe to be their own. Folk psychology and case law support the expectation, held by litigants and legislators alike, that a man will be more inclined to comply with a support order if he believes himself to be the sire than otherwise and, moreover, that such an order is more defensible in terms of natural justice. Thus, establishment of paternity, often on the basis of scientific evidence, is widely and increasingly seen as a requisite for legal imposition of support obligations (e.g., Miller & Garfinkel, 1999), and various policies have been introduced to promote paternity establishment, including public funding of genetic tests.

These considerations raise the question of whether protestations of injustice and failures to comply with court-ordered paternal support obligations may sometimes be inspired or exacerbated by circumstances and cues to which the male psyche responds as probabilistic indicators of nonpaternity. This question is wide open to research. Resemblance of a child to its putative father, for example, may affect a man's willingness to invest in its welfare, and if such paternal discrimination has indeed evolved because it had the effect of facilitating the flow of resources controlled by ancestral men toward their own children, it need not follow that these discriminations will be associated with an articulable suspicion of nonpaternity. Men may respond to other cues. Noncustodial fathers are more inclined to support children who have been given the putative father's name (Furstenberg & Talvitie, 1980), for example, perhaps because such naming represents a maternal commitment to identify one particular man as the sire, and such commitments have at least some statistical validity as paternity cues. Surnames are valid cues of genetic relatedness (e.g., Sykes, 2001), and even total strangers are more likely to comply with a request for assistance if the party making the request shares their name (Oates & Wilson, 2002).

Disinclination to Provide Financial Support to Stepchildren

The observation that descent-based paternal obligation is considered fairer than delict-based rules also raises the issue of the psychology of step-relationship. From an evolutionary theoretical perspective it would be expected that stepparents would not derive the same emotional rewards from parental investment and the welfare of the children as would genetic parents. It is not parental feeling that motivates stepparents to make costly investments in their stepchildren; rather, they invest in the marital relationship with the genetic parent (Anderson, Kaplan, & Lancaster, 1999a; Anderson, Kaplan, Lam, & Lancaster, 1999b; Daly & Wilson, 1997; Rohwer, Herron, & Daly, 1999). It follows that there may be anomalies in the laws that are intended to serve the "best interests of the child."

For example, in 1999, the Canadian Supreme Court ruled[1] that a stepfather who treats his partner's child from a prior union as his own invites a legal imposition of continued child support obligations should the marital union dissolve. Despite the clarity of the ruling, numerous stepparents since have requested the termination of their support obligations to former stepchildren.[2] The Divorce Act of Canada[3] and child support guidelines were recently reviewed by a family law committee with the following conclusion:

> Courts have adopted a variety of approaches to this issue. In light of the resulting inconsistencies some people have argued that the regulations should give judges explicit direction about determining the amount of support for step-children. However, allocating child support among natural parents and stepparents is quite a complex task, which is largely driven by the facts of each case. During consultations, most respondents were concerned that a rigid formula could create unfair results. For these reasons, this section should not be amended. (Minister of Justice and Attorney General of Canada, 2002)

If potential stepparents (or their legal advisors) are aware of this implication that parent-like investments and solicitude will hold them liable for continued support should the relationship end, and if the tacit negotiations in courtship and (re)marriage are indeed conducted in the shadow of any sort of conscious or nonconscious apprehension of the risk that the union may not be permanent, then the Divorce Act and case law treating a stepparent as a person "in the place of a parent"[4] could be producing unintended and counterproductive disincentives: The shadow of obligations extending beyond marital dissolution may be exacerbating, rather than countering, step-parental ambivalence and withholding, and perhaps even undermining the security and stability of reconstituted families. Judicial commentary on a recent Supreme Court case briefly alludes to this tension: "Individuals may be reluctant to be generous toward children for fear that their generosity will give rise to parental obligations," and furthermore, "Superficial generosity

---

[1] Chartier v. Chartier (1999) S.C.R., January 28, 1999.

[2] For example, *Clarke* v. *Clarke* [1998] B.C.J. No. 2370 (S.C.) *Oliver* v. *Oliver* (2000), 6 R.F.L. (5th) 389 (B.C.S.C.); *Dutrisac* v. *Ulm* (2000), 75 B.C.L.R. (3d) 159, 6 R.F.L. (5th) 132 (C.A.) *Greenhalgh* v. *Greenhalgh* [2000] B.C.S.C. 163 (S.C.); *Russenberger* v. *Rebagliati* (2000), 5 R.F.L. (5th) 130 (B.C.S.C.).

[3] *Divorce Act*, 1985, c.3 (2nd suppl), s. 2.

[4] *Divorce Act*, 1985, c.3 (2nd suppl), s. 2.

given merely because a person seeks the attention of a child's parent should be discouraged because the rejection experienced by the child when that financial and emotional support is abandoned is not beneficial to society in general and to the child in particular" (Chartier v. Chartier [1999] S.C.R., January 28, 1999).

From an evolutionary perspective, steprelationship is in one sense analogous to cuckoldry: A child raised by a couple is a potential vehicle of fitness for one party but not the other. It is different from cuckoldry, however, in that this asymmetry is out in the open, and has ideally entered into the negotiation of entitlements and reciprocities in the remarriage. Nevertheless, the presence of stepchildren is an important risk factor for marital disruption and violence (Campbell et al., 2003; Daly, Singh, & Wilson, 1993; Daly, Wiseman, & Wilson, 1997) and the stepchildren themselves incur greatly elevated risk of severe assault (Daly & Wilson 1985, 1988a,b; 2001a). Step-parenthood is one of several forms of "fictive," or nominal, kinship in which people find themselves placed, not always altogether willingly, in interpersonal statuses that are artificial analogues of kinship statuses. It would be very surprising if the appropriate relationship-specific psychology were fully activated by such experiences, because the interests of those with whom one interacts are seldom identical to one's own. Natural selection has presumably acted to buffer people against being the manipulanda of others' social agendas. Nevertheless, it is to be expected that the genetic parent in a stepfamily will be inclined to do what he or she can to induce stepparent and stepchildren to feel and act more like genetic relatives than their own inclinations might otherwise dictate.

Interests and Conflicts of Interest

As we noted at the outset, if a primary function of law and public policy is the regulation of actual or potential conflicts of interests, then correct apprehension of those interests is crucial. An evolutionary psychological framework identifies the distal basis of the interests of individuals as reproduction, because reproductive consequences are the currency of natural selection and hence the criteria by which adaptations, including the most basic human perceptions of self-interest, have evolved (Daly & Wilson, 1997). However, this does not imply that the attainment or violation of individuals' interests can be measured by their reproductive success. Because human motives, emotions, and cognitive processes have been "designed" by natural selection, they should be interpretable (and to some degree predictable) as effective means to reproductive ends in ancestral environments, but their subjective value is autonomous.

For laws and policies to be effective in protecting people against violations of their interests, those interests as well as the reasons why they conflict must be identified (Strahlendorf, 1991). An evolutionary approach can help to clarify why an individual's goals, desires, tastes, and motives may be in conflict with those of another, and point to ways in which the intensity and detailed substance of these conflicts may vary systematically in relation to sex, lifestage, context, and relationship of the parties. Husbands and wives are partners in procreation, for example, and because they derive equal increments in their Darwinian fitness from successful reproduction, one might predict that spousal harmony will generally be enhanced by the presence of children of the present union and diminished by the presence of children of former unions. In addition, discord due to adultery may be anticipated, and a sexual asymmetry in that men seem to be more inclined to seek extramarital sex than women (because it was more likely to enhance the total reproductive success of our male than our female ancestors), and yet exhibit more jealous concern about the sexual fidelity of their spouses than women (because only males have been vulnerable to mistakes in identifying their children).

SOURCES OF MARITAL CONFLICT

Marriage is a universal social institution, albeit with myriad variations in social and cultural details (Murdock, 1967; Van den Berghe, 1979). A review of the cross-cultural diversity in marital arrangements reveals certain common themes: some degree of mutual obligation between husband and wife, a right of sexual access (often but not necessarily exclusive), an expectation that the relationship will persist (although not necessarily for a lifetime), some cooperative investment in offspring, and some sort of recognition of the status of the couple's children. The marital alliance is fundamentally a reproductive alliance: Recognized marriage has invariably been restricted to heterosexual couples, and the relationship categories that proscribe marriage in any particular society are generally coincident with those that proscribe sexual relations (Thornhill, 1991). The fact that certain religious authorities have failed to recognize marriages of impotent or otherwise reproductively incompetent persons speaks to the implicit assumption of these religious institutions that marital alliances are fundamentally reproductive alliances, and the consideration that it can also be described as an economic union does not undermine the conclusion that its reproductive function is primary, because the complementary economic endeavors of marital partners have historically and cross-culturally served the purpose of raising a family.

In referring to marriage's reproductive function, we are not simply talking of its historical origins. Marital ambitions, sentiments, and behavior continue to exhibit signs of "design" for reproduction. For example, youth has always been more relevant to a woman's mate value (which is largely a function of her reproductive value) than to a man's, and social status has greater impact on a man's mate value than a woman's; accordingly, when choosing marriage partners, men everywhere place more emphasis on a candidate's youth than do women (e.g., Kenrick & Keefe, 1992), and women everywhere place more emphasis on a candidate's social standing than do men (e.g., Buss, 1989). The fit between the emotions of the partners and marital alliance's reproductive function is even clearer when we consider responses to infidelity. Adultery by either partner threatens the other's expected fitness, but for slightly different reasons: A woman whose husband philanders or aspires to polygyny suffers a diminution in his investments in her children and herself, whereas a man with an adulterous wife risks misdirecting his parental investments to enhance rivals' fitness. It might thus be anticipated that the sexual jealousy of women and men would be qualitatively different, with male jealousy more focused on the sexual act and female jealousy focused on the alienation of material resources, and that is exactly what a diversity of evidence indicates (Buss, 2000; Buss, Larsen, Westen, & Semmelroth, 1992; Daly, Wilson, & Weghorst, 1982; Teisman & Mosher, 1978).

If marriage is fundamentally to be understood as a cooperative reproductive partnership, in which the children are equally valuable to the fitness of both parents, then how is marital conflict to be understood in evolutionary perspective? To answer this, we must first note that reproductive partnership does not impart perfect commonality of interests. One reason that it does not is because personal reproduction is only one component of fitness (Hamilton, 1964). Marriage partners have separate kindred, in whom they are likely to retain their benevolent interests, and each may then resent the other's continued nepotistic investment of time, attention, and material resources in collateral kin. This is the widely recognized "in-law" problem.

Moreover, even if marriage partners eschew collateral nepotism, their reproductive alliance may be fragile. If both parties want out, conflict may be minimal, but the inclination to separate is probably more often asymmetrical (Daly & Wilson, 2000). This can arise because the partners have, or perceive themselves to have, different "mate values" in the marriage market and hence unequal opportunities for striking a better deal (Buss & Schmitt, 1993; Petrie & Hunter, 1993). Moreover, regardless of whether either party is tempted to end the marriage, there may be conflict over the husband's inclination to be a polygamist, when feasible. More generally, even monogamously married men are often tempted to allocate resources to extramarital mating effort rather than to the wife and children at home. This, of course, is one source of wifely grievance about inequitable investment in the marriage and may again contribute to asymmetrical inclinations to end the marriage. More generally, power asymmetries and resultant dissatisfactions are important direct sources of conflict.

We are invoking reproductive partnership and conflicts as the natural selective underpinnings of the psychology of sexual partnership, but it is necessary to note that although the couple's joint venture is functionally reproductive its substance includes all the mundane business of subsistence.

Marital Conflict and Male Sexual Proprietariness

Anthropologists have maintained that marriage originated as (and in much of the world continues to be) a contract between kin groups of men, in which a woman, with her sexual, reproductive, and productive potential, is bestowed by her natal group upon a groom in exchange for benefits from the groom and his kinsmen (e.g., Lévi-Strauss, 1969). Some may protest that senior women also participate in negotiating marital exchanges, but that does not gainsay the fact that brides are treated as valuable property and marriage commonly entails the transfer of proprietary entitlements. Murdock (1967) tabulated various aspects of the practices of 860 distinct human societies (where "a" society usually corresponds to a language), and he noted that a net transfer of valuable goods ("bridewealth") and/or services from the groom's family to the bride's was characteristic of marriage in 580 (67%) of them. A net movement of wealth in the opposite direction ("dowry") was customary in only 3% of societies, and in the remaining 30%, no asymmetrical transfer of wealth was essential or typical. Modern industrial societies, where the importance of kinship has largely withered, fall into this last group, but they often retain vestiges of proprietary transactions, as when a man "gives" his daughter in marriage.

Having acquired a wife, to what is a man entitled? His proprietary rights may include control of the fruits of her labor, but this is far from universal. What a husband gains in all societies is legitimate sexual access to his wife and the opportunity to sire her children (Wilson & Daly, 1992), and in most cases these rights are exclusive (or are his to bestow). Some anthropologists have been so impressed by the labor value of children and by the utility of having a large kin group as to assert that it is not the opportunity to sire their wives' children that men value, but the opportunity to claim them as kin once they are born. However, this argument is refuted by the ethnographies, in which it is difficult to find even an anecdote involving rival claims of paternity, whereas men's efforts to *deny* paternity and escape its attendant obligations abound. The argument is also refuted by the failure of delict- versus descent-based support obligations, discussed earlier. Men are profoundly concerned that the children in whose welfare they invest are their own, and are often enraged to discover otherwise (Daly & Wilson, 1988a, 1988b).

The proposition that men's sexual proprietariness evolved to defend their probability of paternity implies that female infidelity has been a genuine threat to male fitness. Men certainly feel and act as if there were some risk that their wives might deceive them in this domain (Daly et al., 1982; Wilson & Daly, 1992), but it could be suggested that their apprehension is unfounded, perhaps even a fantastic projection of their own inclinations. An evolutionist might have hypothesized that women would be monogamous in their inclinations, for as we noted earlier, a male's expected fitness increases as the number of his sexual or marital partners increases, but it is not so obvious why the same should be true for females; the factors that limit female fitness are usually constraints of time and energy, rather than a limitation in the number of male partners. Nevertheless, there are a number of theoretical and empirical reasons to believe that woman's psyche has not evolved to be strictly monogamous (Gangestad & Simpson, 2000; Gangestad, R. Thornhill, & Garver, 2002; R. Thornhill & Gangestad, 1996; Simpson & Gangestad, 1991), and survey data confirm the proposition that although men may be more inclined to engage in extramarital sex than women, the latter are not uninterested. According to a 1990 British national probability survey of 18,876 men and women, for example, 19.8% of married or cohabiting men and 10.1% of married or cohabiting women reported two or more heterosexual partners in the past year (A. M. Johnson, Wadsworth, Wellings, Field, & Bradshaw, 1994.), and when people are asked how much infidelity they would like to engage in, sex differences are typically larger, but both sexes still profess adulterous inclinations (Buss, 1994).

Violence Against Wives

One of the foci of our own research is epidemiological investigation of the demographic and situational correlates of violence against wives. Emerging from this research, and giving it direction, is the assumption that violence and threats of violence are coercive tools, which men are especially apt to use in response to perceived threats of temporary or permanent usurpation of their sexual monopoly of their wives. The cues by which men apprehend these threats may vary from very indirect probabilistic indicators of such a risk (or even the delusion thereof) to irrefutable evidence (Wilson & Daly, 1993a, 1993b).

In our research on marital violence, we have treated the relatively rare phenomenon of lethal violence against wives as a window on the broader phenomenon of marital conflict. Killings are extreme manifestations of conflict, to be sure, but they hold an advantage for researchers in the fact that their detection and reportage is relatively unbiased with respect to social class and other attributes that confound analyses of the risk of nonlethal manifestations of conflict. Whether lethal and nonlethal violence against wives exhibit similar patterns of risk in relation to demographic and situational factors is an answerable question (Campbell et al., 2003; H. Johnson & Hotton, 2003; Wilson & Daly, 1998a; Wilson, H. Johnson, & Daly, 1995).

The ostensible motive in the majority of uxoricides is the husband's aggrieved intolerance of the alienation of his wife, either through (suspected or actual) adultery or through her quitting the marriage. Daly and Wilson (1988b) reviewed several studies of well-described spousal homicide cases from a diversity of societies, and in each sample, such sexual proprietariness was apparently the primary motivational factor in over 80% of the cases; see also Allen (1990), Campbell (1992), Mahoney (1991), and Polk (1994). Crawford and Gartner (1992) compiled data from police and coroner's files on 551 women killed by intimate partners in Ontario between 1974 and 1990. Among several conclusions, they stated that "the predominant motive for intimate femicides appears to be offenders' anger or rage over estrangement from their partners" (p. vii). The uxoricide rate for wives who were no longer coresiding was substantially higher than for coresiding wives in Canada, in the state of New South Wales in Australia, and in Chicago (Fig. 9.1; see also H. Johnson & Hotton, 2003, for very similar rates for Canada for 1991–2000). The rates at which separated wives are slain by husbands is substantially greater than the rates for those coresiding, notwithstanding the reduced access and hence "opportunity" for a crime of passion. It must be noted, however, that this contrast must substantially underestimate the risk of lethal assault associated with estrangement, because denominators for the rates portrayed include separations of all durations, whereas the period of risk is apparently concentrated in the immediate aftermath of separation. Among the Australian cases, 47% of the wives were killed within 2 months of terminating coresidency and 91% within one year (Wallace, 1986). Among uxoricides of estranged wives in Hamilton, Ontario, between 1974 and 1995, 9 of 10 estranged registered-married wives were killed within 3 months of separating (Daly, Wiseman, & Wilson, 1997). A recent review of the statistics of fatal and nonfatal assaults of estranged

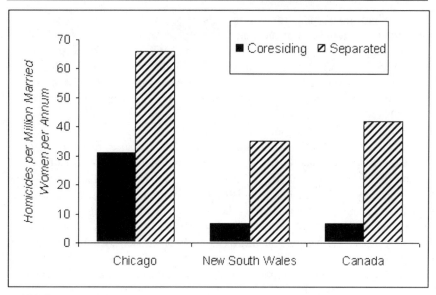

FIG. 9.1.   Married women are more likely to be killed by husbands from whom they are separated than while coresiding. Uxoricides in Chicago 1965–1990; in New South Wales, Australia, 1968–1996; and in Canada 1974–1990. Adapted from Wilson and Daly 1993.

wives in Canada (Hotton, 2001) provides much more extensive evidence of these risks. Estrangement is also a significant risk factor among battered women for being killed (Campbell et al., 2003).

A policy-relevant implication of these findings is that strong passions and a substantial risk of violence are associated with female-initiated separation. Those who work in women's shelters have long been aware that danger attends the decision to leave a violently proprietary husband, and a substantial proportion of a shelter's budget may be devoted to protecting the building and its occupants against the wrath of estranged husbands. Estranged wives are likely to be the target of stalking by proprietary husbands (e.g., Burgess, Harner, Baker, Hartman, & Lole, 2001).

Estrangement implies a permanent dissolution of the union, but even the discovery of a single act of wifely infidelity is an exceptional provocation, likely to elicit a violent rage (Daly & Wilson, 1988b; Wilson & Daly, 1993b). Indeed, such a rage is widely considered so compelling as to mitigate the responsibility of violent cuckolds (Daly et al., 1982). In Anglo-American common law, for example, killing upon the discovery of a wife's adultery has been deemed to be the act of a "reasonable man" and to warrant a reduced penalty (Edwards, 1954). Violent sexual jealousy is considered normal or at least unsurprising both in societies in which the cuckold's violence is seen as a reprehensible loss of control (e.g., Dell, 1984) and in those where it is seen as a praiseworthy redemption of honor (e.g., Bresse, 1989; Chimbos, 1993; Safilios-Rothschild, 1969). These phenomena may be interpreted as being indicative of the cross-cultural ubiquity of misogyny and patriarchy, but such interpretations beg the question of the sources of the specific content of violent men's perceived grievances. Men are apparently much less likely to assault their wives for profligacy or stupidity or sloth, and they cannot invoke these failings as provocations in the courtroom. In fact, the only provocations that have been invested with the same power as wifely adultery to mitigate a killer's criminal responsibility in the Anglo-American commonlaw tradition are physical assaults upon himself or a relative (see, e.g., Dressler, 1982).

Granting the motivational relevance of jealousy to transitory rages and hence to the violent incidents themselves, however, it is still pertinent to ask whether those husbands who are especially proprietary and controlling are also the husbands who are especially violent. In 1993, Statistics Canada surveyed a national probability sample of 12,300 women, 8,385 of whom were currently residing with a spouse, about their experiences of sexual harassment, threats, and sexual and physical violence by marital partners and other men (H. Johnson & Sacco, 1995). Among other things, the women were also asked to assess the applicability of five statements about "autonomy-limiting" aspects of some men's behavior to their own husbands.

Each of the five autonomy-limiting behaviors was attributed substantially more often to husbands who were also reported to have behaved violently than to nonviolent husbands (Table 9.1). Moreover, women who had experienced relatively serious violent incidents, as defined by their affirmation of one or more of a set of particularly violent acts, were much more likely to affirm each of the five items than were women who had experienced only lesser violence. The validity of the seriousness criterion is supported by the fact that among those women who were interviewed further about one incident of violence perpetrated by a coresiding spouse, the percentage reporting having incurred an injury requiring medical attention was 72% for incidents that met the criterion of serious violence and 18% for incidents that did not (Wilson et al., 1995). In addition, wives reported being fearful for their lives in 56% of the incidents that met the "serious" criterion versus 9% of the violent incidents that did not.

Women were also asked "How many different times did these [violent] things happen?," and the more violent episodes a woman had experienced, the greater was her likelihood of affirming that her husband had engaged in the autonomy-limiting behaviors as well (Table 9.2). Thus, the testimony of Canadian women suggests that especially proprietary, controlling husbands are indeed especially violent husbands. Rather than wife assault being one of an alternative set of controlling tactics of proprietary men, it appears to go hand in hand with other tactics of control.

Conflict between Spouses over Parental Investment

Many variables that are relevant to changes in maternal solicitude toward a child should be similarly relevant for fathers. The paternal case, however, is different from the maternal one, in at least three ways, all of which suggest that there will be a sexual asymmetry in the time course of changes in parental affection:

TABLE 9.1

Percent of Canadian Wives Affirming the Applicability of "Autonomy Limiting"
Items to the Behavior of Their Current Husbands
(Registered and Commonlaw Unions Combined), in Relation to Perpetration
of Violence by the Husband. Adapted from Wilson, Johnson, and Daly 1995.

	Violence?		
Statement	None N = 6,990	Only "Non-serious" N = 1,039	"Serious" N = 286
"He is jealous and doesn't want you to talk to other men."	3.5 %	13.0	39.3
"He tries to limit your contact with family or friends."	2.0	11.1	35.0
"He insists on knowing who you are with and where you are at all times."	7.4	23.5	40.4
"He calls you names to put you down or make you feel bad."	2.9	22.3	48.0
"He prevents you from knowing about or having access to the family income, even if you ask."	1.2	4.6	15.3
Mean (± SD) autonomy-limiting index (range 0–5)	0.17 ± 0.53	0.74 ± 1.08	1.78 ± 1.51

TABLE 9.2

Average Autonomy-Limiting Index Values for Wives Who Have Experienced
Different Numbers of Violent Incidents During Their Current Marriages
(Registered or De Facto). Adapted from Wilson, Johnson, and Daly, 1995

	Mean ± SD
No violence (N = 6,990)	0.17 ± 0.53
Single incident (N = 788)	0.65 ± 1.02
2–10 incidents (N = 390)	1.13 ± 1.26
11 or more incidents (N = 154)	2.20 ± 1.50

1. Women's reproductive life spans end before those of men, so the utility of alternative reproductive efforts declines more steeply as a function of own age for women than for men.
2. Dependent children impose different opportunity costs on mothers and fathers, a nursing infant constraining mother's immediate alternative reproductive prospects much more than father's, for example, and the magnitude of this differential impact on mother versus father declines with time since birth.
3. Phenotypic and other evidence of paternity may surface after infancy and is expected to be relevant to paternal but not maternal solicitude.

These three considerations suggest that a mother's valuation of a child relative to her valuation of herself is likely to rise more steeply with time since the child's birth than is the corresponding quantity for the father (Daly & Wilson, 1988a; Wilson & Daly, 1993c). These considerations suggest sex differences in marital conflict. Fathers, more than mothers, are likely to divest or reduce their investment in their children. Fathers, more than mothers, are likely to be interested in pursuing alternative reproductive opportunities, and the time course over the adult life span for pursuing these alternative mateships will be different for mothers and fathers.

Stepfamily Life.   There is abundant evidence that "reconstituted" families are disproportionately susceptible to a wide range of problems, including professed dissatisfaction by all parties, running away, poor scholastic performance and dropping out, early departure from home, and family violence (Daly & Wilson, 1996, 1998; Wilson & Daly, 1987). These problems are sometimes attributed to the insidious effects of the "Cinderella myth," but this puts the matter backwards. Taking on parental duties is generally perceived as a cost of remarriage, not a benefit, and single parents appear to be disadvantaged in the marriage market. Moreover, econometric analyses indicate that the presence of children of the current marriage has the effect of reducing the divorce rate for first and subsequent marriages alike, whereas the presence of children of former marriages raises it (Becker, Landes, & Michael, 1977; White & Booth, 1985). The implication drawn by Nobel Prize winning economist Gary Becker and others is that one's own genetic children must be considered to have positive utility in their own right, rather than being valued as means to the end of wealth accrual, whereas stepchildren have negative utility.

Even when a step-parental role is voluntarily undertaken, investment in the children remains a contested issue. Messinger (1976), for example, asked remarried Canadians with children from previous marriages to rank the areas of "overt conflict" in each of their marriages. "Children" and "money" topped the list for the remarriages, but were hardly ever mentioned for the failed first marriages, and it was clear from the interviewees' elaborations that these two ostensibly distinct issues were really one and the same: The mother wanted more of the stepfather's resources invested in her children than he was inclined to contribute. There is also abundant evidence that parental investment is withheld from stepchildren (e.g., Case, Lin, & McLanahan, 2000; Case & Paxson, 2001), including Canadian evidence (Biblarz, Raftery, & Bucur, 1997), and that stepchildren leave home at substantially younger ages than children living in homes of comparable means, with their genetic parents, again including Canadian evidence (Davis & Daly, 1997; Mitchell, 1994).

These facts are unsurprising to evolutionists. Because children are the principal vehicles of fitness for both mother and father, we may expect that children will tend to be sources of parental harmony: Anything that helps or hurts a given child's well-being has the same impact on the fitness of both parents, with the result that mother's and father's evaluations of various hypothetical futures are likely to converge. But whereas children of the present union facilitate consensus on the crucial question of how the couple's resources should be allocated, children from former unions may be expected to have exactly the opposite effect, as it seems they do. The conflicts and "ambivalence" characteristic of step-relationship are predictable consequences of putting people into a relationship that is structurally analogous to, and must serve as a partial substitute for, the most intimate of loving relationships, namely that of parent and child.

The fact that children in stepfamilies are at greater risk of being abused or killed suggests that mistreatment of stepchildren is itself a likely source of marital conflict. This is a question that had not previously been addressed before our studies of the violence against wives in Hamilton, Ontario (Fig. 9.2). Women with children sired by former partners sought refuge at a shelter for women from assaultive husbands at a per capita rate about five times greater than did same-age mothers whose children were all sired by the present father (Daly et al., 1993). We also estimated that wives with children from prior unions were more likely to have been killed than wives whose children were sired by the killer: 55% of the 20 mothers (32 uxoricides in total) were killed by husbands/stepfathers (Daly et al., 1997). This homicide dataset is small and local, but the phenomenon may be ubiquitous; a replication of the phenomenon has recently been reported for Houston, Texas, with a much larger dataset (Brewer & Paulsen, 1999). A recent multisite study of risk factors predicting lethal outcomes for battered wives (Campbell et al., 2003) found that stepchildren were a significant factor in elevating the risk of uxoricide.

CONCLUSIONS

A common misunderstanding of taking an evolutionary psychological approach to understanding human psychology and behavior is to suppose that it must entail hypothesizing that the specific behavioral phenomena under study are, or once were, adaptive (fitness-promoting). In actuality, they may be maladaptive and yet these "mistakes" are no less the products of evolved psychological processes and mechanisms than are the "successes." The aim of evolutionary thinking about psychology and behavior is to formulate hypotheses that reflect the selection pressures or social and ecological challenges that designed the psyche to respond in a contingent manner to experiences and to situational and physiological cues so as to solve the particular adaptive problem in ancestral environments. The challenge is to

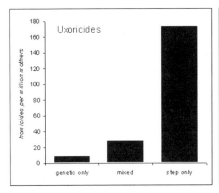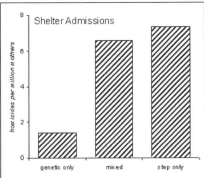

FIG. 9.2.   Partner violence against women residing with a male partner and minor children (< 18 years of age) in relation to the paternity of her children. Adapted from Daly et al., 1993, 1997.

identify the level of abstraction of the hypothesized trait or psychological process that would correctly characterize the environmentally contingent adaptation in ancestral environments.

One of the most important implications of taking an evolutionary psychological approach to the study of marital conflict is that conflict domains are highly relationship specific, and often asymmetrical. Husbands and wives have systematically and predictably different perspectives on what constitutes a betrayal of the marital relationship. Mothers and fathers have systematically and predictably different perspectives on the allocation of reproductive effort to parenting and to the pursuit of alternative reproductive opportunities. From a policy perspective, an evolutionary psychological approach offers a framework for evaluating the possible ramifications of particular policies, regulations, and laws that pertain to sexual and marital relationships.

ACKNOWLEDGMENTS

We thank the Social Sciences and Humanities Research Council of Canada, the Harry Frank Guggenheim Foundation, and the Natural Sciences and Engineering Research Council of Canada for financial support.

REFERENCES

Allen, J. A. (1990). *Sex and secrets: Crimes involving Australian women since 1880.* Melbourne: Oxford University Press.

Anderson, K. G., Kaplan, H., & Lancaster, J. (1999a). Paternal care by genetic fathers and stepfathers I: reports from Albuquerque men. *Evolution & Human Behavior, 20*, 405–431.

Anderson, K. G., Kaplan, H., Lam, D., & Lancaster J. (1999b). Paternal care by genetic fathers and stepfathers II: Reports by Xhosa high school students. *Evolution & Human Behavior, 20*, 433–451.

Becker, G. S., Landes, E. M., & Michael, R. T. (1977). An economic analysis of marital instability. *Journal of Political Economy, 85*, 1141–1187.

Beckerman, S., & Valentine, P. (2002). *Cultures of multiple fathers. The theory and practice of partible paternity in lowland South America.* Gainesville, FL: University Press of Florida.

Biblarz, T., Raftery, A. E., & Bucur, A. (1997). Family structure and social mobility. *Social Forces, 75*(4): 1319–1339.

Bresse, S. K. (1989). "Crimes of passion: The campaign against wife killing in Brazil, 1910–1940. *Journal of Social History, 22*, 653–666.

Brewer, V., & Paulsen, D. (1999). A comparison of U.S. and Canadian findings for uxoricide risk for women with children sired by previous partners. *Homicide Studies, 3*, 317–332.

Burgess, A. W., Harner, H., Baker, T., Hartman, C. R., & Lole, C. (2001). Batterers stalking patterns. *Journal of Family Violence, 16*, 309–321.

Buss D. M. (1989). Sex differences in human mate preferences: evolutionary hypotheses tested in 37 cultures. *Behavioral & Brain Sciences, 12*, 1–49.

Buss D. M. (1994). *The evolution of desire.* New York: Basic Books.

Buss D. M. (2000). *The dangerous passion: Why jealousy is as necessary as love and sex.* New York: The Free Press.

Buss, D. M., Larsen, R. J., Westen, D., & Semmelroth, J. (1992). Sex differences in jealousy: Evolution, physiology, and psychology. *Psychological Science, 3*, 251–255.

Buss, D., & Schmitt, D. (1993). Sexual strategies theory: an evolutionary perspective on human mating. *Psychological Review, 100*, 204–232.

Campbell, J. C. (1992). Wife battering: Cultural contexts versus Western social sciences. In D. A. Counts, J. K. Brown, & J. C. Campbell (Eds.), *Sanctions and sanctuary: Cultural perspectives on the beating of wives* (pp. 229–249). Boulder, CO: Westview Press.

Campbell, J., Webster, D., Koziol-McLain, J., McFarlane, J., Block, R., Campbell, D., Curry, M. A., Gary, F., Wilt, S., & Manganello, J. (2003). Risk factors for femicide in intimate partner relationships: Results from a multisite case control study. *American Journal of Public Health, 93*, 1089–1097.

Case, A., Lin, I.-F., & McLanahan, S. (2000). How hungry is the selfish gene? *Economic Journal, 110*, 781–804.

Case, A., & Paxson, C. (2001). Mothers and others: Who invests in children's health? *Journal of Health Economics, 20*(3), 301–328.

Chimbos, P. D. (1993). A study of patterns in criminal homicides in Greece. *International Journal of Comparative Sociology, 34*, 260–271.

Crawford, M., & Gartner, R. (1992). *Woman killing: Intimate femicide in Ontario 1974–1990.* Toronto: The Women We Honour Action Committee.

Daly, M., Singh, L. S., & Wilson, M. I. (1993). Children fathered by previous partners: A risk factor for violence against women. *Canadian Journal of Public Health, 84*, 209–210.

Daly, M., & Wilson, M. (1985). Child abuse and other risks of not living with both parents. *Ethology & Sociobiology, 6*, 197–210.

Daly, M., & Wilson, M. I. (1988a). Evolutionary social psychology and homicide. *Science, 242*, 519–524.

Daly, M., & Wilson, M. I. (1988b). *Homicide.* Hawthorne, NY: Aldine de Gruyter.

Daly, M., & Wilson, M. (1996). Violence against stepchildren. *Current Directions in Psychological Science, 5*, 77–81.

Daly, M., & Wilson, M. I. (1997). Crime and conflict: Homicide in evolutionary psychological perspective. *Crime and Justice, 22*, 251–300.

Daly, M., & Wilson, M. (1998). *The truth about Cinderella.* London: Weidenfeld & Nicolson.

Daly, M., & Wilson, M. I. (2000). The evolutionary psychology of marriage and divorce. In L. Waite, M. Hindin, E. Thompson, & W. Axinn (Eds.), *Ties that bind: Perspectives on marriage and cohabitation* (pp. 91–110). Hawthorne, NY: Aldine de Gruyter.

Daly, M., & Wilson, M. (2001a). An assessment of some proposed exceptions to the phenomenon of nepotistic discrimination against stepchildren. *Annales Zoologici Fennici, 38,* 287–296.

Daly, M., & Wilson, M. (2001b). Family violence: an evolutionary psychological perspective. *Virginia Journal of Social Policy and Law, 8,* 77–121.

Daly, M., Wilson, M., & Weghorst, S. J. (1982). Male sexual jealousy. *Ethology and Sociobiology, 3,* 11–27.

Daly, M., Wiseman, K. A., & Wilson, M. (1997). Women with children sired by previous partners incur excess risk of uxoricide. *Homicide Studies, 1,* 61–71.

Davis, J. N., & Daly, M., (1997). Evolutionary theory and the human family. *Quarterly Review of Biology, 72,* 407–435.

Dell, S. (1984). *Murder into manslaughter.* Oxford, England: Oxford University Press.

Dressler, J. (1982). Rethinking heat of passion: A defense in search of a rationale. *Journal of Criminal Law and Criminology, 73,* 421–470.

Edwards, J. Ll. J. (1954). Provocation and the reasonable man: Another view. *Criminal Law Review,* 898–906.

Furstenberg, F. F., & Talvitie, K. G. (1980). Children's names and paternal claims: Bonds between unmarried fathers and their children. *Journal of Family Issues, 1,* 31–57.

Gangestad, S. W., & Simpson, J. A. (2000). The evolution of human mating: Trade-offs and strategic pluralism. *Behavioral and Brain Sciences, 23,* 573–587.

Gangestad, S. W., Thornhill, R., & Garver, C. E. (2002). Changes in women's sexual interests and their partners' mate-retention tactics across the menstrual cycle: Evidence for shifting conflicts of interest. *Proceedings of the Royal Society of London B, 269,* 975–982.

Hamilton, W. D. (1964). The genetical evolution of social behaviour. I and II. *Journal of Theoretical Biology, 7,* 1–52.

Hotton, T. (2001). Spousal violence after marital separation. *Juristat, 21*(7).

Johnson, A. M., Wadsworth, J., Wellings, K., Field, J., & Bradshaw, S. (1994). *Sexual attitudes and lifestyles.* Oxford, England: Blackwell Scientific.

Johnson, H., & Hotton, T. (2003). Losing control: Homicide risk in estranged and intact intimate relationships. *Homicide Studies, 7*(1), 58–84.

Johnson, H., & Sacco, V. (1995). Researching violence against women: Statistics Canada's national survey. *Canadian Journal of Criminology, 37,* 281–304.

Kenrick, D., & Keefe, R. C. (1992). Age preferences in mates reflect sex differences in reproductive strategies. *Behavioral and Brain Sciences, 15,* 75–133.

Lévi-Strauss, C. (1969). *The elementary structures of kinship.* Boston: Beacon Press.

Mahoney, M. R. (1991). Legal images of battered women: Redefining the issue of separation. *Michigan Law Review, 90,* 1–94.

Messinger, L. (1976). Remarriage between divorced people with children from previous marriages: A proposal for preparation for remarriage. *Journal of Marriage & Family Counseling, 2,* 193–200.

Miller, C., & Garfinkel, I. (1999). The determinants of paternity establishment and child support award rates among unmarried women. *Population Research and Policy Review, 18,* 237–260.

Minister of Justice and Attorney General of Canada. (2002). Children come first: A report to parliament reviewing the provisions and operation of the *Federal Child Support Guidelines* (Vol. 2). Ottawa: Her Majesty the Queen in Right of Canada.

Mitchell, B. A. (1994). Family structure and leaving the nest: A social resource perspective. *Sociological Perspectives, 37,* 651–671.

Murdock, G. P. (1967). *Ethnographic atlas.* Pittsburgh, PA: University of Pittsburgh Press.
Oates, K., & Wilson, M. (2002). Nominal kinship cues facilitate altruism. *Proceedings of the Royal Society of London B, 269,* 105–109.
Petrie, M., & Hunter, F. M. (1993). Intraspecific variation in courtship and copulation frequency—An effect of mismatch in partner attractiveness. *Behaviour, 127,* 265–277.
Polk, K. (1994). *When men kill: Scenarios of masculine violence.* Cambridge, England: Cambridge University Press.
Rohwer, S., Herron, J. C., & Daly, M. (1999). Step parental behavior as mating effort in birds and other animals. *Evolution &. Human Behavior, 20,* 367–390.
Safilios-Rothschild, C. (1969). 'Honor' crimes in contemporary Greece. *British Journal of Sociology, 20,* 205–218.
Sass, S. L. (1977). The defense of multiple access (exception plurium concubentium) in paternity suits: A comparative analysis. *Tulane Law Review, 51,* 468–509.
Simpson, J. A., & Gangestad, S. W. (1991). Individual differences in sociosexuality: Evidence for convergent and discriminant validity. *Journal of Personality and Social Psychology, 60,* 870–883.
Strahlendorf, P. W. (1991). *Evolutionary jurisprudence: Darwinian theory in juridical science.* Unpublished JDS thesis, School of Law, University of Toronto.
Sykes, B. (2001). *The seven daughters of Eve.* New York: Norton.
Teismann, M. W., & Mosher, D. L. (1978). Jealous conflict in dating couples. *Psychological Reports, 42,* 1211–1216.
Thornhill, N. W. (1991). An evolutionary analysis of rules regulating human inbreeding and marriage. *Behavioral & Brain Sciences, 14,* 247–262.
Thornhill, R., & Gangestad, S. W. (1996). The evolution of human sexuality. *Trends in Ecology & Evolution, 11,* 98–102.
Van den Berghe, P. L. (1979). *Human family systems.* New York: Elsevier.
Wallace, A. (1986). *Homicide: The social reality.* Sydney: New South Wales Bureau of Crime Statistics and Research.
White, L. K., & Booth, A. (1985). The quality and stability of remarriages: The role of stepchildren. *American Sociological Review, 50,* 689–698.
Wilson, M. (1987). Impacts of the uncertainty of paternity on family law. *University of Toronto Law Review, 45,* 216–242.
Wilson, M., & Daly, M. (1987). Mistreatment of stepchildren. In R. J. Gelles & J. B. Lancaster (Eds.), *Child abuse and neglect: Biosocial dimensions* (pp. 215–232). Hawthorne, NY: Aldine de Gruyter.
Wilson, M., & Daly, M. (1998a). Lethal and nonlethal violence against wives and the evolutionary psychology of male sexual proprietariness. In R. E. Dobash & R. P. Dobash (Eds.), *Violence against women: International and cross-disciplinary perspectives* (pp. 199–230). Thousand Oaks, CA: Sage Publications.
Wilson, M., & Daly, M. (1998b). Sexual rivalry and sexual conflict: Recurring themes in fatal conflicts. *Theoretical Criminology, 2*(3), 291–310.
Wilson, M. I., & Daly, M. (1992). The man who mistook his wife for a chattel. In J. Barkow, L. Cosmides, & J. Tooby (Eds.), *The adapted mind* (pp. 289–322). New York: Oxford University Press.
Wilson, M. I., & Daly, M. (1993a). An evolutionary psychological perspective on male sexual proprietariness and violence against wives. *Violence and Victims, 8,* 271–294.
Wilson, M. I., & Daly, M. (1993b). The psychology of parenting in evolutionary perspective and the case of human filicide. In S. Parmigiami & F. vom Saal (Eds.), *Infanticide and parental care* (pp. 73–104). London: Harwood Press.
Wilson, M. I., & Daly, M. (1993c). Spousal homicide risk and estrangement. *Violence & Victims, 8,* 3–16.
Wilson, M. I., Johnson, H., & Daly, M. (1995). Lethal and nonlethal violence against wives. *Canadian Journal of Criminology, 37,* 331–361.

The Pornography Debate: What Sex Differences in Erotica Can Tell About Human Sexuality

Catherine Salmon
University of Redlands

> To encounter erotica designed to appeal to the opposite sex is to gaze into the abyss that separates the sexes. —(Salmon & Symons, 2001)

T he pornography debate has been a long one and it shows no signs of letting up. People have made the claim that pornography is bad for men, dangerous for women, harmless, a waste of money, bad for people in the industry itself, and a reflection of how some men see (or objectify) women. Many of these claims have not been based on actual research, although some have. Many people are uncomfortable with the whole topic, feeling that sex is not appropriate for public discussion, that there's something inherently "bad" about the idea of pornography. But in order to reasonably address the issues behind this debate, and perhaps one day end it entirely, it is necessary to understand the male sexual psychology that makes the pornography industry so successful and how it differs from (and at times may resemble) pornography, or erotica as it is often called, that is produced for female consumption.

Evolutionary psychology can provide a great deal of insight into this area. Much of the research in the field over the past two decades has focused on mating and sexual behavior and the psychological mechanisms that produce such behavior. A more complete understanding of male sexual psychology, its implications, and its connection to pornography will allow humans, as a society, to properly evaluate the issues and determine if there really is a problem that needs to be addressed and if there is, how best to solve this problem in light of evolved human desires and dispositions.

Many kinds of data can illuminate male and female sexual psychologies. Male-oriented pornography and female-oriented romance novels are multibillion dollar global industries, whose products, both visual and written, have been shaped in free markets by the purchasing and rental choices made by millions of men and women who have paid hard earned money for what they desire. Analysis of such erotica can provide insight into the essential nature of male and female psychosexuality. One advantage, from a psychological perspective, of conducting research on commercial erotica is that the design features—that is, the essentials—of porn and of romances constitute unobtrusive measures of male and female sexual psychologies. Real life heterosexual interactions inevitably involve compromise, blurring the differences between male and female sexual desires and dispositions. Erotica has no need for such compromises, because it is targeted at sex-specific audiences.

One way in which erotica can be used to illuminate human sexual psychology is to compare commercially successful products with less successful ones. Sales figures and royalty checks provide reliable information about men's and women's psychology. Another approach is to attempt to identify the essential ingredients of erotica genres. A third approach is to analyze smaller, more esoteric erotic genres and to compare them to mainstream forms.

This chapter examines mainstream erotica for men and women and how it illustrates male and female sexual psychologies. It also discusses political and personal issues related to erotica. In particular, it looks at the claims that pornography increases violence against women, and that it influences men's attitudes toward women in a negative way. Implications for private policy or decisions related to a partner's use of erotic material and its possible impact on relationships are also explored.

UNOBTRUSIVE MEASURES

Many different kinds of studies can provide information about male and female sexual psychologies. One such method involves combining questionnaire studies with unobtrusive measures. Unobtrusive measures are research methods that do not require the cooperation of respondents and do not themselves contribute to the response (Webb et al., 1966). One well-known example of the use of unobtrusive measures is the work of Daly and Wilson (1998) on homicide. They used police statistics on child abuse and homicide to illuminate the psychology of parental love, drawing attention to the conditions (stepparent, offspring quality, etc.) that influence parental solicitude.

Another example focuses on research on human waist-to-hip ratio (WHR). A number of evolutionists have suggested that in ancestral human populations, selection favored males who were sexually aroused by visually detected characteristics of female bodies that reliably indexed high "mate value." Among human females, WHR provides reliable information about health, age, hormonal status, parity, and fecundity; hence, human males can be expected to have evolved psychological mechanisms specialized to extract and process this information (Singh, 1993). Because female mate value varies inversely with WHR, other things being equal, female sexual attractiveness also can be expected to vary inversely with WHR. Singh (1993, 1994) tested this hypothesis using both unobtrusive measures and experimental data.

Based on analyses of the measurements of *Playboy* centerfold models and Miss America contest winners over the last 30 to 60 years, Singh (1993) concluded that "a narrow waist set against full hips [WHR in the .68–.72 range] has been a consistent feature of female attractiveness, whereas other bodily features, such as bustline, overall body weight, or physique, have been assigned varying degrees of importance over the years" (p. 304).

The early focus in this chapter is on commercially available erotica, mainly male-oriented pornography and female-oriented romance novels. They are the primary components of commercial erotica.

Commercial pornography exists in every industrialized society and in many developing societies as well. Worldwide sales of sexually explicit magazines, books, and videos net approximately $56 billion annually (Morais, 1999). Sexually explicit videos are stocked by two thirds of American video rental stores (U.S. Department of Justice, 1986) and, in 1998, Americans rented nearly seven million "adult" videotapes (Morais, 1999), and 8,948 hard-core videos hit the U.S. market. The growth of the porn industry has been marked by successes that have acquired almost mythical proportions. The film *Deep Throat*, which brought fellatio into the spotlight in 1972, cost a mere $25,000 to make and became a classic of the genre, generating more than $100 million in profit (Cook, 1978). Estimated revenues in the United States (in 1998) range from $35 million for Vivid Video (makes 90 feature-length movies a year) to $318 million for Playboy Enterprises (adult television, video, and publishing).

Arcand (1991) suggested that it is "essential to know whether there is such a thing as a pornography consumed exclusively by women, and whether it is fundamentally different from that preferred by men" (p. 49). The answer is yes and it is the romance novel.

Romance novels account for 40% of mass market paperback sales in the United States, generating annual revenues of $4 to $6 billion. In the last year, almost 3,000 romances were published in North America, where more than 45 million women are romance readers. Harlequin Enterprises, one of the largest publishers of romances, boasts annual worldwide sales of over 190 million books, attesting to the enormous appeal of these narratives to women everywhere.

One advantage to conducting research on commercial erotica is that the design features of porn and of romances constitute unobtrusive measures of male and female sexual psychologies. Real-life heterosexual interactions inevitably involve compromise and therefore blur differences between male and female sexual desires and dispositions. Erotica, aimed at either a male or female audience, has only to please one sex at a time.

One way in which erotica can be used to illuminate human sexual psychology is to compare commercially successful products with less successful ones. Sales figures and royalty checks provide reliable information about women's psychology. Best-selling romance novels, for example, almost never feature gentle, sensitive heroes, because women readers prefer to fantasize about strong, confident men who ultimately are tamed only by their love for the heroine. *Gone with the Wind* is a classic example of the popularity of a strong hero; by the end of the novel, Scarlett's affection has shifted from the sensitive but rather helpless Ashley to the powerful Rhett Butler. The popularity of Russell Crowe's character of Maximus in *Gladiator* is another example of the appeal of strong heroes. Romance writers who have experimented with gentle, sensitive heroes have not been rewarded in the marketplace. Within the last few years, there was a sensitive new age guy line of romances, and it failed rather quickly.

Another unobtrusive measures approach is to attempt to identify the essential ingredients of erotic genres. For example, a common characteristic of pornographic videos is attempted humor; but, humor is not an essential ingredient. Many thousands of humorless porn videos are commercially successful. In contrast, impersonal sex is an essential ingredient of porn videos.

PORNOGRAPHY

Because printed narratives and color photographs cannot match the visual and auditory realism offered by film, movies are the preferred medium for modern-day male consumers of sexually explicit material. Analyses of contemporary sexually explicit films reveal a fairly narrow range of themes and content.

The utopian male fantasy realm depicted in pornography, "pornotopia," has remained essentially unchanged over time. In pornotopia, sex is all about lust and physical gratification, totally lacking in courtship, commitment, durable relationships, or mating effort. It is a world in which women are eager to have sex with strangers, easily sexually aroused, and always orgasmic. Where else would a man meet not one but two beautiful strangers in an elevator who proceed to perform oral sex on him? Porn videos contain minimal plot development, focusing instead on the sex acts themselves and emphasizing the display of female bodies, especially close-ups of sexually aroused facial expressions, breasts, and genitals. The majority focus almost entirely on sex, routinely representing "lesbianism, group sex, anal intercourse, oral-genital contact, and visible ejaculation" (Hebditch & Anning, 1988, p. 49). Nonsexual interpersonal behavior is almost completely excluded. A content analysis of 50 random films reveals fellatio to be the most frequent act, followed by vaginal intercourse, with cunnilingus a distant third (Brosius, Weaver, & Staab, 1993). Sex scenes typically culminate with a male ejaculating on a female's body. The fact that videos and, in the last few years, the Internet so thoroughly dominate male-oriented erotica testifies to the deeply visual nature of male sexuality. Men tend to be sexually aroused by "objectified" visual stimuli. As a consequence, porn videos do not require the existence of a point of view (POV) character to be effective, and scenes of a woman masturbating alone, or engaging in sexual activity with another woman, are relatively common. The male viewer can imagine taking the sexually aroused woman out of the scene and having sex with her. Female porn stars manifest cues of high mate value in that they are young and physically attractive. Pornotopia, in short, is a world of low cost, impersonal sex with an endless succession of lustful, beautiful, orgasmic women.

THE ROMANCE NOVEL

Although the romance novel has been called, with some justification, "women's pornography," it is really the opposite of male oriented porn. The goal of a romance novel's heroine is never sex for its own sake, much less impersonal sex with strangers. The basis of a romance novel's plot is a love story in which the heroine overcomes obstacles to identify, win the heart of, and ultimately marry the one man who is right for her. Which is why there are no romance serials featuring the same heroine, as there are endless iterations of James Bond or other male-oriented adventures; each romance must end with the establishment of a permanent union. Unlike male-oriented porn, the existence of a POV character with whom the reader subjectively identifies is an essential feature of romance fiction. The heroine is usually the main POV character, although the POV can shift back and forth between heroine and hero.

Romances vary dramatically in the extent to which sexual activity is depicted, from not-at-all to highly explicit descriptions. Although the description of sexual activities is common in romances, it is not an essential ingredient. When sex is described, it serves the plot rather than dominating it. The hero discovers in the heroine a fulfilling focus for his passion, which binds him to her and ensures his future fidelity. Sex scenes depict the heroine's control of the hero, not her sexual submissiveness. Sexual activity is described subjectively as opposed to objectively, primarily through the heroine's emotions, rather than through her physical responses or through visual imagery. The emotional focus of a romance is on love, commitment, and domesticity. Its final goal is the creation of a perfect union with the heroine's ideal mate, one who is strong yet nurturing (Radway, 1984).

The Hero

The characteristics of the heroes of successful romances can shed a great deal of light on the psychology of female mate choice. As previously mentioned, these romances almost never feature gentle, sensitive new age kind of guys.

Gorry (1999) analyzed every description of the heroes of 45 romance novels. Each of the novels in her sample had been independently nominated for its excellence by at least three romance readers or writers. In all, or almost all, of the romances Gorry analyzed, the hero was older than the heroine, by an average of 7 years. Heroes were always described as taller than the heroine. The adjectives used most frequently to describe the physical characteristics of heroes were muscular, handsome, strong, large, tanned, masculine, and energetic. All of these focused on his good qualities from an attractive protector and provider perspective.

Gorry also found that romance heroes exhibited cues of what she called physical and social "competence." Heroes were described as sexually bold, calm, confident, and impulsive. In a majority of novels, the hero was described as "intelligent," although some lacked formal education.

The characteristics of heroes that were described most consistently had to do with their feelings for the heroines: He desires her sexually; he declares his love for her; he wants her more than any other woman he has ever seen; he has never loved a woman in the way he loves her; he thinks about her all the time; he is sexually jealous and possessive of her; he treats her gently; he wants to protect her. These feelings are exactly what would appear in a list of universal aspects of the experience of romantic love.

The essential characteristics of the hero of a successful romance novel have to do primarily with his physical appearance, physical and social competence, and intense love for the heroine. In contrast, being rich and having high socioeconomic standing, although more common perhaps among romance heroes than among men in general, are not essential characteristics of the hero. In Gorry's research, heroes had a high social rank or occupation in about half the novels. When considering the psychological adaptations that underpin human female mate choice, it is worth considering that money, social classes, and formal education did not exist for the overwhelming majority of human evolutionary history. The heroes of successful romance novels may or may not be rich or aristocratic, but they consistently possess characteristics that would have made them highly desirable mates during the course of human evolutionary history; they are tall, strong, handsome, healthy, intelligent, confident, competent, "dangerous" men whose love for the heroine ensures that she and her children will reap the benefits of these highly desirable qualities.

Donald (1992) summed up these aspects of the hero and his appeal very nicely: "Until very recently in our historic past, strong, successful, powerful men had the greatest prospects of fathering children who survived. If a woman formed a close bond with a man who was sensible, competent and quick-witted, one high up in the family or tribal pecking order, a man with the ability to provide for her and any children she might have, the chances of her children surviving were greater than those of a woman whose mate was inefficient" (p. 82).

Basically, the realm of the romance novel, which might be called "romantopia," is a utopian, erotic female counterfantasy to pornotopia. Just as porn actresses exhibit a suspiciously male-like sexuality, romances are exercises in the imaginative transformation of masculinity to conform with female standards. The essential ingredients of porn and romance novels imply the existence of deep and abiding differences between male and female mating psychologies.

WHY SUCH SEX DIFFERENCES?

But if over the course of human evolutionary history most successful reproduction occurred within marriages, and most marriages were monogamous partnerships, how is it possible for male and female sexual psychologies to differ as dramatically as commercial erotica would seem to imply?

The answer is that ancestral men and women differed qualitatively in some of the adaptive problems that they encountered in the domain of mating. However similar men's and women's typical parental investments may have been, the sexes differed dramatically in their minimum possible investments. If a man fathered a child in whom he did not invest, he could have reproduced at almost no cost. Even if such opportunities did not come along often in ancestral human populations, capitalizing on them when they did come along was so adaptive that males evolved a sexual psychology that makes low cost sex with new women exciting both to imagine and to engage in and that motivates men to create such sexual opportunities. Pornotopia is a fantasy realm, made possible by evolutionarily novel technologies, in which impersonal sex with a succession of high mate value women is the norm rather than the rare exception.

Ancestral females, by contrast, had nothing to gain and much to lose from engaging in impersonal sex with random strangers and from seeking sexual variety for its own sake, and they had a great deal to gain from choosing their mates carefully. The romance novel is a chronicle of female mate choice in which the heroine expends time and effort to find and marry a man who embodies the physical, psychological, and social characteristics that constituted high male mate value during the course of human evolutionary history.

Personal sexual fantasies reflect the same sex differences as commercial erotica. Female sexual fantasies are more likely than male ones to contain familiar partners and to include descriptions of context, setting, and feelings associated with the sexual encounter. Female sexual fantasies are more contextual, emotive, intimate, and passive, whereas male sexual fantasies are more ubiquitous, frequent, visual, specifically sexual, promiscuous, and active (Ellis & Symons, 1990). Sex differences in commercial erotica are, not unexpectedly, a mirror of the sex differences in personal sexual fantasies.

There is, however, no commercial erotic genre that combines the ingredients of pornotopia and romantopia. Such a genre would double the potential audience and perhaps the potential profit. After all, women are sexual as well as romantic beings, fully capable of being physically aroused by hard-core sex scenes. (In fact, a significant proportion of porn video rentals are to women—almost all of whom use them to enhance sexual activities with their partners, not to enhance solitary masturbation.) Also, the evidence from romance novels would seem to imply that women, like men, prefer erotica in which the sexual partners are new to each other rather than being an established couple. And choosing mates carefully and establishing long-term mateships were problems faced by both sexes, not just females, throughout human evolutionary history.

Many commercially successful romantic comedies and romantic adventures do, in fact, appeal to both sexes, and men and women alike can enjoy the literary works of a Jane Austen or a movie like *Sense and Sensibility*, but the unisex appeal of such films and novels is gained at the cost of failing to embody many of pornotopia's and romantopia's essential ingredients. One could imagine a film genre that combined a number of the ingredients of romantopia, pornotopia, and mainstream commercial cinema. Romantic adventures with complex plots, great dialogue, fascinating characters, award winning acting, attractive stars, happily-ever-after endings, and hard-core sex scenes.

But even if such films were produced, they would not eliminate the markets for porn and romances, because some of the essential ingredients of pornotopia and romantopia are mutually exclusive. Most obviously, impersonal sex, the core fantasy at the heart of pornotopia, is incompatible with romantopia. The "plot" of a porn film or video is rarely more than a feebly connected sequence of sex scenes, each of which typically ends with an external ejaculation, the so-called money shot. A porn video has as almost as many climaxes as it does scenes, but a romance novel has only one climax, the moment when the hero and the heroine declare their mutual love for one another. Table 10.1 provides a very vivid illustration of this incompatibility. It is very difficult if not impossible to imagine any of these adult video titles or romance novel titles appearing on the other list.

IMPLICATIONS FOR PUBLIC POLICY

Webster's New Collegiate Dictionary defines pornography as "the depiction of erotic behavior intended to cause sexual excitement." Much of the public debate over pornography has been muddled by concerns of what is and what is not pornography and the issues of obscenity and erotica. And different cultures vary in their attitudes about, and tolerance for, material with sexual content (Randall, 1989). In a multicultural modern society, does there need to be a public policy on pornography? What form should such policies take? And what about private policies?

There are many ways in which evolutionary psychology can inform public policy. But perhaps the most useful way is the way in which it informs about what is or what can be. Much public policy (if not most) is concerned with the way "we" would like the world to be. It is used to try and shape the world (or a particular society or country) into an "ideal" form. In other words, policy is a purposive course of

TABLE 10.1
Successful Porn Videos for Men and Romance Novels for Women

Successful Porn Video Rental Titles	Successful Romance Novels
Angels with Sticky Faces	To Love and Cherish
4-Eyed Whores	One Perfect Rose
Horny Housewives in Heat	A Precious Jewel
Nasty Nympho Nurses	Reason to Believe
Rocco Invades Poland	On Mystic Lake
All Alone and No One to Bone	Lord of Danger
Adventures of Mr. Tootsie Pole	My Beloved Scoundrel
The Aphrodisiac	Baby Be Mine
Cherry Poppers—The College Years	For My Lady's Heart
The 69th Sense	A Knight in Shining Armor

Note: Their titles provide a stark illustration of the differences between erotica produced for men and women. The porn titles were taken from *Best Adult Video Guide* and the romance titles were taken from *All About Romance*.

action followed by an actor or set of actors in dealing with a problem or matter of concern (Anderson, 1975). Once an ideal ("should") is decided on, the question is whether it will be easy or very difficult to achieve. It is this question that evolutionary psychology can address.

The policy process can be thought of in the following simple way. People have assumptions about human nature and how the world works. They act on these assumptions and the outcome of their decisions will be successful when their assumptions about human nature are correct. When these assumptions are wrong, there will be costs to these decisions, costs that can sometimes, although not always, be unreasonably high.

So in a sense, taking an evolutionary perspective toward public policy is very practical. Evolved preferences can suggest values and goals, but they will also enlighten as to evolved constraints on people's preferences, emotions, and behaviors, all factors that will strongly influence the outcome of policy decisions.

The public debate over pornography has been going on for years and it is beyond the scope of this chapter to detail that history. The debate has covered everything from the treatment of women within the industry (although many would argue the men have a harder time of it in terms of performance pressure than the women), to the image of women it presents and the impact of that image on men in the general population as well as the effects on women in the general population themselves. Diamond (1985), for example, suggested that pornographic material demeans women by depicting them as "malleable, obsessed with sex, and willing to engage in any sexual act with any available partner" (p. 53).

In fact, like prostitution, porn is often said to evidence male contempt for, or lack of respect for, women. But there exists an ideal test case for such claims: gay male porn. If these claims were accurate, gay male porn would be expected either not to exist at all, or, if it did exist, to differ in significant ways from straight male porn (e.g., it might emphasize the development of enduring relationships or be less relentlessly focused on genitals). But, in fact, gay and straight porn are essentially identical, differing only in the sex of the actors. In fact, gay porn often gives the impression of being more "real" than straight porn does: For one thing, the actors in gay porn almost invariably seem to be having a genuinely good time, which is not always true of the actresses in straight porn; for another, the impersonal sex depicted in gay porn is not very different from the real-life sexual relations of many gay men.

There has been a great deal of research into the issue of negative attitudes toward women on the part of men after viewing pornography. However, Davis (1997) claimed that men who viewed sexually explicit films did not have negative attitudes toward women's rights, nor were they more accepting of marital or date rape. In examining convicted sex offenders' experiences with porn, Marshall (1989) concluded that they did not differ from those of other incarcerated males. And, interestingly, when Kutchinski (1991) examined the incidence of rape in several societies that have lenient attitudes toward pornography, he concluded that increased availability was not associated with increased reports of rape in Denmark, Sweden, West Germany, or the United States (but see contradictory finding by Baron & Straus, 1984). But the question of effects of nonviolent sexually explicit material remains open (Linz, 1989).

More informative seems to be the work on violent pornography. A review of laboratory studies (Linz, 1989) suggests that exposure to nonviolent pornography does not seem to have adverse effects on attitudes toward rape and rape victims. Consistent negative effects were only found in subjects exposed to violence against women or violence and sex. There is agreement in general that exposure to sexual violence has negative effects on viewers (Allen et al., 1995; Linz et al., 1987; Linz & Malamuth, 1993) but that it is the violence not the sex per se that has the negative effects. And in fact, extreme sexual violence is fairly uncommon in pornography (Monk-Turner & Purcell, 1999).

But the real question that needs to be asked in terms of public policy and pornography is what are "we" trying to achieve? Should pornography disappear because some people are uncomfortable with the graphic portrayal of sexual activity? Or is there a different goal? Perhaps the hope is to reduce levels of violence against women? Or is it to improve men's attitudes toward women and women's issues? Will eliminating pornography change these things? The research certainly does not suggest so. Eliminating violence against women in media products, including pornography, seems a more logical step.

Pornography is about sex, and not about violence or the degradation of women. If there is one thing all porn videos have in common, it is the portrayal of women engaged in some form of sexual activity. An evolutionary perspective on male sexuality points out that modern pornography is exactly what should be expected given that men have evolved to find things like the sight of a young attractive naked woman arousing, and that a variety of such women is just as much or more appealing. The pornography industry is as successful as it is because it is a world where male sexuality runs wild, unchecked by the real-life compromises men must make in their sexual relationships with women. In many ways, pornography imposes a male-like sexuality on females, a fantasy of sexual utopia for men. But consider the other side, the romance novel, or "porn" for women. It imposes a female-like sexuality on men that is in many ways perhaps no more "realistic" than that of pornotopia. But no one is out there lobbying to ban romance novels because of the harm they do to women's attitudes toward men.

A consideration of the place of the porn/adult video industry in terms of where people spend their money is also worth some thought. Table 10.2 gives approximate sales figures in U.S. dollars for a variety of industries from cosmetics ($3 billion) to sports ($100 billion) to Hollywood ($11 billion), but it also points out an interesting fact. Harlequin, one of the biggest players in the romance novel game, is posting around 1 billion in sales per year, whereas Playboy Enterprises—dealing mostly in adult television, video, and magazines—is bringing in a bit over $300 million. Is pornography as prevalent as it is often portrayed?

Perhaps, not surprisingly, much of the opposition to pornography comes from women. It is interesting to consider why that is the case. It might be because they are the ones "hurt" by pornography, or because they are trying to protect the young women in the industry. But there is an alternative. Look at social exchange between men and women in terms of women gaining control over men and gaining resources by regulating men's access to sexual gratification. If pornography is an alternative source of such gratification for men, it (as does prostitution) reduces women's bargaining power in such a sexual/economic arena (see Baumeister & Twenge, 2002, for a discussion of female suppression of female sexuality).

TABLE 10.2
A Comparison of Industry Revenues

Industry/Individual Company	Approximate Sales in $U.S.
Harlequin	1 billion*
Playboy Enterprises	318 million*
Porn/Adult movie industry	20 billion*
Diet industry	50 billion*
Cosmetics	3 billion[+]
Cosmetic surgery	10 billion[+]
Mainstream film video	11 billion*
Sports industry	100 billion[+]

Note: This table highlights the amount of money spent on various industries/company products by both men and women; *worldwide; [+]U.S. statistics.

It seems unlikely that the demise of pornography would solve any of the problems/issues that are usually raised in debates on the subject. And the costs of trying to enforce such a ban should also be considered. Human nature should always be taken into account when considering public policy. Will a policy even be enforceable? What will the costs be of enforcing it? Would time and money be better spent elsewhere? Perhaps it would be better to work to decrease levels of violence in the media. Will enforcing a ban on pornography create other undesirable behaviors? All these questions need to be carefully considered in light of what is known about male sexuality.

IMPLICATIONS FOR PRIVATE POLICY

The issues to be discussed here are a little different. On a personal level, women often express concern over a partner's regular purchasing of *Playboy* or watching pornographic videos. In particular, there is a verbalized concern that these things will effect their relationships or that they are an indication that their partner is not satisfied with them and their sex life.

Should they be concerned? In a way, yes, and in another way, no. Kenrick and some of his colleagues (Kenrick, Gutierres, & Goldberg, 1989) conducted several studies that relate to the question of the impact of viewing pornographic images on an existing relationship. For example, in one study, they had men involved in a monogamous relationship view a series of images. Before and after looking at the images, the men were asked to rate their commitment to their partner. Those males that viewed images of attractive models reported being less committed to their partner after the viewing. In another study, they used *Playboy* centerfolds as the images and got the same results.

Now what this implies is that it is not the viewing of naked women or porn specifically that women should be concerned about, but rather their partners seeing lots of images of very attractive women in general. If, ancestrally, men were living in small groups of 50 to 100 people, then they would regularly see about 25 to 50 women, some of whom would be older, few who would be as attractive as the typical supermodel today. Maybe one or two would be. Regardless, the number of extremely attractive women in the population would be small and he would evaluate the attractiveness of his mate with regard to the other available females (the ones he sees face to face). Modern media filled society bombards men and women with images of beautiful women, perhaps giving men an unrealistic view of how many attractive available women are out there. So women should not be any more concerned about their partner viewing pornographic material than they should be over repeated exposure to attractive women on television or in advertising in general.

CONCLUSIONS

This chapter has used a comparison of romance novels and pornography to highlight differences in sexual psychology between the sexes. A more complete understanding of male and female sexual psychology is essential to completely grasp the nature of the pornography debate and the roles to be played by public and private policy. Taking an evolutionary psychological approach to the development of public policies toward pornography (if more or better public policies need to be made, and many would argue that they do) should lead to the development of more successful policies because they will take into account basic aspects of human nature. Such aspects have often been ignored to date in dealing with these issues.

REFERENCES

Allen, M., D'Allessio, D., & Brezgel, K. (1995). A meta-analysis summarizing the effects of pornography II. *Human Communication Research, 22*, 258–283.

Anderson, J. (1975). *Public policy-making.* New York: Praeger.

Arcand, B. (1991). *The jaguar and the anteater: Pornography and the modern world.* New York: McClelland & Stewart.

Baron, L., & Straus, M. A. (1984). Sexual stratification, pornography, and rape in the United States. In N. M. Malamuth & E. Donnerstein (Eds.), *Pornography and sexual aggression* (pp. 185–209). Orlando, FL: Academic Press.

Baumeister, R. F., & Twenge, J. M. (2002). Cultural suppression of female sexuality. *Review of General Psychology, 6*, 166–203.

Brosius, H. B., Weaver, J. B., & Staab, J. F. (1993). Exploring the social and sexual "reality" of contemporary pornography. *Journal of Sex Research, 30*, 161–170.

Cook, J. (1978, September 18). The X-rated economy. *Forbes*, 81–92.

Daly, M., & Wilson, M. (1998). *The truth about Cinderella: A Darwinian view of parental love.* London: Weidenfeld & Nicolson.

Davis, K. A. (1997). Voluntary exposure to pornography and men's attitudes toward feminism and rape. *Journal of Sex Research, 34*, 131–137.

Diamond, S. (1985). Pornography: Image and reality. In V. Burstyn (Ed.), *Women against censorship* (pp. 40–57). Vancouver, Canada: Douglas & McIntyre.

Donald, R. (1992). Mean, moody and magnificent. In J. A. Krentz (Ed.), *Dangerous men and adventurous women*. Philadelphia: University of Pennsylvania Press.

Ellis, B. J., & Symons, D. (1990). Sex differences in sexual fantasy: An evolutionary psychological approach. *Journal of Sex Research, 27*, 527–555.

Gorry, A. (1999). *Leaving home for romance: Tourist women's adventures abroad.* Unpublished doctoral dissertation, University of California at Santa Barbara.

Hebditch, D., & Anning, N. (1988). *Porn gold: Inside the pornography business.* London: Faber & Faber.

Kenrick, D. T., Gutierres, S. E., & Goldberg, L. (1989). Influence of erotica on ratings of strangers and mates. *Journal of Experimental Social Psychology, 25*, 159–167.

Kutchinski, B. (1991). Pornography and rape: Theory and practice? Evidence from crime data in four countries where pornography is easily available. *International Journal of Law and Psychiatry, 14*, 147–164.

Linz, D. (1989). Exposure to sexually explicit materials and attitudes toward rape: A comparison of study results. *The Journal of Sex Research, 26*, 50–84.

Linz, D., & Malamuth, N. (1993). *Communication concepts 5: Pornography.* Newbury Park, CA: Sage.

Linz, D., Donnerstein, E., & Penrod, S. (1987). The finds and recommendations of the attorney general's commission on pornography: Do the psychological "facts" fit the political fury? *American Psychologist, 42*, 946–953.

Marshall, W. D. (1989). Pornography and sex offenders. In D. Zillman & J. Bryant (Eds.), *Pornography: Research advances and policy considerations* (pp. 185–214). Hillsdale, NJ: Lawrence Erlbaum Associates.

Monk-Turner, E., & Purcell, H. C. (1999). Sexual violence in pornography: How prevalent is it? *Gender Issues, 17*, 58–68.

Morais, R. C. (1999). Porn goes public. *Forbes, 163*, 214–221.

Radway, J. (1984). *Reading the romance: Women, patriarchy, and popular literature.* Chapel Hill: University of North Carolina Press.

Randall, R. S. (1989). *Freedom and taboo: Pornography and the politics of self-divided.* Berkley: University of California Press.

Salmon, C., & Symons, D. (2001). *Warrior lovers: Erotic fiction, evolution and female sexuality.* London: Weidenfeld & Nicolson.

Singh, D. (1993). Adaptive significance of waist-to-hip ratio and female physical attractiveness. *Journal of Personality and Social Psychology, 65,* 298–307.

Singh, D. (1994). Is thin really beautiful and good? Relationship between waist-to-hip ratio (WHR) and female attractiveness. *Personality and Individual Differences, 16*, 465–481.

U.S. Department of Justice. (1986). *Attorney general's commission on pornography: Final report.* Washington, DC: U.S. Government Printing Office.

Webb, E., Campbell, D. T., Schwartz, R., & Sechrest, L. (1966). *Unobtrusive measures: Non-reactive research in the social sciences.* Chicago: Rand McNally.

Why Don't Men
Pay Child Support?
Insights From
Evolutionary Psychology

∾

Todd K. Shackelford
Viviana A. Weekes-Shackelford
Florida Atlantic University

Profound changes have occurred in the structure of the human family over the past several decades in the United States and much of the Western industrialized world. These changes have altered drastically the contexts in which children are raised, and include significant increases in cohabitation, nonmarital fertility, and divorce (Bumpass, 1990; Sweet & Bumpass, 1987; J. Q. Wilson, 2002). About 30% of all children in the United States today—at least 20 million children—do not live with their genetic father, and one in two children born in the United States today will live in a single-parent household for some period of time before adulthood (U.S. Bureau of the Census, 2001; and see Bumpass & Sweet, 1989; Norton & Miller, 1992; J. Q. Wilson, 2002).

A sizable literature addresses the effects of family structure on children's health and well-being. These studies consistently reveal that not living with both genetic parents negatively impacts children's lives (e.g., Daly & M. Wilson, 1985, 1988, 1998; McLanahan & Sandefur, 1994). Children living with just one genetic parent are more likely to receive less schooling, to have nonmarital births, and to live in poverty as adults than are children living with two genetic parents. Previous work suggests that a key culprit of the pitfalls of living in a single-parent household is lack of income of the single parent, nearly always the mother. Due to low income potential of their mother and the receipt of little or no child support from their father, a majority of these children live in economic poverty (see, e.g., Garfinkel & McLanahan, 1986; Holden & Smock, 1991; J. Q. Wilson, 2002).

In the United States in the 1990s, just half of resident parents who had been awarded child support orders received full payments, one fourth received partial payments, and one fourth received no payments (U.S. Bureau of the Census, 1995). Child support payments can have a substantial impact on the health and well-being of children residing with single parents (e.g., Fox & Blanton, 1995; Geary, 2000; Seltzer, Schaeffer, & Charng, 1989). To improve the economic lot of children living with single parents, in the United States and other industrialized countries over the past two decades, national efforts have sought to make more effective and efficient the payment of adequate child support by the noncustodial parent to the custodial parent (for reviews, see Baker, 2000; Garfinkel, McLanahan, & Robins, 1986; Garfinkel, Meyer, & McLanahan, 1998; J. Q. Wilson, 2002). These national efforts have promoted, inspired, and funded research designed to identify the predictors of child support payment—including the identification of which men do not pay and why they do not pay.

Most of the research designed to identify the determinants of child support payments or the failure to make child support payments has been sociological research, focusing on broad, macrolevel predictor variables, such as state-level payment enforcement policies (for reviews, see Fox & Blanton, 1995, and Garfinkel, Meyer, & McLanahan, 1998). A handful of researchers have recognized the need to identify the determinants of child support payments for individual men, focusing on the predictive value of relatively more specific variables at the levels of psychology and interpersonal relationship dynamics, such as the perceived quality of the former spouse relationship (see, e.g., Meyer & Bartfeld, 1998).

This chapter first briefly reviews what is known about child support payments (which men pay or do not pay and why or why not). This review highlights the sociological, macrolevel focus of previous work on the determinants of child support payment. The next section of the chapter highlights the value of addressing these issues from a psychological perspective, focusing on psychological processes that occur at the individual level. It then argues that research and policy will benefit by embracing an explicitly evolutionary psychological perspective (Buss, 1999; Tooby & Cosmides, 1992), in which the modern dilemmas of child support payment and receipt are investigated with a respect and appreciation for the recurrent adaptive problems confronted by ancestral mothers, fathers, and children. It outlines several evolutionary psychological hypotheses regarding the determinants of child support payment and, where applicable, discusses how previous research informs these hypotheses. Finally, it reviews various proposed solutions for increasing men's compliance with child support orders, and evaluates the likely success of these proposals. It concludes that an evolutionary psychological perspective not only can inform research into the determinants of child support payments, but also the social policies that might increase the reliability with which these payments are made.

WHAT DO WE KNOW ABOUT CHILD SUPPORT PAYMENTS?

Over the past two decades, sociologists and policy analysts have made great progress in identifying several macrolevel predictors of child support payment, as well as a few microlevel psychological or relationship-level predictors of child support payment. This section highlights what is known empirically about who pays child support, who does not, and why some men pay child support whereas others do not. The remainder of this chapter assumes that mothers are the custodial parents and fathers are the noncustodial parents responsible for child support payments. Although there are custodial fathers and noncustodial mothers responsible for child support payments, these family situations are relatively rare (see, e.g., Garfinkel, Meyer, & McLanahan, 1998).

Marital Status of Former Partners

Previous research identifies that the marital status of the former partners is a key predictor of the reliability and amount of child support payments made by the noncustodial father to the custodial mother. Women previously married to the child's father are substantially more likely to receive a greater amount of child support from the child's father and to receive this support more reliably than are women who were not married to the father, in part because previously married women are more likely to request and to be awarded such support (see, e.g., Laakso, 2002; Meyer & Bartfeld, 1996, 1998; Seltzer, 1991). There are many potentially confounding variables that might account for the relation between marital status and receipt of child support, however, including the fact that men who father children outside of marriage, compared to men who father children in marriage, have less education and make less money (see reviews in Garfinkel, McLanahan, Meyer, & Seltzer, 1998; Johnson, Levine, & Doolittle, 1999; Wilson, 2002). In addition, men who father children outside of marriage may be less certain of their paternity and, as a consequence, may be less willing to pay support for children to whom they may not be genetically related (Baker & Bellis, 1995). This possibility is addressed later in the chapter.

Parental Income and Education

Using data at the local, state, and national levels, several studies have documented that men with higher incomes and more education are more likely to fulfill their child support obligations (e.g., Arditti, 1992; Arditti & Keith, 1993; Hill, 1992; Meyer & Bartfeld, 1996; Seltzer et al., 1989; Smock & Manning, 1997; Teachman, 1991). Thus, one unsurprising determinant of making child support payments is the ability to pay them. That men with more education are more compliant with child support orders probably reflects the association between education and income, although there also may be an independent effect of education. Perhaps men with more education appreciate the economic and social value to their children of their child support payments more than do men with less education. There also is at least one study that has documented that the mother's income positively predicts child support payments. Using data collected from 220 couples as part of the Panel Study of Income Dynamics, Smock and Manning (1997) found that the incomes of both the nonresident parent (father) and resident parent (mother) are associated with greater child support payments. And at least one study indicates that custodial mothers with more education are more likely to receive child support owed to them (Seltzer, 1991).

Father's Proximity to Children and Visitation Frequency

Another focal point of previous research has documented that men who live closer to and, perhaps as a consequence, more frequently visit their noncustodial children also are more likely to meet their full child support obligations (e.g., Seltzer, 1991; Seltzer et al., 1989; but see Arditti, 1992; Arditti & Keith, 1993). What previous research has not yet determined is the direction of causality. Is the likelihood of child support payment higher as a consequence of living closer to and more frequent visits with children? Or perhaps men who meet their child support obligations feel entitled to visit more frequently in order to monitor the mother's spending of the child support monies. Or perhaps child support payment, living closer to children, and more frequent visitation with children are only spuriously associated, simultaneously caused by another variable, such as certainty of paternity—that is, men's assessment that they are genetically related to the children (e.g., Baker, 2000; Baker & Bellis, 1995).

Quality of Former Spouse Relationship

Using reports from a small sample of 59 divorced parents, Wright and Price (1986) documented that the quality of the relationship between the custodial and noncustodial parent (defined as co-parental communication, honesty, and type of relationship preferred) predicts compliance with child support orders. Arditti (1992, and see Arditti & Keith, 1993) randomly sampled 125 divorced fathers from court records in one Virginia county, and found that men who do not report attempting to avoid their former spouse also report paying more child support. Using a nationally representative sample of ever-divorced mothers ($N = 644$) from the National Longitudinal Study of the High School Class of 1972, Teachman (1991) found that fathers who contribute economically to their noncustodial children also report better relationships with the custodial mother.

In each of these studies, the key variable, "quality of relationship with former spouse," is not well defined, sometimes asking little more than a single question about how much the parents like each other, or how well they get along. Future research will need to clearly define "quality of the former spouse relationship" in a way that might allow for people in the helping professions to work with parents to improve the relationship, with the goal of increasing compliance with child support orders. An intriguing possibility addressed later in the chapter is whether the "quality" of the former spouse relationship, and the associated child support payments, might be predicted by the noncustodial father's continued sexual access to the mother (see, e.g., Weiss, 1975).

Remarriage and New Children

Several studies have investigated whether the remarriage and birth of subsequent children to one or both former spouses affects the reliability and amount of child support received by the custodial parent. Most of these studies have focused on the remarriage and birth of subsequent children to the noncustodial father. Studies focusing on the father's remarriage have produced mixed results, with some studies documenting that the father's remarriage is associated with lower or less reliable child support payments (e.g., Teachman, 1991), other studies documenting that his remarriage is associated with higher or more reliable child support payments (e.g., Seltzer, 1991), and still other studies finding no relation between the father's remarriage and the reliability or amount of child support payments (e.g., Hill, 1992; Meyer & Bartfeld, 1996; Smock & Manning, 1997). Fewer studies have addressed how the mother's remarriage affects the reliability and amount of child support payments made by the noncustodial father. These studies also have produced mixed results (e.g., Hill, 1992; Mandell, 1995; Seltzer, 1991).

Apparently just a single study has tested specifically the hypothesis that the birth of new children to the noncustodial father affects his support payments to children from a previous relationship. Using data from two waves of the National Survey of Families and Households, Manning and Smock (2000) analyzed reports by 133 noncustodial fathers with children under 18 at both waves living with mothers, and to whom the fathers made child support payments. Manning and Smock (2000) provided evidence that fathers "swap" or trade-off economic investment in current and previous children, but only when the trade-off is between new genetic children living in the father's household and existing genetic children living outside the father's household. These findings are consistent with a sizable literature indicating differential investment in stepchildren and genetic children (see, e.g., Daly & M. Wilson, 1988, 1995, 1996; M. Wilson, Daly, & Weghorst, 1980).

Other Correlates of the Reliability and Amount of Child Support Paid by Noncustodial Fathers to Custodial Mothers

A handful of studies conducted using data collected at the local, state, and national levels have identified a few additional correlates of the reliability and amount of child support paid by noncustodial fathers to custodial mothers. Using a sample of 180 divorced, custodial mothers, Seltzer et al. (1989) found that the amount of time since the divorce is associated with decreases in child support payments. Using data from the National Survey of Families and Households, which includes 1,350 cases in which the respondents are mothers in households with children under 18 and in which the father was living in another household, Seltzer (1991) found that mothers with younger children are more likely to receive child support than are mothers with older children (but see Meyer & Bartfeld, 1996). This relation might be confounded with other variables, however, including the time since divorce and the remarriage of one or both parents.

In summary, previous research conducted by sociologists and policy analysts has identified several predictors of the reliability and amount of child support paid by noncustodial fathers. These include the marital status of the former partners, parental income and education, the father's proximity to his children and the frequency with which he visits them, the quality of the former spouse relationship, and the remarriage and subsequent reproduction of one or both parents. Most of this previous research is empirically driven rather than designed to test specific hypotheses derived from integrative, coherent theories about human nature and psychology. The focus of this previous research instead has been on macrolevel sociological variables. One consequence of this broad focus is that there exists a large gap in knowledge about the determinants of child support payments that can be redressed by a focus on psychological processes. The next section of the chapter reviews what could be known about child support payments as a consequence of taking a psychological approach, in general, and an evolutionary psychological approach, in particular.

WHAT COULD WE KNOW ABOUT CHILD SUPPORT PAYMENTS?

Insights from the Psychological Sciences

Sociologists, political scientists, and policy analysts have made great progress over the past several decades in identifying several predictors of the reliability and amount of child support payments made by noncustodial parents to custodial parents. This progress was reviewed in the first section of this chapter. Yet there is much more that could be discovered about child support payments—who makes them and why, who does not make them and why not—by stepping outside the broad brushstrokes of the disciplines that focus on macrolevel descriptions and explanations. A focus on individual-level psychology and behavior may provide additional valuable insight into the problems, pitfalls, and challenges of child support.

Given similar educational backgrounds and similar incomes, for example, why might one man reliably provide child support whereas another does not? If two men have both remarried and had children by a new partner, how might we account for the fact that one man consistently provides support to the children by his first wife, whereas the other man does not (and assuming other key variables are controlled statistically, including, e.g., the income and education of the men)? As a final example, why might a noncustodial father reliably pay the child support he owes for a few months, even a few years, and then rescind that support when his former wife remarries? These are questions that are difficult to address, much less answer, by the macrolevel frameworks offered by disciplines such as sociology. Instead, the answers to these questions require a focus on individual-level psychology and behavior of noncustodial parents and custodial parents. The previous research reviewed in the first section of this chapter relies primarily on large samples of parents for which little detailed information is available. Few studies have collected detailed information from parents and children that might help to explain the many exceptions to the macrolevel findings identified by previous work (see Haskins, 1988; Mandell, 1995).

What is known about child support payments, therefore, has been generated by researchers working with existing databases that often include little detailed information about hundreds or thousands of cases. Few of these studies are informed by a coherent theory of human nature and psychology—in part, due to the apparent irreverence for such theory by the standard social scientists that fill the ranks of sociology and other macrolevel social science disciplines (see Tooby & Cosmides, 1992) and, in part, because working with these large archival databases seems to lend itself to number crunching at the expense of rigorous theoretical analyses. If society wishes to improve the flow of investment by noncustodial parents to their children, then other disciplines must be considered that can help add to the knowledge base of who pays child support, who does not pay child support, and why some noncustodial parents pay whereas others do not. The psychological sciences require a focused attention to the underlying information- processing mechanisms that generate the behaviors that sociologists and policy analysts have identified as correlates of child support payment or nonpayment. In order to identify the determinants of child support payment or nonpayment, an effort must be made to understand the mechanisms that generate the observed behaviors, and the environmental inputs that activate those mechanisms.

The psychological sciences and their focus on information-processing mechanisms—including the input into those mechanisms, the decision rules that determine the functioning of those mechanisms, and the output generated by those mechanisms—are always implicitly evolutionary psychological, and sometimes explicitly evolutionary psychological. This is because the only known cause of complex design or adaptation is evolution by natural selection (Buss, Haselton, Shackelford, Bleske, & Wakefield, 1998; Symons, 1987, 1992; Tooby &

Cosmides, 1992; Williams, 1966). The next section briefly addresses child support from an explicitly evolutionary psychological perspective. The intention is to open the door to explicitly evolutionary psychological discussions of child support—who pays, who does not pay, and why some men pay and some men do not pay. Much of the discussion is speculative and theoretical, with little or no relevant empirical work yet conducted. The intention in the following discussion is to suggest that an evolutionary psychological perspective might help add to the knowledge base of the determinants of child support payment and nonpayment.

Insights from Evolutionary Psychology

A modern evolutionary perspective suggests that in order to understand a behavior, a critical avenue of investigation is the underlying evolved psychology that generates that behavior. A careful consideration of the adaptive problems that ancestral humans were likely to have faced recurrently will help to identify the evolved psychological solutions to those adaptive problems. The modern case of a noncustodial father's formalized, state-regulated, and enforced child support payments can be conceptualized as a specific case of a man's continued investment in offspring produced by a woman to whom he was previously mated, but to whom he is no longer mated. The adaptive problem of whether and how much to invest in offspring has been a key focus of the evolutionary sciences over the past several decades, beginning with Trivers' (1972) seminal contribution (and see Dawkins & Carlisle, 1976; Maynard Smith, 1977; McNamara, Houston, Székely, & Webb, 2002).

In his theory of parental investment and sexual selection, Trivers (1972) noted two fundamental features of sexually reproducing species. First, the sex with greater minimum parental investment (i.e., investment necessary for an offspring to reach reproductive maturity) will be the choosier sex, displaying more stringent mate preferences and greater discrimination about with whom to mate. The sex with lesser minimum parental investment, in contrast, will be the less choosy sex, displaying less stringent mate preferences, greater eagerness to mate, and lesser discrimination about with whom to mate. In humans, as in most sexually reproducing species, females are burdened with greater minimum parental investment than are males and, therefore, females are more choosy than are males about with whom to mate (for a review of work on humans, see Buss, 2004). Second, greater intrasexual competition for sexual access to the more choosy sex will characterize the lesser investing sex. Again, as in most sexually reproducing species, human males display more intense intrasexual competition than do human females (for a review of work on humans, see Daly & M. Wilson, 1988).

A key consequence of these mating dynamics is that the sex with lesser minimum parental investment is more likely to abandon the other mate and any offspring produced by the pair. In humans, as in most sexually reproducing species, the sex more likely to abandon the other parent and offspring is the male. Single parenthood in humans is, of course, strikingly likely to be defined by a female attempting to raise offspring without the investment of an adult male. Human males are far more likely to abandon their offspring than are human females, and this is true both for marital and nonmarital relationships (for recent statistics, see J. Q. Wilson, 2002).

Relationship dissolution is likely to have been a recurrent feature of human evolutionary history, and children produced in the defunct relationship are likely to have resided with one parent and that parent's family, with variable investment by the noncustodial parent. As in modern times, ancestral children are likely to have resided primarily with their mother and to have received variable continued investment from their nonresident father. Whether they received continued investment from their father will have been a function of several key variables. The following paragraphs discuss some of these potential predictors of continued investment by the noncustodial father in his children. The discussion first addresses the continued investment of a man in children produced in a stable, marriage-like relationship. It then addresses the investment of a man in children produced in less formal, sometimes short-term, noncommitted relationships, including brief sexual affairs.

Investment by Noncustodial Fathers in Children Produced in a Stable Mateship

One hypothesis for why noncustodial fathers might decrease or terminate investment in their children is that they may be suspicious as to whether the resources they invest are reaching their children. Resources intended for noncustodial children might instead be used by the custodial mother for a variety of purposes that do not include direct investment in the children. Fathers who are not meeting their court-ordered child support obligations frequently report a concern for how the custodial mother is spending the money, suspecting that it is not being used to raise the children (see, e.g., Haskins, 1988; Mandell, 1995).

From an evolutionary psychological perspective, these concerns of noncustodial fathers might be reframed as concerns that the custodial mother is using the resources provided by the noncustodial father for such activities as increasing her own mate value, channeling resources to a new partner, to children with a new partner, or to the children of a new partner produced in a previous relationship of that new partner. There is at least one study suggesting that a mother's remarriage is followed by a reduction or less reliable payment of child support by the noncustodial father (Hill, 1992). This macrolevel research does not explain why these men reduced or terminated child support payments when the custodial mother remarried. Future work can profitably investigate the evolved psychology that generates decreased investment by the noncustodial father upon the custodial mother's remarriage.

Fathers may decrease or terminate investment in their noncustodial children because they are uncertain of the benefactors of that investment. There are many other reasons why a father might decrease or terminate investment in his noncustodial children. When his relationship with the custodial mother ends, he is faced with the adaptive problem of attracting a new mate, and this often requires resources (see Buss, 2004). It is hypothesized, therefore, that investment that once was channeled to offspring of a previous mate may now be used to attract a new mate, with the result that child support payments are lower or less reliably made.

Once a new mate is attracted and acquired, the noncustodial father now is faced with the adaptive problem of retaining that new mate, and this also often requires investment and resources (see, e.g., Buss, 1988; Buss & Shackelford, 1997; Flinn, 1988). Therefore, the investment that once was channeled to offspring of a previous mate may now be used to retain a new mate, with the result that child support payments are lower or made less reliably by the noncustodial father. No previous work has tested directly this hypothesis. A few studies have investigated whether a father's remarriage is accompanied by a decrease in the reliability or amount of child support payments. These studies have produced mixed results that are difficult to interpret with respect to the mate retention hypothesis, because it is not clear whether and to what extent "father's remarriage" assesses efforts to retain a newly acquired mate (Hill, 1992; Meyer & Bartfeld, 1996; Seltzer, 1991; Teachman, 1991).

If a noncustodial father remarries, then he may produce offspring with his new mate, and these new offspring will require his investment. This investment in new offspring may result in decreased investment in his noncustodial offspring. Most previous macrolevel research on this question has used father's remarriage as a proxy for the production of new offspring, with the conflicting results noted earlier. Manning and Smock (2000) provided the first direct test of the hypothesis that fathers "swap" investment in noncustodial children for investment in new, custodial children (Furstenberg, 1995; Furstenberg & Cherlin, 1991; Furstenberg, Nord, Peterson, & Zill, 1983; Furstenberg & Spanier, 1984). The results generated by Manning and Smock (2000) indicate that fathers do trade-off investment in noncustodial children for investment in new, custodial children, but only when the trade-off is between new genetic children living in the father's household and existing genetic children living outside the father's household. This pattern of findings is consistent with the work of Daly, Wilson, and others that documents a powerful evolved psychology of differential parental investment such that investment in genetic children is greater and more reliable than is investment in stepchildren (see, e.g., Wilson et al., 1980; Daly & Wilson, 1988, 1995, 1996).

Another evolutionarily informed hypothesis about the failure of fathers to invest in their noncustodial children is that, in short, these children may not be their own. In humans, as in all mammals, fertilization occurs internally to females. Males, therefore, can never be certain that the offspring produced by their partner is genetically their own. This is known as the adaptive problem of paternity uncertainty, and it has no parallel in human females, who can always be certain of maternity. Human male ancestors are likely to be those males who, following the dissolution of a relationship, invested preferentially in noncustodial children who were most likely to be their own genetic children. No research has directly tested this hypothesis in the modern case of decreased or terminated investment by fathers in noncustodial children.

Previous research indicates that child support payments are received more reliably when the former spouses have a better relationship (see, e.g., Arditti, 1992; Arditti & Keith, 1993; Teachman, 1991; Wright & Price, 1986). The key variable, quality of relationship with former spouse, is not well defined, however, sometimes asking little more than a single question about how much the parents like each other. It is hypothesized that the "quality" of the former spouse relationship, and the associated child support payments, varies with the noncustodial father's continued sexual access to the mother (see, e.g., Weiss, 1975). Previous research (reviewed in Buss, 2004) provides clear evidence that women sometimes trade sexual access for resources and that men sometimes trade resources for sexual access. It is hypothesized that continued sexual access to the mother of his noncustodial children will predict positively a man's continued investment in those children.

Investment by Noncustodial Fathers in Children Produced Outside of a Stable Mateship

The previous discussion presented several evolutionarily inspired hypotheses about the predictors of continued investment by fathers in noncustodial children produced in a stable, marriage-like relationship. Millions of single mothers in fact never were involved in a long-term committed relationship with the noncustodial father (see, e.g., Baker, 2000; Garfinkel, McLanahan, & Robins, 1986; Garfinkel, Meyer, & McLanahan, 1998; J. Q. Wilson, 2002). It is likely that the same predictors of decreased or terminated investment by fathers in noncustodial children apply to children produced in these nonmarital relationships. However, paternity uncertainty may be particularly relevant for understanding a man's investment in noncustodial children produced in a short-lived or sexually nonexclusive relationship.

In summary, this section has presented the argument that, to complement previous research generated by disciplines such as sociology that focus on macrolevel variables, a psychological approach, in general, and an evolutionary psychological approach, in particular, will produce valuable knowledge about the determinants of child support payments. The next section reviews several proposals for improving the reliability and amount of child support payments made by noncustodial fathers.

ADDRESSING INSUFFICIENT, UNRELIABLE, OR NONEXISTENT RECEIPT OF CHILD SUPPORT BY CUSTODIAL PARENTS

Many different proposals have been offered concerning how to increase the reliability with which noncustodial fathers channel child support to custodial mothers. Few such proposals have been or are ever likely to be successful, in part because the researchers and policymakers that have generated most of these proposals have ignored the evolutionary psychological foundations of child support payments. This section first reviews several standard social science proposals for how to increase the reliability with which child support is paid. If these proposals have been implemented, then the discussion notes whether research exists that has tested the effectiveness of these implemented proposals. If no such research exists, then the likely effectiveness of such proposals, based on what is known about evolved psychology, is noted.

One proposal for how to solve the problems of child support that is widely respected by standard social scientists is what can be termed the *socialization proposal*. This proposal states that all that must be done to increase the reliability with which noncustodial fathers pay child support is to socialize or train these men to appreciate that paying child support is not a "feminine" behavior, but instead that it is a "masculine" behavior, and that "real" men take care of their noncustodial children. According to the socialization proposal, noncustodial fathers in arrears for court-ordered child support "are not necessarily hard-hearted and narcissistic individuals. They are men faced with issues and tasks that are most difficult for them to handle effectively because of the gender-typed socialization occurring in our culture" (Fox & Blanton, 1995, p. 277).

No such socialization proposal has been implemented formally, so the results of empirical tests of the effectiveness of this proposal cannot be reported. Although it is possible that some noncustodial fathers might benefit from such socialization training, a first step will have to be the provision of specific details about the sort of training envisioned. What exactly is meant by "socialization," and by "masculine" and "feminine" behaviors, for example? How specifically might such training be implemented? By whom? Who will pay for this training? What happens when a man has new children by a new partner? Does a "real" man continue paying the same amount of child support at the expense of and to the detriment of his new children, assuming a limited set of expendable resources? The socialization proposal will have several difficulties with which to contend if it is to be implemented successfully.

Meyer and Bartfeld (1998) argued that payment and compliance with child support orders can be increased by enforcing existing orders via income withholding, but also by helping men get gainful employment. Meyer and Bartfeld (1998) reviewed previous research indicating that many men who do not meet child support obligations do not skirt these duties maliciously, but instead do not have the required income to pay, and often do not have gainful employment. According to Meyer and Bartfeld (1998), therefore, one way to increase the reliability with which child support is paid by noncustodial fathers is to provide training to underemployed or unemployed men so that they might be able to meet these child support obligations.

As with the socialization proposal, no empirical work has addressed the effectiveness of this "employment training" proposal. Job training that leads to better jobs or perhaps to any job should increase the reliability with which child support is paid by noncustodial fathers. What this proposal does not address is what to do about the majority of nonpayers or partial payers that already have the income to make child support payments, but elect not to make these payments (see, e.g., Meyer & Bartfeld, 1996). What is needed is research at the level of psychology to better understand the decisions of these men: Why do some of them make partial payments, some full payments, and some no payments at all? A complete answer is not likely to be found in the average incomes of these different groups of men. What is necessary are careful, empirical investigations of decision making by these men that include identification of the social and cultural cues to which these men are responding. Evolved psychological mechanisms lie dormant unless triggered by evolutionarily relevant stimuli (see, e.g., Buss, 1999) and, therefore, a comprehensive evolutionary psychological perspective on child support payment must identify these social and cultural stimuli.

A proposal to increase the reliability with which noncustodial fathers pay child support that has been implemented involves punitive measures for failing to pay this support (e.g., revocation of driver's license) and direct withholding from paychecks and income tax returns. These enforcement policies have met with mixed success. Meyer and Bartfeld (1996), for example, provided evidence that paycheck withholding is effective, but that the bulk of benefits that might be achieved (in terms of increased reliability and amount of child support payments) already have been realized for this strategy in Wisconsin, the state from which the researchers collected the relevant information. Lin (2000) provided evidence that paycheck withholding works for those fathers that perceive that their child support obligation is not fair. For men that perceive that their child support obligation is fair, withholding the child support from their paychecks does not improve the reliability or amount of child support payments made by noncustodial fathers. Beller and Graham (1993) presented evidence that immediate withholding, criminal penalties, tax intercepts, and the ability to place liens against property increase the amount of child support paid. Baker (2000) reviewed evidence that all of these punitive and nonvoluntary payment enforcement strategies can be effective, but they clearly are not always effective for all men who owe child support.

Lin (2000; see Arditti, 1992) supplied evidence that compliance with child support obligations is higher if noncustodial fathers perceive the obligation to be financially fair. Lin (2000) suggested, therefore, that one way to increase the reliability and amount of child support payments is to change fathers' perceptions of the fairness of the obligations. One way to increase perceptions of fairness, according to Lin (2000), is to decrease the monetary value of the obligations. An alternative method for increasing perceptions of fairness without lowering child support is "to standardize child support obligations, reduce deviations from child support guidelines, and fully implement routine income withholding. If the child support system employed more uniform guidelines and if fewer exceptions were made, a compliance 'climate' or 'norm' might develop, similar to that in the social security and income tax systems" (p. 396). The proposal recommended (but not yet formally implemented) by Lin (2000) is nevertheless open to social cheating (as are the social security and income tax systems), whereby some noncustodial fathers continue to avoid full or even partial payment of court-ordered child support. A key question for this proposal, therefore, will be how to monitor and punish failures to pay child support obligations in full.

This chapter closes with a brief review of what might be the most controversial proposal for improving the reliability and amount of child support paid by noncustodial fathers. However, it may be the most successful strategy, although it will be challenging to implement. Baker (2000) suggested that the first step to ensuring that every child receives financial support from a mother and a father is compulsory paternity testing of children at birth. The identified genetic mother and father will be charged a "child tax" for each child assigned to them. These taxes will be paid to the government and subsequently distributed to the resident parent or parents. Most of the time, of course, this means that a man and a woman who live together and who have children together will receive their child taxes back from the government, which they will then use to cover the expenses of the genetic children they share and that live with them in the same household. Sometimes, however, the genetic father will not be the man with whom a woman lives (about 1 in 10 such fathers, on average; see Baker & Bellis, 1995, for a review of the relevant research). The genetic father will be assessed the child tax (assuming he is identified), and these monies will be distributed to the genetic mother to help care for her children. This is the crux of Baker's (2000) proposal, without the many complicating details. The interested reader is referred to Baker (2000) for a detailed discussion of this controversial but promising proposal.

According to Baker's (2000) proposal, children will receive financial support from their genetic mother and father, and hugely expensive governmental programs no longer will be needed to support children without investing fathers. As Baker (2000, p. 27) noted, therefore, "For everybody's benefit—mother, father, child, and Treasury—routine and probably compulsory paternity testing at birth seems a future inevitability." At the same time, however, not everyone will be happy with this new system. As Baker (2000) pointed out,

> Some people—women who can skillfully confuse paternity, men who can successfully cuckold others, and deadbeat dads—will be worse off. All would have found opportunities better suited to their talents in [ancestral] environments in which their vulnerable prey would have been armed only with their ancient guile. Such exploiters will be curbed, not helped, by future developments, but even they would be hard pressed to argue that the future system is less fair than the past. (p. 29)

CONCLUSIONS

Unreliable, partial, or nonexistent child support payments by noncustodial fathers is a scourge of the modern, industrialized world. Working from a standard social science model, sociologists and policy analysts have identified a few macrolevel predictors of who pays child support, who does not, and why some noncustodial fathers pay whereas others do not. This chapter has argued that a comprehensive understanding of child support payment or lack thereof requires, in addition to analyses at the sociological level, analyses informed by an appreciation of evolved4 psychological mechanisms and the adaptive problems these mechanisms were designed to solve. Several proposals have been reviewed that have been offered for improving the reliability and amount of child support paid by noncustodial fathers. A successful social policy for rectifying the woes of child support will be built upon an appreciation of and respect for human evolved psychology.

ACKNOWLEDGMENT

The authors thank Aaron Goetz, Rick Michalski, and an anonymous reviewer for helpful comments that improved this chapter.

REFERENCES

Arditti, J. A. (1992). Factors related to custody, visitation, and child support for divorced fathers: An exploratory analysis. *Journal of Divorce and Remarriage, 17*, 23–42.
Arditti, J. A., & Keith, T. Z. (1993). Visitation frequency, child support payment, and the father–child relationships postdivorce. *Journal of Marriage and the Family, 55*, 699–712.
Baker, R. (2000). *Sex in the future.* New York: Arcade.
Baker, R. R., & Bellis, M. A. (1995). *Human sperm competition.* London: Chapman & Hall.
Beller, A. H., & Graham, J. W. (1993). *Small change.* New Haven, CT: Yale University Press.
Bumpass, L. (1990). What's happening to the family? *Demography, 27*, 483–498.
Bumpass, L., & Sweet, J. (1989). Children's experiences in single-parent families: Implications of cohabitation and marital transitions. *Family Planning Perspectives, 21*, 256–260.
Buss, D. M. (1988). From vigilance to violence: Tactics of mate retention in American undergraduates. *Ethology and Sociobiology, 9*, 291–317.
Buss, D. M. (1999). *Evolutionary psychology.* Needham Heights, MA: Allyn & Bacon.
Buss, D. M. (2004). *The evolution of desire* (rev. ed.). New York: Basic Books.
Buss, D. M., Haselton, M. G., Shackelford, T. K., Bleske, A. L., & Wakefield, J. C. (1998). Adaptations, exaptations, and spandrels. *American Psychologist, 53*, 533–548.
Buss, D. M., & Shackelford, T. K. (1997). From vigilance to violence: Mate retention tactics in married couples. *Journal of Personality and Social Psychology, 72*, 346–361.
Daly, M., & Wilson, M. (1985). Child abuse and other risks of not living with both parents. *Ethology and Sociobiology, 6*, 197–210.
Daly, M., & Wilson, M. (1988). *Homicide.* Hawthorne, NY: Aldine de Gruyter.
Daly M., & Wilson, M. I. (1995). Discriminative parental solicitude and the relevance of evolutionary models to the analysis of motivational systems. In M. Gazzaniga (Ed.), *The cognitive neurosciences* (pp. 1269–1286). Cambridge, MA: MIT Press.
Daly, M., & Wilson, M. I. (1996). Violence against stepchildren. *Current Directions in Psychological Science, 5*, 77–81.
Daly, M., & Wilson, M. (1998). *The truth about Cinderella.* London: Weidenfeld & Nicholson.
Dawkins, R., & Carlisle, T. R. (1976). Parental investment, mate desertion and a fallacy. *Nature, 262*, 131–133.
Flinn, M. V. (1988). Mate guarding in a Caribbean village. *Ethology and Sociobiology, 9*, 1–28.
Fox, G. L., & Blanton, P. W. (1995). Noncustodial fathers following divorce. *Marriage and Family Review, 20*, 257–282.
Furstenberg, F. F. (1995). Changing roles of fathers. In P. L. Chase-Lansdale & J. Brooks-Gunn (Eds.), *Escape from poverty* (pp. 189–210). Cambridge, England: Cambridge University Press.

Furstenberg, F. F., & Cherlin, A. (1991). *Divided families.* Cambridge, MA: Harvard University Press.

Furstenberg, F. F., Nord, C. W., Peterson, J., & Zill, N. (1983). The life course of children of divorce: Marital disruption and parental contact. *American Sociological Review, 48,* 656–668.

Furstenberg, F. F., & Spanier, G. B. (1984). *Recycling the family.* Beverly Hills, CA: Sage.

Garfinkel, I., & McLanahan, S. S. (1986). *Single mothers and their children.* Washington, DC: The Urban Institute.

Garfinkel, I., McLanahan, S. S., Meyer, D. R., & Seltzer, J. A. (Eds.). (1998). *Fathers under fire.* New York: Russell Sage Foundation.

Garfinkel, I., McLanahan, S. S., & Robins, P. (Eds.). (1986). *Child support and child well-being.* Washington, DC: The Urban Institute.

Garfinkel, I., Meyer, D. R., & McLanahan, S. S. (1998). A brief history of child support policies in the United States. In I. Garfinkel, S. S. McLanahan, D. R. Meyer, & J. A. Seltzer (Eds.), *Fathers under fire* (pp. 14–30). New York: Russell Sage Foundation.

Geary, D. C. (2000). Evolution and proximate expression of human paternal investment. *Psychological Bulletin, 126,* 55–77.

Haskins, R. (1988). Child support: A father's view. In S. Kamerman & A. Kahn (Eds.), *Child support* (pp. 306–327). Beverly Hills, CA: Sage.

Hill, M. (1992). The role of economic resources and remarriage in financial assistance for children of divorce. *Journal of Family Issues, 13,* 158–178.

Holden, K., & Smock, P. (1991). The economic costs of marital disruption: Why do women bear a disproportionate cost? *Annual Review of Sociology, 17,* 51–78.

Johnson, E. S., Levine, A., & Doolittle, F. C. (Eds.). (1999). *Fathers' fair share.* New York: Russell Sage Foundation.

Laakso, J. H. (2002). Key determinants of a mother's decision to file for child support. *Families in Society: The Journal of Contemporary Human Services, 83,* 153–162.

Lin, I.-F. (2000). Perceived fairness and compliance with child support obligations. *Journal of Marriage and the Family, 62,* 388–398.

Mandell, D. (1995). Fathers who don't pay child support: Hearing their voices. *Journal of Divorce and Remarriage, 23,* 85–116.

Manning, W. D., & Smock, P. J. (2000). Swapping families: Serial parenting and economic support for children. *Journal of Marriage and the Family, 62,* 111–122.

Maynard Smith, J. (1977). Parental investment: A prospective analysis. *Animal Behaviour, 25,* 1–9.

McLanahan, S., & Sandefur, S. (1994). *Growing up with a single parent.* Cambridge, MA: Harvard University Press.

McNamara, J. M., Houston, A. I., Székely, T., & Webb, J. N. (2002). Do parents make independent decisions about desertion? *Animal Behaviour, 64,* 147–149.

Meyer, D. R., & Bartfeld, J. (1996). Compliance with child support orders in divorce cases. *Journal of Marriage and the Family, 58,* 201–212.

Meyer, D. R., & Bartfeld, J. (1998). Patterns of child support compliance in Wisconsin. *Journal of Marriage and the Family, 60,* 309–318.

Norton, A., & Miller, L. (1992). *Marriage, divorce, and remarriage in the 1990s.* Washington, DC: U.S. Bureau of the Census.

Seltzer, J. A. (1991). Relationships between fathers and children who live apart: The father's role after separation. *Journal of Marriage and the Family, 53,* 79–101.

Seltzer, J. A., Schaeffer, N. C., & Charng, H.-W. (1989). Family ties after divorce: The relationship between visiting and paying child support. *Journal of Marriage and the Family, 51,* 1013–1032.

Smock, P. J., & Manning, W. D. (1997). Nonresident parents' characteristics and child support. *Journal of Marriage and the Family, 59,* 798–808.

Sweet, J., & Bumpass, L. (1987). *American families and households.* New York: Russell Sage Foundation.

Symons, D. (1987). If we're all Darwinians, what's the fuss about? In C. Crawford, D. Krebs, & M. Smith (Eds.), *Sociobiology and psychology* (pp. 121–146). Hillsdale, NJ: Lawrence Erlbaum Associates.

Symons, D. (1992). On the use and misuse of Darwinism in the study of human behavior. In J. H. Barkow, L. Cosmides, & J. Tooby (Eds.), *The adapted mind* (pp. 137–159). New York: Oxford University Press.

Teachman, J. D. (1991). Contributions to children by divorced fathers. *Social Problems, 38*, 358–371.

Tooby, J., & Cosmides, L. (1992). The psychological foundations of culture. In J. H. Barkow, L. Cosmides, & J. Tooby (Eds.), *The adapted mind* (pp. 19–136). New York: Oxford University Press.

Trivers, R. L. (1972). Parental investment and sexual selection. In B. Campbell (Ed.), *Sexual selection and the descent of man: 1871–1971* (pp. 136–179). Chicago: Aldine.

U.S. Bureau of the Census. (1995). *Child support and alimony: 1989 (Current Population Reports, Series P-60)*. Washington, DC: U.S. Government Printing Office.

U.S. Bureau of the Census. (2001). *Living arrangements of children: Fall 1996 (Current Population Reports, Series P-70)*. Washington, DC: U.S. Government Printing Office.

Weiss, R. S. (1975). *Marital separation*. New York: Basic Books.

Williams, G. C. (1966). *Adaptation and natural selection*. Princeton, NJ: Princeton University Press.

Wilson, J. Q. (2002). *The marriage problem*. New York: HarperCollins.

Wilson, M., Daly, M., & Weghorst, S. J. (1980). Household composition and the risk of child abuse and neglect. *Journal of Biosocial Science, 12*, 333–340.

Wright, D. W., & Price, S. J. (1986). Court-ordered child support payment: The effect of the former-spouse relationship on compliance. *Journal of Marriage and the Family, 48*, 869–874.

Evolutionary Life History Perspective on Rape

❧

Randy Thornhill
Craig T. Palmer

L ife history theory is a subtheory of evolution, a set of fact-based principles for productively studying the lifetimes of all organisms (Charnov, 1991, 1993; Roff, 1992; Stearns, 1992). This chapter focuses on life history theory's application to the evolution and ontogeny (development within the individual) of human individual differences in life course decisions about reproductive investment versus survival investment, and the condition-dependence of these decisions. It argues that life history theory's factual and theoretical foundations provide a basis for social policy that may substantially reduce rape. In life history terms, rape is a type of reproductive effort, specifically a mating effort. Investment in survival and in the timing, type, and magnitude of reproductive effort expenditure has evolved to be highly sensitive to information received by the developing individual of its intrinsic and extrinsic mortality. When survival prospects are perceived during development to be dismal or uncertain, individuals devalue the future, divesting in survival and expending more and earlier reproductive effort, including risky effort such as, in men, rape and other forms of sexual coercion to force sexual access. But when survival prospects are good, the same individuals value the future and adjust their survival and reproductive efforts accordingly.

Developmental events that studies indicate influence people's perception of the reliability of the future (setting their time preference in reproductive effort expenditure to current vs. future) are childhood stress versus security, disease versus health, high versus low local mortality, and reduced or uncertain versus adequate or stable resources and parental solicitude. The quality and quantity of parental care is influenced by a diversity of factors: poverty, father absence, divorce, parental incompetence, and parental illness. Although most of human life history decision making is not conscious, there is evidence that people have significant, conscious understanding of their personal survival prospects and this awareness affects their time preference and associated life history allocations.

The practical implications of the life history approach for reducing the incidence of coercive sex derive from two related procedures. First, obtain detailed knowledge of how and when the relevant psychological adaptations assess environmental information about mortality and then use these evolved cues to set an individual's life history parameters, especially a man's risk taking and impulsiveness about mating endeavors. Second, if desired, these environmental cues could then be reduced or eliminated by social policy, providing men with security about their future. There is considerable evidence that this security is instantiated in the human psyche by predictable and adequate material and social resources in the rearing environment.

This chapter is not the first treatment of human rape in terms of life history theory. Relevant discussions can be found in Thornhill and Palmer (2000) and especially in Chisholm (1999b), who discussed social policy implications of the life history approach to rape. This chapter endorses and extends Chisholm's view that the life history approach to rape is a critical insight. The approach simultaneously explains rape's existence as well as variation among men in rape proneness. Causal knowledge of both is necessary for developing effective policy concerning the problem of rape.

The promise of the life history approach to rape can be evaluated adequately only if certain barriers are removed. Research on human life history must move beyond the recent controversy surrounding the role of genetic variation in life history traits (e.g., MacDonald, 1997, & Rowe, 2000, vs. Belsky, 1997, & Chisholm, 1999b). There are no scientifically legitimate grounds for the controversy. Genes and environment are not alternative explanations for a man's impulsive, nonempathic sexual pursuits. Ontogenetically, such pursuits are the product of both causes, even when there is genetic variation among men. Also, an individual's genetic quality itself may act as a trigger of its life history events, but never without environmental causation acting in concert. Genetic engineering to remove genes that affect rape is out of the question on moral and practical grounds. However, environmental modifications using social policy that remove environmental causes can eliminate antisocial pursuits. Understanding this would focus future research appropriately on the environmental developmental cues responsible for rape.

Another barrier is that scholars interested in how science can be used to inform effective social policy against sexual coercion must understand that human values ultimately are a product of past Darwinian selection. Cameron (2001; also see Alexander, 1987; E. O. Wilson, 1998) sketched the history of scholarly views on the source of values, what people consider to be important in their lives, even the purpose of an individual's life. The modern evolutionary view on the ultimate origin of values is in contrast to transcendental secularism and religion that have proposed sources completely outside the human psyche. It is also in contrast to social Darwinism, which has seen values as intrinsic properties of the evolutionary process. Morals do not have divine origin or secular transcendental origin ("culture"), nor are they instantiated in natural laws. Instead, values are caused ultimately by past Darwinian selection and proximately by life course developmental experiences that have their effects because the ontogenetic mechanisms are designed by selection to incorporate them. Personal values are part of the individual's phenotype, as important for an individual's Darwinian fitness as the liver or heart. The evolved function of a person's value system is social navigation and acquiring resources, and converting those resources into descendants. Accordingly, people's values are coordinated with the specific problems that they face in their personal social niche.

Social niches are significantly diverse in terms of the effectiveness and value of long-term vs. short-term social relationships and associated emotional and behavioral skills. Chisholm (1999b) was on-target in viewing the human capacity of possessing values as a life history adaptation with variable expression among men contingent on proximate developmental experiences that were predictive of personal mortality in past evolutionary generations. Different mortality information results in different value systems of men affecting their relative proneness to sexual coercion.

Consider two men. One man has rape-prone ideology. He believes that women really want to be raped and ask for it in their behavior. He lacks skills for enduring relationships. He values women primarily for sexual gratification and as a tally of his prowess with which he competes with his male peers. He also values aggression and violence as means of interpersonal conflict resolution. His lack of empathy results in disregard for the pain and suffering he inflicts on women. He values immediate gratification, exhibiting low self-control or high impulsiveness and high risk taking in his pursuits. His social relationships are exploitative and short term. He trusts no one as his experiences have only been with others who are, like him, in pursuit of short-term social relationships. He has a career of sexual coercion, including rape, beginning in his teens and continuing until he dies at age 21 as a result of lethal conflict about status and women with some local men who share his value system. Evidence points to his ontogeny being impoverished in resources and opportunities and without parental or other role models engaged in enduring sexual and social relationships.

The second man does not have this value system about women and is empathetic. He does not view violence as a legitimate means of conflict resolution with women and male competitors. His time preference is future oriented and he thus has high self-control and low impulsiveness. His relationships are enduring, trusting, and altruistic. He dies at age 77 from the cumulative effects of aging. His sexual career involves no sexual coercion. Evidence indicates that his ontogeny was the opposite of the first man's.

Both men see their own view as self-evident, moral reality. Both are proximately caused by specific experiences during ontogeny because this is the way Darwinian selection has designed the development of values. Both are genetically and environmentally caused, as a result of how the ontogenetic process unfolds during its construction of each and every trait of an individual. Each man's ideology fits his particular social niche.

Which value system is morally right? The answer is found in the general opinion of people in modern society: Sexual coercion is immoral and illegal. Hence, the moral system favors the interests and values of the second man over those of the first man. As Alexander (1987) emphasized, moral issues involve conflicts of interests. Societal moral systems (e.g., systems of law) serve one set of interests over another.

Evolutionary biology explains why people have conflicts of interests about values and the nature of these conflicts. It cannot give moral judgments. Moral systems of the Western world reflect the "democratic process" weighted very heavily in favor of the interests of the socially powerful people in a given society (Alexander, 1979, 1987). In democracies, people vote for and otherwise support the rules of conduct that are in their evolved self-interests.

Evolutionary biology can enter only after socially desired goals are identified. Its role is to provide knowledge that may help in achievement of the goals. The social problem of rape, like all other social problems, has causes. Understanding what causes a problem is essential for solving it. Evolutionary knowledge importantly informs the study of all life in that it provides the general or ultimate explanation that can productively guide the investigation of the partial or proximate causes.

LIFE HISTORY THEORY

The fact that Darwinian selection is the main engine of evolution and the ultimate cause of adaptation, when coupled with the fact that genes, but not individual organisms, have evolved by Darwinian selection to survive, gives deep and profound insight about the function of organisms' lifetimes. Individual lifetimes are for producing descendants/genetic continuation. Lifetimes ultimately have evolved because they maximized genetic propagation, which is synonymous with reproductive success, in the environment of evolutionary adaptedness (EEA). Reproductive success or genetic propagation of the individual is advanced by producing offspring, and by tending to offspring and other individuals who contain its own genes (nondescendant kin). The evolutionary function of lifetimes is not to achieve maximum happiness, security, or health; these are proximate means of achieving genetic continuity. Under some circumstances, as is explained later, insecurity and reduced health concerns also are proximate means of reproductive success.

Life history adaptations are events or features that have been favored by past selection because they advanced the reproductive success of individuals. Thus, these adaptations are proximate mechanisms of genetic propagation. Other life history events are by-products of these adaptations. By-products are indirectly selected and arise incidentally from the directly selected adaptations. (See Thornhill & Palmer, 2000, for further discussion of by-products.)

To argue that a given human life history feature is not a product of evolution would be to engage in mysticism. Life histories of organisms are molded by Darwinian selection and reflect a mix of adaptations and incidental effects. For example, in humans (as in almost all species of animals) there is a sex difference in mortality, with males dying at higher rates than females. Obviously, past selection did not directly favor males who died earlier than females. The sex difference is a by-product of selection for greater male than female risk taking, which leads incidentally to male-biased mortality. Selection itself is differential reproductive success (sometimes through differential survival) stemming from individual trait differences. Relatively more risk taking among males led to greater access to status and resources and thereby greater access to reproductive-aged female mates who produced offspring. Risk-taking did not evolve because it led to injury and death of risk-takers, but because it increased net reproductive success despite its costs to survival.

We have considered 10 hypotheses that might connect rape to evolutionary history in specific ways (Thornhill & Palmer, 2000). It is not equivocal that rape is a product of evolution. The view that human rape is not ultimately a product of evolution is the nadir of intellectual dishonesty or of ignorance about biology. The scientific issue is how, specifically, to connect rape to evolutionary history in order to understand it more completely. After rejecting 8 of the 10 hypotheses on evidentiary and logical grounds, we emphasized that human rape is either an adaptation for raping or an incidental effect of men's sexual adaptation for obtaining mates without investment in them or commitment toward them. If rape is a by-product, then its existence is a result of indirect Darwinian selection in the past. If rape is a product of direct selection, then there will exist in men's sexuality adaptation functionally specialized for rape. Either way, however, rape is a manifestation of men's mating effort because it arises from some sort of sexual psychological adaptation. Thus, its connection to life history theory can be explored without full knowledge of how selection created human rape behavior. That rape is not motivated by sexual desire is a popular view that is scientifically false (see Thornhill & Palmer, 2000, for discussion and review of evidence).

LIFE HISTORY TRADE-OFFS

Central to life history theory is the principle of allocation: Available energy is finite and thus the energy used for one activity or to build one structure cannot be used for another. During the life cycle, energy is obtained and used for repair and maintenance of the body, growth, storage of information in memory, storage of energy (e.g., in fat), the construction of adaptations (e.g., human language adaptations arise at ages 1–3 years and sexual adaptations at adulthood), and reproduction. Organisms face trade-offs in energy use because energy used for one purpose (making a stronger heart) cannot be used for another (aiding offspring). Selection in all organisms will act on how the energy is used, and specifically favor individuals who use it in ways that maximize reproductive success in the niche their evolutionary legacy has granted them.

A trade-off is an allocation problem in that increasing one type of benefit lowers another benefit. A fundamental trade-off in life histories is current reproduction against future reproduction. Reproducing now lowers future reproduction because reproduction has a cost in terms of reduced future survival or fertility.

A second, basic trade-off stemming from the principle of allocation is between offspring number and quality. Parents who invest a great deal in individual offspring necessarily can produce few offspring. Production of many offspring is at the expense of investment in each offspring.

Another formulation of the principle of allocation is in terms of life effort. Lifetimes involve a continuous series of efforts. The principle of allocation is relevant in that investment in one form of effort typically cannot be used for another. Effort is the time, risk, and energy invested in an activity (e.g., mating) or to make a structure (e.g., muscles). Effort is divisible into two, broad categories: (a) *somatic* (body) *effort*, which involves body growth, maintenance and repair, and storage of information and energy, and (b) *reproductive effort*, which involves reproduction.

Somatic effort evolves when it increases the efficiency of subsequent reproductive effort. Somatic effort in people includes a diversity of efforts from constructing the immune and digestive systems to acquiring information and skills for social competition (e.g., acquiring education or social skills).

Reproductive effort is further divisible into parental effort (also called parental investment), the effort involved in aiding the survival of one's offspring; extra-parental effort, the effort involved in reproduction through aid to genetic relatives other than offspring; and mating effort, the effort involved in creating offspring. Courtship and copulation by men and women are mating effort. Nursing offspring and paying for a child's education are parental effort. Nepotism toward siblings or their offspring is extra-parental effort (Alexander, 1987; Low, 2000).

The principle of allocation and the associated trade-offs determine the action of selection on life history traits and therefore the life history adaptations that evolve. For example, increased likelihood of adult mortality selects for individuals who not only reproduce before they die, but expend all reproductive effort before death (i.e., selects for high investment in early reproductive effort). Reproduction lowers residual reproductive capacity, the ability of an individual to reproduce in the future, because of the cost of current reproduction through either reduced future survival or future fertility. Increased probability of death reduces the prospect for enhancing later reproduction by somatic effort. On the other hand, high survival prospects select for increased somatic effort and delayed and reduced reproductive effort. Because somatic effort enhances future reproduction, survival is necessary for this benefit to be realized. Studies of diverse species ranging from plants, insects, crustacea, fish, birds and mammals have provided findings consistent with life history theory's predictions that high mortality is associated with relatively early onset of reproduction, more overall reproductive effort, less somatic effort, and less parental effort per offspring. The opposite patterns have been found under low mortality.

SCORPIONFLY RAPE: AN ALTERNATIVE MATING EFFORT

Scorpionflies of the genus *Panorpa* provide an opportunity to examine the evolution of male mating effort in a group of animal species in which male parental and extra-parental efforts are absent (male reproductive effort is exclusively in the form of mating effort), male reproductive effort can be meaningfully measured, male reproductive effort varies among species and populations, individual males exhibit different types of mating effort in different contexts, and adult mortality could be quantified.

Thornhill (1981) tested the prediction that increased adult male mortality results in the evolution of increased male reproductive effort. This prediction was tested by a comparison of male mating effort across species and populations and by analysis of each of the two alternative male mating behaviors—rape and nuptial gift giving.

Adult *Panorpa* scorpionflies are scavengers and feed on dead arthropods such as insects. The nine species of *Panorpa* studied overlap almost completely in their feeding ecology in their natural habitats. They eat the same things and in the same places in the habitat. They compete intensely for food, both within and between species, and losing in this competition reduces longevity of the losers. The reduction in longevity is related to increased movement in the habitat, increased occupation of suboptimal habitats, increased weight loss, and greater exposure to the important predators, web-building spiders. About 65% of observed predation of *Panorpa* over a 5-year period was by web-building spiders, despite scorpionflies' defenses against the spiders. Increased competition for food forces scorpionflies into spider webs to secure food by stealing it from spiders.

Males conditionally adopt mating effort types, either nuptial gift giving or rape. The nuptial gift is given to a female by a male in exchange for mating. The gift is either a dead arthropod or a hardened salivary mass that the male makes with large, specialized salivary glands that only males possess. Males must feed on dead arthropods in order to produce a salivary mass. Rape involves no gift; males that lose competition for food adopt rape. Experiments reveal that males prefer to use nuptial gifts and that females prefer gift-givers as mates. Rape is associated with much lower male mating success than providing a nuptial gift.

A major factor affecting a male's ability to win competition for food is body size. A male's body size is set at adulthood. He may change in weight, but not in size. Small males lose in competition for food and, as a result, feed and die in spider webs to a greater extent than large males. Small males also employ more rape behavior than large males.

In this research, male reproductive effort was measured by the ratio of salivary gland dry weight to total dry weight of body. This measure is similar to a typical measure of female reproductive effort in life history research as the ratio of clutch weight (birds or insects) or litter weight (mammals) to total body weight. Salivary glands of male scorpionflies make up a large proportion of a male's body weight and represent a morphological investment in current reproduction. Given that males use their salivary glands in the context of gaining access to mates, these structures are analogous (i.e., involve similar selection pressure) to antlers of male deer, horns of certain male beetles, and courtship and mating behaviors of animals.

In the scorpionflies, both across species and across populations of single species, increased average adult mortality was positively associated with increased average mating effort measured as the ratio of salivary gland weight to total body weight. This was the case with each of three estimates of adult life span.

Also, on the finer scale of males within a single population, life history theory successfully predicted mating effort. Residual reproductive capacity declines with male body size within a species of scorpionflies. So the smaller the male, the less likely he can compete successfully for food, and the more likely he will feed and die in spider webs. Thus, the smaller the male, the more the male engages in the most dangerous form of mating effort entering spider webs. Rape by males also probably carries greater risks than consensual mating and thus may be a more dangerous form of mating effort. Rape has the hazard of male injury in the physical struggle that ensues between the male and female. Although small males are more likely to employ rape than large males, large males use rape when food is unavailable, that is, when their survival and hence residual reproductive capacity decline. Moreover, large males are more successful at raping females than small males (Thornhill, 1987).

Selection creates both species-typical (often sex-specific) life history traits as well as life history traits that are expressed conditionally by individuals. In scorpionflies, the variation in male reproductive effort across species probably represents different life history adaptations. However, the variation across male sizes within a species and even within an individual male in use of food in spider webs and raping are condition-dependent tactics of a single male adaptation possessed by all males. It is contingent life history traits that are of interest in considering people's life course decisions.

HUMAN LIFE HISTORY

A key variable affecting reproductive and somatic efforts is mortality. As adult mortality increases, earlier, larger reproductive efforts, accompanied by reduced somatic efforts, are anticipated by theory and observed in fact across many kinds of organisms. Juvenile mortality patterns can have a complex effect on reproductive effort, but life history theory clearly predicts that if mortality rates increase in both adult and juvenile age groups, then early, large reproductive efforts are expected (Charlesworth, 1980).

An important factor influencing mortality in humans is socioeconomic (SES) level. Ellis (1994a, 1994b) reviewed the literature on the effect of SES on health and associated survivorship. Across 165 studies that ranged across the globe (from India, Scandinavia, and the United States) and various decades, low SES was associated with relatively higher juvenile and adult mortality. In some cases, middle SES showed somewhat lower health and survival than upper SES, but in other cases the difference was pronounced only between low SES and middle-upper SES. The decline in health in low-SES environments was found regardless of the measure of health or SES. Chisholm (1999b) reviewed additional studies that reveal the consistent positive association between SES and health/survival.

There are many proximate causes of reduced human health and survival: disease, limited access to medical care, infanticide and other homicide, accidents, and reduced nepotistic investment in children (e.g., parental absence or neglect). Regardless of the source of extrinsic mortality, the human organism is expected to be designed to respond conditionally to it by early, high reproductive effort and associated high risk proneness. Parental investment per offspring is expected to be reduced to obtain many offspring, some of which may survive the uncertain conditions faced. High mating effort is expected because it allows current reproductive success. Concomitantly, parental investment per offspring and extra-parental nepotistic investment should be reduced because its adaptive significance relies on offspring survival to adulthood. Somatic effort is traded off with early and high reproductive effort. Thus, reduced somatic allocation is expected to go to immune function, long-term energy use, and other survival mechanisms. Also expected is reduced interest and time allocated to health care and body maintenance in general.

All these diversions from somatic effort will generate lower phenotypic condition generally and thereby exacerbate the already relatively high mortality in the low SES context. Thus, the well-known, positive association between SES and survival/health is consistent with context-specific (SES-specific), optimal life history allocation.

In the last several years, researchers have begun to apply life history theory to human behavior. Humans, as a species, exhibit relatively long juvenile and adult lives and high levels of extended parental care; both sexes engage in mating effort throughout much of the adult period (Geary, 2000; K. Hill & Hurtado, 1996). There is variation, however, in life history traits across human societies and social strata within a given society. Recent evidence indicates that anticipated survival may be the most important determinant of human life-history variation among SES levels of modern society (see later). Although mortality itself has been examined in some studies, most look at future unpredictability or SES as surrogates of survival prospects faced by people (Chisholm, 1999b). Mortality and its surrogates are closely tied to human risk proneness, as life history theory predicts.

RISK TAKING

Risk proneness is the psychological state of discounting future benefits and prioritizing current benefits. Risk proneness promotes risk taking. Risk taking means engaging in activities with uncertain outcomes. Risk-taking activities include all types of biological endeavors and even a physiological allocation to one system (e.g., muscle) may be risky if it takes away from another system (e.g., immune). Cognitive endeavors such as reasoning and deduction and their associated behaviors also can be risky when they affect survival or other fitness components.

The greater the variation in potential reproductive success from risk taking, the stronger the selection for engaging in risky activities. Male mating effort can capture the rare success in the high-stakes game of male reproductive success. The greater variability in outcome of male mating effort stems from the fundamental asymmetry between the sexes in the minimum reproductive effort necessary for successful offspring production. The human male minimum is the few minutes of time needed to place the energetically cheap ejaculate inside a woman's vagina. By comparison, the human female's minimum is huge: nine months of gestation, birth, and extended lactation and child care. The small male minimum means that men's reproductive success is linearly and positively related to the number of females inseminated who produce offspring. The range of offspring is zero to hundreds in a lifetime. Women's reproductive success, however, is constrained to a relatively small number of offspring by their obligate large investment in each offspring.

The large, sexual asymmetry in minimum effort necessary for successful reproduction is seen in animals in general. This disparity has led to selection favoring males that obtain high numbers of mates. Across species, the same male sexual syndrome is seen: eagerness to copulate, indiscriminate mating, and pursuit of many mates without commitment to the females or investment in the offspring. Males may also include coercion in their battery of tactics for mating. Selection has favored females that expend their limited parental effort cautiously by choosing the ecological circumstances and sire that will increase the chances of the effort leading to successful offspring production. Across species, in general, the same female syndrome is seen: mate choice, parental expenditure dependent on persuasion by males, and attempts to avoid the loss of control of fertilization (and thus of the timing and quality of offspring) that arises from sexual coercion (Thornhill & Palmer, 2000).

Male humans, like males of other species, play a mating game of high stakes in which a few males have many mates and thereby take a large share of reproductive success, and other males have smaller shares, including zero success. It is this reproductive variance in males and the associated selection for risk taking that ultimately accounts for male risk taking being so prominent in human everyday life (M. Wilson & Daly, 1985). Males are overrepresented in the many areas of human life involving inordinate risk taking: intergroup competition (warfare and sports), interindividual physical competition (fighting and other antagonistic behaviors), playing the stock market, gambling (especially when it involves large stakes), criminal activity and other rule breaking, injury and death due to accidents (car crashes, rock climbing, snake handling, skydiving, diving into empty swimming pools, straying into dangerous terrain, gunshot, etc.), neglecting personal health problems, and inventiveness (Campbell, 1995, 1999; Geary, 1998; Miller, 2000; M. Wilson & Daly, 1985). The combination of greater male than female mortality and the low male minimum allocation necessary for successful reproduction makes various high-risk mating efforts adaptive for men, particularly young men. The peak in young men involves the achievement of adulthood and thus the maximum competition for access to resources and status that is attractive to women. The timing also pertains to males entering the period of life of highest mortality relative to females. According to life history theory, if mortality rate increases in an adult age group (male adulthood), then reproductive effort increases just before that age (early adulthood) and decreases after it (middle age and later) (Michod, 1979; Rogers, 1994).

Women also take risks in their mating efforts. Female mortality and criminal behavior also show a peak in the young adult years (Campbell, 1995, 1999). Women compete for mates who have resources and status, and this competition can be intense (Buss, 1994; Campbell, 1995; Geary, 1998). This competition usually involves physical appearance, but also physical conflicts for mates with other young women when stakes are high, that is, when there are few resource-rich potential mates (Campbell, 1995).

The male-specific high variance in reproductive success and associated strong sexual selection for the risk-taking that determined the big winners of many mates (human evolutionary male ancestors) also is the ultimate reason for rape and other forms of sexual coercion. Sexual coercion increases mate number by giving sexual access to females otherwise unavailable (see Thornhill & Palmer, 2000).

This reasoning about rape does not imply that rape or other types of sexual coercion were selected directly in the past and thus are based on a specific adaptation for coercion. All forms of sexual coercion may be incidental effects of directly selected adaptation for obtaining high mate number without much time or emotional investment in each mate. An understanding of male risk-proneness and the environmental factors, including developmental ones, that promote the form of risk taking and other life history traits that lead men to rape could serve as a basis for reducing or eliminating rape through changing those factors.

HUMAN LIFE HISTORY IN MODERN SOCIETY

Survival probability predicts reproductive effort of women in modern society; Chisholm (1999b) fully reviewed the evidence. Geronimus (1987, 1996) found that most teen mothers in the United States are from the urban underclass, a group with relatively poor health and high mortality. This is consistent with the life history prediction that increased mortality will cue a decrease in the age of first reproduction. Burton (1990) also studied the relatively early childbearing in poor neighborhoods. The majority of the women in her study (91%) anticipated their life spans to be relatively short (60 years). Chisholm (1999b) provided data across many nations supporting the positive relation between early offspring production and correlates of high mortality. Higher female fertility also is correlated with increased mortality, as expected from life history theory. M. Wilson and Daly (1997) found across 77 Chicago neighborhoods that, as mortality rate climbed, the age of first offspring production by women decreased and the number of offspring born per woman increased. Neighborhood resource level also correlated with mortality (negatively) and the patterns of female reproductive effort (positively with age of first reproduction, and negatively with total fertility). Similarly, Bereczkei (1998) found that Hungarian Gypsies, who have relatively low rates of survival and fewer and more unpredictable resources, had earlier child production and higher lifetime fertility than non-Gypsy Hungarians living under more secure ecological settings.

Chisholm's (1999a) study of female college students measured expected survivorship by asking women how long they expected to live (average expected life = 82 years). The measure correlated with age of first sexual intercourse. Short life expectancy was associated with earlier first sex, supporting the prediction that perception of prospects for survivorship affects the age of onset of reproductive effort.

Another important factor in generating low and unpredictable resource levels in low SES settings in modern society is father absence or, more generally, reduced paternal investment (Chisholm, 1999b; also Geary, 2000). Presumably, in human evolutionary history, the presence of the father was critical to offspring survival, explaining why relatively large paternal involvement evolved in humans. Certainly, in preindustrial societies, father's investment improves offspring survival (Geary, 2000; K. Hill & Hurtado, 1996). In modern societies, father absence seems to be associated with early menarche and sexual activity in women (Chisholm, 1999b).

In males, age of first sexual intercourse and of first offspring production is earlier in low SES settings as well. Also in low SES environments, sexual intercourse tends to be more concentrated in young men than in men over age 30. Just the reverse is seen in middle-class men (i.e., a delay in sexual intercourse to later in the life cycle; Kemper, 1994). There is also some evidence that father absence may accelerate the onset of adulthood in men (Weisfeld, 1999). These patterns in men are consistent with the prediction that low survivorship probability shifts men's mating effort, and reproductive effort in general, to earlier ages. Kemper (1994) interpreted this as due to class differences in the timing of testosterone production, which may be one of the proximate causes involved.

Engaging in aggression is risky in that it can lead to injury and death. In the study mentioned earlier of the 77 Chicago neighborhoods, homicide rates (mostly men killing men, as in all homicide data) across neighborhoods were strongly negatively correlated with neighborhood life expectancy (range = 54–77 years). The effect of homicide itself on life expectancy was controlled in the analysis, thus, mortality rates were independent of homicide (M. Wilson & Daly, 1997). Durant, Cadenhead, Pendergrast, Slavens, and Linder (1994), in a study of adolescents in low SES environments with high rates of violent crimes, found that perceived confidence of being alive at age 25 was associated with use of violence. The lower the confidence, the greater the current use of violence.

The strong relation between crime incidence and SES is thoroughly documented (e.g., Alexander, 1979; Ellis & Walsh, 2000; Herrnstein & Murray, 1994; J. Q. Wilson & Herrnstein, 1986). Crime is risk-taking behavior. The high crime rate in low SES settings is powerful evidence for low SES factors being causal in the various categories of behavior comprising crime. The centrality of risk taking in crime is documented by the fact that riskier crimes (i.e., those involving violence) show the strongest association with low SES.

The presumed causal factors in low SES settings, according to life history theory, are interrelated: relatively high mortality, low and especially unpredictable resource levels, limited parental investment, and uncertainty in the future. Low resource levels per se are not expected from theory to bring about early and high reproductive effort, because even if resources are scarce, if they are predictable, and mortality is low, the optimal tactic is to stockpile resources and delay reproduction until a resource threshold that will support successful reproduction is reached. It is unpredictability of low resource levels that is expected to impact mortality and thus the conception that the future is not realistic, and the here and now is all that matters. The different effects of low and predictable versus low and unpredictable resources on humans' life history expression may be the reason that MacDonald (1997) found that some low SES settings result in delayed reproduction and onset of sexuality (also see Chisholm, 1999b).

E. M. Hill, Ross, and Low (1997) studied the relationships among risk taking, the early rearing environment, beliefs about unpredictability of the future, and future life span assessment in young adults who were college students or the students' acquaintances. Risk taking was measured in domains of safety, health, sexual behavior, social relations, and finances. Two factors comprised their measures of early rearing environment: adversity (neighborhood crime, family poverty, and parental absence in years 6–13) and family unreliability (frequency and consistency of planned family activities and parental predictability in carrying out these activities and certain other family responsibilities). Belief about unpredictability of the future was measured by combining scores from multiple scales (self-efficacy, causal uncertainty, locus of control, perception of the world as a predicable/unpredictable place in terms of influence on one's life). Future life span assessment was measured by questions about survival and health in eight age categories (20–29, 30–39, 40–49, etc.).

The E. M. Hill et al. (1997) study found the sex differences expected from life history theory. One was in expectation of a long and healthy life; men believed their lives would be shorter. A second was in men's greater risk taking.

Within-sex variation also was consistent with life history theory. Risk taking correlated with family unreliability (+ correlation), with life span assessment (–), with belief in future unpredictability (+), and with adversity in early life (+). They concluded that their results were consistent with the hypothesis "that unpredictable early environments are related to the development of a view of the future as unpredictable and an expectation of short life, and that these beliefs related to risk-taking" (p. 308).

Evidence is accumulating that people infer, store, and act on information about personal survivorship. This is seen in E. M. Hill et al. (1997) as well as in other research already discussed (Burton, 1990; Chisholm, 1999a; Durant et al., 1994; Geronimus, 1987, 1996; see review in Chisholm, 1999b). In humans there is a conscious component to people's life expectancy conception that appears to affect life history traits. M. Wilson and Daly (1997) speculated that this conception may arise from people's knowledge of deaths around them, such as how many relatives have died. The information that goes into the perception of life expectancy in humans, however, probably involves additional factors. Perhaps personal health as well as illness and morbidity in an individual's social environment are important; also, simply the amount and nature of parental care and other nepotism, as well as the general pattern of interpersonal relations in the social environment, typical of either long- or short-term bonds. It is likely, then, that a combination of conscious and unconscious inferences goes into human life span assessment. Certainly in plants and almost certainly in scorpionflies, there is no conscious component to the assessment of mortality that influences the timing and amount of reproductive and somatic effort. Thus, conscious assessment of mortality prospects is not necessary for fine-tuned life history schedules, which makes the consciousness aspect in people's life course of interest.

ATTACHMENT BEHAVIOR

Interpersonal attachment behavior has been tied to life history theory by a number of researchers; Chisholm (1999b) gave a detailed history of this research. The features of risk proneness, current versus future priority, and life expectancy appear to be instantiated in an individual's psyche and serve as proximate causes of reproductive and somatic effort patterns in both sexes. Interpersonal attachment theory connects these proximate psychological mechanisms to types and intensities of attachment that arise during the development of individuals. Accordingly, individuals' attachment style is a life history trait designed for adaptive navigation in their social niche.

Draper and Harpending (1982) first provided evidence that father absence during an individual's development causes a personal attachment approach to mating characterized by low commitment, a short-term perspective, and often high numbers of relationships. They speculated that the window of learning—the critical developmental period—for the father absence emotional and attachment effects is years 5 through 7 or earlier. Even earlier in the literature, Weinrich (1977) interpreted social class differences in attachment-related sexual and parental behaviors as stemming from the greater unpredictability of future income in the low SES setting, as compared to that in higher SES settings.

Belsky, Steinberg, and Draper (1991) and Chisholm (1993) presented evidence that mortality risk and resource availability stemming from parental absence or other ecological factors affect children's attachment styles, and subsequently carry over into adult attachment behavior. Recently, Belsky (1997) and Chisholm (1999a) (also E. Hill, Young, & Nord, 1994) emphasized that attachment is a central component of human life history.

The two major attachment types are secure and insecure. The child's style is seen to come about during both the child's infancy and later childhood and to be caused by early security versus early insecurity. The amount of security causes specific life history tactics to be adopted by children and later by adults. Alternative life history life courses fill different social niches, which were reliably present in human evolutionary history. However, Belsky (1997) emphasized that selection is expected to create enough contingency in decisions of tactic adoption to allow individuals to switch later in life if conditions change (also see later). Life history theory applied to attachment interrelates early family environment, especially resource levels and predictability; the child's relationship with parents and the parents' own relationship; parents' behavior toward their children (investment, reliability, responsiveness, sensitivity); children's and parents' attachment styles (i.e., secure or insecure); age of children's sexual maturity and reproduction; adults' allocation of reproductive effort to emphasize mating effort versus parental effort; and the kind of relationships occurring in the social, developmental environment in general (short term vs. long term).

According to attachment life history theory, in risky, low resource environments, mortality probability is increased for both child and parents, and parents and child will adaptively (in terms of historical environments) attach insecurely. Insecure attachment functions for both child and parents in this setting. The offspring is adaptively fashioned for a childhood and adult ecology in which relationships are short term due to reduced survival. This is the case for all social relationships, not just mating ones. People's social allies, whether mates, relatives, or friends, are temporary under high mortality. Minimum social investment and associated high conflict, manipulation, exploitation, coercion, lack of trust, and selfishness are functional in short-term relationships, but not in enduring, long-term ones. For the parents, insecure attachment to the child promotes the limited investment per child that is optimal in the high-mortality setting. Children so raised grow up to form unstable social relationships, including mating and parental relationships, and focus on many sex partners and high mating effort rather than nepotistic (including parental) effort. These children grow up to be extreme risk-takers and have a preference for the now rather than later. The suite of life history traits that arise under harsh and uncertain development cues includes a value system that guides decision making in a manner that was adaptive historically for the individual facing an impoverished niche and low survival.

In less risky, stable, or high resource environments, mortality is reduced. Accordingly, parent–child relationships are based on secure attachment, which involves more parental investment that is reliably delivered by responsive and sensitive parents. MacDonald (1992) used the construct of "warmth" for the relationship between child and parent under these conditions. Here, too, offspring and parents are attaching adaptively (in reference to evolutionary historical environments). Children are being molded for a lifetime of longer, more enduring, trusting relationships, including mating ones. For the parent, secure attachment focuses interest on the long-term investment in each offspring, who are at low risk of death. The children so raised grow up to focus their reproductive effort on stable pair-bonds and a few children, each receiving high parental care. They also have the ability to delay gratification because of their belief that the future will be favorable to them. The various psychological preferences that arise under developmental cues of ecological and social enrichment comprise the ideology that historically increased reproductive success in this setting.

Conditionality and Heritability of Life History Traits

As mentioned earlier, Belsky (1997) proposed that people should retain after childhood the ability to switch from one alternative life history course to another. This is consistent with the large literature in biology about within-population tactical variation. The greater adaptive value of the ability to switch is thought by biologists to be the reason that alternative condition-dependent tactics are far more common in animals and plants than alternatives based on genetically distinct adaptations (Gross, 1996; Thornhill, 1981; West-Eberhard, 1979). Typically, selection is expected to favor a condition-dependent switch from one alternative to another because a "big winner" alternative usually will exist that will give more reproductive success than other alternatives. The point at which a condition-dependent switch becomes advantageous corresponds to the point where benefit and cost ratios for the alternatives adopted by an individual are equal. The point of switching from one alternative to another may be reached because of conditions encountered during development of a juvenile or in the adult stage, and the switch may or may not be reversible.

This principle of switching is seen, for example, in the alternative, condition-dependent mating efforts of scorpionflies. All adult males are capable of and conditionally employ all behavioral alternatives, and switch from one to another in an adaptive manner. During the evolutionary history of *Panorpa*, selection (in the context of reproductive competition among males) has favored genes that code for an extremely flexible behavioral phenotype. An adult male keeps open options for increased reproduction by adoption of condition-dependent behavioral alternatives. That is, there is a probability that an alternative associated with higher reproductive return can be employed successfully if social and/or environmental conditions change.

It seems reasonable that human life history decisions would have been selected to remain flexible beyond childhood given the potential for change of circumstances affecting optimality of different life history tracks after adulthood. Hence, there is good reason to suggest that economic manipulations to reduce mortality, poverty, and inequality and thereby cue future certainty should begin in the childhood developmental environment. However, consistent, enriched adult environments also are likely to be critical.

MacDonald (1997) reviewed evidence concerning whether human life history traits exhibit heritability. Heritability exists in a trait when trait variation among individuals is due to genetic differences among the individuals. Some life history traits have significant heritability (e.g., age of menarche in women). There is a common tendency to consider condition-dependent life history tactics and heritability of tactics as alternative, causal frameworks (Belsky, 1997; MacDonald, 1997; Rowe, 2000). However, condition-dependence may be triggered by genetic endowment and is anticipated to do so when genetic endowment affects probability of survival (Gross, 1996). For example, an individual with genes for poor health or low intelligence may track developmentally into a high risk life history course because selection has favored the ability to read self's genetic quality and adopt a functional tactic accordingly. Low genetic quality is read adaptively as an intrinsic cue of limited survival. Adoption of relatively low payoff tactics is often referred to as "making the best of a bad job." The bad job can reflect poor phenotypic condition, including poor heritable condition. An individual with high genetic quality, then, would adopt a relatively low risk life history course.

The antisocial life history effects of bad genes for health can be remedied to a great degree by improving health conditions. Genes that increase susceptibility to poor health—physical, mental, and those related to developmental instability—will typically not lead to poor health if nutrition is adequate and stress is low (see Thornhill & Møller, 1997). Also, of course, bad genes for susceptibility to infectious disease cannot reduce health if health programs prevent contact with infectious agents or prevent through health monitoring the agents' chronic effects. The policy implication is straightforward: reduce poverty and social inequality.

Even when there exists two or more genetically distinct life history adaptations in a population, environmental conditions work causally to create each adaptation because genes alone cannot make an adaptation or, for that matter, any bodily feature. Genes are never destiny, because development of the features of the individual involves the equal causal influence of both its genes and its experiences.

SOCIAL STRATIFICATION AND MEN'S MATING EFFORT

In all human societies, competition among males for mates creates differences in social rank among them, but the degree of stratification varies cross-culturally (Low, 2000). Most preindustrial or traditional societies have the mating system of polygyny, in which a minority of men have multiple wives simultaneously (Low, 2000). Men's rank may be stratified by status only, not material resources, as in the Yanamamö, Indians of South America (Chagnon, 1997). In the Yanamamö a man's status, which depends on his bravery in warfare and political strength (size of his male kinship network), predicts his number of wives and children; higher status yields more. Most married men, however, have only one wife. Many men die before marriage, primarily as a result of violent, intervillage raids to obtain women.

In many societies, men are stratified by both status and amount of resources; this takes on extreme forms in modern societies. The United States is one of the world's leaders in the high degree of resource disparity across social strata (see Bernstein, McNichol, Mishel, & Zahradnik, 2000, for the Year 2000 Report of the Center on Budget and Policy Priorities of the Economic Policy Institute). In the United States since World War II, the rural and urban male underclass has grown because of the large number of unemployed and underemployed men resulting from the substantial drop in opportunity for unskilled labor. A similar process has occurred in many other modern states and in the Third World (see Lancaster, 1989). Under high social stratification of modern societies, the totally socially disfranchised men experience greatly elevated mortality in comparison to socially franchised men (Chisholm, 1999b; Ellis, 1994a, 1994b; Weisfeld, 1999; M. Wilson & Daly, 1985, 1997).

The theoretical deduction that high mortality will make mating effort relatively more adaptive than nepotistic effort for men is not inconsistent with the fact that underclass men often invest in their sisters' children and more so than in children born to their romantic partners. This allocation of reproductive effort by men is expected theoretically and observed cross-culturally. When men have low confidence of paternity, genetic relatedness to sisters' children is always a certainty (Alexander, 1979; Gaulin & Schlegel, 1980).

Increased mortality in men is expected to have some specific effects on the type of mating effort expended by men. Investment in a long-term mating relationship, a form of mating effort, was not adaptive historically under high mortality because of the likelihood of both parties' death. Thus, short-term mating relationships, including totally noncommittal matings, are expected to be a priority under high mortality. Short-term sexual relationships of disenfranchised men are expected to include coercive matings and coercive and physically abusive sexual control of mates—coercive sexual proprietariness—because such men's value systems validate coercion and they lack the resources that allow franchised men to control mates' sexuality without coercion. Under social disenfranchisement, high mating effort in impregnating many mates and reproduction early before death were adaptive for men in ancestral settings.

In socially disenfranchised men, this kind of multiple-mate mating effort tends to be accompanied by a psychology that makes it effective. Such men often have a relationship psychology of temporariness, father absence, manipulation, exploitation, absence of trust, and urgency or low impulse control (Barber, 1998; Belsky et al., 1991; Chisholm, 1993; MacDonald, 1997). That is, their psychology is focused on current gratification and discounting the future. A psychology of warmth and caring about offspring and mates and other social allies is adaptive only when there is likely to be a future.

The argument is not that only socially disfranchised men will use sexual coercion. Socially disfranchised men are likely to see rape as appropriate because of the reliable association between being outcast and the experiences that entrain adaptive pursuit of short-term social relationships. Sexual coercion, however, sometimes is used by men with considerable noncoerced sexual access to women (e.g., Jewkes, Levin, Mbananga, & Bradshaw, 2002; Lalumiere & Quinsey, 2000). The evolutionary model purports that sexual coercion is used in relation to perception of benefits and costs, just like other behaviors. There are a variety of circumstances that may lead to physically attractive men and men with social rank finding themselves in circumstances in which they perceive the benefits of sexual coercion exceeding its costs (e.g., teachers who rape their students in South Africa, Jewkes et al., 2002; physically attractive men because they are highly preferred by women, which lowers the cost of rape, Lalumiere & Quinsey, 2000). So even among physically attractive men and high status men, life history theory will predict their use of coercion in mating. The males in these categories who derive from backgrounds of insecure attachment and related variables will be more rape prone than the men in these categories with more enriched backgrounds.

LOW SELF-CONTROL

Gottfredson and Hirschi's (1990) theory of low self-control is a leading theory of crime among criminologists. It purports that low self-control is the cause of most crime and related behaviors. In this theory, low self-control is a psychological state of desires, the thrill of risky behavior, and the de-emphasis of long-term benefits. This characterization accurately describes some important proximate causes of criminal activity, but fails to provide an ultimate understanding of self-control and why it varies among people. Self-control mental mechanisms ultimately came to exist because of past selection. Specifically, life history theory gives the insight that self-control evolved to be variable because mortality is variable. Mortality varies between the sexes and across different ecological settings within a sex. Human evolutionary ancestors were individuals who discounted the future in relation to mortality prospects in the local ecology.

Gottfredson and Hirschi's theory accurately sees socialization as a fundamental cause of self-control. They failed to understand that human socialization involves psychological adaptations that read and evaluate ancestral social environmental cues for guiding the life history of the individual in a way that would have been adaptive in the EEA. Socialization is not the whimsical, arbitrary process of much of social science theory. Instead, it is a critical component of the evolved developmental trajectory that creates human attitudes and goals. And socialization is not a complete cause; it is one category of proximate cause of human mental activity and behavior. Humans have evolved to be socialized, that is, to learn the social environment into which they are born, because social settings varied in human evolutionary history (especially with the evolution of capacity for culture), and dealing effectively with the local social scene is necessary for social success.

It is the functional condition-dependence of human social learning that offers the promise for reducing sexual coercion and many other human problems. Increasing survivorship and cues that the future is a reality are expected to lead to high self-control, low risk taking, father presence, reduced property and sexual crimes and homicide, and higher educational aspirations.

Vila's (1994, 1997) theory of crime, unlike that of Gottfredson and Hirshi, incorporated evolutionary considerations (also see Cohen & Machalek, 1988). Vila's theory is totally consistent with the life history perspective presented herein. As predicted by this perspective, Savage and Vila (2002) found that, across many countries, crime rates correlate negatively with health care availability to infants and older children, child survival, resources available for educational programs (e.g., low student-to-teacher ratio), employment rate, and other indicators of socioeconomic well-being. Thus, across the world, lower survival prospects promote the risk taking that leads to criminal behavior. Social policy that is directed toward improving health and educational and job opportunities may manipulate favorably men's psychology by creating a perception that the future is secure and bright.

EDUCATIONAL ASPIRATION AS A LIFE HISTORY TRAIT

Increasing resource levels in the homes of the underclass is expected from life history theory to generate a positive attitude in children and their parents toward educational achievements. Zvoch (2000) tested this prediction about children's attitudes in a pioneering study of life history theory's relation to personal educational values. He used the socioeconomic rank of the home of rearing of U.S. high school students as a surrogate of local mortality faced by the students, a valid substitute given the consistent, negative correlation between mortality and SES across studies. SES status of the home of rearing is a highly significant predictor of students' educational value system. The lower the SES of children's home, the more negative their attitude about continuing education and years of future education that will be pursued (Zvoch, 2000). Educational interest or disinterest appears to stem from the individual's life history program, which is based on valuation of the current versus future. Time and other resources invested in education are somatic effort. They have a positive effect on the future reproductive capability of the individual. Multiple studies have found that education increases job quality, earnings, and other components of a rewarding life such as neighborhood quality and health care; all these things lead to a personal value system of more parental investment per child and more effective parenting (Zvoch, 2000).

Also, education is expected to increase mate value (attractiveness in the mating market), particularly for men (Buss, 1994). For women, education may result in obtaining a partner with more resources because people tend to pair-bond with others of similar educational level. An education-based increase in mate value in either sex provides more mateship options and thus improves the likelihood of involvement in a long-term mateship with more security and parental investment.

POLICY: ADDITIONAL CONSIDERATIONS

This section further discusses the social policy implications of the knowledge that human life history is evolved and is executed by adaptations that facultatively adjust personal time preference, attachment, reproductive and somatic effort, risk taking, and values. This is not a discussion by social policy experts. Remember that any social policy has many consequences, and the desirability of each is open to debate. In this case, the probable influences of policies on the frequency of rape would be only one of multiple consequences to consider. Policy suggestions are offered as points for discussion by persons who are interested in reducing rape and related social problems and who are willing to acknowledge fully that evolutionary history has designed humans, including their personal values.

As mentioned earlier, central to policy considerations to reduce rape could be reduction of the wealth inequality in modern societies. Such reductions would result in people investing more in somatic efforts: immune function and other bodily survival mechanisms; monitoring and pursuing personal health; less tobacco, drug, and alcohol abuse; and showing more interest in education and in social capital in general, including greater investment in individual offspring and other family relationships. The implications for policy are that social pathology is promoted by poverty and inequality and social health by the opposite. A healthy society is one whose individual members have hope (i.e., they value future benefits over immediate benefits).

Among developed nations, it is not the nations that are rich in terms of total wealth or Gross National Product that have the greatest health and lowest morbidity and mortality. Instead, it is those with the least income differences between rich and poor (for a review of studies, see Chisholm, 1999b) The strong, negative correlation between degree of inequality and health and survival also holds across the United States. The Report of the Center on Budget and Policy Priorities has numerous ideas about how to reduce the economic inequality in the United States, which has increased considerably in recent decades (Bernstein et al., 2000).

Reducing inequality will reduce child and adult stress and environmental uncertainty. According to life history theory, this would increase the prevalence of secure attachment and of a positive attitude toward delayed gratification (i.e., a time preference for the future). These changes would stem from the psyche's reading of less stress and more certainty as cues to greater survivorship. Accompanying these changes would be reduced risk-proneness and impulsiveness, and less delinquency and crime, including sexual crimes.

Health programs would be a major part of the social policy envisioned. Reducing infectious disease incidence and providing the social benefits that reduce the effects of disease once contracted are expected to result in a major increase in the quality of life for many impoverished people. Presumably, their social mobility would be improved significantly due to the positive health effects on developmental stability and associated mental ability and mental health in general (see Thornhill & Møller, 1997). An understanding, through further research, of the nature and timing of environmental problems that reduce the developmental stability of people, especially that in the nervous system, could be very important. Increased availability of health programs to people will be effective only if they are willing to use the health benefits. Thus, it is important to instantiate with social policy a time preference for the future alongside investment in health benefits.

Another complimentary policy approach is increasing father presence in the developmental environments of children. In preindustrial societies, father death or desertion greatly increases the probability of mortality of the family's offspring (see Geary, 2000; K. Hill & Hurtado, 1996). Given that male parental investment evolved in humans because it resulted in increased offspring survival, father removal must have lowered survival of offspring during the last few to several million years of human evolutionary history. This was the period of evolutionary salience in shaping the human-specific adaptations that are unique to humans or at least uniquely expressed in humans (Geary & Flinn, 2001). That father absence itself may be a cue to low survival prospects is seen in its effect across all social strata on truancy, delinquency, and criminal behavior (Barber, 1998; Geary, 2000; Weisfeld, 1999). Of course, father absence increases rapidly as socioeconomic level decreases. Regarding rape, Malamuth and colleagues (Malamuth, 1996, 1998; Malamuth & Heilmann, 1998) found that college men's scores on a scale of men's rape-proneness (e.g., have used coercion in the past and view coercion as valid under some circumstances) is higher in men who derive from family backgrounds of limited paternal investment. This pattern presumably is a result of the negative association between socioeconomic level on the one hand and discounting the future and associated pro-rape ideology on the other.

Starks and Blackie (2000) also indicated that father absence may be related to the rape rate. They examined the relation between divorce rates and rape rate in the United States during the period from 1960 to 1995. These two variables are correlated positively, implying that some condition associated with divorce causes men to rape. The authors' interpretation of the correlation emphasized the effect of sequential monogamy by some men, measurable as divorce rate, on excluding other men from mateships with reproductive-age women because men tend to remarry at higher rates following divorce than women and such men tend to remarry younger women than the wife divorced. Thus, divorce rate correlates directly and positively with the degree to which the reproductive capacity of reproductive-aged women is monopolized by fewer and fewer men.

Divorce, however, also creates father distance from offspring because children of divorce typically reside with their mother. Policy implications pertain to motivating fathers to be more involved and invested in their children after divorce. This could be instituted in laws that encourage father presence and investment following divorce and discourage maternal interference in the father–child relationship. Father presence and investment in the upbringing of boys after divorce might be encouraged by a considerable tax credit to fathers following divorce who reside nearby and directly invest in their sons. Such a tax credit could be modeled after the tax credit in Australia to grandparents who move to reside near their grandchildren, a tax program that benefits grandchildren, parents, and grandparents, and must help cue the life history trait of greater security in the minds of developing children (see Kaplan & VanDuser, 1999).

Rape in war is a ubiquitous and major problem. Like other rape, it is connected to life history theory. Rape in war likely stems importantly from the associated perception of increased mortality in the war context. Society has advocated less tolerance and increased punishment for rape in war, which increases its costs (see Thornhill & Palmer, 2000, for a treatment of rape in war).

Punishments that increase the costs of socially undesirable behaviors such as rape could be used to reduce the likelihood of socially franchised men raping women both in and outside war. Evolution is morally neutral and therefore cannot be a basis for deciding the moral worth of punishing any behavior. Evolution, however, strongly suggests the idea that punishing a behavior that people consider undesirable will reduce the behavior. Whether to use punishment and how severe it should be has to be decided by voters. However, focusing policy on punishment without policy adjustments in socioeconomic inequality, job opportunities, educational support, and health care probably would be largely futile. Unless a brighter future is envisioned, humans are not expected to forego risks, delay reproductive effort, and increase allocations to somatic effort (also see E. M. Hill et al., 1997).

Policymakers also might consider the value of evolution-based educational programs for children and adults. Males and females could be taught the facts about the evolution of humans and simultaneously how these facts may be useful for creating a better world. Along the way and repeatedly, students could be given lessons on how to avoid naturalistic and moralistic fallacies. Perhaps the best way to teach critical, knowledge-based analysis is by giving students intellectually difficult topics such as the evolution of rape and morals. These topics are prone to misinterpretation and thus identify intellectual errors in need of correction (see Thornhill & Palmer, 2000, 2001, for a further discussion of educational programs and their potential value for reducing rape).

ACKNOWLEDGMENT

We thank Catherine Salmon for improving the chapter.

REFERENCES

Alexander, R. D. (1979). *Darwinism and human affairs.* Seattle: University of Washington Press.

Alexander, R. D. (1987). *The biology of moral systems.* New York: Aldine de Gruyter.

Barber, N. (1998). *Parenting roles, styles and outcomes.* Commack, NY: Nova Science Publishers.

Belsky, J. (1997). Attachment, mating, and parenting: An evolutionary interpretation. *Human Nature, 8*, 361–381.

Belsky, J., Steinberg, L., & Draper, P. (1991). Childhood experience, interpersonal development, and reproductive strategy: An evolutionary theory of socialization. *Child Development, 62*, 647–670.

Bereczkei, T. (1998). Kinship network, direct childcare, and fertility among Hungarian Gypsies. *Evolution and Human Behavior, 19*, 283–298.

Bernstein, J., McNichol, E. C., Mishel, L., & Zahradnik, R. (2000). Pulling apart: A state-by-state analysis of income trends. *Economic Policy Institute of Center on Budget and Policy Priorities.*

Burton, L. (1990). Teenage childbearing as an alternative life-course strategy in multi-generation black families. *Human Nature, 1*, 123–143.

Buss, D. (1994). *The evolution of desire.* New York: Basic Books.

Cameron, D. (2001). *The purpose of life.* Bristol, England: Woodhill Publishing.

Campbell, A. (1995). A few good men: Evolutionary psychology and female adolescent aggression. *Ethology and Sociobiology, 16,* 99–123.

Campbell, A. (1999). Staying alive: Evolution, culture and women's intra-sexual aggression. *Aggressive Behavior, 25,* 36.

Chagnon, N. (1997). *Yanomamö* (5th ed.). Ft. Worth, TX: Harcourt & Brace.

Charlesworth, B. (1980). *Evolution in age-structured populations.* Cambridge, England: Cambridge University Press.

Charnov, E. L. (1991). Evolution of life history among female mammals. *Proceedings of the National Academy of Science, USA, 88,* 1134–1137.

Charnov, E. L. (1993). *Life history invariants: Some explorations of symmetry in evolutionary ecology.* New York: Oxford University Press.

Chisholm, J. (1993). Death, hope, and sex. *Current Anthropology, 34,* 1–24.

Chisholm, J. S. (1999a). Attachment and time preference: Relations between early stress and sexual behavior in a sample of American university women. *Human Nature, 10,* 51–83.

Chisholm, J. S. (1999b). *Sex, death and hope.* New York: Cambridge University Press.

Cohen, L., & Machalek, R. (1988). A general theory of expropriative crime: An evolutionary ecological approach. *American Journal of Sociology, 94,* 465–501.

Draper, P., & Harpending, H. (1982). Father absence and reproductive strategy: An evolutionary perspective. *Journal of Anthropological Research, 38,* 255–273.

Durant, R. H., Cadenhead, C., Pendergrast, R. A., Slavens G., & Linder, C. W. (1994). Factors associated with the use of violence among urban black adolescents. *American Journal of Public Health, 84,* 612–617.

Ellis, L. (1994a). Relationships between height, health, and social status (plus birth weight, mental health, intelligence, brain size, and fertility): A broad theoretical integration. In L. Ellis (Ed.), *Social stratification and socioeconomic inequality: Vol. 2. Reproductive and interpersonal aspects of dominance and status* (pp. 145–163). Westport, CT: Praeger.

Ellis, L. (1994b). Social status and health in humans: The nature of the relationship and its possible causes. In L. Ellis (Ed.), *Social stratification and socioeconomic inequality: Vol. 2. Reproductive and interpersonal aspects of dominance and status* (pp. 123–144). Westport, CT: Praeger.

Ellis, L., & Walsh, A. (2000). *Criminology: A global perspective.* Needham Heights, MA: Allyn & Bacon.

Gaulin, S. J. C., & Schlegel, A. (1980). Paternal confidence and paternal investment: A cross-cultural test of a sociobiological hypothesis. *Ethology and Sociobiology, 1,* 301–309.

Geary, D. C. (1998). *Male, female: The evolution of human sex differences.* Washington, DC: American Psychological Association.

Geary, D. C. (2000). Evolution and proximate expression of human paternal investment. *Psychological Bulletin, 126,* 55–77.

Geary, D. C., & Flinn, M. V. (2001). Evolution of human parental behavior and the human family. *Parenting, Science and Practice, 1,* 5–61.

Geronimus, A. (1987). On teenage childbearing and neonatal mortality in the United States. *Population and Development Review, 13*(2), 245–279.

Geronimus, A. (1996). What teen mothers know. *Human Nature, 7,* 323–352.

Gottfredson, M. R., & Hirschi, T. (1990). *A general theory of crime.* Stanford, CA: Stanford University Press.

Gross, M. (1996). Alternative reproductive strategies and tactics: Diversity within sexes. *Trends in Ecology and Evolution, 11,* 92–98.

Herrnstein, R. J., & Murray, C. (1994). *The bell curve: Intelligence and class structure in American life.* New York: The Free Press.

Hill, E. M., Ross L. T., & Low, B. S. (1997). The role of future unpredictability in human risk-taking. *Human Nature, 8*, 287–325.

Hill, E., Young, J., & Nord, J. (1994). Childhood adversity, attachment security, and adult relationships: A preliminary study. *Ethology and Sociobiology, 15*, 323–338.

Hill, K., & Hurtado, A. M. (1996). *Ache life history: The ecology and demography of a foraging people.* Hawthorne, NY: Aldine de Gruyter.

Jewkes, R., Levin, J., Mbananga, N., & Bradshaw, D. (2002). Rape of girls in South Africa. *Lancet, 359*, 319–320.

Kaplan, D. M., & VanDuser, M. L. (1999). Evolution and stepfamilies: An interview with Dr. Stephen T. Emlen. *The Family Journal: Counseling and Therapy for Couples and Families, 7*, 408–413.

Kemper, T. D. (1994). Social stratification, testosterone, and male sexuality. In L. Ellis (Ed.), *Social stratification and socioeconomic inequality: Vol. 2. Reproductive and interpersonal aspects of dominance and status* (pp. 47–62). Westport, CT: Praeger.

Lalumiere, M. L., & Quinsey, V. L. (2000). Good genes, mating effort, and delinquency. *Behavioral and Brain Sciences, 23*, 608.

Lancaster, J. B. (1989). Evolutionary and cross-cultural perspectives on single-parenthood. In R. W. Bell & N. J. Bell (Eds.), *Sociobiology and the social sciences* (pp. 63–72). Lubbock, TX: Texas Tech University Press.

Low, B. (2000). *Why sex matters: A Darwinian look at human behavior.* Princeton, NJ: Princeton University Press.

MacDonald, K. (1992). Warmth as a developmental construct: An evolutionary analysis. *Child Development, 63*, 753–774.

MacDonald, K. (1997). Life history theory and human reproductive behavior: Environmental/contextual influences and heritable variation. *Human Nature, 8*, 327–359.

Malamuth, N. M. (1996). The confluence model of sexual aggression: Feminist and evolutionary perspectives . In D. M. Buss & N. M. Malamuth (Eds.), *Sex, power and conflict: Evolutionary and feminist perspectives* (pp. 269–295). Oxford, England: Oxford University Press.

Malamuth, N. M. (1998). An evolutionary-based model integrating research on the characteristics of sexually coercive men. In J. G. Adair, K. W. Dion, & D. Belanger (Eds.), *Advances in psychological science: Vol. 2. Personal, social, and developmental aspects* (pp. 35–59). Hove, England: Psychology Press.

Malamuth, N. M., & Heilmann, M. F. (1998). Evolutionary psychology and sexual aggression. In C. B. Crawford & D. L. Krebs (Eds.), *Handbook of evolutionary psychology: Ideas, issues and applications* (pp. 515–542). Hillsdale, NJ: Lawrence Erlbaum Associates.

Michod, R. E. (1979). Evolution of life histories in response to age-specific mortality factors. *American Naturalist, 113*, 531–550.

Miller, G. F. (2000). *The mating mind: How sexual choice shaped the evolution of human nature.* New York: Doubleday.

Roff, D. A. (1992). *The evolution of life histories.* New York: Chapman & Hall.

Rogers, A. R. (1994). Evolution of time preference by natural selection. *American Economic Review, 84*, 460–481

Rowe, D. (2000). Book review of *Death, hope and sex: Steps to an evolutionary ecology of mind and morality* by J. S. Chisholm. Cambridge, England: University of Cambridge Press.

Savage, J., & Vila, B. (2002). Changes in child welfare and subsequent crime rate trends: A cross-national test of the lagged nurturance hypothesis. *Journal of Applied Developmental Psychology, 23*, 51–82.

Starks, P., & Blackie, C. (2000). The relationship between serial monogamy and rape in the United States (1960–1995). *Proceedings of the Royal Society of London B, 267*, 1259–1263.

Stearns, S. C. (1992). *The evolution of life histories.* Oxford, England: Oxford University Press.

Thornhill, R. (1981). *Panorpa* (Mecoptera: Panorpidae) scorpionflies: Systems for understanding resource-defending polygyny and alternative male reproductive efforts. *Annual Review of Ecology and Systematics, 12,* 355–386.

Thornhill, R. (1987). The relative importance of intra- and interspecific competition in scorpionfly mating systems. *American Naturalist, 130,* 711–729.

Thornhill, R., & Møller, A. P. (1997). Developmental stability, disease and medicine. *Biological Reviews, 72,* 497–548.

Thornhill, R., & Palmer, C. T. (2000). *A natural history of rape: Biological bases of human sexual coercion.* Cambridge, MA: MIT Press.

Thornhill, R., & Palmer, C. T. (2001). Rape and evolution: A reply to our critics. Preface for paperback edition of *A natural history of rape: Biological bases of human sexual coercion* Retrieved February 1, 2001, from http://mitpress.edu/thornhill-preface.html

Vila, B. (1994). A general paradigm for understanding criminal behavior: Extending evolutionary ecological theory. *Criminology, 32,* 501–549.

Vila, B. (1997). Human nature and crime control: Improving the feasibility of nurturant strategies. *Politics and the Life Sciences, 16,* 3–21.

Weinrich, J. D. (1977). Human sociobiology: Pair-bonding and resource predictability (effects of social class and race). *Behavioral Ecology and Sociobiology, 2,* 91–118.

Weisfeld, G. E. (1999). *Evolutionary principles of human adolescence.* New York: Basic Books.

West-Eberhard, M. J. (1979). Sexual selection, social competition, and evolution. *Proceedings of the American Philosophical Society, 123,* 222–234.

Wilson, E. O. (1998). *Consilience: The unity of knowledge.* New York: Knopf.

Wilson, J. Q., & Herrnstein, R. J. (1986). *Crime and human nature.* New York: Simon & Schuster.

Wilson, M., & Daly, M. (1985). Competitiveness, risk taking, and violence: The young male syndrome. *Ethology and Sociobiology, 6,* 59–73.

Wilson, M., & Daly, M. (1997). Life expectancy, economic inequality, homicide, and reproductive timing in Chicago neighborhoods. *British Medical Journal, 314,* 1271–1274.

Wilson, M., & Mesnick, S. L. (1997). An empirical test of the bodyguard hypothesis. In P. A. Gowaty (Ed.), *Feminism and evolutionary biology: Boundaries, intersections, and frontiers* (pp. 505–511). New York: Chapman & Hall.

Zvoch, K. (2000). *Contextual effects on adolescent educational expectations: A life history perspective.* Unpublished doctoral dissertation, University of New Mexico, Albuquerque, NM.

13

Women in the Workplace: Evolutionary Perspectives and Public Policy

∾

Kingsley R. Browne
Wayne State University Law School

P ublic policy necessarily rests on assumptions about human psychology and behavior. Policymakers make assumptions about the reasons for existing social patterns, and they make assumptions about how individuals will respond to policy modifications. If these assumptions turn out to be incorrect, then chosen policies are likely to be ineffective at best and affirmatively harmful at worst.

Those who fashion policies relating to women in the workplace—whether legislatures, administrative agencies, or courts—have often relied on assumptions about the processes underlying private decisions of men and women that turn out to be untrue. Commonplace comparisons such as "women constitute X% of the workforce but only Y% of (*fill in the blank*)," with the choices being anything from corporate executives to engineers to plumbers to firefighters, convey an implicit message that to the extent that X and Y diverge, something needs fixing. Similarly, comparisons such as "the average woman earns only Z% of the earnings of the average man" imply that the farther that Z is below 100, the bigger the problem. The assumption underlying both of these comparisons is a behavioral one—that men and women will, when presented with the same options, make decisions that are, on average, the same. Differential outcomes, therefore, must be a consequence not of sex differences in free choices, but rather differences in the options that are open to members of the two sexes, either because of invidious discrimination by employers or the cumulative action of a sexist, if not patriarchal, society. That conclusion, in turn, rests implicitly on an even more fundamental biological assumption—that the human brain is sexually monomorphic. In other words, the hardware is the same, but males and females are provided (by society) with different software and different external constraints.

If male and female brains had evolved to be the same in all respects relevant to the workplace, then it would be logical to conclude that employment outcomes of men and women should be the same, on average, in the absence of some sort of differential treatment by employers or other important constituents of society (e.g., parents, teachers, and the all-pervasive entertainment and news media). One of the most robust findings of evolutionary psychology, however, is that the mind is not sexually monomorphic (Buss, 1999; Geary, 1998; Mealey, 2000). Rather, in a host of ways, female and male minds differ in ways that cause females and males, on average, to have somewhat different preferences and abilities. In a free labor market, different preferences and abilities will predictably lead to different workplace choices and behaviors.

NATURAL SELECTION AND PSYCHOLOGICAL SEXUAL DIMORPHISM

Despite the fact that males and females have had to adapt over evolutionary time to the same hostile forces of nature, some selective pressures have operated differently on the sexes. Men and women during the Pleistocene made their livings in different ways, with (generally speaking) men hunting and women gathering. Even if the sexual division of labor had not initially been based on biological differences between the sexes, natural selection has had thousands of generations to reward those members of each sex who were especially talented at the tasks "assigned" their respective sex. Thus, even if the allocation of tasks to each sex had initially been arbitrary (which, given what we know about nonhuman primates and other mammals, is not very likely), one would expect that selection would act over the millennia to cause the talents of the two sexes to diverge to some extent.

This difference in "ordinary" selective pressures (sometimes referred to as "survival selection") was likely dwarfed by the pressures of "sexual selection" (sometimes referred to as "reproductive selection"). Both processes reflect reproductive advantages, but the former operates through facilitating survival so that the organism can reproduce, and the latter reflects mating advantages that the particular organism has relative to others of its own sex. (Cronin, 1991; Miller, 2000). Thus, what were the traits that enabled some men to gain reproductive advantage over other men, and what traits enabled some women to gain reproductive advantage over other women?

The key to the understanding of sexual selection is the concept of *relative parental investment*. As defined by Trivers (1972), "parental investment" is "any investment by the parent in an individual offspring that increases the offspring's chance of surviving (and hence reproductive success) at the cost of the parent's ability to invest in other offspring" (p. 139). Among mammals, there is a substantial asymmetry between the sexes in minimum necessary investment. Both during gestation and for some time thereafter, the female's investment is more critical than the male's. Where such asymmetry exists, members of the sex investing less (males, in the case of mammals) will compete among themselves for access to members of the sex investing more (females, in the case of mammals). Males can directly increase their reproductive success by procuring multiple mates in a way that females cannot.

Throughout evolutionary history, it appears that the route to male reproductive success has been through attainment of high status and control of resources, a path that has tended to provide males with access not only to multiple mates but also to the most desirable ones (Betzig, 1986). The reproductive payoff that comes from achievement of status has left men more inclined than women to strive for status in hierarchies and to engage in the kind of assertive and aggressive risk-taking behavior that is often necessary to acquire resources and rise to the top of hierarchies. From early childhood, males are more oriented than females toward competition, and competition tends to increase the motivation of males but decrease the motivation of females. (Weinberg & Ragan, 1979). Men also exhibit a greater taste for both physical and nonphysical risk than women (Fetchenhauer & Rohde, 2002; Olsen & Cox, 2001). Women, in contrast to men, generally cannot enhance their reproductive success by acquiring wealth or accumulating mates, and in some cases women actually imperil their reproductive success by acquiring political status (Low, 1992). As Smuts (1987) noted, competition among females is at a low level relative to that among males because "the outcome of a single interaction rarely leads to large variations in reproductive success because female reproductive performance depends mainly on the ability to sustain investment in offspring over long periods of time" (p. 402).

Unlike men, women have tended to increase their reproductive success by devoting the bulk of their parental energies to investment in children, through provision of milk and other forms of direct care taking, rather than through acquisition of status and resources. Risk-taking behaviors that may yield reproductive rewards to men are less rewarding to women, because women stand to gain less than men reproductively for engaging in such behaviors, and they stand to lose more, because the life chances of existing offspring are typically imperiled to a greater extent by loss of the mother than by loss of the father (Campbell, 1999). Separation of the mother from the infant poses more danger to the infant (and therefore to the reproductive success of its parents) than separation of the father, binding mothers more tightly than fathers to their children (Maccoby, 1998).

Selection has left a differential imprint on the average cognitive, as well as temperamental, profiles of the sexes, likely as a consequence of the sexual division of labor that is a universal pattern in human societies (Brown, 1991). Consistent differences are found, for example, in some forms of spatial ability, with males showing a consistent advantage, particularly on tests of mental rotation. Women, on the other hand, tend to outperform men in tests of object location. These patterns are reflected in sex differences in navigation, with men more likely to rely on cardinal directions and women more likely to rely on landmarks—patterns consistent with the demands of hunting and gathering, respectively (Silverman & Eals, 1992). Males also tend to outperform females in mathematics, especially at the highest levels of performance, a pattern reflected both in a higher male mean in performance and greater male variability. Although there is no reason to think that selection has acted directly on mathematical ability, such ability may be a by-product of selection for spatial ability (Geary, 1996). Males also substantially outperform females in mechanical reasoning. Females, in contrast, tend to perform better than males in many verbal abilities in broadly representative samples, although the difference shrinks in more select samples (Geary, 1998; Lubinski & Benbow, 1992).

Space considerations preclude presentation here of the amount of detail that could convince the highly skeptical reader that biology has anything to do with these sex differences; that evidence is presented at length elsewhere (Browne, 2002; Buss, 1999; Geary, 1998; Kimura, 1999; Mealey, 2000). The evidence comes from a variety of sources, including psychology, anthropology, and biology. The temperamental and cognitive differences described are found cross-culturally, many appear at a very early age, and they are consistent with sex differences found in other mammals. Moreover, many of them have been linked to exposure to prenatal sex hormones. For purposes of this chapter, the reader is asked to assume that there is ample evidence to warrant the conclusion that these differences exist and have biological roots. The question, then, is how these differences play out in the workplace and how policymakers might respond to them.

THE SEXUALLY DIMORPHIC MIND IN THE WORKPLACE

The importance of temperament, interests, and talent in occupational selection and attainment is hardly counterintuitive, but it is often overlooked. We would expect engineers, actors, insurance agents, nurses, bricklayers, police officers, poets, daycare workers, and lawyers to differ along a number of predictable lines, both temperamental and cognitive. We would not expect professional mountain climbers and accountants to resemble each other in personality, and we would similarly expect substantial differences between a CEO (whether male or female) and the CEO's secretary (whether male or female). Because men and women differ in a variety of traits, we should not expect a random distribution of men and women throughout the labor force.

Any account of women in the workplace must explain not simply why, on some global measure, women have not advanced as far as men. A low-resolution view of the workplace might make such commonly invoked causes as discrimination by employers and a generalized sexism on the part of society plausible candidates. A higher-resolution view of workplace patterns, however, reveals a rich texture that makes such simplistic explanations unconvincing. Patriarchy and discrimination, for example, might be invoked to explain the relatively low number of female physicists, engineers, and mathematicians, but what explains the much higher number of female lawyers, doctors, and biologists, not to mention actual female predominance in such fields as anthropology, sociology, and psychology (Browne, 2002)? Patriarchy and discrimination might account for the disproportionately low representation of women in top executive positions, but what accounts for women's proportionate representation in management generally? Patriarchy and discrimination might account for the fact that full-time female employees earn roughly three quarters the earnings of male employees, but what accounts for the fact that single women have approximately the same earnings as their male counterparts? No plausible theory of employer *discrimination* has been put forward to explain why mothers earn far less than nonmothers, whether male or female, or why longer birth-spacing intervals exacerbate the wage gap (Polachek, 1995).

A more nuanced analysis of the workplace reveals that the variegated patterns are more readily explainable in terms of evolved sex differences than they are by some generalized implied conspiracy against female achievement. Average sex differences in interests and abilities can explain not only why women have failed to make inroads in certain areas, but also why they have made such stunning advances in others.

Dominance Assertion and Status Seeking

The people who are most likely to reach high positions in corporate hierarchies are, not surprisingly, those who are most willing, if not eager, to engage in the behaviors necessary to assert dominance over others in the climb for the top. The pyramidal nature of corporations means there are ever-fewer spots in the upper reaches of corporations. Whether corporations purport to encourage competitiveness of executives or discourage it, the jobs will go to those who have stood out from their peers along dimensions that are rewarded by their superiors.

Successful executives of both sexes tend to be competitive, assertive, ambitious, and strongly career oriented (Browne, 1998, 2002). It is immediately apparent, of course, that these traits are typically viewed as masculine, not only in Western society, but cross-culturally as well (Williams & Best, 1990). It should, therefore, come as no surprise to learn that more "masculine" women tend to have greater career success than more feminine women (Wong, Kettlewell, & Sproule, 1985), or that women at high corporate levels are likely to report having been "tomboys" when they were children (Hennig & Jardim, 1977).

The career commitment needed to reach the CEO level is intense, and it is not an exaggeration to say that it requires a "fire in the belly"—not only a drive to perform well individually but also a hunger, if not a need, to lead others. Nicholson (1998) noted that "the most important attribute for leadership is the desire to lead" and that though "managerial skills and competencies can be trained into a person, the passion to run an organization cannot" (p. 146).

No account of workplace achievement can be anywhere close to complete without a consideration of priorities and trade-offs. Many people would like to be CEOs. Some, of course, will not succeed because they lack the talent; some will not do so because they are unlucky. Many others, however, may have the talent but may be unwilling to invest as much of themselves as is necessary to achieve such positions. Single-minded commitment to career, which yields rewards in both occupational status and financial compensation, is in substantial tension with active involvement in the lives of offspring as well as with many other aspects of one's personal life.

In part because of conflicts with family life, but also in part because women on average seem not to get the same psychic reward from achieving status and dominance over others, women are less likely to organize their lives in ways that will lead them to the top. Put another way, women are more likely than men to say "I see what it took for him (or her) to get to that position, and it simply isn't worth it to me."

Risk Taking

Variation in the taste for risk, both physical and nonphysical, has profound workplace implications. A taste for risk is one of the most important traits of the successful executive. A willingness to take moderate risks distinguishes executives from nonexecutives, and it distinguishes more successful executives from less successful ones (MacCrimmon & Wehrung, 1990). The sexes differ substantially in risk preference, as noted earlier, because over evolutionary time male risk-taking was likely to carry greater reproductive payoffs than female risk-taking. As Hennig and Jardim (1977) noted in their study of women in management, "Men see risk as loss or gain; winning or losing; danger or opportunity," whereas "women see risk as entirely negative. It is loss, danger, injury, ruin, hurt" (p. 27). Women are often less willing than men, therefore, to make risky career choices, such as accepting an operational position where failure would be obvious and closely connected with the bottom line, in preference to a staff or administrative position in which success or failure is not quite so obvious.

Variations in risk taking have effects beyond the executive suite. Jobs differ greatly in physical risk, for example, and the riskier jobs tend to be occupied overwhelmingly by men. The most dangerous occupations in the United States are virtually all-male: fisherman, logger, airplane pilot, structural metal worker, taxicab driver, and construction laborer. Every year, over 90% of the occupational deaths in the United States are men (Browne, 2002). Because it often takes additional compensation to get people to risk their lives, physically risky jobs tend, all else being equal, to pay more than safe jobs. Thus, the "risk premium" for dangerous jobs goes overwhelmingly to men, contributing to the "gender gap" in compensation (Filer, 1985; Hersch, 1991).

Physical Strength

Sex differences in physical strength are obvious, and equally obviously are substantially affected by biology. Their importance in the modern workplace, however, is often overlooked. Although automation has diminished the need for strength in many occupations—and with it the male advantage in those occupations—some occupations stubbornly resist automation. No one, for example, has figured out a way to reduce the need for brawn among firefighters (or infantry soldiers, for that matter). Fire hoses full of water, doors that need to be broken through with axes, and citizens in need of rescue all impose substantial physical demands. Sex differences in both physical strength and risk taking are largely responsible for the virtual absence of women in big city fire departments. For example, in 2000, only 36 of 11,000 New York City firefighters were women (Browne, 2002). Similarly, many other blue-collar positions, such as mechanical and construction occupations, continue to require substantial strength (as well as requiring work under unpleasant working conditions). Not surprisingly, then, women's success in white-collar occupations has not been matched in the blue-collar realm, an outcome that is hard to explain for those who believe that workplace patterns are a result of men's keeping the best jobs for themselves.

Just as physically risky jobs must pay a premium, so must jobs requiring a large amount of physical strength. The jobs of garbage collector and parking lot attendant may both be largely unskilled jobs, but there are substantially more people who can collect parking tolls than can sling 30- to 50-pound garbage cans all day, and the effort required of the latter substantially exceeds that required of the former. Even without the more unpleasant working conditions of a garbage collector, then, one would expect garbage collecting to be more lucrative.

Cognitive Abilities

The male advantage in the somewhat related areas of spatial, mathematical, and mechanical abilities has substantial occupational implications. For example, it affects the sex ratio in many occupations. Men overwhelmingly predominate in occupations that require high levels of some or all of these abilities, such as engineer, physicist, mathematician, and mechanic. Quantitative demands of a field also affect its level of compensation. There is a high correlation between the quantitative demands of a field and the starting salaries of college graduates in the field. Indeed, one study found that quantitative demands of fields accounted for 82% of the variance in earnings of new college graduates among various fields (Paglin & Rufolo, 1990).

The verbal advantage of women also has occupational implications. Book editing and public relations, for example, have become predominantly female occupations (Reskin & Roos, 1990). In academic disciplines, women predominate in literature and foreign languages, whereas men predominate in more technical areas (Bellas, 1994). The latter academic fields tend to pay better than the former, in large part because in the latter fields there is more competition with the private sector. There does not, however, appear to be a wage premium for high-verbal fields comparable to that found in math-intensive fields (Paglin & Rufolo, 1990). The lack of such premium is probably due to the fact that although higher levels of verbal ability may lead to incrementally higher levels of performance in some jobs, there is less of a threshold effect than there is in mathematically demanding fields, where some relatively high level of mathematical ability may be required to do the job at all, not just to do it well. Even if there were a premium for high-verbal fields, that would not as clearly translate into a compensation advantage for women, however, because although mean female performance exceeds that of males, male variability is higher, so that female average superiority does not translate into equivalent superiority at the high end (Lubinski & Benbow, 1992).

Nurturance/Attachment to Child

Greater female nurturance has a dual workplace effect. Not only does it affect the distribution of women within occupations, it also affects women's labor market attachment. The "caring professions," such as nursing, social work, and child care, for example, are overwhelmingly female. Even within those fields, the sex ratio varies with the nature of the subfield's demands. For example, although less than 5% of nurses are men, men constitute 42% of nurse anesthetists, a highly paid technical field that involves less social interaction than general nursing (American Association of Nurse Anesthetists, 2001). Moreover, even in largely female occupations, men disproportionately occupy administrative jobs, such as social work supervisor, head librarian, school principal, and nursing director (Zimmer, 1988). Administrators obtain fewer of the social rewards of jobs in these professions, of course, but they obtain more of the status and financial rewards.

Women's greater attachment to their children creates more conflict between work and children than is the case with men. After the birth of a child, women tend to reduce their workplace involvement. They may do so by cutting back on their hours or their travel, by changing to a part-time schedule, or by leaving the workforce altogether. New fathers, in contrast, tend to intensify their work activities and increase their work hours after the birth of a child (Korenman & Neumark, 1992, 1991). This pattern mirrors the pattern of our evolutionary ancestors, with women providing the bulk of the direct parental care and men devoting themselves to provisioning of the family. These responses to parenthood have obvious consequences for both promotion and compensation.

Job Attribute Preferences and Holland Occupational Type

Many of the sex differences described are reflected in sex differences in reported job attribute preferences and in measures of occupational interest. Women generally prefer jobs that have safe working conditions, regular or flexible hours, pleasant physical surroundings, short commutes, and good relations with coworkers and supervisors. Men tend to focus more strongly on income and promotion opportunities (Browne, 2002). Acting on these preferences has obvious economic consequences.

Vocational counselors have long known that the sexes differ markedly on measures of vocational interest such as the Strong Interest Inventory. Men score considerably higher on the factor labeled "Realistic," which reflects a preference for building, working outdoors, and working with things rather than ideas or people. Most blue-collar jobs strongly tap this interest. Similarly, women score higher on the "Social" factor, which describes people who are sociable, helping, instructing, and humanistic. Indeed, one of the most robust sex differences is on the "people–things" dimension, which is consistent with the female preference for people and the male preference for things that is observable even among infants (Lubinski, 2000). Occupations at the extreme "people" end of the spectrum include child-care worker, home economics teacher, community service organization director, and secretary; occupations at the extreme "thing" end of the scale are physicist, chemist, mathematician, computer programmer/systems analyst, and biologist (Harmon & Borgen, 1995). There are predictably few people who would be strongly attracted to jobs in both categories.

Sex differences in temperament, cognitive ability, and occupational type can have a cumulative effect on sex differences in occupational outcomes. Therefore, when people make statements such as "Sure, the sexes differ in strength/mathematical ability, but that difference isn't large enough to explain the small number of female firefighters/physicists" they are technically accurate, but their reasoning is incomplete. It is not just sex differences in strength that account for the skewed sex ratio among firefighters; sex differences in risk preference and in occupational type (firefighter is a highly "Realistic" occupation) are strongly implicated as well. Similarly, it is not just sex differences in mathematical and spatial ability that lead to the skewed sex ratio among physicists; the disparity is also driven by the low social/high theoretical nature of the discipline, as well as the overwhelming career commitment typically required of physicists.

THE POTENTIAL RELEVANCE OF SEX DIFFERENCES TO POLICYMAKERS

What should be made of these differences? Should policymakers be made aware of them? Are they actually relevant to the formation of public policy, or do the differences affect only the realm of "personal decisions"? Does it matter if men, on average, are more inclined to take both physical and nonphysical risks and to scramble for places in hierarchies; or if men exhibit greater spatial, mathematical, and mechanical skill; or if women tend to have greater verbals skills than men; or if women are more tightly bound to their infants than men? The answer to these questions depends on what it is that policymakers are trying to accomplish.

If policymakers are interested in discovering the reasons for observable workplace patterns, then the answers to these questions about men and women are highly relevant. If men are more inclined to devote energies to scramble to higher positions in hierarchies, then that plausibly accounts, at least in part, for men's greater likelihood of achieving such positions. Greater male spatial, mathematical, and mechanical skills might explain at least part of the disparity between the sexes in fields like engineering, physics, mathematics, and automotive mechanics that reward such skills. If women tend to have greater verbal skills, then that may similarly have something to do with the fact that fields such as book editing have become disproportionately female occupations. If women are more tightly bound to their infants, then it might not be surprising to find that the birth of an infant tends to attenuate women's workforce attachment, whereas the same event tends to increase men's labor market activity.

A belief that men and women truly do not differ along these temperamental and cognitive dimensions is likely to lead policymakers to policies different from those prompted by a belief that substantial differences exist. The former view is more likely to lead them, for example, to seek solutions in more stringent antidiscrimination laws aimed at employers and educational institutions, because it is these entities that may be assumed to have caused sexually monomorphic minds to be distributed so asymmetrically in the workplace. In contrast, a belief that men and women differ substantially in their psyches is more likely to encourage—although not logically compel—a conclusion that current workplace arrangements are an unproblematic consequence of sexually dimorphic minds.

Because values must be brought to bear on facts in order to arrive at an appropriate set of policies, a particular view of the scientific evidence of psychological sex differences does not by itself compel any specific policy. Take two examples from opposite ends of the spectrum. A belief that workplace disparities are caused by the free choices of individuals guided by their own preferences and predispositions does not logically foreclose governmental attempts to equalize outcomes, because it is possible to believe that equality of outcomes is of paramount importance no matter what the cause of perceived inequalities. Similarly, a belief that workplace disparities are entirely a consequence of discrimination by employers does not logically compel the strengthening, or even the existence, of antidiscrimination laws, because it is possible to believe that the freedom of employers to construct their workforces as they see fit is of paramount importance. Both of these positions, however, although not logically inconsistent with the hypothesized facts, are what would be labeled as "outside the mainstream" of contemporary American thought—to the left of it in the former case and to the right in the latter.

It is precisely because there is a clearly identifiable philosophical "mainstream" that the debate over facts is so contentious. Those who argue, for example, that any wage gap is too much understand that political support for their position depends on convincing policymakers that the existence of the gap demonstrates the existence of an invidious cause, most commonly asserted to be discrimination by employers. Similarly, those arguing against intervention do not contend that intervention is inappropriate whatever the cause; instead, they argue that causes other than discrimination are more likely responsible. The debate over the inclusion of women in military combat positions proceeds in a similar fashion (Browne, 2001). The central argument of opponents of sexual integration in the military is that, for a host of reasons, inclusion of women will diminish military effectiveness. Again, it is possible, logically, to say that even if women would reduce military readiness, the benefits of their inclusion, whether the symbolic trappings of citizenship or individual self-fulfillment, outweigh whatever impairment results. However, other than among a few academics who flirt with this argument, this position has not had a prominent place in the debate. The only argument that has a plausible chance of prevailing politically is that women will not weaken the military, even a little bit, because people understand that an even marginally weaker military is likely to lead to more combat deaths, and most people's attachment to abstract notions of equality does not take them so far.

The importance of the interaction between values and facts is often confused. Accusations of the "naturalistic fallacy" (see Crawford, chap. 1 in this vol.) often greet those who suggest that scientific facts are relevant to policy making. The suggestion of biological explanations for why women are less inclined to seek CEO positions or tend to earn less money or gravitate toward certain female-dominated occupations is interpreted, at least for rhetorical purposes, as suggesting that what is natural is good, that what is ought to be, or that any attempts to alter the current situation are doomed to failure. The scientific evidence is not introduced for any of these normative or prescriptive purposes, however. Rather, its function is to explain how, in a labor market that allows individuals to assort according to their own talents and tastes, statistical asymmetries are a predictable result and why policies based on an incorrect or incomplete understanding of the reasons for existing patterns are likely to be ineffective, harmful, and unjust.

Ironically, those who level accusations of the naturalistic fallacy seem to be those most prone to constructing a link between facts and values. One could look long and hard without finding a proponent of the view that demonstrating the biological roots of a phenomenon establishes its desirability, yet those who oppose biological explanations often assert, or at least assume, that a description of biological origins implicitly incorporates a value judgment. For example, Kay (1990) asserted that "sociobiologists use sexual difference as a natural evolutionary justification for continued female exploitation" (p. 75). This assertion equates two things that simply should not confused: a *description* of the origins of a phenomenon and a *justification* of it. External values must be applied to the facts to determine whether or not a given phenomenon is in some sense "justified."

POLICYMAKERS OFTEN HAVE AN INADEQUATE UNDERSTANDING OF MEN AND WOMEN

It is instructive at this point to look at a few examples of how the ignorance of policymakers about sex differences has led them astray. By "astray," I do not mean that their decisions are misguided because their values are faulty. Rather, their decisions are misguided, according to *their own* stated values and the principles they are applying.

In class-wide cases of employment discrimination, deviations from proportional representation are often taken as presumptive proof of discrimination (Browne, 1993). The rationale for this practice, according to the Supreme Court, is that "absent explanation, it is ordinarily to be expected that nondiscriminatory hiring practices will in time result in a work force more or less representative of the … composition of the population in the community from which employees are hired" Teamsters v. United States, 431 U.S. 324, 339-340 n. 20 (1977). Statistical imbalances, therefore, do not in and of themselves violate the law; they are legally relevant because they are interpreted as proof that the employer is discriminating. Thus, in the case of Catlett v. Missouri Highway and Transportation Commission, 828 F.2d 1260 (8th Cir. 1987), the court held that the state had discriminated in hiring for highway-maintenance positions—jobs that entailed mowing highway rights-of-way, plowing snow, filling potholes, maintaining rest areas, and servicing equipment. During the period of time covered by the lawsuit, it had hired 8 women and 89 men. The court held that based on the percentage of women in the overall labor force, the highway department would have hired 46 women and 51 men if it had not been discriminating, thus ruling that 38 (unidentified) women had been discriminatorily denied positions. The highway department's argument that women were not very interested in these positions was labeled "conjecture," notwithstanding the fact that very few women applied for the job, and those who did had a slightly higher likelihood of being hired than male applicants.

Similarly, the Equal Employment Opportunity Commission (EEOC) pursued litigation against retailer Sears, Roebuck and Company for 15 years for its supposed pattern of discrimination against women in hiring for commission sales jobs, EEOC v. Sears, Roebuck & Co., 839 F.2d 302 (7th Cir. 1988). Although the EEOC could not identify a single woman who claimed to have been a victim of discrimination, it contended that discrimination was established by the fact that only 30% of commission sales employees were female compared with over approximately 75% of its noncommission sales employees. Sears ultimately prevailed on the basis of uncontradicted evidence that women were not as interested as men in these fiercely competitive positions where the economic risk of poor performance rests immediately on the employee. But, it took 135 days of trial involving 20,000 pages of transcripts, 49 witnesses, and 2,172 exhibits consisting of another 22,000 pages, in addition to resisting the appeal of the EEOC in the Seventh Circuit, for it to do so.

Despite uncontradicted evidence of women's lesser interest in commission sales jobs and despite the EEOC's failure to identify a single victim of discrimination, the three-judge panel of the Seventh Circuit was not unanimous. The dissenting judge expressed outrage that Sears could prevail by demonstrating that women tend to be the way that people think that women tend to be:

> These conclusions, it seems to me, are of a piece with the proposition that women are by nature happier cooking, doing the laundry and chauffeuring children to softball games than arguing appeals or selling stocks. The stereotype of women as less greedy and daring than men is one that the sex discrimination laws were intended to address. 839 F.2d at 361. (Cudahy, J., dissenting)

Most academic commentary on the Sears case endorsed Judge Cudahy's approach (Browne, 1995).

With all due respect to Judge Cudahy and his followers, the sex discrimination laws were not intended to *repeal* stereotypes; stereotypes, after all, are factual generalizations that generally contain a substantial element of truth (Jussim, McCauley, & Lee, 1995), and among the many functions of the law, repealing facts is not one of them. There is a stereotype that men are taller than women, but the law is incapable, by fiat, of making women as tall as men, just as it is incapable of creating the same taste for risk in females that males exhibit, or, for that matter, establishing that two plus two equals five. Contrary to Judge Cudahy's view, the discrimination laws were intended to prohibit employers from acting on stereotypes, treating applicants and employees as members of a group rather than as individuals. There is a large gulf, however, between an employer's saying "we will not hire women because women, on average, are not as competitive as men and because they are risk averse" and its saying, as Sears did, "we tried to hire women, but we could not hire as many as the EEOC thought we should hire, because women are not very interested in the jobs apparently because the jobs are both competitive and risky."

Congress could declare (subject to constitutional limitations) that even if women are not as interested in these jobs as men, women still must make up 50% of every segment of every employer's workforce irrespective of differential interest. However, that would require a dramatic redefinition of the concept of discrimination, which heretofore has focused primarily on process rather than exclusively on outcome. Yet, it must be acknowledged that a regime that strongly presumes that men and women will sort themselves in the same way and that views statistical disproportionality as strong evidence of discrimination has much the same effect as a law that explicitly commands that result.

Universities have been similarly animated by a concern for lack of proportional representation of women, especially in the sciences. There may be good reasons for attempting to attract more women (and more men, for that matter) to science. However, much of the motivation behind programs giving special benefits to female students appears to be that the low number of female students, particularly in fields such as physics and mathematics, indicates that either the universities have been doing something wrong or, even more fundamentally, that there is something wrong with the discipline. Thus, people who have studied women in science make such declarations as "But we can't fix the girls, we have to fix science, to get it to be something they want to do" or that "we really have to rethink our whole notion of what science is and how it functions" (Holloway, 1993, p. 96). Again, the notion seems to be that in a just world, men and women would be attracted in equal numbers to all occupations (although there have been few calls to "fix" nursing to make it equally attractive to men).

The "gender gap in compensation" is likewise held up as proof that the discrimination laws are not working. The fact that, on average, a full-time female employee earns only about three quarters of the wages of a full-time male employee is routinely invoked as demonstrating the need for tougher wage discrimination laws or affirmative action plans. In 1999, for example, President Clinton, in urging stronger penalties for wage discrimination, declared that "75 cents on the dollar is still only three-quarters of the way there, and Americans can't be satisfied until we're all the way there" ("Clinton Seeks More Money," 1999). Despite the routine invocation of the wage gap as evidence of discrimination, however, few economists believe that much of it is actually due to wage discrimination at all. Many of the contributors to the gap have already been mentioned. For example, women have a greater preference than men for safe but low paying jobs, and women are less likely to be found in lucrative highly quantitative fields. Women also work substantially fewer hours than men, with full-time male workers working, on average, 8% to 10% more hours than women, and in some fields the disparity is substantially greater, and they have substantially more extended absences from the workplace than men. (O'Neill & Polachek, 1993).

Many universities have conducted "pay equity" studies to determine whether female faculty are underpaid relative to men and have made "pay equity adjustments" if they are found to be so. Virginia Commonwealth University, for example, found a $10,000 gap between the average salary of male and female faculty. After control for doctoral degree, academic rank, tenure status, and number of years since beginning teaching, the gap narrowed to $2,000. The university then allocated a half million dollars to salary increases for female faculty. When male faculty sued for sex discrimination, the university defended by arguing (as it had to under prevailing law) that the remaining disparity was due to sex discrimination. The Court of Appeals for the Fourth Circuit ultimately ruled that the case must go to trial because the university had not provided uncontroverted evidence that the wage gap was due to discrimination, Smith v. Virginia Commonwealth University, 84 F.3d 672 (4th Cir. 1996). The university had not controlled for many of the factors used by the university in setting salaries under its merit-pay system, such as teaching load, teaching quality, quantity and quality of research and publications, and service to the community. The court rejected the argument that the university could simply assume that these factors did not vary by sex, and, in any event, the plaintiffs had introduced evidence to show that male VCU faculty had a higher scholarly output than female faculty. If productivity measures were excluded from the study, sex differences in productivity would, under the university's statistical model, show up as sex discrimination.

The Fourth Circuit's decision should have been uncontroversial. After all, the question boiled down to whether measures of merit must be controlled for in deciding whether salaries under a merit-pay system were discriminatory. Nonetheless, five judges dissented, arguing that the university's assumption of equal productivity of male and female faculty was a reasonable one, despite the fact that the plaintiffs had introduced evidence that the assumption was unwarranted and despite the fact that virtually all studies of academic productivity show male faculty to be substantially more productive (typically around 50% more) than female faculty (Browne, 2002). The dissent then continued with the breathtaking statement that "even if performance factors could measure and did in fact show differences between the productivity of men and women on the average, the only appropriate conclusion to be drawn is that performance factors improperly favor one sex over the other, not that one sex is actually more productive than the other." Thus, it contended, "as a matter of law" use of performance measures that lead to unequal salaries is illegal sex discrimination.

The *Catlett* majority and the *Sears* and *VCU* dissents can be seen as instantiations of the "moralistic fallacy" or something quite like it. In a "just world," women would have the same interest as men in highway maintenance and commission sales positions, and in such a world, men and women would be equally productive. What ought to be must be, and contrary evidence is not just unpersuasive, it is irrelevant. The *VCU* dissent's contention that measures of productivity must be discarded if it turns out that one sex is judged more productive than the other embodies the same logic as a conclusion that tape measures must be discarded if they show that one sex is taller than the other.

Reflexive suspicion of statistical disparities makes sense only if one starts with the assumption that parity in all statistical measures would be the natural state in a world unblemished by sexism. If it were, then it might be rational to question what it is that employers, universities, and other institutions are doing to females to cause the differential average outcomes for men and women. Yet, the differences in occupational outcomes among employed women, which could possibly be attributable to employers, are mirrored among self-employed women, who work substantially fewer hours and earn substantially less than self-employed men. Indeed, self-employed women, whose freedom to fashion a work environment is less constrained than that of employed women, actually work fewer hours and earn substantially less than employed women (Browne, 2002). Females' leisure preferences, which are similarly unconstrained by employer expectations, also differ substantially from those of males, so much so that sex is the strongest single predictor of adolescent leisure activities (Garton & Pratt, 1991).

CONCLUSIONS

What is the lesson to be drawn from all of this? The principal lesson is not that one specific policy or another is wise or unwise; instead, it is that if policies are to be adopted, then they should be adopted for the right reasons. Much policy analysis relating to women in the workplace is so steeped in the rhetoric of discrimination and sexist societal conditioning that one is hard-pressed to know whether those phenomena are really the presumed cause of the complained-of patterns or if they are simply invoked instrumentally for pragmatic political reasons. An understanding of the evolved differences between the sexes should lead to more rational, and more productive, policy discussions.

Law and other public policies are to a large extent means to respond to and shape human behavior. Although it would be entirely uncontroversial to suggest that zookeepers ought to have a deep understanding of the animals they are managing, the suggestion that policymakers should have a more complete understanding of human nature is often viewed as somewhat exotic if not downright bizarre. Nonetheless, evolutionary psychology offers policymakers a window into the fundamental nature of the human animal and, for that reason, holds out the hope of policies that are more effective than those formed in studied ignorance of human nature.

REFERENCES

American Association of Nurse Anesthetists. (2001). *What is a nurse anesthetist?* Retrieved July 6, 2003, from http://www.aana.com/about/ataglance.asp

Bellas, M. L. (1994). Comparable worth in academia: The effects on faculty salaries of the sex composition and labor-market conditions of academic disciplines. *American Sociological Review, 59,* 807–821.

Betzig, L. (1986). *Despotism and differential reproduction: A Darwinian view of history.* New York: Aldine.

Brown, D. E. (1991). *Human universals.* New York: McGraw-Hill.

Browne, K. R. (1993). Statistical proof of discrimination: Beyond "damned lies." *Washington Law Review, 68,* 477–558.

Browne, K. R. (1995). Sex and temperament in modern society: A Darwinian view of the glass ceiling and the gender gap. *Arizona Law Review, 37,* 971–1106.

Browne, K. R. (1998). *Divided labours: An evolutionary view of women at work.* New Haven, CT: Yale University Press.

Browne, K. R. (2001). Women at war: An evolutionary perspective. *Buffalo Law Review, 49,* 51–247.

Browne, K. R. (2002). *Biology at work: Rethinking sexual equality.* Rutgers, NJ: Rutgers University Press.

Buss, D. M. (1999). *Evolutionary psychology: The new science of the mind.* Boston, MA: Allyn and Bacon.

Campbell, A. (1999). Staying alive: Evolution, culture, and women's intrasexual aggression. *Behavioral and Brain Sciences, 22,* 203–252.

Clinton seeks more money to reduce gap in wages. (1999, January 31). *New York Times,* sect. 1, p. 19, col. 3.

Cronin, H. (1991). *The ant and the peacock: Altruism and sexual selection from Darwin to today.* Cambridge, England: Cambridge University Press.

Fetchenhauer, D., & Rohde, P. A. (2002). Evolutionary personality psychology and victimology: Sex differences in risk attitudes and short-term orientation and their relation to sex differences in victimizations. *Evolution and Human Behavior, 23,* 233–244.

Filer, R. K. (1985). Male–female wage differences: The importance of compensating differentials. *Industrial and Labor Relations Review, 38,* 426–437.

Garton, A. F., & Pratt, C. (1991). Leisure activities of adolescent school students: Predictors of participation and interest. *Journal of Adolescence, 14,* 305–321.

Geary, D. C. (1996). Sexual selection and sex differences in mathematical abilities. *Behavioral and Brain Sciences, 19,* 229–284.

Geary, D. C. (1998). *Male, female: The evolution of human sex differences.* Washington, DC: American Psychological Association.

Harmon, L. W., & Borgen, F. H. (1995). Advances in career assessment and the 1994 Strong Interest Inventory. *Journal of Career Assessment, 3,* 347–372.

Hennig, M., & Jardim, A. (1977). *The managerial woman.* Garden City, NY: Anchor Press/Doubleday.

Hersch, J. (1991). Male–female differences in hourly wages: The role of human capital, working conditions, and housework. *Industrial and Labor Relations Review, 44,* 746–759.

Holloway, M. (1993). A lab of her own. *Scientific American, 269*, 94–103.

Jussim, L. J., McCauley, C. R., & Lee, Y. T. (1995). Why study stereotype accuracy and inaccuracy? In Y. T. Lee, L. J. Jussim, & C. R. McCauley (Eds.), *Stereotype accuracy: Toward appreciating group differences* (pp. 189–214). Washington, DC: American Psychological Association.

Kay, H. H. (1990). Perspectives on sociobiology, feminism, and the law. In D. L. Rhode (Ed.), *Theoretical perspectives on sexual difference* (pp. 74–85). New Haven, CT: Yale University Press.

Kimura, D. (1999). *Sex and cognition.* Cambridge, MA: MIT Press.

Korenman, S., & Neumark, D. (1991). Does marriage really make men more productive? *Journal of Human Resources, 26*, 282–307.

Korenman, S., & Neumark, D. (1992). Marriage, motherhood, and wages. *Journal of Human Resources, 27*, 233–255.

Low, B. S. (1992). Sex, coalitions, and politics in preindustrial societies. *Politics and the Life Sciences, 11*, 63–80.

Lubinski, D. (2000). Scientific and social significance of assessing individual differences: "Sinking shafts at a few critical points." *Annual Review of Psychology, 51*, 405–444.

Lubinski, D., & Benbow, C. P. (1992). Gender differences in abilities and preferences among the gifted: Implications for the math-science pipeline. *Current Directions in Psychological Science, 1*, 61–66.

Maccoby, E. E. (1998). *The two sexes: Growing up apart, coming together.* Cambridge, MA: Belknap Harvard.

MacCrimmon, K. R., & Wehrung, D. A. (1990). Characteristics of risk taking executives. *Management Science, 36*, 422–435.

Mealey, L. (2000). *Sex differences: Developmental and evolutionary strategies.* San Diego, CA: Academic.

Miller, G. F. (2000). *The mating mind: How sexual choice shaped the evolution of human nature.* New York: Doubleday.

Nicholson, N. (1998). How hardwired is human behavior? *Harvard Business Review, 76*(4), 134–147.

Olsen, R. A., & Cox, C. M. (2001). The influence of gender on the perception and response to investment risk: The case of professional investors. *Journal of Psychology and Financial Markets, 2*, 29–36.

O'Neill, J., & Polachek, S. (1993). Why the gender gap in wages narrowed in the 1980s. *Journal of Labor Economics, 11*, 205–228.

Paglin, M., & Rufolo, A. M. (1990). Heterogeneous human capital, occupational choice, and male–female earnings differences. *Journal of Labor Economics, 8*, 123–144.

Polachek, S. W. (1995). Human capital and the gender earnings gap: A response to feminist critiques. In E. Kuiper & J. Sap (Eds.), *Out of the margin: Feminist perspectives on economics* (pp. 61–89). New York: Routledge.

Reskin, B. F., & Roos, P. A. (1990). *Job queues, gender queues: Explaining women's inroads into male occupations.* Philadelphia: Temple University Press.

Silverman, I., & Eals, M. (1992). Sex differences in spatial abilities: Evolutionary theory and data. In J. H. Barkow, L. Cosmides, & J. Tooby (Eds.), *The adapted mind: Evolutionary psychology and the generation of culture* (pp. 533–549). New York: Oxford University Press.

Smuts, B. (1987). Gender, aggression, and influence. In B. B. Smuts, D. L. Cheney, R. M. Seyfarth, R. W. Wrangham, & T. T. Struhsaker (Eds.), *Primate societies* (pp. 400–412). Chicago: University of Chicago Press.

Trivers, R. L. (1972). Parental investment and sexual selection. In B. G. Campbell (Ed.), *Sexual selection and the descent of man* (pp. 136–179). Chicago: Aldine.

Weinberg, R. S., & Ragan, J. (1979). Effects of competition, success/failure, and sex on intrinsic motivation. *Research Quarterly, 50,* 503–510.

Williams, J. E., & Best, D. L. (1990). *Measuring sex stereotypes: A multination study* (rev. ed.). Newbury Park, CA: Sage.

Wong, P. T. P., Kettlewell, G. E., & Sproule, C. F. (1985). On the importance of being masculine: Sex role, attribution, and women's career achievement. *Sex Roles, 12,* 757–769.

Zimmer, L. (1988). Tokenism and women in the workplace: The limits of gender-neutral theory. *Social Problems, 35,* 64–77.

Is Psychopathy Pathology or a Life Strategy?: Implications for Social Policy

∾

Kirsten N. Barr
Vernon L. Quinsey
Queen's University

Persistently antisocial individuals have long been of interest to mental health and criminal justice professionals. In the 20th century, the construct underlying persistent antisociality has been labeled psychopathy, dyssocial personality disorder, and antisocial personality disorder. Although mental health professionals have long recognized those individuals called psychopaths in this chapter, there has been substantial disagreement about the etiology and nature of their condition (Cleckley, 1976; Hare, 1996; Walker, 1973), leading it to be variously considered a type of mental illness, a form of insanity, and a moral deficit.

Psychopathy is considered a personality disorder. Personality disorders, in contrast to other psychiatric diagnostic categories (e.g., depression, anxiety, or schizophrenia) are unusual in that their existence is rarely disturbing to the individuals who possess them. Generally, psychopaths are brought to the attention of mental health professionals by the criminal justice system, or by family members or friends, who are the ones who suffer from contact with psychopathic individuals. Behaviorally, psychopathy is characterized by persistent, repetitive, flagrant, and remorseless violation of the rights of others and the mores and rules of society. Interpersonally, psychopaths have been described as lacking conscience and empathy, and willing to gratify their own needs and desires without considering the consequences for themselves or others. Although it is certain that many psychopaths develop extensive criminal histories and are responsible for a disproportionate percentage of crime, it remains unclear as to what proportion of them never incurs arrests or convictions. In fact, it is their propensity for criminal lifestyles that has allowed a greater understanding of this disorder, because the vast majority of research done with psychopathic individuals has been conducted in prisons and penitentiaries (Hare, 1996).

DIAGNOSIS

The most popular, reliable, and valid measure used to assess psychopathy is the Revised Psychopathy Checklist (PCL–R; Hare, 1991, 1996). The PCL–R contains 20 items that were written to reflect Cleckley's (1976) conception of the prototypical psychopath. Clinicians and researchers using the PCL–R provide ratings on a 3-point scale, indicating whether the individual does, does not, or does somewhat match the description of a prototypical psychopath. The PCL–R consists of two distinct, but related, factors. The first is the Emotional/Interpersonal factor, which is defined by superficial charm, grandiose sense of self-worth, pathological lying, manipulativeness, lack of remorse, shallow affect, lack of empathy, and failure to accept responsibility. The second is the Social Deviance factor, which is defined by need for stimulation, parasitic lifestyle, poor behavioral controls, early behavioral problems, juvenile delinquency, lack of realistic long-term goals, impulsivity, irresponsibility, and revocation of conditional release. There are also three items that do not load on either factor: promiscuous sexual behavior, many short-term marital relationships, and criminal versatility (Hare et al., 1990). Scores on the PCL–R predict both violent and nonviolent future criminal offences (Hare, 1996).

The other main approach to identifying persistently antisocial individuals in North America employs the formal diagnostic criteria for Antisocial Personality Disorder (APD) outlined in the *Diagnostic and Statistical Manual* (*DSM–IV*; APA, 1994). In order to maximize interrater reliability, the *DSM–IV* criteria were designed to focus largely on behaviors rather than on inferred personality traits. This decision has been criticized for focusing mainly on criminal activity and antisocial behavior rather than on personality traits (Hare, 1996). Hare noted that many individuals who are diagnosed with the *DSM–IV* APD are not, in fact, psychopaths, and some psychopaths may not be captured by the APD criteria if they have the personality traits but not the extensive criminal history. However, Skilling and her colleagues (Skilling, Harris, Rice, & Quinsey, 2002; Skilling, Quinsey, & Craig, 2001) conducted analyses designed to assess whether psychopaths constitute a discrete class among male criminal offenders. They found that if the *DSM* criteria were scored on the same 3-point scale as the PCL–R items, rather than a categorical yes-or-no approach, then the same offenders were identified as highly antisocial by both methods. Thus, at least among male offenders, those who are characterized by persistent, serious antisocial behavior according to either method are those who have the highest probability of being psychopaths.

CONCEPTUALIZATIONS OF PSYCHOPATHY

Etiological Theories of Psychopathy

There are currently two main conceptualizations of psychopathy in the literature. The first view is that psychopathy is a mental disorder or illness. This view asserts that there is something *wrong*, some malfunction in the mental makeup of psychopathic individuals that causes them to behave the way they do. Thus, the diagnostic category APD is included in the *DSM–IV* (APA, 1994). APD is very closely related to the construct of psychopathy, both conceptually and, as already pointed out, empirically. The second view, derived from evolutionary psychology, is that psychopathy is an adaptation that evolved in a certain proportion of individuals as a result of particular selection pressures. That is, natural selection led to the creation of a niche for individuals who are deceitful, manipulative, lacking in empathy and remorse, and who are willing to exploit any and all opportunities (and other people) to gratify their own needs and desires. Clearly, this is quite a radical departure from the pathology view, in that psychopathy is considered a *normal*, if uncommon, evolutionary outcome. But how would this selection have come about?

A Darwinian perspective suggests that psychopathy may involve a life history strategy in which mating effort, rather than parental effort, is preferentially pursued. That is, psychopaths focus on procuring as many partners as possible, as opposed to investing in their offspring. From this perspective, the constellation of behaviors characteristic of psychopathy are seen as by-products of the behaviors necessary to enact this high mating effort strategy. For example, manipulativeness may help psychopaths initiate numerous shallow relationships, promiscuity may increase the number of offspring psychopaths produce, and a lack of conscience may allow psychopaths to leave relationships, shrugging off parental responsibilities (Kinner, 2003; Mealey, 1995; Quinsey & Lalumière, 1995). Quinsey, Harris, Rice, and Cormier (1998, p. 230) proposed that "psychopathy can be considered to be a life history strategy consisting of short-term mating tactics, an aggressive and risky ('warrior-hawk') approach to achieving social dominance, and frequent use of nonreciprocating and duplicitous (cheating) tactics in social exchange." Frank (1988) argued that psychopathy arose because of frequency dependent selection. The existence of a group of cooperating individuals provided a niche for more exploitative individuals to prosper. These individuals would prosper as long as there were not too many of them.

Ellis and Walsh (1997) described two theories of genetically based mating strategies pertaining to the study of criminal or antisocial behavior: the Cheater (or Cad vs. Dad) Theory and the *r/K* Theory. According to the Cheater Theory, because of their higher biological investment in offspring, women have evolved psychological mechanisms and tendencies to choose men who also appear willing to invest heavily in their offspring. To counter these strategies, a certain proportion of men would likely evolve tendencies to be deceptive. These men would appear willing to offer paternal investment until they gained the opportunity to impregnate a desired female, after which they would evade and shirk their parental responsibilities. Ellis and Walsh suggested that these cheaters would be characterized as deceptive, irresponsible, and opportunistic—traits that are also common to descriptions of prototypical psychopaths. The *r/K* Theory suggests that there is a continuum of reproductive strategies, which is anchored by the two most common strategies: having few offspring but investing heavily in rearing them to reproductive age (the *K* strategy), or having many offspring but foregoing the heavy investment (the *r* strategy). Ellis and Walsh proposed that most humans use the *K* strategy, but that persistently criminal or antisocial individuals use the *r* strategy. Their criminal behavior, then, is a phenotypic side effect of a genetically encoded strategy.

Pathology View: Predictions and Support

Prediction 1: Psychopaths Should Be Distinguishable from Nonpsychopaths on Some Biological Features Related to the Presumed Pathology. The pathology view has led to considerable research aimed at finding differences between psychopaths and nonpsychopaths, especially in terms of neural functioning (see Fishbein, 2000, for an extensive review of biological theories of antisocial behavior). One theory is that psychopathy consists of some "minimal brain dysfunction"—that is, some neurological dysfunction that is subtle enough that sufferers are not diagnosed with organic brain syndromes, but serious enough to cause substantial differences in personality and behavior. A number of potential neurological and neuropsychological differences have been detected that are putative candidates for these etiological factors.

Psychopaths differ from nonpsychopathic offenders and nonoffender controls on psychophysiological indexes, such as electroencephalogram (EEG) readings and skin conductance (Raine, 1997). One interpretation of the psychophysiological evidence is that psychopaths are chronically underaroused. Chronic underarousal early in life may result in disinhibited temperaments and preferences for novel, stimulating situations. These preferences, in turn, can lead to impulsive, antisocial, and violent behaviors in adolescence and adulthood. An alternative, but not mutually exclusive, explanation is that early and chronic underarousal may prevent psychopaths from learning from punishment and acquiring the fear of negative events that nonpsychopaths develop early in life. This fearlessness then enables psychopaths to engage in behaviors that have aversive consequences—consequences that would inhibit most people (Gray, 1987; Newman & Wallace, 1993). Newman and his colleagues (Newman & Wallace, 1993; Patterson & Newman, 1993) proposed, based on this theory, that psychopaths were characterized by a syndrome of disinhibition—that they were sensation-seekers who were not limited by the inhibitory mechanisms that restrain the behavior of most people. This would then cause them to behave in an impulsive, irresponsible, and reckless manner.

Disinhibition is related to brain chemistry. Serotonin is an inhibitory neurotransmitter that plays a role in the regulation of appetite, sleep, mood, sexual behavior, and aggression. Many studies have found inverse relationships between antisocial behavior and measures of serotonergic activity, suggesting that serotonin normally acts to inhibit antisocial impulses (Berman, Kavoussi, & Coccaro, 1997; Coccaro, Kavoussi, & McNamee, 2000). The relationships that have been observed in personality-disordered men and violent offenders have also been found in children with attention deficit hyperactivity disorder, oppositional defiant disorder, and conduct disorder. It is noteworthy that these childhood conditions have all been statistically linked to persistently antisocial behavior in adulthood.

Neuropsychological functions associated with the frontal lobe of the cerebral cortex may also be different in psychopaths (Giancola, 2000; Henry & Moffitt, 1997). In both incarcerated and nonincarcerated samples, there is a link between verbal deficits, executive function deficits, and antisocial behavior. Typically, differences are found between controls and violent, aggressive, or sexual offenders in blood flow or glucose metabolism in the frontal lobe. Importantly, these neuropsychological deficits emerge before the development of antisocial behavior. These deficits could fit into Moffitt's (1993) model of life course persistent antisociality, in which subtle neurological dysfunctions predispose youths to interpersonal rejection and academic failure, thereby increasing their risk of early and prolonged antisocial behavior.

Prediction 2: Psychopathy Is a Manifestation of Neuropathology. This Neuropathology May Reflect a Developmental Disturbance Similar to Those Involved in Commonly Recognized Psychopathologies Such as Schizophrenia. Psychopathy is evident early in life. Fledgling psychopaths are deceptive, truant, and defiant of teachers' authority in elementary school, and engage in arson, cruelty to animals, vandalism, physical confrontations, and property crimes in adolescence (Lynam, 1996). Moffitt (1993) claimed that two groups of children engage in antisocial behavior: those who begin early and persist in their misbehavior into and throughout adulthood (life-course-persistent antisociality), and those who begin when they are somewhat older, misbehave for a few years, then desist in late adolescence (adolescence-limited antisociality). Numerous longitudinal studies have found that age of onset is a reliable predictor of the seriousness and persistence of antisocial behavior (e.g., see Loeber & Farrington, 1998). Children who begin antisocial behavior earlier have more lengthy and diverse antisocial careers. Lynam described a path that may be particularly risky for the development of adult psychopathy: a dual diagnosis of hyperactivity-impulsivity-attention problems (HIAP) and conduct problems (CP) provides a double hazard. Either diagnosis on its own merely increases the risk of mild antisocial behavior. However, children with both kinds of problems are on a developmental pathway that may culminate in adult psychopathy. The neuropsychological and psychophysiological correlates of psychopathy, described later, have also been observed in children with HIAP-CP.

A number of studies have linked developmental disturbances with later aggressive and violent behavior. These disturbances can take place at any time during the development of the brain. Prenatal studies, covering gestation up to the seventh month, include both maternal factors (e.g., maternal illness, malnutrition, or stress) and fetal factors (e.g., exposure to toxic or harmful substances like alcohol, drugs, or unusual levels of circulating hormones). One method of assessing potential intrauterine insults is to measure minor physical anomalies (MPAs). These are minor abnormalities in physical development that, because the brain develops in tandem with various physical characteristics, are presumed to reflect possible brain abnormalities. Both longitudinal and cross-sectional prenatal studies have showed that MPAs are linked to violent criminal arrests (but not property arrests) and violent recidivism (Brennan & Mednick, 1997; Kandel, Brennan, Mednick, & Michelson, 1989). In addition, MPAs have been linked to several behavior disorders that predict later antisociality, as well as other mental illnesses, such as schizophrenia. Firestone and Peters (1983) and Fogel, Mednick, and Michelsen (1985) found that MPAs were linked to hyperactivity in boys, and other researchers have found associations between MPAs and problem behavior among preschool and school-age children (e.g., Burg, Rapoport, Bartley, Quinn, & Timmins, 1980; Halverson & Victor, 1976; O'Donnell & Van Tuinan, 1979).

Perinatal studies cover the period surrounding birth, from the seventh month of gestation to 28 days after birth. Several perinatal studies have linked birth complications (e.g., anoxia during delivery, use of forceps, breech delivery) with later outcomes, including antisociality. Perinatal complications have been linked to impulsive criminal offences; however, the data on this relationship remain contradictory. Perinatal insults have also been connected to the later commission of serious, violent offences (Brennan & Mednick, 1997).

Postnatal studies (covering the period starting 4 weeks after birth) involve any harmful events that may affect the brain after the perinatal period, and can include such factors as head injury sequelae, mineral toxicity, and nutritional deficiency. The factors that may mediate the relationship between these developmentally risky events and later antisociality include neurological dysfunction, changes in hormone levels, or changes in the functioning of neurotransmitter systems. Studies of postnatal developmental risks have found several factors that are related to aggression and violent (but not nonviolent) offending, including head injuries, mineral toxicity, dietary deficiencies, and various other medical factors (Brennan & Mednick, 1997). However, the aforementioned research does not focus on psychopathy specifically. The one study that did examine psychopathy and indexes of developmental perturbations (Lalumière, Harris, & Rice, 2001) found that, as expected, nonpsychopathic offenders scored higher than did nonoffenders on both obstetrical complications and fluctuating asymmetry. However, psychopathic offenders actually scored *lower* than the other offenders on these indexes, and in fact, were within the same range as nonoffenders. This suggests that although developmental insults may be related to some types of violence, especially impulsive violence, they are not causative factors in psychopathy.

Prediction 3: There May Be a Genetic Basis to Psychopathy as There Is with Other Mental Disorders (e.g., Schizophrenia, Depression).   Many studies of the heritability of violent, criminal, or antisocial behavior have been conducted. In studies of impulsivity and aggression in children, the data show a mean heritability estimate of up to .80, although this could be somewhat inflated by methodological problems (Goldman & Fishbein, 2000). In adolescents, studies generally show conflicting or null results, however, this is likely due to the large number of adolescence-limited delinquency cases (Moffitt, 1993). In adults, heritabilities range from .41 to .72 (Goldman & Fishbein, 2000). Finally, Coccaro et al. (2000) and Mason and Frick (1994) reviewed a large number of twin studies of criminal behavior in children and adults, and estimated the overall heritability to be between .30 and .50. Carey and Goldman (1997) pointed out that heritability estimates are generally higher when the variables studied are more general psychological constructs (e.g., aggression, psychopathy) than specific, socially defined constructs (e.g., violent crimes). Clearly, a significant proportion—perhaps as much as half—of the behavioral variation in antisociality in the population is due to genetic variation.

Molecular genetic techniques have become available that allow researchers to directly investigate the makeup of the human genome, searching for particular genetic markers associated with violent behavior. To date, at least two genotypes have been identified that are linked to violence. Each has a single mutation: The first involves a mutation in the gene for aldehyde dehydrogenase and the second involves a mutation in the gene for monoamine oxidase (MAO), which leads to Brunner's syndrome (Carey & Goldman, 1997). Caspi et al. (2002) conducted an extremely thorough prospective study of the effects of MAO activity genotype and serious childhood maltreatment on later antisocial and violent behavior. Although the main effect of MAO genotype on violent behavior was not significant, the main effect of maltreatment and the interaction between the genotype and exposure to maltreatment were significant. Breaking these effects down, Caspi et al. found that men with low MAO activity and childhood maltreatment had significantly higher scores on a measure of violent dispositions, and significantly more APD symptoms than did the comparison men. In addition, men with low MAO activity and childhood maltreatment were 2.8 times more likely to develop conduct disorder, and were 9.8 times more likely to be convicted of a violent offence, than were the comparison men. The authors suggested that interactions such as this one may explain the common, but discrepant, finding that maltreatment is very common in persistently antisocial men, but that most maltreated children do not grow up to be antisocial. That is, those children that inherit genotypes that predispose them to antisocial behavior will respond much more strongly to environmental risk factors for antisociality, such as maltreatment.

Life Strategy View: Predictions and Support

Consider now the evidence that psychopathy may be a life history strategy. There is a considerable body of research that suggests that psychopathy could be a disorder, but none of the data discussed earlier necessarily prove that it is a disorder (Kinner, 2003; Mealey, 1995; Quinsey & Lalumière, 1995). The *DSM* criteria describing personality disorders would seem to indicate that it is, however Wakefield (1992a, 1992b) criticized the *DSM* and proposed different criteria for delineating a mental disorder. First, he suggested, a disorder must cause some harm, dysfunction, or disability to the individual. Second, the disorder should be the result of a mental mechanism that is an adaptation to some particular problem in the evolutionary context, and that has malfunctioned in some way. By these criteria, it is less certain that psychopathy can be considered a disorder. Psychopaths do not generally feel a sense of subjective distress over their condition (not including the distress they feel as a result of societal constraints). Furthermore, the evidence presented earlier does not necessarily indicate a malfunctioning mechanism. Physiological, neurochemical, and neuropsychological *differences* do not necessarily imply *dysfunctions*.

Brain-based or psychiatric features are not the only differences that have been observed between psychopaths and nonpsychopaths. Psychopathy is currently considered a personality disorder, an Axis II diagnosis. Axis II disorders are described in terms of inflexible, problematic personality traits and behaviors that, although not necessarily subjectively distressing, can be detrimental to the individuals possessing them. However, the so-called detriment generally consists of the negative reactions of *others* to the trait or behavior. For example, a personality trait that is common in psychopathy is Machiavellianism, which is a willingness to manipulate and exploit others, and to engage in deception and rule-breaking to gain influence or rewards. Individuals high in Machiavellianism espouse attitudes typified by the adages "It's a dog-eat-dog world" and "I have to look out for number one first." Psychopaths exhibit particularly high levels of Machiavellianism relative to normal samples (Christie & Geis, 1970; Mealey, 1995; Mealey & Kinner, 2003). But Mealey and her colleagues noted that this does not necessarily harm the psychopath, and in some senses could be beneficial—after all, in many areas this trait would be considered advantageous.

Prediction 1: There Must Be a Genetic Basis for Psychopathy.   W h e r e a s the pathology view asserts that there may be a genetic basis for psychopathy, in the life history view there must be. The research discussed above clearly points to a genetic contribution to psychopathy—perhaps as much as half of the population variability in antisociality is due to genetic variation (Coccaro et al., 2000; Mason & Frick, 1994). However, this does not automatically mean that psychopathy is a disorder. Genetic variation is the raw material for evolution; it provides the basis by which natural selection pressures can cause change over time. The fact that a trait shows genetic variation in the population can indicate that some or all of the alleles underlying the trait evolved because they conferred some fitness advantage. Theoretically, if an allele confers a fitness advantage, the allele will become more common in the population. But the potential advantage of an allele is not necessarily an either/or proposition (*either* the allele is advantageous *or* it is not). Sometimes an allele confers an advantage only in a particular context. Frequency dependent selection is one example of this phenomenon.

Frequency dependent selection (FDS) occurs when the benefits an allele confers depend on the allele's frequency in the population. In negative FDS, specifically, an allele has a high fitness value only when it is rare; as it becomes more common, the fitness value decreases. An obvious example of negative FDS is the maintenance of a balanced sex ratio in the population caused by the reproductive advantage conferred on members of the rarer sex. Psychopathy could be another such situation; the genotype that creates these deceptive manipulators may provide them fitness advantages only as long as they are few, and cooperators many.

Mealey (1995) described a sociobiological model that suggests that psychopathy (or sociopathy, in her terminology) is a reproductive strategy, at least for some psychopaths. That is, psychopaths are presumed to be engaging in a particular reproductive strategy, with the well-known interpersonal characteristics that this entails, rather than suffering from a mental disorder. This strategy is considered a short-term, high mating effort strategy. Quinsey and Lalumière (1995) formulated a similar theory, however they suggested that these short-term mating tactics could be shifted to more long-term, investment-oriented tactics, depending on the environmental contingencies. That is, they suggested that the short-term mating strategy is a facultative, as opposed to an obligate, algorithm. They noted that this means that the short-term mating strategy is unlikely to be genetic, but a considerable body of work suggests that psychopathy has a substantial genetic component. Mealey resolved this discrepancy in her model. She differentiated between primary psychopaths and secondary psychopaths. Her primary psychopaths are those who are *born* psychopaths—that is, they have inherited whatever adaptation leads to the constellation of reproductive behaviors that are collectively called psychopathy. Secondary psychopaths are those whose behavior might be elicited by environmental contingencies; that is, they may have a predisposing capability of engaging in such a strategy, but the behavior is *released* when contextual factors evoke it.

Prediction 2: There Should Not Be an Increased Incidence of Developmental Perturbations in Psychopathy.   As discussed earlier, there is evidence that some antisocial individuals have developmental perturbations that are linked to their behavior. However, the data also suggest that psychopaths are antisocial not because they suffered from some developmental insult, but because they have a predisposition to be antisocial. Indeed, in the only study to explicitly separate psychopathic from nonpsychopathic offenders (Lalumière et al., 2001), psychopaths were lower on indexes of developmental problems than nonpsychopathic offenders, and scored similarly to nonoffender controls. Thus, it is unlikely that psychopathy represents a developmental neuropathology.

Prediction 3: Psychopaths May Begin their Reproductive Careers Earlier than Nonpsychopaths (e.g., Earlier First Intercourse, Earlier First Pregnancy). A number of researchers have found that antisocial behavior and early age of sexual initiation share a number of predictors, and may also reflect the same underlying trait. In a factor analysis of traits related to individual differences in antisocial behavior, Quinsey, Book, and Lalumière (2001) found that, although number of sexual partners and preference for variety in sexual partners loaded on a factor labeled Mating Success, age at first intercourse loaded on a factor labeled Antisociality. Other variables loading on the Antisociality factor were physical aggression, elementary school maladjustment, school suspension, family and personal history of alcohol problems, conduct disorder symptoms, and juvenile arrests. Thus, there was clearly a correlation between individuals' histories of antisocial behavior and age at first intercourse. This relationship is so close that items whose manifest content clearly involves antisociality (e.g., "My friends respect me because they know I'm a little wild and crazy") behave well in a scale designed to measure male mating effort (Rowe, Vazsonyi, & Figueredo, 1997).

In general, boys and men are more likely to engage in antisocial behavior than are girls and women. This finding is robust both temporally and geographically; that is, this pattern is found in every place and during any period in which official crime statistics were kept. Men are also more likely than are women to engage in short-term mating tactics and to invest their energy more highly into mating effort (Buss & Schmitt, 1993). For these reasons, most studies of persistently antisocial and/or psychopathic individuals use males. Therefore, first consider the evidence for a relationship between antisociality and early reproductive career onset in boys and men.

In a longitudinal study of 206 boys at risk for negative outcomes, Capaldi, Crosby, and Stoolmiller (1996) found that antisocial behavior was the most significant predictor of age at first intercourse. Those boys who scored above the median on antisocial behavior in grade 4 were twice as likely as were boys scoring below the median to have intercourse by grade 11. Other significant predictors were parental antisocial behavior, poor parental supervision, parental transitions, and substance use. In addition, early intercourse was significantly related to number of juvenile arrests, with those boys who began having intercourse early being arrested significantly more often than later-starting boys. Fagot, Pears, Capaldi, Crosby, and Leve (1998) found that young fatherhood was significantly predicted by low parental income and socioeconomic status, parental antisocial behavior, boys' antisocial behavior, deviant peers, and low academic achievement. When the 35 young fathers were compared to nonfathers on risk factors assessed in grade 12, the fathers showed significantly higher arrest rates, higher drug and tobacco use, and higher high school dropout rates than nonfathers. Overall, those boys who had the least prospect of gaining resources by virtue of their low parental socioeconomic status and low academic achievement were also those most likely to become young fathers. In addition, when these boys' children were assessed at age 2, 58% of them were not living with their fathers and 40% had no contact with their fathers, showing that boys who became young fathers did not inevitably invest heavily in their children.

Stouthamer-Loeber and Wei (1998) conducted a prospective, longitudinal study of the risk factors for delinquency and fatherhood among 506 adolescent boys. Those boys who became fathers before age 19 were more than twice as likely to have been classified as seriously delinquent, and all of the predictors of young fatherhood also predicted serious juvenile delinquency. In fact, throughout the study, the predictors of young fatherhood were consistently a subset of the predictors of delinquency. These variables included early onset of sexual intercourse, positive attitudes and exposure to drugs and delinquency, association with drug abusing and delinquent peers, cruelty to other people, untrustworthiness, and truancy, suspension, and negative attitudes toward school. In addition, young fathers were more than four times as likely to be still considered serious delinquents in the year after the birth as were nonfathers, showing that fatherhood did not diminish their antisocial behavior.

However, even though the base rate of female antisocial behavior is lower, women's reproductive behavior is easier to study because maternity is certain. That is, short of an early miscarriage, a woman knows when she has become pregnant and given birth, whereas men may not be aware of all of their children. Thus, consider next the evidence for an overlap of antisociality and early mating efforts in girls. Serbin et al. (1998) conducted a longitudinal study of 853 inner-city women at risk for various negative outcomes. They found that women who have antisocial features tend to have children earlier, and to have more children at younger ages. In addition, these young mothers, as compared to women who have children when they are older, show fewer positive parenting behaviors. Serbin et al. interpreted these findings as reflecting intergenerational transfer of risk. However, in an evolutionary framework, these results could instead be seen as depicting an alternate mating strategy in which more children are borne at younger ages, but parental investment efforts are lower.

Hardy, Astone, Brooks-Gunn, Shapiro, and Miller (1998) assessed the continuity of age at first birth over three generations. They found remarkable continuity of age of first birth. Women who had teen mothers were significantly more likely to become teen mothers themselves, and those whose mothers delayed childbearing were significantly more likely to have done so as well. In this study, the children of teen mothers were significantly less likely to complete high school, to be physically and mentally healthy, to be financially independent, and to be free from substance use and criminal behavior. In addition, there was a "double-dose" effect: The worst outcomes in these areas were for children whose mothers and grandmothers were both teens at their first births. These children were more likely to have intercourse early (before 16 years), to have been charged or arrested with a crime, and to leave home at a young age (before 17 years). Finally, Lanctôt and Smith (2001) assessed the relationship between sexual and nonsexual deviance in 196 adolescent girls, asking whether the risk factors for both types of deviance were similar. They found that girls with high levels of early sexual behavior had significantly higher drug and alcohol use and committed more status offences than did girls with lower levels of early sexual activity. In addition, girls who became pregnant as adolescents had higher rates of status offences and drug and alcohol use than did sexually active girls who did not become pregnant. Early sexual behavior, early status offences, and early drug and alcohol use shared numerous predictors in this sample. The authors concluded, therefore, that early sexual behavior and early nonsexual deviance likely reflect the same underlying trait.

Therefore, the patterns for boys and girls are the same. The data show a strong and significant relationship between antisocial behavior and early onset of sexual intercourse and pregnancy. However, the male and female samples in these studies differ on a number of demographic variables, so direct comparisons are difficult. Fortunately, several researchers have investigated this relationship in samples that include both boys and girls.

R. Jessor, Costa, L. Jessor, and Donovan (1983) conducted a longitudinal, prospective study designed to predict adolescents' age at first intercourse. They theorized, based on their problem-behavior theory, that adolescents who engage in antisocial behavior would also begin intercourse at a younger age. A total of 403 participants (172 boys and 231 girls) participated throughout their school years and provided data again at a 7-year follow-up. Although there were some differences between the male and female participants' sexual behaviors (e.g., context of initial sexual intercourse, proportion of participants who were married or living common law), the age of onset for boys and girls did not differ significantly, and the data patterns were remarkably consistent across the sexes. After preliminary analyses in which the authors compared male and female participants and found few differences, they conducted the remaining analyses on the combined sample. A number of psychosocial indices, measured initially when all participants were still virgins, reliably predicted the age of onset of intercourse. For example, lower academic achievement, greater social criticism, higher tolerance for deviance, more positive views and higher rates of drug use, less parental support, greater influence of friends relative to parents, more parental and friend approval of problem behavior, more friend-modeled problem behavior, and less involvement in conventional behavior were all associated with earlier age of onset. Thus, adolescents who are already engaging in problem and antisocial behavior also tend to engage in sexual intercourse significantly earlier than do their more conventional peers.

Based on this relationship between sexual and nonsexual deviance, Rowe, Rodgers, Meseck-Bushey, and St. John (1989) conducted a sibling study examining the familial nature of an underlying proneness to deviance. A genetic basis for age at first intercourse had earlier been found in a retrospective twin study: Monozygotic twins were more similar in their age at first sexual intercourse than were dizygotic twins (Martin, Eaves, & Eysenck, 1977). Thus, Rowe et al. suggested that a heritable trait underlying age of onset of sexual behavior could be the same trait that underlies deviance proneness. Using samples of high school and university students and their siblings, the authors collected data on age at first intercourse, level of various sexual and presexual activities, and nonsexual deviance. They found that individuals who engaged in sexual intercourse earlier also exhibited more antisocial behaviors. In addition, the correlations between one sibling's deviance and the other sibling's age at first intercourse and level of sexual activities were strong. Not only was age at first intercourse predictable from the participants' own levels of deviant behaviors, it was also predictable from the siblings' levels of deviance. These patterns were very similar across the sexes. Finally, the authors used structural equation modeling to compare nonsexual and sexual deviance between brothers and sisters. Their results suggested that the same latent (likely genetic) trait is responsible for both female and male deviance proneness, and this trait underlies both sexual and nonsexual deviance across the sexes.

Bingham and Crockett (1996) conducted a longitudinal analysis of the relationship between timing of first sexual intercourse and psychosocial development of 414 adolescents (216 girls and 198 boys). Their results were consistent across the sexes: For both girls and boys, those who had intercourse earlier showed significantly higher rates of deviance and substance use, lower rates of church attendance, lower school marks and academic expectations, and poorer family relationships than did adolescents who had intercourse later. However, once the authors statistically controlled adolescents' initial values on these variables, these differences disappeared. They concluded that adolescents who initiate intercourse earlier do so because they are already on a more antisocial developmental trajectory. Scaramella, Conger, Simons, and Whitbeck (1998) conducted a prospective, longitudinal study of the predictors of risky behavior and early involvement in a pregnancy in 368 adolescents (191 girls, 177 boys). They found that warm and involved parenting (measured in 7th grade) predicted lower association with deviant peers and higher school achievement in 8th grade. All of these variables, in turn, predicted lower levels of substance abuse, delinquency, and pregnancy in 12th grade. The authors initially performed these analyses separately for the two sexes, but combined them after finding almost identical results for both groups. They concluded that the pathway to early involvement in a pregnancy could be considered "a consequence of a general tendency toward deviance" (p. 1242) for both boys and girls.

Although the aforementioned studies all include individuals with high rates of antisocial behavior and traits, none of the studies assessed psychopathy explicitly. Without such a specific assessment, it is not possible to know whether or how many of the participants might be considered psychopaths. However, some researchers suggest that cumulative scores on continuous measures of antisocial behavior and traits can be interpreted as reflecting the probability that any given person is a member of the persistently antisocial, possibly psychopathic, taxon (e.g., Skilling et al., 2001). This is in contrast to using cutoff scores, which often are not empirically derived. When cumulative scores are used, those individuals who show the most extreme manifestations of antisocial behaviors and traits are also considered those with the highest probabilities of being antisocial taxon members.

Prediction 4: Psychopaths Should Show Higher Mating Effort than Do Non-psychopaths (i.e., Higher Number of Sexual Partners, Sexual Coercion of Reluctant Partners, etc.).   Quinsey and colleagues (Quinsey & Lalumière, 1995; Seto, Khattar, Lalumière, & Quinsey, 1997) showed that psychopaths engage in higher mating effort (e.g., more short-term sexual partners and "one night stands"). In addition, when reluctant or hesitant partners frustrate their efforts, psychopaths are more likely to use coercion to obtain sexual access. They are also less likely to verify that their partner is using contraception (Seto et al., 1997). In a sample of adolescents who sought routine medical attention, those diagnosed with antisocial personality or conduct disorder symptoms had higher numbers of sexual partners, and a higher likelihood of having unsafe sexual encounters than did comparison adolescents (Lavan & Johnson, 2002). Rowe et al. (1997) also found that high mating effort individuals were more sexually active, showing that their mating efforts are successful. These authors also noted that mating effort had a familial component.

Prediction 5: Psychopaths Should Show Other Indications of a Short-Term Mating Strategy (e.g., Low Birthweight, Higher Rates of Premature Delivery, Births in Rapid Succession, Frequent Twinning, etc.; Ellis & Walsh, 1997). There is some evidence for this prediction, although the studies cited here did not assess these outcomes specifically as a function of psychopathy. Fagot et al. (1998) found that the youngest fathers in their sample of at-risk boys were more likely than a comparison sample of fathers to have children born prematurely. Serbin et al. (1998) found that women in their high risk category (who had been aggressive and withdrawn as children) were significantly more likely to be teen mothers, to be multiparous by age 24, and to have closely spaced births (i.e., less than 2 years between children). Hardy et al. (1998) found that girls whose mothers and grandmothers were both teens at their first births were more likely to have teenage births themselves. In addition, their mothers were more likely to have grown up in large (4 or more children), poor families. Although these data are suggestive, further research is needed in this area, especially research that specifically assesses these outcomes as a function of psychopathy.

Comparing these two views of psychopathy, we can see that many of the data are consistent with both views. That is, several of the predictions from both views are similar or identical. However, there is one major difference between them: If psychopathy is a disorder, then psychopaths would be expected to have fewer offspring; if it is a life strategy, then psychopaths should have as many or more offspring as nonpsychopathic individuals. This question, therefore, provides a means for definitively establishing the correctness of one of these two competing theories.

UNDERSTANDING THE EVOLUTION
OF THE PSYCHOPATHIC LIFE STRATEGY

By definition, all evolutionarily stable strategies must confer fitness advantages. In addition, because all strategies involve trade-offs, the advantages must either balance or outweigh the costs incurred by the strategists. What are the potential costs and benefits of a psychopathic life history strategy?

Benefits of the Psychopathic Life Strategy

Psychopaths may have more children or have children earlier than do nonpsychopaths or else the strategy would likely not persist through evolutionary time. Data show that highly antisocial youths have children earlier than less antisocial youths (e.g., see Prediction 3). Furthermore, male psychopaths can come closer to their desired number of sexual partners (i.e., many) than can men who invest more in their offspring (Quinsey & Lalumière, 1995; Seto et al., 1997). An advantage of having many mates is that some may have better genes than might the one potential mate that an individual could secure if he mated monogamously. Another boon of the short-term mating strategy is that, for male psychopaths at least, they do not have to engage in the perpetual negotiation that takes place when men's and women's relationship needs conflict; they need only negotiate long enough to ensure conception. Finally, there may be other short-term gains from this strategy that cooperators cannot access. For example, in the noniterated version of the Prisoner's Dilemma game, defectors get more resources than they would if both members cooperated. As long as the cooperators outnumber the defectors, there is a short-term competitive advantage to being a defector, and the defectors who can successfully exploit several cooperators have the chance to amass potentially considerable resources.

It is also important to note that there are potential nonreproductive advantages. Psychopaths strive for status in intermale competitions (Ellis, 1998; Wilson & Daly, 1985) In fact, Ellis also described the *Coincidental Status-striving Theory* in which women are more attracted to, and have preferences for, high status men. Therefore, the men who can compete successfully for more resources are also those who end up attracting more potential mates. In other words, it may not be the mating effort per se that results in higher reproductive success for antisocial individuals, but the efforts they expend in acquiring social dominance and material resources. These efforts are not limited to honest efforts; psychopaths are known for their criminal versatility, and their criminal careers often include charges of theft, robbery, fraud, and embezzlement (e.g., Hare, 1996; Rowe et al., 1997). Psychopaths also have a well-documented propensity to commit crimes of violence (Quinsey et al., 1998). Morrison and Gilbert (2001) found that primary psychopaths in a maximum security psychiatric hospital in England viewed themselves as socially dominant, and the perception of social dominance was highly correlated with responding aggressively to interpersonal provocation.

Costs of the Psychopathic Life Strategy

The psychopathic life history strategy also incurs costs. In general, one requirement of negative frequency dependent selection is that the frequency of an allele (or a phenotype) stay at or near its optimal level. Considering psychopathy, the strategy of cheating and exploiting others only works as long as most of the others are cooperators. That is, if most members of the population are cooperators, then they will expect to interact with cooperators as well, and thus can be exploited by the pyschopath. If psychopaths, or cheaters, become more common, then cooperators will start to evolve strategies to detect or prevent cheating, and will not interact so trustingly with others. This removes the niche that provided the initial advantage to psychopaths.

More particularly, in the language of game theory, the psychopath risks encountering other defectors. If both players defect, neither will acquire any resources, and they may both experience losses. Even if psychopaths consistently encounter cooperators (or the same cooperator), they may develop a reputation that deters others from interacting with them. Psychopaths may therefore also risk being shunned or exiled—a serious consequence in the evolutionary context, when the social bonds between fellow hunters and gatherers may have been all that stood between any given individual and starvation. Even if psychopaths remain in the community, they risk conflicts with others: with other males who may be fighting for a particular mate or resource, with other males whom they have cuckolded, or with the family members of short-term mates they have exploited. Intrasexual mate competition, sexual jealousy, and intrafamilial defense of members' sexual integrity are well documented, both in various animal species and in humans. Additionally, the existence of cheaters (also sometimes called sneakers or satellites) is well documented in other animal species (mammalian, amphibian, piscine, etc.; e.g., see Ellis, 1998).

For reasons such as these, psychopaths often die young. Their impulsive, risk-taking, sensation-seeking behavior can result in serious injury and death, and these risky activities start to peak early in their reproductive career. They therefore run the chance of being injured or killed before having the chance to reproduce. In this way, psychopaths can be considered like somewhat exaggerated young men, who tend to be antisocial, aggressive, highly interested in sex, and boastful and conceited during adolescence (Moffitt, 1993; Wilson & Daly, 1985). In fact, these characteristics are so common to adolescent males that Wilson and Daly dubbed the pattern "young male syndrome." However, psychopaths become like young men earlier and stay in the high mating effort, risk-taking mode longer (or forever). In terms of the coincidental status-striving theory proposed by Ellis (1998), there are also costs involved in competing with conspecific males for resources. As Ellis put it (p. 89), "Traits that have been subjected to natural selection often over-shoot as well as under-shoot the exact optimum in terms of their reproductive advantage." In other words, individuals can become so persistently competitive that they aggravate others around them to the point of inviting retaliation or exile.

Finally, even if psychopaths achieve reproductive maturity and impregnate one or more mates, there is no guarantee that the young will survive without the father's support of the mother. In the evolutionary context, pregnant or lactating women were extremely vulnerable to starvation because of the increased difficulty they would have foraging, and to aggression from other men who might take advantage of this vulnerability. Thus, pregnant women who found themselves without a supportive mate could potentially miscarry, deliberately abort, or have children who failed to thrive and mature.

POLICY IMPLICATIONS

In considering social policy issues concerning psychopathy, it is important to remain cognizant of three basic facts. The first is that crime rates, most convincingly indexed by homicide, have fallen dramatically in Europe and North America from medieval times until after the first third of the 20th century (Gurr, 1989). After a brief and modest increase, North American crime rates have tended to continue their decline over the last decade (Donohue & Levitt, 2001). The second fact is that crime is only one of a number of important social problems (e.g., child maltreatment, gross inequities in wealth, substance abuse, mental illness, etc.) to which crime is related. Third, psychopaths, although the most persistent serious offenders, contribute only a fraction of all criminal offences. Consideration of these three factors suggests that alarmist or draconian pseudo-solutions to the crime problem are not worthy of consideration. Rather, policies should be sought that deal with the broader issues of social justice and social order, as opposed to those focusing solely on crime or on psychopaths. Thus, in addition to trying to change psychopaths' behavior and trying to decrease people's susceptibility to victimization by psychopaths, social and economic measures must be used to ameliorate a number of social problems. Important goals here are the diversion of facultative (or secondary) psychopaths from an antisocial developmental path, and shortening the criminal careers of adolescent-limited offenders.

Social Hygiene and Crime Reduction

A number of societal factors provide a niche that may encourage antisocial behavior from both obligate (or primary) psychopaths and facultative (or secondary) psychopaths. Thus, potential solutions involve social change to try to remove this niche. This is a primary prevention strategy—that is, the purpose is to prevent individuals from developing the condition in question, antisociality. Removal of the niche that supports antisocial behavior may reduce its occurrence.

Gross disparities in wealth are related to crime. It is often those who not only do not possess the resources, but who also have little hope of procuring any in the immediate future, who engage in antisocial behavior. This behavior is often an attempt to procure resources by cheating the system. Obvious examples are theft and robbery to gain material resources, or sexually aggressive or assaultive behavior to create reproductive opportunities. If resources were allocated more equitably, this could result in a significant decrease in antisocial behavior, via two mechanisms. First, the secondary psychopaths might be prevented from following an antisocial developmental trajectory if the niche that encouraged cheating were removed.

Second, the primary psychopaths' genotypes may be subject to gene-environment interactions that might change the sexual behavior of persistently antisocial individuals, decreasing their mating effort. The disparity in wealth can also be decreased by increasing public access to educational opportunities, which would distribute employment potential more equitably. If postsecondary educational and vocational training were more equally available across all social classes, this could provide the means of obtaining the resources necessary for maintaining independence and supporting families to those who are least likely to be successful in competitive situations.

Secondary prevention methods, which target individuals at risk for developing a condition and provide interventions to interrupt the condition or shorten its duration, can also be used. Teenage parenthood is an important risk factor for future antisocial behavior of the offspring. Thus, one obvious prevention measure would be to increase public access to contraception, family planning, and abortion. This would be especially salient for the youngest teen parents, who may be differentially giving birth to fledgling psychopaths. In nations in which information regarding contraception is readily available (e.g., the Scandinavian countries), there are much lower frequencies of unplanned teen pregnancies and births. These nations also have lower rates of both general and property crimes. The opposite is true in nations, such as the United States, in which birth control information is not universally accessible. A decrease in the proportion of juvenile and repeat offenders in a given youth cohort could be achieved by providing easy access to contraceptive information and measures. In fact, some researchers have argued that one of the main factors responsible for the decreases in the American crime rate since 1991 was the 1978 judicial decision that increased the availability of abortion to economically disadvantaged mothers (Donohue & Levitt, 2001). In addition, public access to health care, especially for young mothers and children, could reduce persistent antisociality caused by neurodevelopmental insults incurred during fetal or postnatal development. Many of these insults are avoidable through preventive health care (e.g., proper nutrition for pregnant women and for developing children, prompt and adequate treatment for such acute events as infections, fevers, or head injuries). Poor people disproportionately lack access to adequate medical attention in many nations.

A crucial focus for social programs, highlighted in Caspi et al.'s (2002) research, is child maltreatment. Although most mistreated children do not become antisocial, a very significant proportion of persistently antisocial individuals have abuse and neglect in their backgrounds. And as Caspi et al. showed, if abused children also have a particular genotype, the combination of factors dramatically increases the chance of violence and criminality in adulthood. Some methods of decreasing the rate of child maltreatment include prevention programs that selectively target at-risk families, parenting training offered as part of standard prenatal care, and better funding for social services agencies that must intervene when abuse is discovered. Again, although abuse and neglect cross all social classes, the poor are at higher risk because of their lack of resources. For example, parents may have insufficient funds to provide appropriate day care, or insufficient time to provide stimulating environments and interactions for the children if they must work low-paying jobs, or they may lack funds to enroll in parenting classes if these are not provided freely. It might even be beneficial to provide parenting classes early in secondary school, especially given that those individuals who have the greatest risk of becoming young parents are also at increased risk of dropping out of school before finishing grade 12. If such classes were provided early enough that most adolescents were still in school, then at least a segment of potential parents who are traditionally likely to provide negative and inadequate parenting might learn better coping and child management strategies.

Yoshikawa (1994) reviewed a large number of studies that aimed to reduce or prevent delinquency via early interventions. This review showed that interventions targeting such risk factors as family socioeconomic status, parenting skills, child–parent attachment, child welfare and maltreatment, child cognitive ability, school adjustment, and early child emotional competence could all effect decreases in later juvenile offending. In addition, Tremblay and Craig (1995) described a number of studies in which paraprofessionals carried out home visits and taught at-risk families skills to maximize their children's nutrition, health, development, and safety. These programs reduced important predictors of early delinquency, such as impulsivity and attention problems, cognitive problem-solving deficits, low school achievement, and early disruptive behavior. Of note is the fact that these interventions began in the infancy or preschool years. The authors concluded that the interventions most likely to reduce juvenile antisocial behavior are multimodal in nature, last for relatively long periods, and begin early in the child's life.

Tertiary prevention strategies focus mainly on rehabilitation and restoration of proper function, and on minimizing the negative effects of the condition. One tertiary prevention strategy worthy of consideration is the use of alternatives to incarceration for young offenders. Because many adolescents who engage in antisocial behavior are likely to desist from criminal behavior as they grow older, it is important to avoid overcriminalizing this somewhat normative behavior and foreclosing education and employment opportunities. Restitution programs have shown some success with young offenders, and can serve to emphasize personal and social responsibility (see Loeber & Farrington, 1998). These programs have the added benefit of providing some reparation for the victim, although this is more realistic for property than for violent offences. It would be useful to evaluate such alternate strategies for persistent, but nonpsychopathic, adult offenders. However, diversion strategies require that it be possible to accurately identify those offenders who are likely not dangerous, to ensure the safety of society by preventing more dangerous offenders from being allowed into the community while they still pose a high risk of reoffending. Actuarial measures, such as the Violence Risk Appraisal Guide (VRAG; Quinsey et al., 1998) provide a direct means of estimating the long-term risk of future violent and sexual offending, and can aid in dispositional decisions about male offenders. Treatment and supervisory resources (including incarceration) are most effectively used when directed toward the highest risk offenders (Andrews et al., 1990).

When all other prevention and intervention strategies are exhausted with serious offenders, incapacitation is the only available strategy to prevent further harm to society. It is useful to build a procedure for considering individuals' actuarial risk assessments into the sentencing part of the judicial process, so that the length of a sentence can be based on individuals' likelihood of recidivating as well as on the nature of the offences. Some procedures like this have already been established. For example, in Canada, when a violent offender is being sentenced and is considered to be at high risk for committing further violent and/or sexual offences, the Crown can instigate Dangerous Offender proceedings. Once an offender is declared a Dangerous Offender, the court has the option to give an indefinite sentence. Psychopaths are differentially likely to be among the most dangerous offenders.

Psychopaths

The available evidence on psychopathy supports the possibility of a genetic basis for a life history strategy involving high mating effort, social defection, high risk acceptance, and aggression. However, genes are not necessarily destiny. Nevertheless, prevention and intervention strategies, however well implemented, are unlikely to eliminate psychopathy. This section discusses additional programs and policies that seem necessary to deal with psychopaths. There are two ways to reduce the impact of psychopaths on society: change their behavior or change society's susceptibility to their behavior. Given that psychopaths generally do not feel subjective distress regarding their own behavior, it would seem prudent to implement the latter change, even while attempting to bring about the former.

Although psychopaths, like everyone else, appear to decide their future actions based on cost–benefit analyses, their analyses are relatively little affected by a consideration of how their actions might affect others' interests (Mealey, 1995). Given that psychopaths are adept at cheating and deception, the likelihood is that in the past they were often able to exploit and manipulate others without any major or immediate consequences. This, Mealey suggested, is one area in which the overall incidence of antisocial behavior should be decreased. According to Mealey, "A society must establish and enforce a reputation for high rates of detection of deception and identification of cheaters, and a willingness to retaliate. In other words, it must establish a successful strategy of deterrence" (p. 537). This strategy, then, requires better detection and deterrence methods.

A number of factors have been identified that influence the ability to detect cheaters. The factors that make cheaters more difficult to identify include urbanization of communities, increases in population, looser social ties within communities, lower participation in social organizations, ease of travel and relocation, more competitive societies, and increased reliance on electronic communication methods (see Mealey, 1995, for a more complete list). In other words, any factor that increases the potential for anonymity and decreases the chance that psychopaths' reputations will precede them will give them freer reign to manipulate and exploit the system for their own ends. To counteract the many features of 21st-century life that do facilitate antisocial behavior, stronger communities, and better communication between different communities, are necessary. Although many politicians and pundits have talked about increasing globalization, its community aspects lag far behind its economic aspects. Some social commentators have discussed the increasing need for an international code of law, and better cooperation between nations in detecting and punishing criminals. In the wake of recent foreign terrorist attacks in several nations, some efforts in this vein have begun. For example, nations are negotiating agreements to share information between their respective criminal investigation agencies, to identify potential criminals and terrorists who cross national boundaries. Face, fingerprint, and retinal recognition software is becoming more common at airports, border crossings, and security-sensitive locations. If efforts to track and monitor potentially psychopathic cheaters or criminals across jurisdictions are continued, and are widely publicized, then this may deter those individuals who commit antisocial acts not for ideological purposes, but solely for personal gain. In addition, if more power were accorded to national and international watchdog agencies (e.g., securities violations auditors, U.N. weapons inspectors, international war crimes tribunals) to compel cooperation and access, and to impose sanctions on violators, then this might serve a deterrent function for those who seek personal gain and fame on a national or international stage. However, some of these strategies may be difficult to implement, for reasons of liability, civil rights, and sheer logistics. Thus, it is also important to focus on harm avoidance techniques that individuals can use in their own lives to minimize the potential for exposure to, and damage from, psychopaths.

Research on learning and psychopathy suggests that psychopaths do not learn from the same tasks or in the same way as do nonpsychopaths. On the other hand, when the contingencies are salient and relevant to them, they show no learning deficits (Patterson & Newman, 1993). They seem primed to learn best from reward-based positive reinforcement tasks or paradigms, rather than from negative reinforcement or punishment. That is, psychopaths may be more motivated to work for reward and less likely to stop and reflect (i.e., learn) after punishment when they are already focused on reward. This inability to switch from an approach response to an avoid response makes them less likely to learn from real-life situations in which consequences are mixed—their attention to short-term gains prevents them from avoiding the long-term costs (Patterson & Newman, 1993). Given that differential learning is evident very early between children with and without such psychopathy precursors as conduct disorder or hyperactivity-impulsivity problems, it is clearly advisable to start young. A stringent program of incentives and positive reinforcement could help parents or teachers teach fledgling psychopaths to pay more attention to contingencies and to delay gratification (Lynam, 1996).

A significant body of research suggests that psychopaths may suffer from an overall hypoarousal of the nervous system (Mealey, 1995; Patterson & Newman, 1993). That is, their baseline level of stimulation is aversively low, and their behavior may, in part, reflect their attempts to change this by seeking novel and exciting stimuli. Sensation-seeking has been consistently linked with the use of alcohol and drugs, interpersonally antisocial behavior, and criminal activity. If psychopaths behave this way to avoid boredom and underarousal, then one intervention may be to direct them into more interesting, exciting, or stimulating fields of work, such as acting, fire-fighting, racing, and so forth (Mealey & Kinner, 2003).

Tertiary programs that are successful for nonpsychopathic offenders are often less successful or have detrimental effects for psychopaths. For example, Ogloff, Wong, and Greenwood (1990), Rice, Harris, and Cormier (1992), and Seto and Barbaree (1999) all found that insight-oriented, talk-therapy programs that were effective in reducing recidivism rates in nonpsychopathic offenders actually *increased* recidivism rates among psychopathic offenders. This differential response to treatment means evaluation studies need to be conducted that assess psychopaths and nonpsychopaths separately.

ACKNOWLEDGMENTS

The first author was supported by a fellowship from the Social Sciences and Humanities Research Council and the second by a Senior Research Fellowship from the Ontario Ministry of Health. The authors would like to thank Martin Lalumière and an anonymous reviewer for comments on an earlier draft of this chapter.

REFERENCES

American Psychiatric Association. (1994). *Diagnostic and statistical manual of mental disorders* (4th ed.). Washington, DC: Author.

Andrews, D. A., Zinger, I., Hoge, R. D., Bonta, J., Gendreau, P., & Cullen, F. T. (1990). Does correctional treatment work? A clinically relevant and psychologically informed meta-analysis. *Criminology, 28*, 369–404.

Berman, M. E., Kavoussi, R. J., & Coccaro, E. F. (1997). Neurotransmitter correlates of human aggression. In D. M. Stoff, J. Breiling, & J. D. Maser (Eds.), *Handbook of antisocial behavior* (pp. 305–313). New York: Wiley.

Bingham, C. R., & Crockett, L. J. (1996). Longitudinal adjustment patterns of boys and girls experiencing early, middle, and late sexual intercourse. *Developmental Psychology, 32*, 647–658.

Brennan, P. A., & Mednick, S. A. (1997). Medical histories of antisocial individuals. In D. M. Stoff, J. Breiling, & J. D. Maser (Eds.), *Handbook of antisocial behavior* (pp. 269–279). New York: Wiley.

Burg, C., Rapoport, J. L., Bartley, L. S., Quinn, P. O., & Timmins, P. (1980). Newborn minor physical anomalies and problem behavior at age 3. *American Journal of Psychiatry, 137*, 791–796.

Buss, D. M., & Schmitt, D. M. (1993). Sexual strategies theory: An evolutionary perspective on human mating. *Psychological Review, 100*, 204–232.

Capaldi, D. M., Crosby, L., & Stoolmiller, M. (1996). Predicting the timing of first sexual intercourse for adolescent males. *Child Development, 64*, 344–359.

Carey, G., & Goldman, D. (1997). The genetics of antisocial behavior. In D. M. Stoff, J. Breiling, & J. D. Maser (Eds.), *Handbook of antisocial behavior* (pp. 243–254). New York: Wiley.

Caspi, A., McClay, J., Moffitt, T. E., Mill, J., Martin, J., Craig, I. W., Taylor, A., & Poulton, R. (2002). Role of genotype in the cycles of violence in maltreated children. *Science, 297*, 851–853, (Suppl.), 1–6.

Christie, R., & Geis, F. L. (1970). *Studies in Machiavellianism*. New York: Academic Press.

Cleckley, H. (1976). *The mask of sanity* (5th ed.). St. Louis, MO: Mosby.

Coccaro, E. F., Kavoussi, R. J., & McNamee, B. (2000). Central neurotransmitter function in criminal aggression. In D. H. Fishbein (Ed.), *The science, treatment, and prevention of antisocial behaviors* (pp. 6-1–6-16). Kingston, NJ: Civic Research Institute.

Donohue, J. J., III, & Levitt, S. D. (2001). The impact of legalized abortion on crime. *Quarterly Journal of Economics, 116*, 379–420.

Ellis, L. (1998). Neodarwinian theories of violent criminality and antisocial behavior: Photographic evidence from nonhuman animals and a review of the literature. *Aggression and Violent Behavior, 3*(1), 61–110.

Ellis, L., & Walsh, A. (1997). Gene-based evolutionary theories in criminology. *Criminology, 35*, 229–276.

Fagot, B. I., Pears, K. C., Capaldi, D. M., Crosby, L., & Leve, C. S. (1998). Becoming an adolescent father: Precursors and parenting. *Developmental Psychology, 34*, 1209–1219.

Firestone, P., & Peters, S. (1983). Minor physical anomalies and behavior in children: A review. *Journal of Autism and Developmental Disorders, 13*, 411–425.

Fishbein, D. H. (Ed.). (2000). *The science, treatment, and prevention of antisocial behaviors*. Kingston, NJ: Civic Research Institute.

Fogel, C. A., Mednick, S. A., & Michelsen, N. (1985). Hyperactive behavior and minor physical anomalies. *Acta Psychiatrica Scandinavica, 72*, 551–556.

Frank, R. H. (1988). *Passions within reason: The strategic role of the emotions*. New York: Norton.

Giancola, P. R. (2000). Neuropsychological functioning and antisocial behavior—implications for etiology and prevention. In D. H. Fishbein (Ed.), *The science, treatment, and prevention of antisocial behaviors* (pp. 11-1–11-16). Kingston, NJ: Civic Research Institute.

Goldman, D., & Fishbein, D. H. (2000). Genetic bases for impulsive and antisocial behaviors—can their course be altered? In D. H. Fishbein (Ed.), *The science, treatment, and prevention of antisocial behaviors* (pp. 9-1–9-18). Kingston, NJ: Civic Research Institute.

Gray, J. A. (1987). *The psychology of fear and stress* (2nd ed.). New York: Cambridge University Press.

Gurr, T. D. (1989). Historical trends in violent crime: Europe and the United States. In T. D. Gurr (Ed.), *Violence in America: Vol. 1. The history of crime* (pp. 21–54). London: Sage.

Halverson, C. F., Jr., & Victor, J. B. (1976). Minor physical anomalies and problem behavior in elementary school children. *Child Development, 47*, 281–285.

Hardy, J. B., Astone, N. M., Brooks-Gunn, J., Shapiro, S., & Miller, T. L. (1998). Like mother, like child: Intergenerational patterns of age at first birth and associations with childhood and adolescent characteristics and adult outcomes in the second generation. *Developmental Psychology, 34*, 1220–1232.

Hare, R. D. (1991). *The Hare Psychopathy Checklist–Revised*. Toronto, Ontario: Multi-Health Systems.

Hare, R. D. (1996). Psychopathy: A clinical construct whose time has come. *Criminal Justice and Behavior, 23*(1), 25–54.

Hare, R. D., Harpur, T. J., Hakstian, A. R., Forth, A. E., Hart, S. D., & Newman, J. P. (1990). The revised psychopathy checklist: Reliability and factor structure. *Psychological Assessment: A Journal of Consulting and Clinical Psychology, 2*, 338–341.

Henry, B., & Moffit, T. E. (1997). Neuropsychological and neuroimaging studies of juvenile delinquency and adult criminal behavior. In *Handbook of antisocial behavior* (pp. 280–288). New York: Wiley.

Jessor, R., Costa, F., Jessor, L., & Donovan, J. E. (1983). Time of first intercourse: A prospective study. *Journal of Personality and Social Psychology, 44*, 608–626.

Kandel, E., Brennan, P. A., Mednick, S. A., & Michelson, N. M. (1989). Minor physical anomalies and recidivistic adult violent criminal behavior. *Acta Psychiatrica Scandinavica, 79*, 103–107.

Kinner, S. (2003). Psychopathy as an adaptation: Implications for society and social policy. In R. Bloom (Ed.), *Evolutionary psychology and violence: A primer for policy makers and public policy advocates* (pp. 57–82). Westport, CT: Praeger.

Lalumière, M. L., Harris, G. T., & Rice, M. E. (2001). Psychopathy and developmental instability. *Evolution and Human Behavior, 22*, 75–92.

Lanctôt, N., & Smith, C. A. (2001). Sexual activity, pregnancy, and deviance in a representative urban sample of African American girls. *Journal of Youth & Adolescence, 30*, 349–372.

Lavan, H., & Johnson, J. G. (2002). The association between Axis I and II psychiatric symptoms and high-risk sexual behavior during adolescence. *Journal of Personality Disorders, 16*, 73–94.

Loeber, R., & Farrington, D. P. (1998). *Serious and violent offenders: Risk Factors and successful interventions.* Thousand Oaks, CA: Sage.

Lynam, D. R. (1996). Early identification of chronic offenders: Who is the fledgling psychopath? *Psychological Bulletin, 120*, 209–234.

Martin, N. G., Eaves, L. J., & Eysenck, H. J. (1977). Genetical, environmental and personality factors influencing the age of first intercourse in twins. *Journal of Biosocial Science, 9*, 91–97.

Mason, D. A., & Frick, P. J. (1994). The heritability of antisocial behavior: A meta-analysis of twin and adoption studies. *Journal of Psychopathology and Behavioral Assessment, 16*, 301–323.

Mealey, L. (1995). The sociobiology of sociopathy: An integrated evolutionary model. *Behavioral and Brain Sciences, 18*, 523–599.

Mealey, L., & Kinner, S. (2003). Psychopathy, machiavellianism, and theory of mind. In M. Brune, H. Ribbert, & W. Schiefenhovel (Eds.), *The social brain: Evolution and pathology* (pp. 355–372). New York: Wiley.

Moffitt, T. E. (1993). Adolescence-limited and life-course-persistent antisocial behavior: A developmental taxonomy. *Psychological Review, 100*, 674–701.

Morrison, D., & Gilbert, P. (2001). Social rank, shame and anger in primary and secondary psychopaths. *Journal of Forensic Psychiatry, 12*, 330–356.

Newman, J. P., & Wallace, J. F. (1993). Diverse pathways to deficient self-regulation: Implications for disinhibitory Psychopathology in children. *Clinical Psychology Review, 13*, 699–720.

Patterson, C. M., & Newman, J. P. (1993). Reflectivity and learning from aversive events: Toward a psychological mechanism for the syndromes of disinhibition. *Psychological Review, 100*, 716–736.

O'Donnell, J. P., & Van Tuinan, M. (1979). Behavior problems of preschool children: Dimensions and congenital correlates. *Journal of Abnormal Child Psychology, 7*, 61–75.

Ogloff, J. D., Wong, S., & Greenwood, A. (1990). Treating criminal psychopaths in a therapeutic community program. *Behavioral Sciences and the Law, 8*, 81–90.

Patterson, C. M., & Newman, J. P. (1993). Reflectivity in syndromes of disinhibition. *Psychological Review, 100*, 716–736.

Quinsey, V. L., Book, A. S., & Lalumière, M. L. (2001). A factor analysis of traits related to individual differences in antisocial behavior. *Criminal Justice and Behavior, 28*, 522–536.

Quinsey, V. L., Harris, G. T., Rice, M. E., & Cormier, C. A. (1998). *Violent offenders: Appraising and managing risk.* Washington, DC: American Psychological Association.

Quinsey, V. L., & Lalumière, M. L. (1995). Evolutionary perspectives on sexual offending. *Sexual Abuse: A Journal of Research and Treatment, 7,* 301–315.

Raine, A. (1997). Antisocial behavior and psychophysiology: A biosocial perspective and a prefrontal dysfunction hypothesis. *Handbook of antisocial behavior* (pp. 289–304). New York: Wiley.

Rice, M. E., Harris, G. T., & Cormier, C. (1992). Evaluation of a maximum security therapeutic community for psychopaths and other mentally disordered offenders. *Law and Human Behavior, 16,* 399–412.

Rowe, D. C., Rodgers, J. L., Meseck-Bushey, S., & St. John, C. (1989). Sexual behavior and nonsexual deviance: A sibling study of their relationship. *Developmental Psychology, 25,* 61–69.

Rowe, D. C., Vazsonyi, A. T., & Figueredo, A. J. (1997). Mating-effort in adolescence: A conditional or alterative strategy. *Personality and Individual Differences, 23,* 105–115.

Scaramella, L. V., Conger, R. D., Simons, R. L., & Whitbeck, L. B. (1998). Predicting risk for pregnancy by late adolescence: A social contextual perspective. *Developmental Psychology, 34,* 1233–1245.

Serbin, L. A., Cooperman, J. M., Peters, P. L., Lehoux, P. M., Stack, D. M., & Schwartzman, A. E. (1998). Intergenerational transfer of psychosocial risk in women with childhood histories of aggression, withdrawal, or aggression and withdrawal. *Developmental Psychology, 34,* 1246–1262.

Seto, M. C., & Barbaree, H. E. (1999). Psychopathy, treatment behavior, and sex offender recidivism. *Journal of Interpersonal Violence, 14,* 1235–1248.

Seto, M. C., Khattar, N. A., Lalumière, M. L., & Quinsey, V. L. (1997). Deception and sexual strategy in psychopathy. *Personality and Individual Differences, 22,* 301–307.

Skilling, T. A., Harris, G. T., Rice, M. E., & Quinsey, V. L. (2002). Identifying persistently antisocial offenders using the Hare Psychopathy Checklist and DSM antisocial personality disorder criteria. *Psychological Assessment, 14,* 27–38.

Skilling, T. A., Quinsey, V. L., & Craig, W. M. (2001). Evidence of a taxon underlying serious antisocial behavior in boys. *Criminal Justice & Behavior, 28,* 450–470.

Stouthamer-Loeber, M., & Wei, E. H. (1998). The precursors of young fatherhood and its effect on delinquency of teenage males. *Journal of Adolescent Health, 22,* 56–65.

Tremblay, R. E., & Craig, W. M. (1995). Developmental prevention of crime. In C. Tonry & D. P. Farrington (Eds.), *Building a safer society: Strategic approaches to crime prevention* (Vol. 19, pp. 151–236). Chicago: University of Chicago Press.

Wakefield, J. C. (1992a). The concept of mental disorder: On the boundary between biological facts and social values. *American Psychologist, 47,* 373–388.

Wakefield, J. C. (1992b). Disorder as harmful dysfunction: A conceptual critique of DSM-III-R's definition of mental disorder. *Psychological Review, 99,* 232–247.

Walker, N. (1973). *Crime and insanity in England.* Edinburgh, Scotland: University of Edinburgh.

Wilson, M., & Daly, M. (1985). Competitiveness, risk taking, and violence: The young male syndrome. *Ethology and Sociobiology, 6,* 59–73.

Yoshikawa, H. (1994). Prevention as cumulative protection: Effects of early family support and education on chronic delinquency and its risks. *Psychological Bulletin, 115,* 28–54.

Cultivating Morality and Constructing Moral Systems: How to Make Silk Purses From Sows' Ears

ॐ

Dennis L. Krebs
Simon Fraser University

Most people would agree that the key to fostering harmonious social relations, enhancing the quality of our lives and ensuring the continuing existence of humanity lies in the cultivation of morality. Most people also would agree on the four main steps we need to take to cultivate morality. First, we need to define the behaviors we consider moral, which entails specifying the types of behavior we will target. Second, we need to determine what we have to work with, which entails identifying the mental mechanisms that give rise to moral and immoral behaviors, mapping their design, and determining what activates and inhibits them. Third, we need to determine how children acquire morality-producing mechanisms, how the mechanisms develop, and why different people end up with different mechanisms or with mechanisms designed in different ways. Finally, based on this knowledge, we need to design interventions that are equipped to maximize the acquisition and activation of mechanisms that give rise to moral behaviors and minimize the acquisition and activation of mechanisms that give rise to immoral behaviors.

Faced with the task of cultivating morality, few people would expect much help from evolutionary psychology. In this chapter, I will argue that, contrary to such expectations, an evolutionary analysis of how moral dispositions evolved in the human species can help us understand the nature of morality, the ways in which moral mechanisms are designed, and how such mechanisms can be activated most optimally. Metaphorically, an evolutionary analysis of morality can teach us how to make silk purses from sows' ears.

SILK PURSES: DEFINING MORALITY

Someone once wrote that morality is a concept that everyone possesses but no one understands. Viewing morality from an evolutionary perspective helps clarify what morality is by inducing us to ask what it was for—that is, to say how the mechanisms that give rise to it evolved in the human species. To answer this question, imagine several hominid groups in ancestral environments. What social strategies would most effectively have helped members of such groups survive, reproduce, and propagate their genes? Clearly, in hostile environments, banding together and cooperating for the purposes of hunting, building shelters, and protecting themselves against predators and antagonistic groups of hominids could have had greater adaptive potential than more individualistic strategies. Members of groups who worked together cooperatively could have reaped significantly more fitness-enhancing benefits than individuals could have by working alone or by competing against the others. So, it might seem, cooperative strategies should have evolved in the human species without impediment.

This is not so. Assume that you are a member of a group in which all members except one inherit mental mechanisms that induce them to contribute their share to cooperative endeavors and to take their share of the spoils. The deviant member inherits a mutant strategy that inclines him to take more than his share of fitness-enhancing benefits and suffer less than his share of fitness-reducing costs. As a result, he produces more offspring than the more cooperative members of his group, half of whom, on average, inherit his selfish strategy. His selfish offspring produce more offspring than their cooperative peers, inducing an exponential increase in the proportion of selfish members in the group until, eventually, there are no cooperative members left.

This evolutionary scenario is not only sad, it is self-defeating. As the number of cooperative members diminishes, so also do the resources produced through cooperation. For example, if no one is willing to make the sacrifices necessary to kill large game, to build group shelters, or to protect the group against predators, then everyone suffers. Inasmuch as interactions between selfish individuals pay off more poorly than interactions between cooperative individuals, the benefits of selfishness decrease in proportion to the increase in the number of selfish members of the group.

Reaping the benefits of cooperation was one of the most important adaptive problems faced by hominid ancestors (Krebs, 1998, 2000a, 2000b, 2000c). This problem is intrinsically moral in nature. As Rawls (1971) put it,

> Although a society is a cooperative venture for mutual advantage, it is typically marked by a conflict as well as by an identity of interests. There is an identity of interests since social cooperation makes possible a better life for all than any would have if each were to live solely by his own efforts. There is a conflict of interests since persons are not indifferent as to how the greater benefits of their collaboration are distributed, for in order to pursue their ends, each prefers a larger to a lesser share. (p. 4)

A sense of morality evolved in the human species to solve this adaptive problem. The biological function of morality is to enable individuals to maximize their benefits from interactions with others by upholding fitness-enhancing systems of cooperation. Viewing morality in these terms helps us understand its nature. Morality boils down to individuals giving their share (doing their duties) and taking their share (exercising their rights), treating others fairly as they would like to be treated, and resisting the temptation to maximize their gains at the expense of others. To accomplish this, members of groups form social contracts. This conception of morality has been espoused in nonbiological terms by many scholars. To quote Rest (1983), morality consists in "standards or guidelines that govern human cooperation—in particular how rights, duties, and benefits are [to be] allocated" (p. 558). Morality involves "the equilibrium of individuals in society ... each reciprocating with other individuals according to rules that balance the benefits and burdens of cooperation" (Rest, 1983, pp. 572–573).

Kohlberg (1984) and other developmental psychologists found that children's conceptions of morality change in stage-like ways as they develop. In terms of the evolutionary model I outlined, such conceptions uphold increasingly broad and complex systems of cooperation. Stage 1 moral judgments uphold hierarchical systems of cooperation by prescribing deference to authorities. Stage 2 moral judgments uphold egalitarian systems of concrete reciprocity. Stage 3 moral judgments uphold systems of cooperation based in relatively long-term mutually beneficial affectionate relations between spouses, family members, friends, and ingroup members. Stage 4 moral judgments uphold systems of indirect reciprocity necessary to maintain social systems in complex societies. Finally, Stage 5 moral judgments uphold ideal systems of cooperation that maximize benefits for all: the greatest good for the greatest number. Kohlberg (1984) assumed that higher stage, later developing conceptions of morality are better—more moral—than earlier developing, lower stage, conceptions.

I have argued that the sophisticated systems of cooperation upheld by high stage moral judgments have the greatest potential to maximize net benefits for the individuals upholding them (Krebs, 2000a). In general, the more complex a system of cooperation, the greater the potential gains in trade. An important implication of this argument is that there is no necessary inconsistency between maximizing biological benefits and behaving morally. However, there is a catch: In general, the more complex a system of cooperation, the more susceptible it is to exploitation by cheaters.

To summarize, I believe that viewing morality from an evolutionary perspective helps clarify what it is by orienting us to the functions it was designed to perform. Conceptions of morality—silk purses—are ideas about how individuals can most optimally foster their interests in mutually beneficial cooperative exchanges with other individuals. I turn now to a consideration of what natural selection gave us to work with—the sows' ears.

SOWS' EARS: DETERMINING WHAT THERE IS TO WORK WITH

The main reason why some people assume that evolutionary theory has little to contribute to an understanding of morality is because they believe that moral qualities cannot evolve. They assume that all naturally selected dispositions are, by definition, selfish and immoral. As revealed in the following quotes, such "born bad" conceptions have been promulgated by eminent evolutionary theorists.

> Nothing resembling the Golden Rule or other widely preached ethical principles seems to be operating in living nature. It could scarcely be otherwise, when evolution is guided by a force that maximizes genetic selfishness. (Williams, 1989, p. 195)

> Be warned that if you wish, as I do, to build a society in which individuals cooperate generously and unselfishly toward a common good, you can expect little help from biological nature. Let us try to teach generosity and altruism, because we are born selfish. (Dawkins, 1989, p. 3)

I believe these theorists are wrong for at least three reasons. First, genetically selfish dispositions and other maladaptations can evolve (Crespi, 2000). Second, dispositions that were genetically selfish in ancestral environments need not necessarily be genetically selfish in current environments (see Crawford, chap. 1 in this vol.). And third, as explained by Janicki (chap. 3 in this vol.) and others (e.g., Alexander, 1987; de Waal & Flack, 2000; Sober & Wilson, 1998), genetically selfish dispositions are not necessarily individually selfish or immoral. It is possible for individuals to propagate their genes (i.e., to behave in genetically selfish ways) by caring for, cooperating with, and helping others (i.e., by behaving in individually unselfish and moral ways). The question is, what kinds of strategy— individually selfish strategies or individually unselfish strategies—were most adaptive in ancestral environments? Were individuals who behaved selfishly more likely than individuals who behaved unselfishly to survive, to reproduce, and to propagate their genes?

I believe the answer to this question is: What you see is what we got. If you observe people, you will see them behaving in both selfish and unselfish ways. Such behaviors stem from dispositions that have evolved in the human species; they are activated in contexts in which they paid off in ancestral environments.

With respect to unselfish dispositions, I believe at least four types (deferential, cooperative, caring, and docile)[1] are equipped to give rise to moral behaviors. These dispositions are the sows' ears, or the raw material with which those who seek to cultivate morality have to work. It is important to understand how these dispositions are designed, how they develop, and how they are activated; and this, in large part, entails understanding how they were selected in ancestral environments. In other papers I have offered explanations for the evolution of moral dispositions (Krebs 1998, 2000a, 2000b, 2000c; Krebs & Janicki, 2003). I will briefly summarize these explanations, then address their implications for public policy and personal decisions.

THE NATURAL SELECTION
OF DECISION-MAKING MECHANISMS

It is helpful to frame questions about the evolution of moral and immoral dispositions in the following way. Assume that our hominid ancestors inherited decision-making mechanisms designed to solve the adaptive problems they faced. Buss (1999, p. 49) characterized such mechanisms as sets "of procedures within the organism that [are] designed to take in a particular slice of information and transform that information via decision rules into output that historically has helped with the solution to an adaptive problem." Buss (1999) suggested that evolved mechanisms are activated by information relevant to the specific adaptive problems they were designed to solve and the decision rules they contain operate on "if–then" contingencies.

Assume further that different individuals may inherit mechanisms that contain different kinds of decision rules, or strategies, and such individuals (therefore strategies) compete against each another. By definition, winning strategies increase in frequency, or evolve, and losing strategies decrease in frequency, or go extinct. The question is, which strategies were best equipped to solve the adaptive problems faced by individuals motivated to foster their inclusive fitness through interactions with other members of their group?

Axelrod and Hamilton (1981) modeled such adaptive problems in Prisoners Dilemma games. In the simplest version of such games, players are required to select one of two strategies: either to behave selfishly or to behave cooperatively. If both players make cooperative choices, then each propagates three offspring. If both players make selfish choices, then each propagates one offspring. If one player makes a selfish choice and the other makes a cooperative choice, then the selfish player propagates five offspring and the (now) altruistic player propagates none. It is easy to think of contexts in which modern humans face such choices and to see the moral dilemma inherent in them.

---

[1]Self-regulatory mechanisms also give rise to moral behaviors, but I will not discuss them in this chapter.

THE EVOLUTION OF SELFISHNESS

Clearly, selfishness is the winning strategy in one-move Prisoner's Dilemma games and on every specific move of many-move games. If your opponent makes a cooperative choice, you will propagate two more offspring by adopting a selfish strategy than by adopting a cooperative strategy. If your opponent makes a selfish choice, you will propagate one more offspring by adopting a selfish strategy than by adopting a cooperative strategy. On these contingencies, selfish strategies become more frequent, or evolve, and cooperative strategies go extinct. It is on this logic that the eminent evolutionary theorists I cited earlier concluded that moral dispositions cannot evolve.

Let us conclude without further ado that selfish dispositions have evolved in all species. All animals, including humans, behave selfishly in some circumstances. Viewed in evolutionary terms, individuals invoke selfish strategies in the "if" conditions in which they paid off in ancestral environments, which are modeled in one-move Prisoners Dilemma games. However, it does not follow that such strategies are optimal in all conditions. Indeed, as I will explain, there is little question that other, less selfish and more moral, strategies are equipped to reap greater adaptive benefits than selfish strategies in some "if" conditions or contexts, and that such strategies have evolved.

THE EVOLUTION OF DEFERENCE

Players in Axelrod and Hamilton's model of natural selection were of equal power, but in the groups formed by most social species members vary in power. Imagine individuals competing with members of their group for a resource, say some food or a potential mate. The strategy that is most optimal will depend on an individual's relative power. If the person is more powerful than the competitor, the person's best bet might well be to adopt a selfish strategy and take more than a fair share. However, if the person is weaker than the competitor, this strategy could be lethal. In such cases, discretion could well be the better part of valor. Better for individuals to subordinate their interests to those who are more powerful than them and to live to fight another day.

There is a spate of evidence that deferential dispositions have evolved in many species (see Alcock, 1998, for a review). Primates are especially sensitive to indications of social power (Boehm, 2000; Cheney & Seyfarth, 1985). Deferential dispositions are rooted in fear systems, with perhaps a touch of awe. Dominance and submission, especially in males, is regulated by increases and decreases in androgens.

Deference is linked to morality in all traditional psychological models. Piaget (1932) suggested that the fear and awe young children feel for the apparent omnipotence and omniscience of adults plays a pivotal role in determining their moral orientation. Freud (1925) believed that children internalize the superegos of their parents because they fear being punished by them. Learning theorists such as Aronfreed (1968) argued that fear-reduction plays an important role in the process of socialization. Kohlberg (1984) defined his first stage of moral development in terms of "avoidance of punishment and the superior power of authorities" (p. 624).

THE EVOLUTION OF COOPERATION

As implied in Prisoner's Dilemma simulations of evolution, unconditionally cooperative strategies cannot evolve because they are susceptible to exploitation by selfish strategies. However, as revealed in Axelrod and Hamilton's (1981) research, a conditionally cooperative strategy called Tit for Tat can. Tit for Tat is based on the decision rule, "Open with a cooperative move, then copy the move made by your partner." Although Tit for Tat loses to selfish strategies on the first move, it cuts its losses quickly and draws with them on the remaining moves. In a population containing a sufficient number of Tit for Tat strategies, Tit for Tat can defeat selfish strategies in the long run, even though it does not defeat them on any move, by reaping the relatively high payoff benefits of drawing with other Tit for Tat strategies, or cooperating with cooperators. As the proportion of Tit for Tat strategies increases in the population, so also do the payoffs from the strategy. In general, to evolve, a strategy must pay off well against itself.

Following the publication of Axelrod and Hamilton's (1981) findings, investigators changed parameters in Axelrod and Hamilton's game and examined the fecundity of other strategies. In general, the closer the environments approximated the actual conditions of evolution, the greater the benefits of conditionally altruistic strategies. For example, games that allowed for the inevitable errors that occur in social exchanges found that strategies such as "Two Tits for a Tat," "Generous Tit for Tat," "Contrite Tit for Tat," and "Forgiving Tit for Tat" fared better than Tit for Tat because they were equipped to break self-defeating blood feuds precipitated by one selfish mistake (see Krebs, 2000a, and Ridley, 1996, for reviews of relevant research). Simulations that enabled players to observe other players and keep track of their strategies (called "image scoring") favored the evolution of altruism through indirect reciprocity (Nowak & Sigmund, 1998). Allowing players to trade resources of relatively little value to them for resources of greater value to them is even more conducive to the evolution of cooperation (Trivers, 1971). In chapter 3, Janicki reviewed evidence in support of the conclusion that mechanisms that induce people to invest heavily in friends have evolved because of the long-term adaptive benefits of such relationships. A friend in need is a friend indeed.

Dugatkin (1997), Trivers (1971), and others have adduced evidence that mechanisms giving rise to reciprocity have evolved in many species. The exchange of blood in vampire bats (Wilkinson, 1990) is a particularly interesting example. There can be no question that cooperation was instrumental in the evolution of the human species (Tooby & DeVore, 1987). According to Leakey and Lewin (1977),

Throughout our recent evolutionary history, particularly since the rise of a hunting way of life, there must have been extreme selective pressure in favor of our ability to cooperate as a group.... The degree of selective pressure toward cooperation ... was so strong, and the period over which it operated so extended, that it can hardly have failed to have become embedded to some degree in our genetic makeup. (p. 45)

Piaget (1932) adduced data in support of the idea that hierarchical relations between parents and children tend to give rise to a "heteronomous" moral orientation based on "constraint," or deference, whereas egalitarian relations among peers help children acquire a more autonomous moral orientation based on cooperation. Based on observations of boys playing marbles in schoolyards, Piaget concluded that children discover the benefits of cooperation and reciprocity naturally, without intervention from adults. Modern researchers such as Youniss, McLellan, and Strouse (1995) adduced evidence in support of these ideas.

I believe that Piaget's conclusion that children tend to adopt different strategies in relations with adults from those they adapt in relations with peers is correct; however, I believe it is more a matter of degree than a dichotomy. A growing body of evidence suggests that newborn infants inherit mechanisms that induce them to cooperate with their caregivers in mutually beneficial ways: "As 20 years of infancy research have persuasively documented, babies appear to be born into the word with a cognitive system preadapted to mutuality of expectation, to intersubjectivity, and to interaction" (Wozniak, 1993, p. 82). And although relationships among children may, in general, be more egalitarian than relationships between children and adults, children differ in power and form dominance hierarchies (F. F. Strayer & J. Strayer, 1976), as depicted dramatically in *Lord of the Flies*.

THE EVOLUTION OF CARE

Deferential and cooperative dispositions go a long way in accounting for moral behaviors, but according to some scholars, they do not go far enough. Psychologists such as Gilligan (1982) criticized models of moral development for neglecting care-oriented dispositions, which they argued play a more prominent role in the moral orientation of women than of men. Evolutionary perspectives lead us to suspect that the original function of care-oriented mechanisms was to induce parents to nurture their offspring.

In Axelrod and Hamilton's (1981) Prisoner's Dilemma simulations of social evolution, players reproduced asexually and offspring entered new generations as self-sufficient adults (or more exactly as strategies or genes). In contrast, in the real world, most species reproduce sexually and offspring are born dependent or altricial. If parents who inherited mechanisms that induced them to care for their offspring contributed more offspring to future generations than parents who inherited more selfish mechanisms, caring mechanisms would have evolved. Flinn and Low (1986), MacDonald (1997), and J. B. Lancaster and C. S. Lancaster (1987) suggested that mechanisms giving rise to exceptionally high levels of parental investment have evolved in the human species due in large part to the prolonged dependency of human infants.

Infants from many species form attachments to their caregivers. Bowlby (1980) accounted for such attachments in terms of their adaptive value. Developmental psychologists tend to assume that children's attachment to their parents stems from the same psychological system as parents' attachment to infants. However, MacDonald (1997) adduced evidence that the psychological mechanisms that mediate attachment behaviors in infants are regulated primarily by fear and are oriented to safety (i.e., rooted in deferential dispositions), whereas parental investment is regulated primarily by positive feelings of warmth (i.e., rooted in caring dispositions). The biological function of attachment behaviors in infants is to foster their own survival. The biological function of attachment behaviors in parents is to propagate the complement of their genes invested in their offspring. There is a great deal of evidence that the type of attachment children form with their parents exerts a significant effect on their social and moral development (see Thompson, 1998, for a review).

With respect to morality, the problem with dispositions that induce parents to nurture their offspring is that the caring behaviors to which they give rise are restricted to their offspring. However, in one of the most influential insights in evolutionary biology, Hamilton (1964) explained that the principle that accounts for the evolution of parental investment can be extended to explain why members of many species help other relatives as well. What counts in evolution is the propagation of genes. If individuals share genes, then they are able to propagate replicas of their genes by helping others, just as parents propagate replicas of their genes by helping their offspring. Thus, according to Hamilton (1964), behaving altruistically pays off biologically when the fitness costs to altruists are less than the fitness benefits to recipients multiplied by their degree of relatedness, or the probability that they possess replicas of the helper's genes. Recently, Sober and Wilson (1998) explained how the range of recipients who evoke care-oriented behaviors could be expanded even further through group selection.

Research on empathy and altruism is consistent with the conclusion that the care-oriented mechanisms inherited by humans may be activated by a relatively wide range of recipients (see Batson, 1991). Recipients need not necessarily be related to donors, they need only possess the characteristics that constituted cues to kinship in ancestral environments—cues such as similarity, familiarity, and proximity. Further, there is evidence that people identify with ingroups, favor ingroup members, and are disposed to sacrifice their interests for the sake of the group (see Brown, 1986, and Tajfel, 1982, for a review of supporting evidence). The key challenge for those who would foster morality by inducing people to care for others is to find ways to expand the circle of people equipped to activate the mechanisms.

THE EVOLUTION OF DOCILITY

Another limitation of Axelrod and Hamilton's (1981) game theory simulations of evolution was that strategies were fixed at the beginning of the game and could not change. There was no room for learning. Clearly, learning and modeling play an important role in the acquisition of morality. The explanatory power of any model of moralization that neglects these processes will be limited. Viewed in phylogenetic context, human infants are unique in their capacity to learn and human adults are unique in their capacity to teach.

Evolutionary models of morality are often contrasted with social learning models, giving rise to nature versus nurture dichotomies. However, knowledgeable theorists from both schools of thought know better. Consider, for example, the following statement by Bandura (1989, p. 52).

> Genetic factors and neural systems affect behavioral potentialities and place constraints on capabilities. Both experiential and physiological factors interact, often in intricate ways, to determine behavior. Even in behavioral patterns that are formed almost entirely through experience, rudimentary elements are present as part of the natural endowment.... Action patterns regarded as instinctual, because they draw heavily on inborn elements, require appropriate experience to be developed. Sensory systems and brain structures are alterable by environmental influences.... Dichotomous thinking, which separates activities neatly into innate and acquired categories, is seriously inaccurate.

A biological analysis of morality draws attention to the fact that the mental mechanisms that induce humans to teach and the mental mechanisms that enable them to learn are evolved mechanisms. Simon (1990) outlined the adaptive benefits of "docility," which he defined as a disposition that induces individuals to learn what others teach and to believe what others say. In refinements of Axelrod and Hamilton's (1981) game theory simulations, researchers found that strategies such as "Pavlov" that contained the capacity to learn from experience were able to defeat less flexible strategies (see Ridley, 1996). Indeed, even fixed strategies such as Tit for Tat can be defined in terms of principles of learning such as "if a behavior is followed by punishment, change it; if a behavior is followed by reward, repeat it." Modeling enables individuals to avoid the costs of trial and error by copying behaviors that have biologically beneficial consequences.

Although Simon (1990) argued that docile dispositions are designed in ways that induce individuals to behave in altruistic ways that decease their fitness, I believe the logic of evolution and evidence from social learning theory supports the conclusion that humans are selective in the people they model and the behaviors to which they conform. As suggested by Flinn and Alexander (1982), social learning mechanisms are guided by rules such as "imitate those who appear successful," and "accept advice and instruction from those with an interest in [your] success" (p. 394). Similarly, Boyd and Richerson (1985) suggested that social learning mechanisms are affected by "biases," which incline people (a) to copy those who are fit, admired, respected, of high status, wise and so on, (b) to copy behaviors that have the greatest promise of enhancing their fitness, and (c) to copy behaviors that are most frequent in the population. Consistent with these suggestions, researchers have found that the probability of modeling is affected by factors such as the status, nurturance, and power of models, the similarity between observers and models, and whether the behaviors emitted by models are rewarded or punished (Burton & Kunce, 1995, pp. 151–152).

Summary

In a chapter in the *Handbook of Child Psychology* dealing with socialization, Bugental and Goodnow (1998) suggested that "socialization processes may be parsed into different social domains on the basis of biological influences" (p. 408). They argued that the "often observed differences in socialization in different contexts (e.g., attachment-based relationships, compliance-oriented socialization, negotiated relationships between peers, etc.) may have evolved as a function of the distal advantages they served" (p. 409). Although I divide the social domains in a slightly different manner from Bugental and Goodnow (1998) (viewing attachment in children as stemming primarily from the deference system and viewing social identity as an aspect of the care and cooperation systems), our approaches converge. The basic point of agreement is that to understand how children acquire a sense of morality, it is important to recognize that moral dispositions stem from several evolved psychological systems that are designed in different ways and activated in different social contexts.

Individual Differences

Although evolutionary models are concerned mainly with species-specific characteristics, they are attentive to variations in genomes that contribute to individual differences in evolved dispositions. Researchers have found that several aspects of temperament, such as warmth, emotional responsiveness, and fearfulness are highly heritable in both children and adults (MacDonald, 1997; Plomin, DeFries, & McClearn, 1997). Evolutionary theorists do not assume that genotypic differences induce differences in behavior directly. They assume that although it is possible to account for substantial portions of the variance in phenotypic behaviors by attending to genetic differences among individuals, genes interact with a host of other factors to produce their effects. Behavioral geneticists such as Plomin et al. (1997) assumed that inherited differences induce individuals to behave in ways that affect their social environments, which in turn produce differences in social behavior.

MAKING SILK PURSES FROM SOWS' EARS: CULTIVATING MORALITY

Virtually all evolutionary theorists would agree that to foster the development of healthy individuals, the complement of genes they inherit must be nurtured in optimal interuterine environments. A large proportion of social problems are caused by a small number of abnormal individuals, many of whom were doomed from the start because they were assaulted in the womb. As exemplified by fetal alcohol syndrome, teratogenic agents can drastically disrupt social adjustment. Less dramatically, factors such as excess emotionality in mothers, low birthweight, complications during childbirth, and stress in families—all of which are more prevalent in lower socioeconomic strata than in higher socioeconomic strata—are associated with behavior disturbance later in life (Field, Dempsey, & Shuman, 1981; Kopp, 1983).

All children have the right to a healthy prenatal environment, injury-free childbirth, and supportive early environment, and social systems equipped to ensure that all pregnant mothers receive optimal care payoff for everyone in the end. Societies should establish ways of identifying pregnant women and ensuring that they and the infants they bear receive the resources they need. Pregnant women have no more right to abuse the fetuses they carry than mothers have to abuse newborn infants. If necessary, alcoholic or drug addicted mothers who cannot kick their habits should be institutionalized, monitored, and nurtured while they are pregnant for the sake of their children.

Some people think that preserving the sanctity of genes, and perhaps programs of eugenics, are just about the only guidance that evolutionary approaches have to offer those motivated to improve the human condition. This belief is based in the assumption that evolutionary models posit a direct, unalterable relation between genes and behavior (Lickliter & Honeycutt, in press). However, as implied in the model of morality advanced in this chapter, evolutionary approaches do not make such genetically deterministic assumptions (see Krebs, in press, for a review of evidence relevant to this issue). Evolutionary psychologists assume that genes interact with extra-genetic factors to design psychological mechanisms that operate in terms of "if–then" decision rules. The "ifs" in question refer to environmental conditions, which is mainly what those who seek to cultivate morality have to work with.

As explained by Bugental and Goodnow (1998),

> The utility of biological approaches comes from the window they provide on the basic "design" features in the ways we are set up for socialization. They suggest the distinctive regulatory processes that govern socialization within different domains, thus accounting for the limitations consistently found in providing any general-purpose explanations for socialization processes.... An awareness of biological influences on social processes allows us insight into why some socialization processes are more easily implemented than others. (p. 414)

In terms of the present model, socializing agents have four main regulatory processes to work with. The key challenge for those who seek to cultivate morality is to structure environments in ways that constrain the development and activation of selfish mechanisms and foster the development and activation of deferential, caring, cooperative and docile mechanisms. In large part, fostering the development of mechanisms of morality entails expanding and refining the "if" conditions that activate them.

There are two important implications of the evolutionary model I am advancing. I have discussed the first, that the best way to induce people to behave morally is to structure their environments in ways that ensure that behaving morally pays off better than behaving immorally, or more exactly in ways that activate mechanisms that fostered the inclusive fitness of their hominid ancestors. Second, it is misguided to attempt to induce people to behave in ways that are inconsistent with evolved dispositions and strategies. Although it might be appropriate for philosophers to derive ideal moral principles—what people ought to do—with no constraints from what people can do, it is a waste of time for socializing agents to attempt to induce people to behave in accordance with moral principles that are inconsistent with the dispositions they inherit. Better to recognize that people inherit dispositions that fostered their biological interests and structure social systems in ways that induce members to foster their interests in cooperative rather than exploitative ways. Indeed, it could be argued that inducing individuals to sacrifice their interests for the sake of others subverts moral systems by disrupting the balance of justice.

Social Domains

As individuals develop, they participate in an increasingly broad array of groups and social systems. Bronfenbrenner (1995) categorized such groups in terms of four embedded systems. The *microsystem* contains families, schools, peer groups, and neighborhoods. The *mesosysem* contains interactions among aspects of the microsystem. The *exosystem* contains social institutions such as health care, day care, welfare, legal assistance, and the mass media. Finally, at the broadest level, the *macrosystem* contains societal and cultural influences such as urbanization and global economies.

Most interventions aimed at cultivating morality have focused on the microsystem; and within the microsystem, most interventions have focused on parent–child relations (Weissberg & Greenberg, 1998). From an evolutionary perspective, this focus is justifiable. In general, the smaller and simpler the group, the easier it is to ensure that cooperative strategies pay off better than selfish strategies. Families are an especially promising context for the cultivation of morality because members have a vested genetic interest in each other's welfare, family members interact with each other repeatedly, and the strategies family members invoke are relatively easy to track.

It also is relatively easy to cultivate morality in institutions such as day care centers and schools because the groups in question are relatively closed systems in which it is relatively easy to institute systems of cooperative exchange and hold those who cheat on them accountable. Such groups are probably similar to the groups in which cooperative mechanisms evolved. However, as the size of groups increases into societies and nations, the groups diverge from the structure of ancestral groups in which cooperative mechanisms were selected and designed, and therefore from the conditions that activated them. Although the payoffs from cooperative exchanges tend to increase with the size and complexity of a group, so also does the difficulty of reckoning just deserts and ensuring that cheaters do not prosper. I turn now to a consideration of the types of intervention that, from the perspective of the evolutionary analysis advanced in this chapter, seem optimal for the cultivation of morality in families, child-care centers, schools, and societies.

Cultivating Morality in Families

Virtually all socialization theories assume that early interactions between parents and children play the central role in children's acquisition of morality, and this assumption is supported by a spate of research (see Grusec & Lytton, 1988, and Kochanska & Thompson, 1998, for reviews). In most socialization theories, parents are viewed as the instruments of socialization and children are viewed as the objects. The task of parents is to teach their children what it means to be moral and to train them to behave accordingly. In contrast, from the perspective of evolution, families are groups that contain members who are evolved to behave in ways that enhanced the inclusive fitness of their ancestors. Families are like other groups in that they usually contain hierarchical relations between parents and children as well as more egalitarian relations among siblings, and members adopt strategies to foster their interests. But the family is a special group in at least three ways. First, it is everyone's first group. Second, it is most people's most stable group. And third, in general, the biological costs of treating family members selfishly and the biological benefits of treating family members altruistically are greater than they are in other groups because, as explained earlier, helping relatives may foster the helpers' genetic interests.

As explained by Trivers (1972) and others, from the moment of conception, offspring and parents compete with one another for resources and cooperate for mutual gain. Individuals attempt to interact with others in ways that, in effect, activate the psychological mechanisms that benefit them. The outcomes each experiences are a function of the interaction between the strategies each invokes. Neither overly selfish nor overly generous strategies are optimal. The key lies in constructive coordination that produces mutual gains.

Parenting Practices

There is wide agreement among developmental psychologists that the key to the moralization of children lies in parenting practices. The general conclusion reached by research on the effects of parenting styles is that overly authoritarian and overly permissive styles are less conducive to the development of morality than more authoritative styles (see Grusec & Lytton, 1988, and Hoffman, 1999, for reviews). With respect to discipline, power assertion and love withdrawal have been found to be less effective than induction. Modeling has been found to exert a significant influence on prosocial and antisocial behavior (Grusec & Lytton, 1988).

From the perspective of the present analysis, all forms of discipline have their place. Power assertion affects deferential dispositions. Love withdrawal affects caring dispositions and attachment. Induction affects cooperation. Modeling affects the docility system. The challenge for parents is to create the "if" conditions that induce optimal activation of all four systems. Research on the effects of parenting practices suggests some guidelines.

With respect to deference, investigators have found that "discipline practices that are completely devoid of force are ineffective because they elicit insufficient anxiety to signal the importance of the parental intervention, to orient the child to the message, and to provide motivation to change. But too much force can be detrimental to moral internalization" (Kochanska & Thompson, 1998, p. 68). To be effective, punishment must be relatively moderate, consistent, and administered as immediately as possible after transgressions (Aronfreed, 1968). If punishment consistently follows transgressions, children are quick to learn the "if" (you misbehave), "then" (you will be punished) contingencies.

With respect to care, researchers have concluded that a "mutually-responsive, positive parent-child orientation promotes the child's broad internalization of parental values" (Kochanska, 1997, p. 64). Too much care, or pampering, fosters the cultivation of selfishness. Too little care, or neglect, fosters insecure and avoidant attachments, which are associated with subsequent social problems.

With respect to induction, evolutionary models view the ideas parents preach to children as signals designed to, in effect, persuade and manipulate them (Krebs & Janicki, 2003). From an evolutionary perspective, attempting to persuade children to sacrifice their interests for the sake of others should be less effective than attempting to persuade them to foster their interests in mutually beneficial ways, which often entails explaining why cooperative strategies pay off better than selfish strategies in the long run. Finally, with respect to modeling, children should be affected by the biases described by Flinn and Alexander (1982) and Boyd and Richerson (1985).

The idea that successful parenting involves the optimal activation of several evolved systems implies a more complex model of moralization than traditional models that focus on only one system and attempt to identify the best form of discipline. And this is only the beginning. The practices that parents employ are affected by their temperaments and by the temperaments of their children. For example, parents who inherit psychological systems that react strongly to stress are inclined to employ strong forms of physical punishment (Rothbart & Ahadic, 1994) and children who experience relatively little distress following misdeeds tend to evoke harsh forms of punishment (Dienstbier, 1984). And different parenting practices are optimal for children with different temperaments. For example, Kochanska (1997) found that gentle, nonpower-oriented discipline was optimal for the development of conscience in temperamentally fearful children, but caring and cooperative parenting practices worked better for temperamentally fearless children.

From the perspective of the evolutionary model I am advancing, the key to successful parenting lies in the coordination of the psychological systems possessed by parents and children in mutually beneficial cooperative exchanges. Authorities on child development rooted in other theoretical approaches have reached similar conclusions. For example, Maccoby (1984) concluded that "parent-child social-ization [involves] inducing the child into a system of reciprocity—the formation of a mutually binding, reciprocal, and mutually responsive relationship" in which "partners in a communal or mutually reciprocal relationship feel invested in and responsible for each other's welfare" (Kochanska & Thompson, 1998, pp. 64–65).

Finally, to add another layer of complexity, practices that were optimal at one stage of development may not be optimal at other stages. As concluded by Bugental and Goodnow (1998),

> Relationships between the same individuals operate according to different "rules" based upon the changing nature of their relationship and the changing nature of the immediate context. Thus, the interaction between a given parent and child may be governed by attachment principles when the child is highly dependent (common in infancy and recurring at later times of stress). The struggles between the parent and the same child as a toddler (or early adolescence) may more typically involve power-based principles. During collaborative activity (work or play) involving the parent and the child, interactions are more likely to involve principles of reciprocity. At other times, the dyadic relationship may be based upon their shared identity as a family or as community members. (pp. 400–401)

Implications for Public Policy

The public policy implications of this analysis involve investing in interventions that foster effective parenting throughout the life span. P. A. Cowan, Powell, and C. P. Cowan (1998) reviewed research on the effectiveness of parenting interventions in the United States. Consistent with the present model, they reached the following three conclusions. First, "it makes good sense to increase efforts devoted to the creation of prevention programs for parents. Interventions early in the life of a family, or early in the development of family problems, give promise of staving off more serious problems farther along the family developmental trajectory" (p. 50). Second, "recent research on the effects of parenting programs provides support for complex, contextual, systemic theories of parenting effects" and "multidomain interventions." And third, "children at each age and stage have characteristic developmental tasks ... and parents need to learn to respond appropriately to infants, toddlers, and adolescents, because what works and can be understood at one age may not be effective in another" (p. 53).

In my view, social systems should be structured in ways that ensure that all potential parents receive instruction on pregnancy, childbirth, and optimal parenting practices. Literature and videotapes on these topics should be made available to all newlyweds. Experts should visit the homes of all pregnant women and new mothers to ensure they receive the assistance they need.

CULTIVATING MORALITY OUTSIDE THE FAMILY

Many people assume that it is unnatural for people other than mothers to assume responsibility for rearing children, but this assumption is false. To quote Lamb

(1998), "Exclusive maternal care throughout the period of dependency was never an option in what Bowlby (1980) called the 'environment of evolutionary adaptiveness,' and there are no societies today in which it is the typical practice. Indeed, exclusive maternal care … was seldom an option in any phase of human history; it emerged as a possibility for a small, elite segment of society during one small portion of human history" (p. 76). What is natural is for children to interact with and be cared for by a group of people that includes their parents, older siblings, members of their extended families, and nonrelatives from their ingroups (Whiting & Whiting, 1975).

Child-Care Centers

When I try to imagine large scale interventions equipped to foster moral development in young children who do not have access to interactions with siblings, peers, and adults other than their parents, I can think of none with more potential than the implementation of child care centers, especially for high risk kids. Child-care centers are pervasive in Scandinavian and Eastern European countries, where citizens believe that societies have a responsibility to foster the welfare and socialization of their children. Good child-care centers provide a safe environment for children, adequate nutrition, plentiful resources, and stimulating activities. At child-care centers, children interact with adults, older children, and younger children, who may come from many ethnic groups and cultures. The child-care profession tends to attract caring adults who receive training in parenting practices. Such workers serve as models for children and their parents. In child-care contexts, children can be offered guidance in cooperative activities and ways of resolving their conflicts of interest. Deferential, cooperative, caring, and docile mechanisms can be activated in optimal ways.

This potential notwithstanding, research on the effects of day care on children's attachments, peer relationships, and social development has produced mixed results. Based on an extensive review of the literature, Lamb (1998, pp. 115–116) reached the following conclusions. First, relationships with peers and care providers "can affect children's later social behavior, personality maturity, and cognitive development for good or for ill, depending on the quality and stability of these relationships." Second, as might be expected, "the quality of care received both at home and in alternative care facilities appears to be important." Moreover, "poor quality care can have harmful effects on child development" and "improvements in quality appear to have significant positive effects even at the highest end of the [age] range sampled, suggesting there is no threshold beyond which quality of care no longer matters." And, finally, "nonparental care is likely to be most beneficial when it complements the quality of family care most successfully, and most likely to be harmful when there are differences in ideology, belief, and behavior."

In a nutshell, evolutionary theory encourages child-care workers to structure their centers in ways that enable the children to discover the benefits of cooperation and the costs of selfishness. If children with day-care experience are less compliant than those reared exclusively at home, then this may not be a bad thing. According to many theorists, autonomy, coupled with respect for the rights of others, is essential for moral development.

Peer Relationships

According to Piaget (1932) and other developmental psychologists, peer relationships are critical for the cultivation of autonomous and cooperative moral orientations. The paucity of peers in relatively small modern families may constitute a constraint on moral development. Children in such families may become good at interacting with (and manipulating) adults, but fail to develop the social skills necessary to coordinate with peers. For optimal moral development, I believe children should interact with older and younger peers from an early age. For children who do not have brothers and sisters, this could take place within the family context, extended families, preschool play groups, neighborhoods, or child-care centers. As children grow older, they are inevitably faced with the challenge of developing cooperative relationships with their peers at school.

Schools

Most people define the role of schools in socializing children in terms of induction. They assume that teachers should teach moral values to children in much the same way they teach other subjects. In my view, this assumption is dead wrong. To teach morality to children, teachers must emphasize the problems morality is equipped to solve—problems that pertain to the maximization of mutual benefits through cooperation and effective ways of resolving conflicts of interest. This said, I believe even such pragmatic forms of induction are relatively impotent. Children may learn them in the same way they learn other subjects taught in schools, and they may be able to repeat them when asked, but by and large, they remain on a verbal plane, exerting relatively little effect on behavior.

To be effective, school programs designed to foster moral development must offer opportunities for students to actively practice the principles they and others preach. Role-playing opportunities take one step in this direction. Structured team activities and games take another, but such steps are relatively small. Following the failure of school-based moral discussion groups, moral educators guided by cognitive-developmental theories concluded that, to constitute effective agents of morality, schools needed to be restructured in ways that actively involved students in the decision-making processes (Higgins, Power, & Kohlberg, 1984; Kuhmerker, 1991). To this end, Kohlberg and his colleagues designed alternative schools in which students were given responsibility for creating and enforcing their own rules. Children who participated in such democratic schools displayed significantly greater gains in moral development than children who attended more conventional schools (Higgins et al., 1984).

The alternative schools created by Kohlberg and his colleagues were designed in ways that are consistent with interventions implied by evolutionary models of morality. Members of groups participate in the creation of rules that foster their mutual interests. Such participation encourages identification with the group, which lowers the threshold for the activation of care-oriented behaviors. Participants decide on the sanctions that follow violations of rules and acts of selfishness. As members of cooperative systems in which they have invested, students are more highly motivated to uphold the system by detecting, reporting, and punishing transgressors. Kohlberg and his colleagues found that, in addition to advances in moral development, students in such schools acquired a stronger sense of responsibility (Higgins et al., 1984).

Societies

From the perspective advanced in this chapter, interventions designed to cultivate morality in societies should be designed in accordance with the same principles as interventions designed to cultivate morality in child-care centers, schools, and other institutions. Members of societies should create maximally beneficial systems of cooperation and derive rules that define their rights and duties in such systems. Societies should structure their environments in ways that make following rules and upholding cooperative systems pay off better than cheating, which among other things necessitates the creation of mechanisms equipped to detect and to punish cheaters. As discussed, the gains in trade from systems of cooperation in large-scale societies are potentially greater than the gains in trade from cooperative exchanges in smaller groups. Common currency such as money enables all members of societies to, in effect, trade items of relatively little value to them for items of greater value. However, it is significantly more difficult to implement such systems of cooperative exchange in large-scale societies than in smaller groups for at least four reasons.

First, it is more difficult to activate care-based mechanisms in large societies than it is in smaller groups because fewer members of large societies possess characteristics such as similarity, familiarity, and proximity that constitute the "if" conditions for the activation of caring mechanisms. Second, it is significantly more difficult to define rights and duties and reckon costs and benefits in large societies than in smaller groups. Consider, for example, the difference between bartering with another individual or engaging in a Tit for Tat exchange and deciding whether carpenters should make more dollars per hour than mechanics. Third, it is more difficult to detect cheaters in large groups practicing indirect reciprocity than it is in smaller groups practicing direct reciprocity. Finally, members of societies have less incentive to punish transgressors. In general, societies do a very poor job of ensuring that punishments are administered as immediately as possible after transgressions in consistent and fair ways. Courts take years to make decisions. Criminals who are caught in the act are often set free. Wealthy transgressors buy their way out of penalties.

I believe that the ambivalence members of societies have toward the detection of transgressions and the imposition of punishments is built into the mechanisms they inherit. Consider, for example, people's ambivalence to photo radar and traffic tickets. The technology exists to detect every single speeder or red-light runner. If drivers knew for sure they would be caught and punished for violating traffic rules, then they would obey them. Thousands of lives would be saved. Yet people resist such sure-fire methods of detection. When asked why, people will allude to Big Brother types of danger. Such arguments are warranted when systems of detection are imposed on citizens by totalitarian authorities, but are not appropriate when people decide to impose such systems on themselves for their mutual benefit. Evolutionary theory implies that the source of such ambivalence lies in the constraints such interventions impose on the freedom of individuals to exploit systems of cooperation.

Reporting transgressors and administering punishments entails a cost—sometimes small and sometimes large. In relations between individuals in relatively small groups, the costs of detecting transgressions and administering punishments may be outweighed by the gains. It is relatively easy for individuals to discover that someone has cheated them one on one, and it is relatively easy to punish cheaters by getting even, severing relations with them or sullying their reputation through gossip. However, the larger the group and the more indirect the effects of one member's behavior on others, the less the value to each member of detecting transgressors, and the more reluctant members are to assume responsibility for administering punishments (Boyd & Richerson, 1985). Individuals also experience an ambivalence with respect to transgressions committed by members of their ingroups against other groups or society at large. Codes of silence often prevail.

Overcoming Obstacles to the Cultivation of Morality in Societies.   Evolutionary theory offers four forms of guidance for those who seek to foster morality at a societal level. First, societies should expand the circle of those who activate caring mechanisms, which can be accomplished by increasing the prevalence of kin recognition cues. For example, we could expand the number of people perceived as similar by labeling them in the same ways (e.g., Canadians), by encouraging them to share forms of dress and culture, by teaching them the same language and dialect, and so on. We could foster people's sense of proximity to and familiarity with members of their societies through the mass media (see Huston & Wright, 1998, for a review of the literature on the impact of the mass media).

Second, societies should ensure that members participate in the derivation of the rules that guide the allocation of resources. Permitting powerful authorities to define rules opens the door to dictatorship and totalitarianism. Rules imposed from the outside tend to be only as effective as the sanctions invoked to enforce them, and they tend to drive transgressions underground. People need to be as directly involved as possible in the creation of the rules that govern the systems of cooperation in which they participate. Delegating this responsibility to the elected official tends to depersonalize it.

Third, societies should create effective ways to detect and punish cheaters. Detection can be improved through methods such as video surveillance, photo radar,

Block Watches, DNA analysis, alcohol detectors in cars, publication of the identities of repeated sex offenders, and through programs such as America's Most Wanted. The effectiveness of punishment can be enhanced by reforming the court system in ways that increase the immediacy and consistency of punishment.

Finally, societies should maximize the exposure of their citizens to moral models. Inasmuch as docility mechanisms are activated by frequently observed behaviors or behaviors emitted by successful and powerful models, and inasmuch as members of societies are exposed to such models through the mass media, societies are in a position to regulate the models to which their members are exposed.

CONCLUSIONS

In this chapter, I offered an explanation for the origin of morality in the human species and explored the implications of this explanation for the cultivation of morality in today's world. I suggested that the biological function of morality is to help members of groups reap the benefits of cooperative exchanges by helping one another and resisting the temptation to behave selfishly. I questioned the conclusion that all evolved dispositions are inherently selfish in nature, explained how deferential, cooperative, caring, and docile dispositions could evolve, and adduced evidence that such dispositions give rise to moral behaviors.

In the second half of the chapter, I explored the implications of the evolutionary analysis advanced in the first half of the chapter for the cultivation of morality. I argued that the key to the cultivation of morality lies in determining the "if" conditions that activate moral dispositions and structuring environments in ways that optimize their activation. In large part, this entails ensuring that cooperative strategies pay off better than selfish strategies. Noting that individuals become members of increasingly large and complex groups as they develop, I offered reasons why it is easier to cultivate morality in family, child-care, and school contexts than in society at large. We have the wherewithal to fashion silk purses from the sows' ears of evolution, but to accomplish this challenging task, we must determine realistically what we have to work with and design interventions accordingly.

REFERENCES

Alcock, J. (1998). *Animal behavior: An evolutionary approach* (6th ed.). Sunderland, MA: Sinauer Associates.
Alexander, R. D. (1987). *The biology of moral systems.* New York: Aldine de Gruyter.
Aronfreed, J. (1968). *Conduct and conscience.* New York: Academic Press.
Axelrod, R., & Hamilton, W. D. (1981). The evolution of cooperation. *Science, 211,* 1390–1396.
Bandura, A. (1989). Social cognitive theory. *Annals of Child Development, 6,* 1–60.
Batson, C. D. (1991). *The altruism question: Toward a social-psychological answer.* Hillsdale, NJ: Lawrence Erlbaum Associates.
Boehm, C. (2000). Conflict and the evolution of social control. In L. D. Katz (Ed.), *Evolutionary origins of morality* (pp. 79–101). Exeter, UK: Imprint Academic.
Bowlby, J. (1980). *Attachment and loss: Vol. 3. Loss.* New York: Basic Books.

Boyd, R., & Richerson, P. J. (1985). *Culture and the evolutionary process.* Chicago: University of Chicago Press.

Bronfenbrenner, U. (1995). Developmental ecology through space and time: A future perspective. In P. Moen, G. H. Elder, Jr., & K. Luscher (Eds.), *Examining lives in context* (pp. 619–647). Washington, DC: American Psychological Association.

Brown, R. (1986). *Social psychology* (2nd ed). New York: The Free Press.

Bugental, D. B., & Goodnow, J. J. (1998). Socialization. In W. Damon & N. Eisenberg (Eds.), *Handbook of child psychology* (Vol. 3, 5th ed., pp. 389–462). New York: Wiley.

Burton, R. V., & Kunce, L. (1995). Behavioral models of moral development: A brief history and integration. In W. M. Kurtines & J. L. Gewirtz (Eds.), *Moral development: An introduction* (pp. 141–172). Boston: Allyn & Bacon.

Buss, D. (1999). *Evolutionary psychology: The new science of the mind.* Boston: Allyn & Bacon.

Cheney, D. L., & Seyfarth, R. M. (1985). Social and non-social knowledge in vervet monkeys. *Philosophical Transactions of the Royal Society of London, 308,* 187–201.

Cowan, P. A., Powell, D., & Cowan, C. P. (1998) Parenting interventions: A family systems perspective. In I. E. Sigel & K. A. Renninger (Eds.), *Handbook of child psychology* (Vol. 4, 5th ed., pp. 3–72). New York: Wiley.

Crawford, C. B., & Anderson, J. L. (1989). Sociobiology: An environmentalist discipline? *American Psychologist, 44,* 1449–1459.

Crespi, B. J. (2000). The evolution of maladaptation. *Heredity, 84,* 623–629.

Dawkins, R. (1989). *The selfish gene.* Oxford, England: Oxford University Press.

de Waal, F. B. C., & Flack, J. C. (2000). "Any animal whatever": Darwinian building blocks of morality in monkeys and apes. In L. D. Katz (Ed.), *Evolutionary origins of morality: Cross-disciplinary approaches* (pp. 1–29). Exeter, UK: Imprint Academic.

Dienstbier, R. A. (1984). The role of emotion in moral socialization. In C. Izard, J. Kagan, & R. B. Zajonc (Eds.), *Emotions, cognitions, and behaviors* (pp. 484–513). New York: Cambridge University Press.

Dugatkin, L. A. (1997). *Cooperation among animals: An evolutionary perspective.* New York: Oxford University Press.

Field, T. M., Dempsey, J. R., & Shuman, H. H. (1981). Developmental follow-up of pre-and postterm infants. In S. L. Friedman & M. Sigman (Eds.), *Preterm birth and psychological development.* New York: Academic Press.

Flinn, M. V., & Alexander, R. D. (1982). Culture theory: The developing synthesis from biology. *Human Ecology, 10,* 383–400.

Flinn, M. V., & Low, B. S. (1986). Resource distribution social competition, and mating patterns in human societies. In D. I. Rubenstein & W. Wrangham (Eds.), *Ecological aspects of social evolution: Birds and mammals* (pp. 217–243). Princeton, NJ: Princeton University Press.

Freud, S. (1925). *Collected papers.* London: Hogarth.

Gilligan, C. (1982). *In a different voice: Psychological theory and women's development.* Cambridge, MA: Harvard University Press.

Grusec, J. E., & Lytton, H. (1988). *Social development: History, theory, and research.* New York: Springer-Verlag.

Hamilton, W. D. (1964). The evolution of social behavior. *Journal of Theoretical Biology, 7,* 1–52.

Higgins, A., Power, C., & Kohlberg, L. (1984). The relationship of moral atmosphere to judgments of responsibility. In W. M. Kurtines & J. L. Gewirtz (Eds.), *Morality, moral behavior, and moral development* (pp 74–106). NY: Wiley.

Hoffman, M. L. (1999). *Empathy and moral development.* Cambridge, England: Cambridge University Press.

Huston, A. C., & Wright, J. C. (1998). Mass media and children's development. In I. E. Sigel & K. A. Renninger (Eds.), *Handbook of child psychology* (Vol. 4, 5th ed., pp. 999–1058). New York: Wiley.

Kochanska, G. (1997). Multiple pathways to conscience for children with different temperaments: From toddlerhood to age five. *Developmental Psychology, 33*, 228–240.

Kochanska, G., & Thompson, R. A. (1998). The emergence of conscience in toddlerhood and early childhood. In J. E. Grusec & L. Kuczynski (Eds.), *Parenting and children's internalization of values: A handbook of contemporary theory* (pp. 53–77). New York: Wiley.

Kohlberg, L. (1984). *Essays in moral development: Vol 2. The psychology of moral development.* New York: Harper & Row.

Kopp, C. (1983). Risk factors in development. In J. Campos & M. Haith (Eds.), *Handbook of child psychology* (Vol. 2, pp. 1081–1182). New York: Wiley.

Krebs, D. L. (1998). The evolution of moral behavior. In C. Crawford & D. L. Krebs (Eds.), *Handbook of evolutionary psychology: Ideas, issues, and applications* (pp. 337–368). Hillsdale, NJ: Lawrence Erlbaum Associates.

Krebs, D. L. (2000a). The evolution of moral dispositions in the human species. In D. LeCroy & P. Moller (Eds.), Evolutionary perspectives on human reproductive behavior. *Annals of the New York Academy of Science, 907*, 132–148.

Krebs, D. L. (2000b). Evolutionary games and morality. In L. D. Katz (Ed.), *Evolutionary origins of morality: Cross-disciplinary approaches* (pp. 313–321). Exeter, UK: Imprint Academic.

Krebs, D. L. (2000c). As moral as we need to be. In L. D. Katz (Ed.), *Evolutionary origins of morality: Cross-disciplinary approaches* (pp. 139–143). Exeter, UK: Imprint Academic.

Krebs, D. L. (in press). Fictions and facts about evolutionary approaches to human behavior. *Psychological Bulletin.*

Krebs, D. L., & Janicki, M. (2003). The biological foundations of moral norms. In M. Schaller & C. Crandall (Eds.), *Psychological foundations of culture* (pp. 125–148). Hillsdale, NJ: Lawrence Erlbaum Associates.

Kuhmerker, L. (1991). *The Kohlberg legacy for the helping professions.* Birmingham: Doxa Books.

Lamb, M. E. (1998). Nonparental child care: Context, quality, correlates, and consequences. In I. E. Sigel & K. A. Renninger (Eds.), *Handbook of child psychology* (Vol. 4, 5th ed., pp. 73–134). New York: Wiley.

Lancaster, J. B., & Lancaster, C. S. (1987). The watershed: Change in parental-investment and family-formation in the course of human evolution. In J. B. Lancaster, J. Altman, A. S. Rossi, & L. R. Sherrod (Eds.), *Parenting across the life span: Biosocial dimensions* (pp. 187–205). New York: Aldine de Gruyter.

Leaky, R. E., & Lewin, R. (1977). *Origins.* New York: Dutton.

Lickliter, R., & Honeycutt, H. (in press). Developmental dynamics: Towards a biologically plausible evolutionary psychology. *Psychological Bulletin.*

Maccoby, E. E. (1984). Socialization and developmental change. *Child Development, 55,* 317–328.

MacDonald, K. (1997). The coherence of individual development: An evolutionary perspective on children's internalization of values. In J. E. Grusec & L. Kuczynski (Eds.), *Parenting and children's internalization of values: A handbook of contemporary theory* (pp. 362–397). New York: Wiley.

Nowak, M. A., & Sigmund, K. (1998). Evolution of indirect reciprocity by image scoring. *Nature, 393,* 573–577.

Piaget, J. (1932). *The moral judgment of the child.* London: Routledge & Kegan Paul.

Plomin, R., DeFries, J. C., & McClearn, G. E. (1997). *Behavioral genetics.* New York: Freeman.

Rawls, J. (1971). *A theory of justice.* Cambridge, MA: Harvard University Press.

Rest, J. F. (1983). Morality. In J. H. Flavell & E. M. Markman (Eds.), *Handbook of child psychology: Vol. 3. Cognitive development* (4th ed., pp. 556–629). New York: Wiley.

Ridley, M. (1996). *The origins or virtue: Human instincts and the evolution of cooperation.* New York: Viking.

Rothbart, M. K., & Ahadic, S. A., (1994). Temperament and the development of personality. *Journal of Abnormal Psychology, 103,* 55–66.

Simon, H. (1990). A mechanism for social selection of successful altruism. *Science, 250,* 1665–1668.

Sober, E., & Wilson, D. S. (1998). *Unto others: The evolution and psychology of unselfish behavior.* Cambridge, MA: Harvard University Press.

Strayer, F. F., & Strayer, J. (1976). An ethological analysis of social agonism and dominance relations among preschool children. *Child Development, 47,* 980–989.

Tajfel, H. (1982). *Social identify and intergroup relations.* Cambridge, England: Cambridge University Press.

Thompson, R. A. (1998). Early sociopersonality development. In W. Damon & N. Eisenberg (Eds.), *Handbook of child psychology* (Vol 3, 5th ed., pp. 25–104). New York: Wiley.

Tooby, J., & Devore, I. (1987). The reconstruction of hominid behavioral evolution through strategic modeling. In W. G. Kinzey (Ed.), *The evolution of human behavior: Primate models* (pp. 183–237). Albany, NY: SUNY Press.

Trivers, R. L. (1971). The evolution of reciprocal altruism. *Quarterly Review of Biology, 46,* 35–57.

Trivers, R. L. (1972). Parental investment and sexual selection. In B. Campbell (Ed.), *Sexual selection and the descent of man* (pp. 136–179). Chicago: Aldine.

Weissberg, R. P., & Greenberg, M. T. (1998). School and community competence-enhancement and prevention programs. In I. E. Sigel & K. A. Renninger (Eds.), *Handbook of child psychology* (Vol. 4, 5th ed., pp. 877–954). New York: Wiley.

Whiting, B. B., & Whiting, J. W. M. (1975). *Children of six cultures.* Cambridge MA: Harvard University Press.

Wilkinson, G. S. (1990). Food sharing in vampire bats. *Scientific American,* February, 76–82.

Williams, G. C. (1989). *A sociobiological expansion of "evolution and ethics," evolution and ethics* (pp. 179–214). Princeton, NJ: Princeton University Press.

Wozniak, R. H. (1993). Co-constructive metatheory for psychology: Implications for an analysis of families as specific social contexts for development. In R. H. Wozniak & K. W. Fischer (Eds.), *Development in context: Acting and thinking in specific environments* (pp. 77–91). Hillsdale, NJ: Lawrence Erlbaum Associates.

Youniss, J., McLellan, J. A., & Strouse, D. (1995). "We're popular, but we are not snobs": Adolescents describe their crowds. In R. Montemayer (Ed.), *Advances in adolescent development* (Vol. 5, pp. 101–122). Newbury Park, CA: Sage.

CHAPTER

16

Darwinism and Public Policy: The View From Political Science

Robert S. Robins
Tulane University

Political science is a crazy quilt of borrowings from history, philosophy, law sociology, psychology, economics, public administration, policy studies, area studies, international studies, civics, and a variety of other sources. Any real coherence in political science exists only at the broadest conceptual level, in the form of our widely shared interest in power, the "authoritative allocation of values for society," "who gets what, when, how," and the like.   —(Sigelman, 2002, p. viii)

Political science is the systematic study of power in society. Most political scientists would agree that power is desired so that its wielders can acquire what evolutionary history has made enjoyable, namely, influence, wealth, security, and the good regard of others (especially status and affection). For political scientists, public policy is the means by which government is used by those with influence in government to help themselves and others to acquire those things. Darwinists recognize that the pursuit of influence, wealth, security, and status is a proximate cause. The ultimate motivation of people's behavior, however, draws on deeper, evolutionary forces.

Human beings' success in designing effective public policies in large part rests on understanding their own psychological nature; that is, being aware of those mental characteristics that are universal to the human race and that cannot be contradicted or, more often, contradicted only at great cost.

The chapters herein do not set boundaries or give invariable prescriptions for how laws and other public policies may be made. What they do is suggest the costs that will have to be borne by choosing one policy over another. For example, we can legislate that equal numbers of men and women become kindergarten teachers or professional football coaches. They can require that children be raised separately from their parents. Society can pass laws based on the belief that all criminals can be reformed. All these rules have been enacted and enforced at one time or another. All have induced unanticipated consequences that have led to their reversal. The ultimate reason for these failures in public policy has been that each has been made under the assumption that individuals are completely malleable.

The point here is not that such policies cannot, or even should not, be implemented. The point is that they have costs. A Darwinian perspective in the making of policy will indicate what costs must be borne or, perhaps, how a more careful development of policy can minimize those costs. There are always trade-offs in the making of legislation. As Salmon (chap. 10 in this vol.) noted, "Once an ideal ("should") is decided upon, the question is whether it will be easy or very difficult to achieve." An evolutionary perspective is necessary in estimating the likely trade-off.

The areas of public policy described by political scientists are broad indeed. Consulting four mainstream textbooks (Anderson, 1997; McKenna & Feingold, 2002; Peters, 1999; Stone, 1996) and taking notes in local and national newspapers over a 2-week period, the following two clusters of topics appeared:

> *Regarding relations among countries*: Policies concerning military and intelligence cooperation, intellectual property, immigration, human rights, alliances, treaties, trade relations. None of these topics are substantially addressed in this volume.

> *Regarding the politics of the advanced industrial nations of North America*: Airline deregulation, tax policy, national health insurance, unemployment insurance, energy policy, environmental policy, gun control, gay marriage, abortion, campaign finance, antimonopoly legislation, capital punishment, affirmative action, imprisonment law (Barr & Quinsey, chap. 14 in this vol.), school choice, relationships between the sexes, rules concerning psychoactive substances, law (Wilson & Daly, chap. 9 in this vol.; Shackleford & Weekes-Shackelford, chap. 11 in this vol.), who may serve in the military, rape law (Crawford, chap. 1 in this vol.; Thornhill & Palmer, chap. 12 in this vol.), occupational law (Browne, chap. 13 in this vol.), pornography law (Salmon, chap. 10 in this vol.), immigration policy, private charity vs. public support, strike legislation, radio and television broadcasting rules; regulation of business hours, minimum wage, child labor, postal service, drunk driving laws, social security, savings incentives for retirement.

ISSUES OF RIGHT AND WRONG

As well as these two areas, practitioners of political science and public policy are also concerned with broad issues of right and wrong (Badcock, this volume; Barr & Quinsey, this volume; Fiddick, this volume; Holcomb, this volume), even when not directly addressed in government law and rules. Many public policies draw indirectly on ethical obligations (parental obligation for the care of children). Symbolic public policy is especially contentious, such as the prohibition of flag burning. Here are some public policy topics with especially strong components of ethics or symbolism that are touched on in this volume: the development of a civic culture outside of government, democracy and autocracy, freedom of speech, hate speech, assisted suicide, abortion, the practice of religion, capital punishment, the protection of endangered species, just war doctrine, racism, sexism, recreational drug regulation. Arguably, these issues straddle the practical and the theoretical, but the point here is that they vitally affect public policy.

It would be impossible to cover all these issues here, but it is worthwhile to take up several to note how the principle of trade-offs is relevant to each.

Rape

There are a variety of definitions of this term. This chapter restricts analysis to forced sexual intercourse by a man with a woman. The standard, socially dominant, blank slate analysis is that rape is a crime of violence and not of sex. Certainly, the victim experiences the act not as sex, but as violence. For the most part, legislation and other forms of social intervention make that assumption and give scant attention to punishing and preventing the crime by means responsive to its sexual character.

Rapists strongly tend to be in their most virile and sexually active years, and the victims of rape strongly tend to be in the most fertile age range for women. There are other evidences that male sexual urge plays an important role in this crime. Rape, from an evolutionary perspective, is arguably an adaptation. That is, in evolutionary history, coerced sexual intercourse under certain circumstances conferred a reproductive advantage.

Denying the sexual component of rape makes its prevention less likely. Among evolutionarily informed policies that might be added to those already in place would be sterilization for rapists, encouragement of marriage, public information campaigns warning women of behaviors and dress that are likely to be sexually provocative, and that being in certain locations increases the chance of their being raped. These initiatives would, of course, infringe on individual freedom. Although hundreds of millions of people in India, China, and the Muslim world live with similar policies, such authoritarian policies would be difficult to implement in Western democratic societies. As Thornhill and Palmer (chap. 12 in this vol.) argue, rape is likely to be decreased in circumstances of social equality. If so, policies engendering that situation would be a positive factor in decreasing the crime.

Pornography

This is a difficult word to define. The old statements that pornography is more readily recognized than defined and that "I can't tell you what it is, but I know it when I see it" are indicative of its sometimes elusive character. The definition that will be used here is "material designed as its principal, and characteristically as its sole, intent, to stimulate sexual desire—without regard to and frequently in violations of cultural norms." This discussion is limited to pornography directed toward men, in that is by far the area of greatest public debate.

Two questions arise: Does pornography do harm? And, if so, how might this harm be prevented or mitigated, and at what cost?

Material offered in this volume indicates that pornography that does not include violence has no discernable negative effect, except perhaps to make the observer less satisfied with his present mate. The circumstances surrounding pornography are arguably the problem. Thus, material successfully designed to depict erotic situations involving children (i.e., unwilling or manipulated objects as with rape) if socially and legally accepted, legitimize and perhaps stimulate pederasty. It may also be that children's exposure to any form of erotica adversely affects their later sexuality. Therefore, society has an interest in prohibiting, limiting, or discouraging the exhibition of pornography.

Does an evolutionary perspective add anything to this discussion? The current environment exposes men (and women, although that topic is outside this chapter) to a greater variety of attractive sexual partners than was the case in the ancestral environment. Pornography is an especially strong form of such exposure. Arguably, the present aggressiveness of sexually themed entertainment and advertisement is a factor in the weakening of marriage. If marriage is seen as a good thing for society, then limits or prohibition on pornography may be justified. Many believe that pornography is a coarsening influence on society in general. This may be so, but those making the argument must define the terms and demonstrate the consequences with greater precision than that general statement. On the other hand, viewing pornography might provide a sexual outlet for otherwise harmful behavior.

Another question concerning public policy and pornography concerns not the viewers but the performers. Does willing performance in a pornographic production harm the participants? There is no ready answer from evolutionary psychology.

Marriage and Divorce

In terms of public policy, the principal issues regarding marriage and divorce concern property and children. These problems arise most directly in cases where the putative father does not live with a child he believes to be his, where the putative father does not believe or suspects that he is not the child's genetic parent, and where the mother's male household partner knows and acknowledges he is not the father (i.e., stepfather situations).

In the ancestral environment, it is most reasonable to assume that in the overwhelming majority of cases a mother would live in the same band with the father of her children. Mate guarding would be difficult for the male and opportunities for "extra-marital" mating would be available for males and females. Because the members of the band resembled one another, the physical appearance of a child would rarely be a reliable means of suggesting paternity. Male adaptations would have developed to assume responsibility for a child's well-being only where a variety of personal and social cues indicated that it was his child.

Even where the father acknowledged the child, being out of contact for substantial periods of time from the mother and the child would have been rare, and when it occurred there would not have been a means of the father supporting the child. Mother and child would have likely been supported by the mother's relatives.

Thus, although paternal investment would have been selected for, it would be considerably weaker than the mother's, who would have been confident of her maternity and rarely distantly separated from her dependent child. This paternal investment, moreover, would be conditional on the reasoned belief of the male that it is his child.

Because of the characteristically (but not invariable) communal nature of ancestral life, single mother households in the current sense would have been rare indeed. Single mother households in the current environment are, however, far from unusual. Children raised in such households are disproportionately likely to suffer from various forms of social pathology, especially juvenile crime, and are less likely than other children to succeed in life.

In the more prosperous countries, the state assumes part of the burden that the mother's family or the father would have provided in the ancestral environment. To require the father to assume a substantial burden, governments have passed a variety of laws. For delinquent fathers, garnishment of wages, refusal to grant driver's licenses, liens on property, and even imprisonment are regularly applied. "Softer" measures, such as programs to convince men that supporting their children is the manly thing to do, are also employed. These policies work in many cases, and the situation would be worse without them. The fact of nonpaternal support, however, remains a major problem. Is there anything that evolutionary psychology can suggest?

Approximately 12% of putative fathers are not the natural father of the child ascribed to them. This figure varies geographically and perhaps by demographic group. It is also likely that it varies by social circumstances. It is reasonable to speculate that children born into stable marriages are more likely to be their putative father's genetic offspring than those born into unstable marriages and to less regular unions. The males in such circumstances are less confident about the children's paternity. In some cases, economic self-interest probably colors their opinions in the direction of nonsupport.

To increase paternal support, government could institute policies (e.g., tax advantages) to encourage stable marriages. It could also require, as Schackelford and Weekes-Schackelford (chap. 11 in this vol.) suggest in this volume, that a paternity test be made routinely at the birth of each child, and that the parents be informed of the result. Genetic fathers would thus have a near certainty of paternity, where that is the case. This policy, needless to say, would not only be controversial, but its implementation would likely have consequences that cannot be gauged.

As Wilson and Daly (chap. 9 in this vol.) indicate in this volume and elsewhere, there is substantial evidence that children in stepfamilies (where one of the partners is acknowledged as not the genetic parent) are at substantially greater risk of injury or death than are children in households where only a genetic parent is present. Two public policy issues arise here. Single parents (in most cases mothers) should be made aware that their children are at greater risks in such situations. They should also be reminded that they themselves are also at greater physical risk. Secondly, social welfare agencies, as well as law enforcement, should exercise enhanced monitoring of children in these households. Government policies (e.g., tax policy) should be considered to encourage stable unions.

Crime Reduction Policies and Serious Repeat Offenders

Political scientists would not quarrel with the *DSM* definition of psychopathy that Barr and Quinsey (2003) detailed, but, following general usage, would more likely define the behavior as an established preference, without moral consideration, for actions that are exploitative and often violent. Stated less formally, in common parlance, the terms used to describe psychopaths are "cold blooded killers," "Machiavellians," "conscienceless parasites," and "heartless thieves." An evolutionary analysis strongly suggests that the behavior may be a manifestation of "an adaptation to some particular problem in the evolutionary context" (Barr & Quinsey, chap. 14 in this vol.). Society has responded to such hard-core non-reformable offenders by deterrence (increasing the likelihood of detection and the severity of punishment) and by immobilization (imprisonment and execution). Incorrigible offender laws, often called three-strikes laws in which a third conviction for a felony results in a prison sentence well beyond what the crime itself would call for, are examples of societal responses to psychopathic criminals. Certainly, imprisoning or executing psychopaths eliminates them from society.

Deterrence, where feasible, is a milder, preferable, and more humane option. As Barr and Quinsey pointed out, psychopathy as an adaptation is not an invariable response to all situations, although it may be to very many. That is, there is a large element of opportunism in the behavior of even the most hardened psychopath. Thus, another method of lessening this behavior is by informing the public of its possibility and the protective action its members as individuals should take. There is a substantial amount of evidence from the study of societies that have a high level of social integration (strong families, vigorous voluntary associations, i.e., a strong civil society) that these societies have lower levels of all types of crime. Those persons who might be inclined to psychopathic behavior are more likely identified in that there is a generally higher and broader level of social interaction. Conversely, events such as war, rapid urbanization, and inadequate responses to disasters (e.g., famine, flood, and fire) are likely to give psychopaths greater opportunities. Society can, to a substantial degree, eliminate or mitigate such events.

Sex Discrimination in the Work Place

It is very common for advanced industrial societies to have legislation concerning occupational sexual discrimination. The legislation falls into two categories. One type attempts to prevent sexual discrimination (against women in almost all cases) by laying down required procedures (e.g., advertising for positions, consistent use of promotion standards) and those that must be avoided (e.g., systematically assigning one sex to lower paid positions, requiring sexual favors as a condition of employment). Little political controversy exists concerning these general principles or their general aim—equality of treatment. The second type of legislation (sometimes created via judicial interpretation) evaluates the effectiveness of these procedures by their outcome. That is, regardless of the evidence provided as to the punctiliousness of the application of the procedures or any other factors, if the result is not one of near statistical identity, the presumption is made that either the procedures are defective or that they have been improperly and prejudicially applied.

Browne (2003) offered powerful evidence that men, as a sex, are likely to be more desirous of status than women and hence willing to make greater sacrifices to achieve it. Furthermore, there is greater variability among males than females, thus giving males an advantage in achieving positions of greater status, usually including income. Because of a general tendency toward nurturant and cooperative behavior in women and aggressive and competitive behavior in men, there is a sexual sorting in terms of occupational preference. Men are more likely to be found in fields such as commission sales and litigation, and women are more common in areas such as editing and counseling. Men, too, have about 15% greater upper body strength than women, and so are likely to be dominant in physically demanding occupations such as trash collection, fire fighting, and bar room security. Evidence is also available to show that, for the most part, men tend to do better than women on spatial and mathematical problems, and women on verbal ability. There is, of course, substantial overlap between the sexes in these behaviors, and so one would not likely see any employment exclusively occupied by one sex. In all these instances, the behaviors are consistent with what is known of the ancestral environments in which they developed and in the traits that "enabled men to gain reproductive advantage over other men and [the traits that] enabled some women to gain reproductive advantage over other women" (Browne, chap. 13 in this vol.).

As public policy, the problem is easily identified and easily solved. If the desire is simply to assure equal treatment, a process-based approach is sufficient. If the desire is to assure that men and women have equal representation in all or perhaps only on a designated list of positions, then the assignment of quotas is sufficient. There will be small costs in applying the procedure-based approach and substantial costs in applying the outcome-based policy. For example, it will be expensive to provide a sufficient number of women garbage collectors or in arranging the disposal of garbage in such a way as to make the occupation equally attractive to men and women. So too, the provision of gender equality in nursery school teachers will require changes in the nature of nursery schools or in the compensation of male nursery school teachers. But if society chooses to make such arrangements, it can. What it cannot do is to achieve equal representation of the sexes in all or nearly all fields through any process short of quotas. Evolutionary history prevents that from happening.

The Terms of the Debate

The previous examples were specific. But probably the greatest impact that evolutionary psychology will have on public policy will be in changing the terms of the debate: changes in normative political theory and the inclusion of evolutionary perspectives in the methods of inquiry; the oldest branch of political science is that of political theory—why political society is organized as it is and what are its members' duties and rights.

The chapters by Badcock (5), Barr and Quinsey (14), Fiddick (8), and Holcomb (4) in this volume address themselves most directly to these issues. Regarding how the state arose, Locke, Hobbes, Rousseau, and Marx offered ideas, fanciful to the evolutionist, positing that society was created through an act of will or of error. The state—defined broadly as a hierarchy that distributes those things that its members value and in which its members fulfill socially defined functions—exists among other animals and it preceded human emergence. Indeed, it was the state that created the human race and not the reverse.

Central to normative political theory are questions of obligation to others. And central to that topic is the assumption of choice, or free will. In law, as in ethics, responsibility ceases where free will ends. Yet, much of mental life—and so the actions that it produces—is unconscious. This is not to say that "my genes made me do it" but only to acknowledge that people's acts are influenced, and sometimes decisively influenced, by forces outside their control.

Some of these influences are hostile and destructive—an oversuspicion of strangers and those who seem unlike ourselves—but many of them are positive. Caring for the well-being of others is probably the most important of the evolutionarily related adaptations. Or to put it as Harmon Holcomb does, "Moral feelings are social feelings" (chap. 4 in this vol.).

Few believe that normative political theory will ever give decisive and conclusive answers to the enduring questions of politics, such as the conflict between freedom and authority. But what people do say can only be made more helpful by a better understanding of human nature, and that understanding must include consideration of ancestral history.

Ultimately, the greatest impact evolutionary psychology will have will be in the social sciences, not least in political science. That revolution is just beginning. Social scientists overwhelmingly believe that evolution occurred and that occurrence matters, and those who doubt it are ignoramuses—except, that is, when it comes to their own field of inquiry. Human bodies and their brains are the product of evolution, but not their minds, they say. Or, if any consideration is given to evolutionary explanations, the standard of argument for publication is set far, far higher than for social environmental explanations. With the exception of *Politics and the Life Sciences*, no substantial journal of politics is receptive to articles with an evolutionary perspective.

This resistance is not due to a blind prejudice to all new methods. Formal theory has over the past thirty of so years become a major, some might even argue, the dominant method in political science. It is, therefore, notable that the one chapter in this volume that offers an explicitly methodological approach does so via formal theory. Ketelaar (chap. 7 in this vol.) demonstrates how formal theory can be enhanced by an evolutionary perspective, as well as how formal theory can permit people to better see the powerful traces of their ancestry on present behavior.

Ketelaar makes no explicit public policy arguments, but he does offer two insights with arguably important public policy consequences. The first is the type of insight that will intrigue the makers of public policy, because on first view it is counterintuitive, but on second consideration it is quite logical. Society, Ketelaar notes, is divided among various groups with substantially different levels of cooperation and exploitation. Some are very cooperative (the largest number), some are cautiously cooperative, and some are not cooperative at all. There are two other groups. One, a small group of extreme exploiters, is discussed shortly. There may also be a substantial number of super-cooperators. This group (designated as "too nice") is a *negative* influence on productive and amicable social order. By having such a ripe and vulnerable (though small) group of victims, exploiters are encouraged, grow in number and aggressiveness, and so adversely affect all.

What can society do about these nice people? A more aggressive interpretation of the common law principle that a crime is not only committed against an individual, but also against society would lead to the adoption of the rule that crimes experienced or known of must be reported. This is not the rule in the United States, for example, but is in many other countries. Nice people would be permitted to forgive and forget their exploitation, but the courts would not.

The second insight is attractive as a refinement and explanation of a common belief: The behavior of a very small number of aggressive noncooperators can have consequences out of all proportion to their numbers and to the people whom they injure. A few aggressive thieves, a few con men, or, more dramatically, even one serial murderer can adversely change the behavior of very large numbers of people and add a high social and economic cost to society. In late 2002, a serial murderer was, over a period of weeks, shooting people at random in the Washington, DC area. The effects on travel, shopping, police, and other expenses were extraordinary. As of this writing, it appears that two men, one an adolescent, were responsible. The effect of psychopaths or other exploiters goes well beyond the suffering they cause their victims. All of society pays a price. Because psychopaths are habitual in their depredations, this is an argument for increasingly severe punishment for habitual offenders.

CONCLUSIONS

These five fields of public policy certainly do not exhaust the areas that political science could investigate. The explicitly public policy chapters in this volume all deal with either political theory or domestic policy. Much of political science, however, concerns the relations among and between states.

Consider these related topics: nationalism, racism, international cooperation, defense, intellectual, property, immigration, criticism of other countries as to human rights, alliances, treaties and trade, war making, and international law. Yes, the international state system is very different from the pattern of generally hostile bands in the ancestral environment. Or is it? Evolutionists do not find it difficult to acknowledge that people as individuals have within them tendencies and drives derived from distant ancestors, adaptations for the ancestral environments that are destructive in everyday life. Darwin's light has been focused on these problems in this volume. Perhaps the next collection will deal with the evolutionary sources of conflicts among nations and peoples.

REFERENCES

Anderson, J. E. (1997). *Public policy making.* New York: Houghton Mifflin.
McKenna, G., & Feingold, S. (Eds). (2002). *Taking sides: Clashing views on controversial issues.* New York: McGraw-Hill.
Peters, B. G. (1999). *American public policy.* New York: Chatham.
Sigelman, L. (2002). *American Political Science Review, 96*(1), viii.
Stone, D. (1996). *Policy paradox.* New York: Norton.

Author Index

Subject Index

The letters f, t, and n after a page number indicate figures, tables, and notes, respectively.

A

Abuse. *See* Child abuse; Sexual abuse; Spousal abuse and assault; Substance abuse
Accidents, psychology of, 137, 138, 258–259
Adaptations, theory
  adaptability, defined, 39
  adaptation, defined, 25, 36, 37, 39
  adaptiveness, defined, 39
  behavioral adaptations, 17–18, 36–39
  beneficial and detrimental effects, 39
  and genetic variation, 41–42
  in life history theory, 252–253
  See also Psychological adaptations
Adolescents
  and male risk taking, 258–259
  problem behaviors and prevention, 260, 301–306, 310–311
  young male syndrome, 308
  See also Life histories
Adoption, as quasi-normal behavior, 14t, 16, 17
Adultery, 202–208
  See also Paternity certainty
Aesthetics, as mental culture, 109
Age, life history variable, 32–33, 222, 236
  See also Development (ontogeny); Life histories
Aggression, 38, 295–296

See also Competition; Warfare
Altruism
  defined, 27, 31, 53
  emotional bases for prosocial behavior, 57–60, 155
  evolution of, 53–56
  and genetic selfishness, 52–53
  in group selection, 27
  history of, in sociobiology, 51–52
  inclusive fitness, 31–33, 53–54, 327
  reciprocal altruism, 7–8, 33–34, 54–56, 127–128, 153–154
  as social norm, 65–67
  toward non-kin, 61–64
  See also Inclusive fitness; Moral psychology; Reciprocity
Anthropomorphism, defined, 100
Antisocial behavior, 301–306, 310–311
Antisocial personality disorder. *See* Psychopathy
Architecture, as material culture, 111
Art, 109, 111
Artificial intelligence, 178
Asperger's syndrome, 105–107
Assault, spousal. *See* Spousal abuse and assault
Attachment, 262–264, 326–327
Attribution, disposition vs. situation, 137
Autism, as mentalistic deficit, 100–108
Avunculate, and paternity uncertainty, 266
Axis II disorders, defined, 300

in evolutionary theory, 26
as frequency-dependent strategy,
159–160, 162–163
and male mating effort, 265–267
and self-deception, 123–125
sex differences, 258, 277, 279–280
Competitor strategy, 159–160, 160f,
162–163
Computational theory of mind, 170–171
Computer tournaments, in game theory,
55, 147, 150–153
Conflict avoidance, in primates, 81
Conscience. *See* Moral psychology
Consciousness
as adaptive heuristic, 117–119
costs of, 122–123
as mentalistic state, 108
of survival prospects, 262
See also Self-deception
Cooperation
among legal systems, 312–313
cooperative selfishness in friendship,
63–64
Cooperator strategy, 159–160, 162–163
emotional bases for, 155, 157–159
evolution of, 56–57, 320–322
in families, 203–204, 333–334
group selection for, 67–68, 320–322
illusion of control, 130–131
in large groups, 321–322, 335–337
in moral psychology, 323, 325–326
as policy goal, 68
and punishment, 90
social norms, 65–67
super-cooperators, 351
trust and self-deception, 127–128,
138–139
See also Moral psychology; Moral
systems
Cooperator strategy, 159–160, 160f, 162–163
Cost/benefit comparisons
in adaptive decision processes, 37–38,
39
of cooperation, 335–337
of cultural moral norms, 75
of gains in trade, 180–181, 321–322
helping non-kin, 61–64
of maternal care, 210
in moral contexts, 77–79
payoffs in Prisoner's Dilemma, 55,
148–149, 148f
of psychopathy, 306–309, 312–313
of punishment, 18–20, 308

in reciprocal exchange, 34
in risk taking, 43–45
of sexual coercion, 266–267
See also Decision making; Tradeoffs
Crime
antisocial behavior, 301–306, 310–311
genetics of criminal behavior, 299
as policy problem, 309–314, 348–349
priming cheater detection, 138–139
sex differences, 258–259
and survival prospects, 260–261,
267–268
unobtrusive measures, 219
See also Child abuse; Psychopathy;
Rape; Spousal abuse and
assault; Substance abuse
Cross-cultural studies, 203–204, 265, 278
Cuckoldry, 202–208
See also Paternity certainty
Culture
cross-cultural studies, 203–204, 265,
278
cultural evolution, 66–67
legal systems, 110, 189–190
management by public policy, 88–90
mechanistic aspects, 111–112
mentalistic aspects, 108–110
nature/culture dichotomy, 84–85
social norms, 65–67, 75
See also Moral systems

D

Darwinian psychology. *See* Evolutionary
psychology, theory
Deception. *See* Cheating; Self-deception
Decision making
in behavioral adaptations, 37–38
economic fairness in, 57–58
evolution of, 3–20, 323
in moral contexts, 77–79, 83–86
participatory, 336
personal vs. public, 3–5
in Prisoner's Dilemma, 145–166,
323–324
self-deception in, 117–140
See also Cognitive adaptations;
Self-deception
Decomposed games, 159–160, 160f
Deference, 323–325, 333
Delict, theory of, 198–200
Democracy, role in cultivating morality,
338

Silks purses from sows' ears (*quote*) p 339